D0350274

Advance Praise for *Bending Toward Justice*

"For forty years, justice had gone undone in the brutal murder of four young girls in the 16th Street Baptist Church. Forty years of pain and hurt for the families of those young girls and their community. Forty years of the Klan laughing at justice, getting away with the act of a coward.

"Doug Jones said no more. Justice had to be done. Those young girls deserved it. Their families deserved it. The community needed it. It took courage, commitment, and persistence. And—maybe most of all—heart."

—former vice president Joe Biden

"This book describes the painful sacrifice that was required, and may be called for again, for us to move toward true democracy in America. Facing the truth of our dark past with honesty and humility is the only way this nation can heal these deep wounds. But knowing the truth Jones shares in this book can set this nation free to earnestly build a more perfect union."

—Rep. John Lewis

"Doug Jones has proven himself adept at getting right with history against tall odds, whether it's in his prosecution of the 16th Street Baptist Church bombing case or his election to the U.S. Senate. *Bending Toward Justice* is his riveting inside account of arguably the most important cold case prosecution in civil rights history, and a crucial contribution to our understanding of where we are—and he is—today."

—Diane McWhorter, author of the Pulitzer Prize–winning
*Carry Me Home: Birmingham, Alabama—The Climactic
Battle of the Civil Rights Revolution*

BENDING
TOWARD
JUSTICE

BENDING
TOWARD
JUSTICE

THE BIRMINGHAM CHURCH BOMBING THAT CHANGED THE COURSE OF CIVIL RIGHTS

U.S. SENATOR
DOUG JONES

WITH GREG TRUMAN

ALL
POINTS
BOOKS

All Points Books is an imprint of St. Martin's Press.

www.allpointsbooks.com

Designed by Meryl Sussman Levavi

Library of Congress Cataloging-in-Publication Data

Names: Jones, Doug (G. Douglas), 1954– author. | Truman, Greg, author.
Title: Bending toward justice : the Birmingham church bombing that changed the course
    of civil rights / U.S. Senator Doug Jones with Greg Truman.
Description: First edition. | New York : All Points Books, 2019. | Includes index.
Identifiers: LCCN 2018039980| ISBN 9781250201447 (hardcover) | ISBN 9781250201454 (ebook)
Subjects: LCSH: Jones, Doug (G. Douglas), 1954– | Trials (Murder)—Alabama—Birmingham. |
    16th Street Baptist Church Bombing, Birmingham, Ala., 1963. | Birmingham (Ala.)—Race
    relations—History. | African Americans—Civil rights—Alabama—Birmingham—History.
Classification: LCC F334.B69 N445 2019 | DDC 323.1196/0730761781—dc23
LC record available at https://lccn.loc.gov/2018039980

Our books may be purchased in bulk for promotional, educational, or business use. Please contact your local bookseller or the Macmillan Corporate and Premium Sales Department at 1-800-221-7945, extension 5442, or by email at MacmillanSpecialMarkets@macmillan.com.

First Edition: March 2019

10 9 8 7 6 5 4 3 2 1

DEDICATION

In so many ways, *Bending Toward Justice* is about family.

From the families of the victims to the tribe of lawyers and investigators who toiled, in some cases for decades, to ensure justice was done.

And this book, which reflects on my home and history, is dedicated to my loved ones. The people who sustain and invigorate me.

To my eternal benefit and joy, my daily touchstone is my wife, Louise. She has always allowed me to pursue dreams, walking with me every step of the way as my most ardent supporter and most helpful critic; my friend, my love, and an amazing mother.

I am also blessed with three amazing children, Courtney, Carson, and Christopher, who have enriched my life beyond words. My granddaughters—Courtney and her husband Rip Andrews's babies—Ever and Ollie, are the brightest lights in my sky these days.

My sister, Terrie, and her husband, Scott Savage, have been with me every step of the way in recent years as we've cared for my ailing parents. Gloria and Gordon Jones showed me the importance of decency and hard work and passed on the loving tradition of my maternal grandparents, Ruby and Oliver Wesson, and Dad's folks, Charlesie and Edwin Jones.

CONTENTS

FOREWORD

In Harper Lee's American classic *To Kill a Mockingbird*, the author conjures a modest country lawyer from imagination and memory, from pieces of her own father, and sets him against Southern society itself, against prejudice and meanness and the petrified opinions of a doomed but lingering ideal.

The lawyer is asked, in her fictional story, to save a young black man wrongly accused of a terrible thing, and he takes on that task with full knowledge that it will cost him in that society, in an old South that is willing, if not eager, to believe the worst of a man for little other reason than the color of his skin.

The lawyer, more of an old name than old money, cannot, in the end, save the man. His victories are noble ones, but moral ones. It is one of the best books I have ever read in my life, but as a child of the Deep South, a child of Harper Lee's Alabama, I have always been haunted by that book and its lessons. I have never seen much good in a moral victory, at the lip of a grave.

There are just too many ghosts down here, so very many. So many victims gone unavenged. So much justice denied. So many young men, old men now, left free to gloat and preen and even confess, in the company of like-minded men, to their meanness and even murder.

Moral victories, in such a landscape, are a thing of fiction. Harper Lee's great book reminded us of that, beautifully but tragically, and became a kind of sermon for our time.

But it was fiction.

Atticus Finch was just a name in a story.

Men did their evil across the decades and got away with it, while good men stood by and did nothing.

I was four years old when the worst of it happened, the nightmare story of the Jim Crow years. In 1963, children marched for their civil rights in Birmingham, the big city to our west. That fall, elementary and high schools began a court-ordered integration, and the segregationists, seeing their world come to pieces around them, did the unthinkable. They targeted the children themselves.

On September 15, 1963, Ku Klux Klansmen planted a powerful bomb at 16th Street Baptist Church, timed to go off just minutes before Sunday services. In the church basement, four little girls were getting ready for the program that day.

Addie Mae Collins.

Cynthia Morris Wesley.

Carole Robertson.

Denise McNair.

The blast took them from this life and burned their names in history, and the bad men, the worst of cowards, got away with it, for years and years. There were attempts at justice, but the courtrooms in those days were merely turnstiles. The accused smirked around their Winston cigarettes. Police pumped their hands.

It was shameful.

Finally, in 1977, Alabama Attorney General Bill Baxley worked what some lawyers still consider a courtroom master class and brought to trial and convicted a single defendant, Robert Chambliss, the man his friends affectionately called "Dynamite Bob."

It was better than a moral victory. But everyone, from investigators to newspaper reporters to the man and woman on the streets of that city, knew that Dynamite Bob Chambliss did not act alone, knew that somewhere out there, men gathered in the shadows to remember and relive what they had done, and even brag.

In the courtroom that day, as the gavel came down hard on Chambliss, was a young law student who had skipped classes day after day to see it all unfold. He was not some Yankee firebrand. He was a boy from the outskirts of Birmingham, where the smokestacks turned the sky orange and black, and a product of the passive traditions that had allowed such evils to go unpunished, of a world that just turned its face from the fanatics and said they could not be responsible for what that white trash did.

But in the courtroom that day, something broke in young law student Doug Jones.

Or rather, something was welded in place.

He would get them.

He would get as many of them as he could.

He would, someday, assemble the broken pieces of a justice system that had left the families of those four little girls wondering just how much justice there was in a system that treated this horror with such nonchalance. He would scrape and dig and hound, and someday, someday . . .

Almost four decades passed. His legal career had been impressive, and he had risen to become a U.S. Attorney based in Birmingham. The bombing case had always been with him, riding in his own conscience after all that time. If it was still hot to his touch, he knew how it must burn in the guts of the mothers, fathers, sisters, and brothers of the victims of September 15, 1963.

Others, some well-meaning, some thinking of his future, said let it lay.

Nothing is gained by digging all that old stuff up again.

He could hear it in his sleep.

Baxley had gone after them, people cautioned, and look what happened. He could have been Governor, but the old racists rose from their holes and helped vote him down.

Let it lay.

Let it lay.

"I knew I just had to do something," Jones said a thousand times.

I was not in the courtroom the day Jones got the second bomber, an old Klansman named Tommy Blanton, piecing together faded and crumbling evidence and testimony. He read the sworn testimony of ghosts into the record. He plumbed the faded memories of old men and women.

And Tommy Blanton went to prison for the rest of his life. The South might not have changed greatly, but it had changed enough.

The next and final trial, against a defiant old man named Bobby Frank Cherry, was harder. What few witnesses Jones had for Blanton's trial were now gone. The hard evidence had all but faded away, like an old photograph left in the sun.

But one piece of testimony stood out raw and jagged and mean. Cherry had bragged about it, to witnesses. He had believed himself safe, in the company of men who saw the world through the same dark lens.

But the world, for some men, had turned to a better place, leaving him in the ruin of the old one.

I was there that day, when the gavel came down. I heard Jones give a powerful and heartbreaking closing argument that left the now gray-haired relatives of the little girls unable to look up from their clenched fists in their laps.

He told the jury about a doll one of the little girls had. It was white.

It just happened to be white.

You had to learn to resent the difference.

Some men could not live with it. Some people can barely live with it, today.

Sometimes, down here, it seems like we slide backward in time. We have traded Jim Crow for immigration laws that target, again, the most vulnerable. But there are good men and women here determined to stop that slide.

Doug Jones is one of them.

I guess I am prejudiced. Doug Jones is my friend. I have stood beside him in a small boat in Mobile Bay and attempted to catch some speckled trout, and I can tell you right now that as a fisherman he is a fine attorney. We mostly talk football, and shotguns, what we will do, someday, when we have some time off. But we both know we will probably die working. We do not often talk of the trials, or the darkness that settled on this land and lingered there for so long. And sometimes I even forget that the man across from me at the meat-and-three was the avenger of those four little girls.

Maybe it is because the evil that took hold is still too sharp and jagged, so mean that it, too, seems almost like an awful fiction, not something that human beings could actually do to each other in my South. And if that were so, then a man of fiction, a hero of imagination, like Atticus, would suffice.

But the darkness of spirit in this hot and humid place is still very real, still out there in human form, still grinning and plotting and threatening, and maybe no longer as deep in shadow as we have come to believe.

Men like Doug cannot pass into legend or even history.

But their stories need to be told. This book walks us through the life of the man and the case that defined him, and in many ways still defines our state. It is an honor to be some tiny part of it.

I believe every word he writes about it.

If, in it, he claims to be a good fisherman, that is another matter.

RICK BRAGG

AUTHOR'S NOTE

Lawyer jokes are a dime a dozen, and I used to open speeches with one or two. However, after a while, I figured I had to stop using them because the non-lawyers didn't realize I was kidding.

Despite the public often holding attorneys in less than stellar esteem, the law is, in fact, a noble profession. Sure, there are bad apples, but I continue to believe that lawyers have had the greatest positive impact on the country of any profession.

For me, apart from wanting a career that didn't involve the sight of blood, I suspect my high school exposure to courtroom battles on integration, together with a long-held interest in the power of the law, made my career choice inevitable. And once I was on my way, wading through contracts and civil procedure courses at the Cumberland School of Law, I was given the gift of being exposed to a few fine lawyers like Bill Baxley, the former Alabama Attorney General.

Baxley was already one of my heroes, but in 1977 he proved to be more heroic than I could ever have imagined. While he didn't motivate me to become a lawyer, he damn sure made me want to be a very good one who could make a difference.

In November of that year, I skipped a bunch of law school classes to watch Baxley ignore the odds, follow his heart, and use his head to win the unwinnable case. Fourteen years after four African-American girls were killed in the bombing of Birmingham's 16th Street Baptist Church, he secured a murder conviction against "Dynamite" Bob Chambliss, a former Ku Klux Klansman, who, along with several others, had to that point successfully and somewhat brazenly avoided the reach of justice.

As a twenty-three-year-old, I watched Baxley, in the Chambliss case, test the capacity of the court system to do exactly what it was designed to do and came to realize that crusading for a cause was something you could do from the "inside." The tools were already in place for justice to be done; you could be an activist simply by doing your job the right way.

There is a good reason Atticus Finch, the beyond reproach defense lawyer created by Harper Lee in *To Kill a Mockingbird*, is recognized as both the greatest film hero of all time and the best single marketing tool for the legal profession.

Sure, it's fiction, but Finch's passionate closing argument to the jury, as he strives for justice for Tom Robinson, pretty well sums up the great potential of the justice system (and has more than a hint of Baxley about it):

> In this country our courts are the great levelers, and in our courts all men are created equal. I'm no idealist to believe firmly in the integrity of our courts and in the jury system—that's no ideal to me, it is a living, working reality. . . . I am confident that you gentlemen will review without passion the evidence that you have heard, come to a decision, and restore this man to his family. In the name of God, do your duty.

But the legal process is not perfect. The fact that the fictional *Mockingbird* jury of all white men did not restore that good man to his family also illustrates the fallibility of the system we revere. Only by testing its limits can we improve the quality of outcomes.

Baxley took a chance with the Chambliss case that paid off in the courtroom, but he paid a personal price. His run for Governor of Alabama the next year was impacted negatively by his prosecution of an "old white man in his golden years," as the repellent Chambliss was sympathetically characterized. When white, mostly union workers refused to shake Baxley's hand at various industrial plants, he knew the jig was up. The black vote was his, the white, not so much. Baxley lost the Democratic primary that year.

Four years later, in 1982, he returned to politics and was elected Lieutenant Governor, the number two office in the state. Ironically, his rebound was overshadowed by the return of arch-segregationist George

Wallace, voted in as Governor for the fourth time (fifth if you count the 1966 election of his wife/proxy Lurleen).

In 1986, Baxley was defeated for the Governor role once again, thus ending one of the most promising political careers in generations and Alabama's best opportunity to be a "New South" state.

Today, Baxley continues to enjoy a magnificent legal career in private practice in Birmingham, but I believe that Alabamians, by refusing to see past long-held prejudices to elect the man as Governor, blew a golden opportunity to make their state a much better place. Simply, he was brought down for having the temerity to remind Alabama of what had happened fourteen years before.

His chief investigator in the 16th Street bombing case, Bob Eddy, a man lauded by several generations of law enforcement with knowledge of the case, also had a career stumble immediately after Chambliss was convicted. He returned to Huntsville and ran for election as Sheriff of Madison County. But, as with Baxley, it wasn't meant to be. Not everyone appreciated the pride the investigator took in his role in sending an elderly white man to prison for the murder of a young black girl.

It might have been a career killer, but the push to prosecute one of the Klan's worst left an indelible and profound mark on many of the participants and observers at the trial—especially the law student in the balcony.

I was not only mesmerized by Baxley's performance at the time; the case embedded itself in my psyche.

As a young college student, I had received an invaluable career tip from longtime Supreme Court Justice William O. Douglas to go out of my way and watch great trial lawyers ply their trade. I did just that to watch Baxley. He dominated the grand old courtroom in Birmingham, methodically building his case and relentlessly chipping away at lies and denials until a cowering Chambliss couldn't even look the prosecutor in the eye, much less take the stand in his own defense.

It was as if Baxley had intervened before the South could palliate its history once more. In confronting the ugliness, there was an honor and honesty that had been missing from the rhetoric and platitudes that accompanied the reluctant white embrace of civil rights and racial equality.

The arc of history may well bend toward justice, but brushing over hard truths distorts our moral compass. The path to fairness and equality isn't a given; it has to be forged, sometimes through activism or political discourse but most importantly by embracing the possibilities of our justice system.

There will be abuses, oversights, and failures—Atticus Finch could not save Tom Robinson; Baxley got one of the bombers, but several remained free. However, in the broad sweep, it's a process that works because people like Baxley know it's our most powerful tool.

I was raised in a white household in the segregated suburbs of Birmingham at a time when one of the great challenges of desegregation, the integration of schools, was confusing and sometimes infuriating our parents. The peak moment of that period of turmoil was the abhorrent, racially motivated bombing of 16th Street Baptist Church.

Nine miles and a racial barrier had been enough to prevent me from seeing the horror of it all when I was a nine-year-old in suburbia. But a seed was planted, perhaps by osmosis, when I was a kid. By the time I was an adult in a Birmingham courtroom where Baxley methodically and dramatically laid out the case, I fully understood the repugnance of the crime and the maladjusted environment in which it was committed.

I'd like to say that I walked out of the courtroom that November day with the same passion for bringing justice to Chambliss's confederates that drove Baxley. But candidly that was not the case. In my wildest imagination, I did not see myself ever having the opportunity to follow in the former AG's footsteps. One thing, however, was for sure—my (yet to be launched) career as a lawyer would always be grounded in some way by that case.

I wasn't alone. A young lawyer at the time, Caryl Privett, who would play a central role in jump-starting the bombing prosecution process decades later as an interim U.S. Attorney, was watching the trial unfold just a few feet from my vantage point on the balcony.

We were just two of a cluster of lawyers and investigators in Alabama who, from that point on, had the girls' names permanently etched on our minds. It's reflected to this day in the difficulty many of us who worked the case have discussing the victims and the emotional impact of their deaths and the trials.

Eddy, the lead investigator who has seen it all, is a good example. After talking freely about the facts of the Baxley investigation—and the pivotal role he played in assisting my team two decades later—he took a long pause before venturing into evaluating its personal impact.

"I . . . it took a long time, it's something that never really goes away," whispered this jovial gem of a man. Battle-hardened from the Korean War and one of the best criminal investigators in the South, Eddy struggles with the memory of the case like no other.

"We were doing our job, but maybe it was [also] a chance to make up for what had happened. One time, in talking to Baxley, I told him how much I appreciated him trusting me enough to work on that case."

Eddy's voice trailed off for a moment.

"It was bad," he said. "It wasn't something you wanted to be looking into, but it had to be done."

Why, he wondered, would anybody blow up a church with those young girls in it?

"It's still with me. Every day."

He speaks for quite a few of us.

PART
ONE

THE ARC OF HISTORY

My father, Gordon Jones, was named after George Gordon Crawford, President of the Birmingham heavy industry behemoth the Tennessee Coal, Iron and Railroad Company (TCI). Dad grew up in Ensley, a dot on the map, seven miles west of the city, and when he was not quite eighteen, anxious to do his bit for his country, he fudged his age by a few months to enlist in the United States Navy.

On home leave in 1949, he was set up on a blind date with a recent graduate of Minor High School, Gloria Wesson. I guess the date went pretty well. A mere two weeks later, much to the surprise of both families, they were married in the front room of my great-aunt and -uncle's new home in Sylvan Springs, about seventeen semi-rural miles along Route 269 out of the city. The town was close enough to the mines and factories on the outskirts of Birmingham to offer just about every man in the family a manageable commute to work.

They headed to Texas where Dad was stationed, first in Corpus Christi, then Dallas. Toward the end of the four-year stint, Mother became pregnant with me. That propelled the couple back to the bosom of the family in Edgewater, a small mining town on Birmingham's fringes.

I was born on May 4, 1954, thirteen days before the Supreme Court under Chief Justice Earl Warren handed down the landmark *Brown v. Board of Education* ruling.

The decision was arguably the first nail in the coffin of the Jim Crow laws of the old South. It made state laws authorizing "separate but equal" black and white public schools unconstitutional, sparking overdue change and extreme racial anxiety, especially among whites.

Tumultuous transformation was in the wind, but my parents were too busy building the foundations of the family to get caught up in "wider" issues. After a few months of unemployment, Dad found a job with the biggest game in town, U.S. Steel, as had many other family members. At first, he toiled as a laborer at what was then the second-largest steelmaking plant in the country before he rose through the ranks to management. He ended up spending more than sixty-two years at that plant, either as an employee or heading up the local office of one of the company's prime contractors, until retiring at the age of eighty.

In the forties and fifties, heavy industry wasn't just an imposing presence on the outskirts of the city of Birmingham; it dominated the landscape, especially along Routes 80, 269, and 56, arteries that also connected us to relatives like the branches of a family tree.

"U.S. Steel stretched as far as you could see this way and that," Dad recalled recently. "It was very impressive. Twenty-five thousand people, all of them there every day, working three shifts, seven days a week."

The boosters had called Birmingham the Magic City since the late nineteenth century when industrial growth and its population exploded, but truckers in the postwar era knew better. For them, it was Smoke City, the metropolis regularly cocooned by a putrid aerial cocktail.

The billowing smokestacks produced plumes of beautiful filth that were the byproduct of progress, introducing a new level of stability, even prosperity, for the workers and generating lucre for the bold, brilliant, sometimes corrupt, rarely accountable captains of industry.

So enamored of heavy industry was Birmingham that the Magic City had missed a major development opportunity in the forties when Atlanta, then a sister city of about the same size, won the affections of Delta Air Lines to become the company's southern hub. We all know how that has turned out.

A company-built satellite city, Fairfield, was one of the better results of U.S. Steel's efficiency in shaping the lives of its employees. My parents grabbed a chance to settle into the newest community in the vicinity, dubbed Glen Oaks, in 1955.

We were the first family to move into the subdivision. Our little house seemed enormous to me as a young boy, a conspicuous one-level castle on the corner of Rutledge and Glen Oaks Drives surrounded by scores of similar structures. Newly erected or still-under-construction homes lined recently plotted and paved streets, the smell of freshly laid asphalt often mixing with the invigorating scent drifting in from soon-to-be-leveled woods a few blocks away.

When he wasn't working weekend or overnight shifts, Dad would take me up the hill behind the house where the roads had been cut but were still dirt, and on windy days we would fly kites. Mother was ever-present for me and my sister Terrie, who came along in 1957.

Reminiscing today with friends, it's startling how many memories we share. While we thought our tight little community special, it became apparent in later life that the experience of many white families in Birmingham and scores of other towns in the South was similar.

We all seemed to enjoy the same foods, sports, music, and television shows. The vacation spot of choice was Panama City Beach. You'd complete the five-hour drive to the Gulf Coast, and it seemed the first person you'd see, either by arrangement or chance, would be a kid from Glen Oaks.

My other excursions out of the subdivision consisted of summer weeks at the house where my parents had married, with Aunt Laverne, Uncle Jimmy, and my cousins Deborah and Ricky. In the wilds of Sylvan Springs, a boy could wield a BB gun and fancy himself a direct descendant of Daniel Boone or Davy Crockett. The occasional romp in a mudhole was a highlight.

The lack of an interstate highway system made a trip between Birmingham's satellite towns seem like a grand journey. Heading from our suburban enclave into downtown Birmingham required extensive planning and was an all-day affair.

With everyone dressed in their best outfit, it would be lunch at Britling Cafeteria, punctuating Mother's shopping at locally owned department stores such as Pizitz and Loveman's. The highlight would be catching a movie at one of downtown's handsome single-screen theaters—the Alabama, the Ritz, or the Empire. And of course, we ended up on the knees of various in-store Santas around Christmas, when the lights and window decorations added to the excitement and expectation.

Trumping even the movies, the Birmingham Zoo was a prized excursion, a chance to match a few animals to those I'd seen on *Wild Kingdom*, Marlin Perkins's compelling wildlife television show.

The excitement on zoo days started with the drive from Fairfield, through Homewood and down Lakeshore Drive, where we'd cruise by a vision of barely fathomable opulence—a house with a private lake. Who lived like that, with their own lake? Certainly, no one we knew. (The house is gone now, razed to make way for office buildings, but the lake remains, although, through adult eyes, I have to concede it's more like a pond.)

Trips to the zoo took a full day. The apes, giraffes, and big cats were first stops, and a ride on the "Casey Jones Railroad," a miniature train that traversed parts of the more than one hundred acres, was a must.

Especially compelling was the site of the grave where Casey Jones, the fabled train engineer, was supposedly buried, his engineer's cap and boots sticking out of the ground. They don't make attractions like that anymore.

Sixty-Three

My tight circle of neighborhood friends and I had little if any idea that the Birmingham school system was poised to go through unprecedented change as the desegregation process commenced despite violent and widespread objections from whites.

All we knew was we had a brand-new elementary school in Glen Oaks that opened in the fall of 1962, my third-grade year, meaning no more busing to neighboring Forest Hills Elementary. This ensured a quicker and smoother transition between schoolyard sports rivalries and late-afternoon neighborhood pickup games.

Adult heads would shake ever so gently when there were glimpses on the evening news of "trouble" on the streets, usually in some faraway city, though occasionally we'd recognize a Southern landmark or two in footage of the latest bombing. Firemen and police would be depicted taming flames or involved in heated confrontations with black folks.

That would be virtually our only glimpse of non-white faces, other than our "maid," of course. Julia was always there for us, and loved our family like her own. She had a robust and enchanting personality that endeared her to everyone. We kids adored her, and we knew the feeling was mutual.

My family were good people, but like most white folks, they were immersed in the biases of the time. Segregation had been the way of the South for generations, and we were white Southerners. Race wasn't discussed—not around kids—and there was never any ill will openly expressed toward any group. But some things were incontrovertible, even if the political environment was in transition.

There were hints of adult prejudices and preferences. For example, figurines depicting prominent characters didn't come standard with Chevys, so the one perched near the back window of my grandfather's car was conspicuous.

"Who's that?" I remember asking my beloved grandfather, whom we called Paw-Paw.

"Never you mind, it's just a politician," he said, opting not to explain that it was Birmingham's notorious Public Safety Commissioner, Eugene "Bull" Connor, the man responsible for enforcing segregation laws and mores. Connor, a former sports commentator, was a popular figure who had a penchant for riding around on the back of a white tank at the height of civil disturbances while barking instructions to law enforcement officers.

I didn't mind too much that some questions went unanswered. That's just the way things were.

The presidential election of 1960 is the first election I remember. I was all about JFK. He was young, charismatic, and intelligent—exactly what a six-year-old thought the country needed.

Hard to believe today, but JFK won with about sixty percent of the vote in Alabama. A Democrat would only carry Alabama one more time (1976, for Georgia neighbor Jimmy Carter) in the next thirteen presidential elections as race became a dominant factor in elections.

Kennedy's support in Alabama gradually faded when it became clear his administration, with his Attorney General brother Bobby leading the charge, was leaning toward civil rights. Conservative Democrats—representatives of the old Solid South coalition of states and defenders of segregation—were a powerful constituency in Washington, even if times were changing.

In his first year of the presidency, JFK was focused predominantly on the imminent danger of the Cold War, with the Soviet Union flexing its considerable muscle on the world stage. However, civil rights protests had gained national momentum since December 1955, when Rosa Parks defied a local ordinance and refused to give up her seat to a white man on a bus in Montgomery, Alabama.

Parks's act of courage and resistance sparked a young Dr. Martin Luther King Jr. to lead a thirteen-month-long boycott of the Montgomery bus system, establishing a template for peaceful demonstration that spread throughout the South.

The Kennedys knew the king-making power of the support of Southern

Democrats and, reportedly at their father Joe's instruction, avoided ruffling segregationists' feathers. The new President and his Attorney General, tacitly at first, tolerated black activism. When the Freedom Riders rode into Alabama in May 1961, however, the federal administration could not avoid directly addressing the civil rights issue.

A multi-racial group of activists, the Freedom Riders had decided to test whether the 1960 Supreme Court decision *Boynton v. Virginia*, outlawing segregation in restaurants and waiting rooms in bus and train terminals, was being enforced. They embarked on a trek from Washington, D.C., to New Orleans, white and black together, with an African American toward the front of the bus to challenge local seating customs and laws.

On May 14, 1961, white supremacists firebombed a Greyhound bus in Anniston, Alabama, and beat the travelers as they tried to escape the damaged vehicle. Later, a Trailways bus carrying another group of activists arrived in Birmingham. Despite the expectation of confrontation and violence, there were no police on hand as men armed with baseball bats, iron pipes, and chains assaulted the riders. Bull Connor, the city "public safety" czar, had alerted the Klansmen that they would have a quarter hour to coerce the activists into heading back to Washington. Publicly, Connor put a lack of swift police response down to it being Mother's Day.

The nation was outraged, and there were widespread demands for federal action over the incidents. Bobby Kennedy, instead, called for a "cooling off" period. It was by no means an endorsement of the Freedom Riders, but his failure to condemn their "provocative" campaign infuriated many in the South who fumed about interference from "outsiders." As the Kennedys got behind school integration in subsequent years, most of the support from Democrats in the South disappeared to the point that America's youthful leaders were widely vilified.

I was blissfully ignorant of these and other incidents during the Kennedy administration. My admiration for the President stemmed mainly from his support for an ambitious space program. However, I could sense his popularity was waning and instinctively knew, even as an eight-year-old, any positive affirmation of JFK, at school or in social situations, was unlikely to meet with resounding support. Paw-Paw's brusque assessment was he could not vote for him in the presidential election as Kennedy was Catholic. I didn't allow myself to contemplate at length why that was an issue but assumed it was because we were Methodists. But for most, religion was simply a way to gloss over racial issues.

No subject was banned from discussion, probably because my family never really needed to invoke restrictions on me. I knew what not to say—a talent I have tried to exercise judiciously during my professional life.

But there was something mildly discombobulating about 1963. I don't know how noticeable it was at the time—I may just be projecting what I know now onto my memory of those usually languid days—but hints of unrest in Birmingham did seep through.

Of course, Fairfield, like Birmingham and every other Alabama community, had long been segregated: the neighborhoods, churches, schools, and restaurants. It had been that way for generations, and we accepted it without question. Whites lived in Glen Oaks, Forest Hills, Bellwood, and later Fair Oaks, while the black community lived on "The Hill"—the area that circled Miles College, an all-black college founded in 1898 by the Christian Methodist Episcopal Church and named in honor of Bishop William H. Miles.

In postwar years, the city of Birmingham also had a "hill" neighborhood. The Fountain Heights area became known as "Dynamite Hill," as white supremacists launched a campaign of terror to protest the growth of the black population there.

According to police records, the Ku Klux Klan detonated dozens of bombs in churches, houses, and black businesses from 1947 to 1963 and infamously helped earn Birmingham the moniker of "Bombingham."

The KKK-led terrorist attacks in black neighborhoods went up a notch in 1963. As the civil rights movement gathered steam, Klan violence intensified. Nevertheless, media outlets, owned and staffed for the most part by whites, weren't awash with news reports on the incidents. As my father reflected recently, you'd be lucky to hear about protests.

But the swell of unrest in the streets of downtown Birmingham made confronting a few ugly truths inevitable as the civil rights movement's Reverend Fred Shuttlesworth, James Bevel, and the nationally famous Dr. King drew attention to the city's apartheid-like laws in unique nonviolent protests.

On Good Friday 1963, King and his close friend Reverend Ralph Abernathy were handcuffed and incarcerated in the Birmingham jail. Eight white ministers termed King's involvement as "unwise and untimely" and implored him to wait and give the city's newly elected administration (that would not include Bull Connor) a chance to act and quell tensions. In response, MLK penned his legendary "Letter from Birmingham Jail."

On release, King, following suggestions from Bevel, the Southern Christian Leadership Conference's brilliant strategist, agreed to expand the involvement of local children in protests. Kids had already been taking part in the community effort, but Bevel and others believed Birmingham's youth was the best way to deliver the message to the nation about multigenerational injustice in Birmingham and the rest of the South.

Black adults also had special challenges protesting, as their participation often ensured they'd lose their jobs, especially if arrest was a possibility. (It was a probability in Connor's Birmingham.) Youth faced no such retribution.

Reluctantly, and in the face of considerable opposition and notable condemnation, the leaders conspired to stage large-scale children's rallies. Thousands, aged six to eighteen, would be involved, transported from the suburbs into the city any way they could. What originally had been dubbed "Project C" for "Confrontation" became the "Children's Crusade."

Taking their organizational cues from popular radio disc jockeys "Tall Paul" White and Shelley "The Playboy" Stewart, the kids gathered at the 16th Street Baptist Church, where the pastor, Reverend John Cross, had agreed they could meet to pray and plan the peaceful demonstrations.

Police wasted no time arresting the children when they hit the streets, herding them into school buses for a trip to jail. Nevertheless, the protests persisted, with children breaking into groups of fifty or so to march through town, sending the authorities in different directions.

Initially the protests were conducted and controlled relatively peacefully (although dumping schoolchildren in jail cells with real convicts wasn't an experience they would get over easily). Nine hundred and fifty-nine children had been arrested by the end of the day, May 2.

The following day, a thousand more crowded around 16th Street Baptist Church and spilled across the road to Kelly Ingram Park. Connor, knowing his 900-capacity jails already had more than 1,200 inmates (a makeshift holding center had to be set up at the state fairgrounds), decided he was finished with the kid-glove treatment and ordered his troops to take a more menacing approach to crowd control.

Police and fire officers used attack dogs and fire hoses in and around the park to control the crowd. The barely believable photos of German Shepherds being launched at defenseless kids and teenagers being repelled by dangerously powerful blasts of water quickly spread around the world. They even made the often protest-shy local papers (although not page one in the *Birmingham News*).

The effectiveness of the children's marches as a protest tool was immediate and lasting. On May 10, King, Abernathy, and Shuttlesworth announced that they had reached an agreement with city officials to desegregate lunch counters, restrooms, and drinking fountains. An unspecified number of black sales clerks would be employed in Birmingham stores. An uneasy truce was achieved.

Connor, who had refused to vacate his office after being defeated at the polls, erupted like a Klan bomb and predicted swift retaliation. That evening, Robert Shelton, the Imperial Wizard of the Klan, speculated that the settlement would be King's epitaph. On the night of May 11, the residence of Dr. King's brother, A. D. King, was bombed and, minutes before midnight, a bomb exploded at the A.G. Gaston Motel, in the heart of the black business district just a block from 16th Street Baptist Church. Fortunately, the bomb's intended target, MLK, was already home in Atlanta.

Tensions had reached the breaking point, and over the ensuing days riots flared, resulting in injuries to dozens of people.

All the while, Governor George Wallace talked abrasively, generating a frenzy of fear and loathing in the white community. With a civil crisis in the making, President Kennedy relented to public demands and dispatched federal troops to Fort McClellan, near Anniston. Potentially violent intervention looked likely should civil unrest escalate.

But three weeks after fire hoses and dogs were turned on children, there was a circuit breaker for Birmingham that prevented civic breakdown: Connor was finally banished from office. Federal troops stood down. The historic agreement between the Dr. King–led Southern Christian Leadership Conference (SCLC) and the city officials was modest but effective and fueled calls for change elsewhere in the South.

The same month I turned nine, thousands of children, many the same age as me, turned the tide of the civil rights movement. If I knew about it at the time, it was secondhand knowledge. There were no discussions at home or deliberations in the playgrounds of white neighborhoods.

But the adults knew. "The crisis," as my parents and many others still refer to it, generated an unrelenting tension. The pressure to take sides in an atmosphere so inimical to unity was clearly intense.

"In your mind, you didn't want to get involved. You were afraid to because you didn't know which side would turn against you whatever you did. It was very nerve-racking," my mother said. "There were a lot of mean white folks and a lot of mean black ones."

We didn't have too many mean black folks in Glen Oaks. Truth be told, Mother wouldn't have closely encountered many, if any, people of color while going about her daily rituals, except for one.

Julia, our gentle and jovial maid, was at the same time our sitter and my family's main link to the "other side." I particularly remember one day, at the height of the crisis, when she was uncommonly distressed.

Like many others at the time, she felt confused and put-upon. Societal change was underway and the pressure to know your mind and embrace or reject a specific vision of the future was intense. Clearly frightened by the heightened community tension, Julia had heard terrible, inaccurate rumors about the fate of the black community. She stunned my parents when she asked my father: "Mr. Gordon, will you buy me if they put us up for sale?"

My parents thought she was joking, but Jim Crow wasn't just a vague memory in 1963, and the threat of slavery to folks like Julia was yet to be completely erased from nightmares.

"I don't want to go to Africa," she asserted, apparently in the belief she could be deported from the land of her birth. Desperate, she said she could live in a little shed in our backyard if my dad would "buy her," if it came to that.

Mom and Dad assured her there would be no such insanity, no return to the inhumanity of previous generations, that things were going to be OK. In retrospect, though, perhaps her fears weren't entirely unfounded, given the presence of white supremacist groups that wanted to subjugate blacks using tactics every bit as odious as those employed in years past. In fact, one of the darkest, most unbearably sad days for Alabama, the South, and the United States was only a few months away.

I can't recall what I was doing Sunday, September 15, 1963.

I don't really remember when I heard the news that the 16th Street Baptist Church had been bombed, killing four young black girls. I suspect, however, that I had just left my family's regular Methodist Sunday School and church appointment where I am sure there were prayers for "peaceful times" in Birmingham. My guess, though, is my intense personal appeal for divine assistance would have likely focused on the Alabama-Georgia football game scheduled for the following Saturday.

I was nine. I was white. I was loved, and I was lucky.

Desperate and Emboldened

Carol Denise McNair was eleven, black, and loved. In many ways, she was a lot like me.

A neighborhood leader with a hankering for sports, she would organize her friends for after-school baseball games. She would also put together skits for little front-yard performances, charging a penny or two and donating the proceeds to the muscular dystrophy telethon.

In 1963, Denise was a fifth grader at the all-black Center Street Elementary School in Birmingham. Her mother, Maxine, was a teacher there. Denise, or Niecie, as she was alternately called by friends and family, was a bundle of energy. A solid student, active in the Brownies and her church, she was an enchanting mix of innocence and precociousness.

The McNairs were salt of the earth folks who were positive about a future that wouldn't be inhibited by the Jim Crow racial segregation laws that had prevailed since Reconstruction. They had deep community roots anchored by their connection to church groups. Maxine McNair attended 16th Street Baptist, while Denise's dad, Chris, was a leader at St. Paul's Lutheran.

A Tuskegee graduate, Chris worked as a milkman and a schoolteacher before channeling his passion for photography into a career, opening his studio on 6th Avenue South in 1962. He had a rapidly expanding clientele of black and white Alabamians—segregation wasn't going to play a part in his professional or family life.

McNair used his photographic skill to document some of the key moments and figures of the civil rights movement. As one of the few professional black photographers in Birmingham, his work often provided an unusual, up-close perspective, including intimate shots that captured the charisma of Dr. King and the fierceness of a local hero, Reverend Shuttlesworth.

He would often turn his camera on his family with brilliant results, though his favorite photo was a simple snapshot of his radiant daughter in pajamas. It was taken with her little Instamatic, as she held her favorite "talking" doll, a Chatty Cathy.

It was a photo I displayed prominently in a Birmingham courtroom thirty-eight years later when a former Ku Klux Klansman was tried for Denise's murder.

Along with Addie Mae Collins, Cynthia Morris Wesley, and Carole Robertson, Denise was killed when a bomb exploded at the 16th Street Baptist Church on Sunday morning, September 15, 1963.

That unfathomable misery for the girls' families, and for the greater community, came at the beginning of the school year in the wake of the volatile spring and summer in Birmingham. As blacks protested ongoing racial segregation, white supremacists initiated an unprecedented campaign of violence and intimidation.

Extremists had planted the bomb as some sort of last-ditch effort to derail the desegregation of the Birmingham city schools. Indeed, racially integrating education in many ways represented the ultimate defeat for those who were ignorant enough to think that they were involved in a war.

While it is essential to understand the context of their terrorism, it took men with especially dark hearts to commit such an immeasurably wicked act. The girls were slain when they were at their most vulnerable in a place they had the right to feel most secure. Thinking about it infuriates me to this day.

Knowing all that I know now, I am almost embarrassed to say that the scariest thing in my protected little world in the spring and summer of 1963 was the thought that the Yankees wouldn't go back-to-back in the World Series.

African-American kids, on the other hand, had long had bogeymen to worry about. The ghostly hooded figures of the Klan weren't an everyday sight in Birmingham, but their presence was conspicuous enough. They were as bold as they had been at any stage since Reconstruction, when they had first started their campaign of violence and racial hatred.

If a family like mine came upon a rally or stumbled into someone handing out leaflets, we, like most respectable folks (segregationist or not), would have no part of it and move on without incident. But if you were Jewish, Catholic, or African-American, the Klansmen were obviously anything but a benign, easily ignored presence. At the least, they were a manifest reminder of a long, gruesome history of baseless white antipathy toward African Americans and others.

In 1963, the Klan, for the most part, was still considered an unsavory presence on the fringe of Birmingham life, though the white supremacists themselves were clearly emboldened by community anger over court mandates to racially integrate schools. One particularly violent cluster in Birmingham became self-appointed soldiers for the cause as Governor Wallace fueled anti-integration sentiment, his racially charged dog whispers becoming a loud, unmistakable bark.

Otherwise decent people, feeling cornered and confused, directed their anger at the federal government as the administration stepped up its efforts to honor the *Brown v. Board* decision, issued years before, and finally compel schools across the nation to integrate. At some rallies, effigies of the Kennedys were burned. I may have understood little of what was going on, but the "us against them" sentiment and mass community defensiveness were unmistakable. If nothing else, my decision to keep my own counsel about my admiration for JFK was proving wise.

In that wrongheaded climate of desperation and defensiveness, it was inevitable that matters would come to a head. But few would have predicted an act so despicable would be imposed on Birmingham, changing the course of American history and providing provenance for a white nine-year-old's lifelong quest for justice and redemption.

ONE

THE BOMBING

Thursday nights were busy under Highway 280's Cahaba River Bridge, on the outskirts of the city of Birmingham.

The Cahaba River is a small, beautiful estuary that boasts one of the most diverse ecosystems in the country. But to this day, it's bleak down there under 280 at night. The river laps noisily onto the scrappy grassed banks as cars rumble across the bridge above. There is a sense of menace as any movement in the immediate area echoes. The squelch of approaching footsteps through the mud is particularly unsettling.

Back in the sixties, even kids knew snippets about the strange and dangerous people who'd gather there. They were like the trolls of children's storybooks in many imaginations, brutish bogeymen doing all manner of unspeakable things right at the doorstep of civilization.

Turns out that was just about right.

With Friday and Saturday nights reserved for chasing women, harassing blacks, and maybe taking in a movie, Thursdays under the bridge were an opportunity for some of the Klan's most abhorrent to break out the bourbon, moonshine, and hateful rants.

It was a safe place for open discussion, as most of the men correctly believed their homes and cars to be bugged by the FBI. The Klan had historically operated with relative freedom in Birmingham, as many powerful elements in the local and state police forces were KKK sympathizers.

But the Feds, along with their wiretaps and "bugs," were a source of constant concern.

A relentless Klan campaign to terrorize blacks (and to a lesser extent Jews and Catholics) in Birmingham had gone on for decades and accelerated in the early sixties after federal government intervention and court rulings intensified the push to racially integrate schools and dismantle the vestiges of institutional segregation.

The frequent bombings in black Birmingham neighborhoods had shone a national spotlight on the city. The law at the time allowed the FBI and other federal organizations to use wires to listen for potential violent threats with a view to thwarting nefarious plots. Use of the recordings as evidence in a court of law, however, was debatable.

Under the bridge, the Klansmen were free to speculate and plan. And there was much to discuss as fall descended on Birmingham in 1963. Governor Wallace was blowing hard in opposition to desegregation. The same week black kids were poised to attend formerly white schools for the first time in Birmingham, he'd told the *New York Times* that to stop integration, Alabama needed "a few first-class funerals."

Wallace's words were divisive and inflammatory, but many white supremacists were angry that he seemed unable to curtail the federal government's initiatives to desegregate the South.

In June, the Governor's so-called Stand in the Schoolhouse Door to block the entry of two African-American students to the University of Alabama had proved ineffective and, if anything, sparked federal authorities into action, with JFK addressing the nation hours later to outline what would later become legislation as the Civil Rights Act.

The Klan and their sympathizers increasingly believed it was time they took matters into their own hands. Indeed, soon after watching the Kennedy address on television, Mississippi civil rights activist Medgar Evers was fatally shot on the front porch of his Jackson home by white supremacist Byron De La Beckwith.

Prominent among the Birmingham group of incensed Klansmen was Robert Chambliss, also known as "Dynamite Bob," who was responsible for a large proportion of the explosive destruction around Birmingham. His primary target was Dynamite Hill, the old Fountain Heights area. Onetime Klan leader Charles Pearson, a grocer, used to live in the neighborhood. Pearson had paid his most violent friends in perishable goods to cause havoc in response to the neighborhood's evolution from a white enclave to a home to many black families.

The men under the bridge called themselves the Cahaba River Bridge Boys and were associated with a special local Klan pod, Eastview Klavern #13. Believing the larger Klan organization was not doing enough to stem civil rights progress, they perceived themselves as storm troopers for the white supremacist cause and advocated the use of extreme violence.

In the book *Long Time Coming*, Petric Smith (formerly Elizabeth H. Cobbs, Chambliss's niece by marriage) details the "to death" secrecy and loyalty among the group's members and maps some of their connections around the city.

The author identifies some of the core group as Chambliss, Troy Ingram, Thomas "Pops" Blanton and his son Tommy, Bobby Frank Cherry, Herman Cash and his brother Jack, Charles Cagle, and John Wesley "Nigger" Hall. Law enforcement documents from the period pinpoint Hubert Page, a Klansman with extensive political connections, as the group's leader.

They were unified by their commitment to carnage and moved to secretive action by what Chambliss and others perceived to be the wider Klan community going "soft."

The spot under the bridge was their boozing sanctuary. At other times, they would meet in secret at members' homes or gather at the Modern Sign Company shop in downtown Birmingham, owned by sympathizer Merle Snow.

The Modern Sign Shop churned out Confederate flags, banners, and other symbols of Southern white anger and hate, many of which adorned Chevys and Fords cruising Birmingham streets.

The hardcore trolls from under the Cahaba River Bridge plotted random acts of violence to inflict on the black community, including "missionary work" of conspicuous beatings, to send a message.

These were the radical fringe dwellers of an extremist movement. They didn't need an invitation to carry out despicable acts, but with the school year about to commence, howls of protest reached a fevered pitch as white school districts throughout the region prepared to integrate racially.

If Wallace, Connor, and other politicians couldn't do anything, it was up to the Cahaba River Bridge Boys. They felt they had a mandate.

Planting the Bomb

"Just you wait until Sunday morning," one of the Boys sneered under his breath, hinting at what was to come. The Klansmen, often full of piss and vinegar, couldn't help incriminating themselves, implying in earshot of family that an earth-shattering event would rectify the creep of integration.

To the Klansmen of Eastview #13 the white community had been soft on segregation, and now the reality was setting in that their kids would be going to school with "niggers."

Friday night, September 13, marked the end of a momentous week. Blacks had taken their kids into white schools for the first time, and whites throughout Birmingham were angry. The enmity reached a fever pitch at the Modern Sign Shop. Chambliss was there, likely making final adjustments to the bomb he'd been building, perhaps at Troy Ingram's house. The pair were said to be in a constant battle to demonstrate who built the better explosive devices. At some stage, Tom Blanton came by, and former munitions expert Bobby Frank Cherry added his support and expertise to the special project.

Few outsiders were tolerated at such gatherings, and all were bound by the "kiss of death"—the threat of Klan execution should any word of their business leak out.

This bomb would be a Dynamite Bob masterpiece—much larger than the couple of sticks of dynamite used in the past to attack black churches and residences of prominent African Americans. It was rumored that Chambliss had learned to use a fishing bobber and wire as part of a drip method employing a bucket of water as an ignition device, a significant technological advance.

Transporting the bomb, especially because it had a dozen or so sticks of dynamite, would be a challenge, but it would all fit into a single satchel, and the destination, the most famous black church in Birmingham, was only a few blocks away from the sign shop. They'd made the run a few weeks earlier, and all had gone according to plan until a civil defense volunteer shone his headlights in the direction of the car. The Klansmen would be taking extra care this time to avoid detection.

Alibis were constructed, some in coordination with sympathetic cops, friends, lovers, and acquaintances, and a series of distractions around the city in the quiet hours of late Saturday night and early Sunday morning were planned.

On the night of September 14, there was a barrage of phone calls to Chambliss's home, so many that his wife and her sister knew that something was up. Even those not within the inner sanctum seemed to know an attack was imminent, as did a few cops with friendly connections in the

KKK. Klansmen and their associates spread throughout Birmingham, making sure they were "seen" in order to account for their whereabouts.

Finally, a tense quiet descended on the city.

In the sweetly cool early morning hours of Sunday, September 15, one witness could barely believe his eyes as a parade of maybe twenty Chevys and Fords, adorned with Confederate flags, rumbled through downtown and into the black business district around 16th Street Baptist Church. They disappeared quickly.

Earlier in the night, there had been information that a group of blacks armed with shotguns was motoring toward the city. There was nothing to that, but not long after the conspicuous Confederate caravan rolled by, a call came into police headquarters warning that a bomb had been planted at the Downtowner Holiday Inn and would detonate at 3:30 a.m. Police were redirected from patrols to check it out, but there was no sign of any device.

Meanwhile, the Cahaba River Bridge Boys had picked up the bomb, loading it into Tom Blanton's 1957 white-on-blue Chevy. The car's guttural purr in the inky darkness didn't seem to disturb anyone around the church.

Pulling up in front of Poole's Funeral Chapel at the rear of 16th Street Baptist Church, they acted with stealth, mindful of attracting attention. The lights of a passing car came straight at them briefly, but it moved on without stopping.

The weeds and brush underneath the bottom step of the outside stairwell that ran to the back of the main sanctuary on the 16th Street side of the church, just below the magnificent stained-glass window of Christ, offered a perfect location to do the most damage. They placed the bomb there and set it.

It was dark at the side of the building; you could hardly see a few feet in front of you.

With the bomb secured in place, the conspirators hightailed it; the only glitch, a cop in a patrol car spotted them speeding through Ensley and gave chase. Knowing the streets in the area, though, they easily left him behind.

As the sun rose at 6:20 on September 15, 1963, an unseasonably mild though slightly cloudy morning, families throughout the city and its suburbs prepared for a day of worship.

Reverend John Cross, assisted by associate ministers Herbert E. Oden and M. A. Stollenwerck, usually brought the message to the congregation at the 16th Street Baptist Church. This Sunday's 11:00 a.m. gathering would be a special "Youth Worship Service," featuring the active involvement of many young churchgoers. The Sunday School lesson was entitled "A Love That Forgives."

Reverend Cross felt it an appropriate time to focus his young flock on matters of the soul and spirit after the especially tumultuous spring and summer. He had mixed feelings about the church being a staging point for earlier protests and the children being used in the campaign, though he conceded that much good had come of it.

The Children's Crusade marches had started from the church, and it had been used as a gathering place for those planning the protests. The dramatic photos of youths being sprayed by authorities with fire hoses and set upon by police dogs had been taken across the road in and around Kelly Ingram Park and sent all around the world by the news media.

Founded in 1873, 16th Street was the oldest and most prestigious black Baptist church in the city. Located on the same site since 1880, it underwent modifications until completion in 1911. Its unique Romanesque and Byzantine design and construction cost $26,000.

The state's only black architect, Wallace Rayfield, had designed the building. The contractor was T. C. Windham, one of the few African Americans with such a prominent job at the time.

Over the years, national black leaders and civil rights activists such as W.E.B. Du Bois, Mary McLeod Bethune, Paul Robeson, Ralph Bunche, and Dick Gregory had lectured from the pulpit.

Six mass meetings of more than a thousand black protesters and twelve additional workshops to instruct participants how to behave in community marches and sit-ins had been held at the church over the spring and summer. Additionally, there had been weekly meetings encouraging and promoting the urgency of voting rights for the adults.

16th Street's role had made it a target for those who hated the very idea of civil rights.

One day in June, church clerk Myrtle Buycks listened to what sounded like an elderly man on the other end of a call: "This is the KKK. Your church will be bombed tonight," he said.

On Sunday, September 8, church secretary Mabel Shorter received an eerie call from a man who also identified himself as a member of the Klan, telling her the church would be bombed that night. Intimidating calls had also been received at the home of Reverend Cross, whose daughter took one from a woman warning that the church would be blown up.

Although no devices were ever found, Cross had exercised caution, canceling church activities in some cases.

It was full steam ahead on Sunday, September 15, however. The marquee outside the church announced the start of a series of youth services. The church and the youth, both prominent symbols of the movement, were coming together again.

Right on time at 7:00 a.m., janitor Willie Green, a former railroad man, reported to work to clean, sweep, and mop the building. Reverend Cross got there at 8:00, about thirty minutes ahead of Eva Jones, a Sunday School teacher. A few minutes later, secretary Shorter arrived.

Green took his 9:00 a.m. break, checking the main clock in the church to make sure it was synchronized with his watch before heading across the street to the Silver Sands Restaurant for a morning cup of coffee. By that time, in the course of doing his job, he probably would have been one of a few people to trudge up and down the outside stairs at the rear of the church that morning.

There were only six people in the café, including its workers. One of them, waitress Barbara Poellnitz, while taking the order from Green and a couple of other patrons, eyeballed a blue or green car speeding by with a huge rebel flag flapping from the antenna. This is a bad omen, she thought to herself.

At 9:20 a.m. William Grier was driving to church with his wife Mamie in their new blue-and-white Buick Electra. On approach, they noticed a dark green 1955 to 1957 Chevrolet with a large Confederate flag flying from its rear antenna. There appeared to be a single person in the car, the driver, a white man around forty years old. He was cruising around the church. A foreboding gripped them.

Meanwhile, well-dressed families started streaming toward the church for adult and junior Sunday School classes. Mothers had taken special care to groom their children on this special day.

Most early arrivals were there for Sunday School. Children, usually more than two dozen of them, would head to the basement area, where they would break into groups in small rooms off the main assembly area. The girls would often preen for the service in a "ladies' lounge" in the northeastern corner of the basement.

The church had grown so much in recent years that the adult Sunday School classes had to meet in various locations throughout the building. Most adults would bypass the basement and meander up the massive stairs in the front of the building that led directly to the sanctuary.

Claude and Gertrude Wesley planned to make the short trek from their home at 11th Avenue North with their beloved Cynthia Morris, a fourteen-year-old who had come into their life when she was only six. Cynthia was from a large family with a single mother who was having difficulty raising her children, and a social worker had persuaded Mrs. Morris to allow Cynthia to live with the Wesleys, who had no children of their own.

Pushed academically by Mrs. Wesley, a teacher and later a principal at Lewis Elementary, Cynthia played the violin, was in the school band, and sang in the church choir. Noted for her vibrancy and sense of humor, she loved animals and planned to be a veterinarian. She was "a blessing from God," according to the Wesleys.

On Saturday night, Cynthia had been reading news of the death of a baby and was motivated to ask why God would take home such an inno- cent child. Mrs. Wesley replied that God sometimes took buds that would bloom in his heavenly garden.

Cynthia was eager to arrive for her Sunday School class that morning, so Claude Wesley dropped her at the front of the church at 9:30 before parking several blocks away and heading off to take care of some personal business, including getting a shoeshine, before the 11:00 a.m. service.

Cynthia's friend Carole Robertson was also dropped off in front of the church by her father. She was especially excited about the prospect of being an usher for the special service.

The fourteen-year-old—Alvin and Alpha Robertson's third child—was, like sister Diane and brother Alvin Jr., a standout in most everything she did. An honor roll student, she entered Parker High School in 1962, where she sang and played clarinet in the band. A Brownie who had graduated to the Girl Scouts, Carole also joined Jack and Jill of America, a group formed to build leaders among young blacks.

Addie Mae Collins didn't have the benefit of a car ride that day. She was a little disheveled on arrival, having used a pretty purse as a makeshift foot- ball for a fun scrimmage with her sisters on the walk to the church.

The fourteen-year-old was the seventh of Oscar and Alice Collins's eight children and was considered the peacemaker in the family. An eighth grader at Hill Elementary School, she played baseball and was quite the pitcher, blessed with a baffling underhand motion.

Addie Mae sang in the church choir and the night before had starched her white dress and pressed and curled her hair so she would look her best. But the football game with younger sister Sarah and older sibling Janie that broke out on her walk to 16th Street meant Addie Mae needed a touch-up if she was to look her best as an usher at the special service.

The Collins girls arrived a little after 10:00, a bit late for Sunday School.

Janie informed her younger sisters they needed to hurry into the ladies' lounge to make sure they looked appropriate.

Denise McNair was also running a little late and wanted her father to drop her off on his way to his church, St. Paul's Lutheran. But her dad, Chris, was pressed for time.

"Why can't you wait for me?" she asked her daddy, who explained he had duties as St. Paul's Sunday School superintendent.

"Okay Daddy, go ahead," she said. A short time later she hugged her dog Whitey and joined her mother, Maxine, for the drive to 16th Street.

Arriving at 9:55, as the cool, dry day slowly seemed to be transforming into something less desirable under increasingly overcast skies, Maxine parked near the parsonage on 5th Avenue. The two parted at the steps outside the church as Denise went downstairs while her mother climbed the stairs to attend her adult class in the choir loft, almost directly above the ladies' lounge.

A few minutes after reaching her Sunday School class, Denise asked permission from her teacher, Clevon Phillips, to go to the ladies' lounge. Two of the Collins sisters—Addie Mae and Sarah—were already there, along with Cynthia Morris Wesley and Carole Robertson.

Janie Collins and Marsha Stollenwerck were leaving as Denise arrived. Walking toward them to tell the young ladies to return to their class was Bernadine Mathews, fifteen, sent on this mission by her teacher.

Admonishing the girls to hurry up and put on their robes so they could help usher, Bernadine heard Cynthia say, "I just have to push my hair up one more time, and I'll be ready."

Before closing the door, Bernadine responded, "Cynthia, children who don't obey the Lord live only half as long." She then turned and began to walk back to her classroom.

The explosion was heard miles away. "The whole world started shaking. It sounded like it, felt like it," recalled Reverend Cross, who had been enjoying a little pre-service solitude on a pew in the sanctuary at that minute, 10:22 a.m., when the clock in the sanctuary stopped and time stood still.

Pieces of brick, glass, concrete, dust, dirt, and debris fell through the windows of the church into the sanctuary. Flying debris cut many, and scores of worshippers were disoriented by the explosion and devastation around them. Smoke accompanied by a fetid odor swept through the building.

As the crushing sound of the blast subsided, the rising cacophony was a sickening blend of screams for help and pain from children, mothers, and fathers. Reverend Cross quickly ushered the ninety or so members in the main church area out of the building for fear it would buckle.

While the adult Sunday School classes exited from the main entrance, the pastor checked to see if the basement, where the children's class had been due to conclude at 10:30 a.m., had been cleared. There had been at least two dozen kids and teachers in the rooms below the main worship area.

It appeared most of the children in the basement had escaped the building, though some were cut, screaming as they searched for parents outside. Many managed to get out unharmed, ushered to safety by their teachers after lying on the floor under tables to protect themselves from falling ceiling fragments.

Working his way outside, Reverend Cross observed a huge hole where the window to the ladies' lounge had been located. The outside stairs next to that window had been reduced to rubble, and there was a crater descending about eighteen inches into the church's concrete foundation. His heart sank as he realized it was likely someone would have been in the now obliterated lounge at the time of the explosion.

It also occurred to Reverend Cross that another explosion was a possibility. It gave him a moment's pause before he quickly made the decision to enter the devastated area through the gaping hole in the side of the church.

Joined by a few worshippers, he tossed aside debris, choked on dust, and struggled to make out anything still intact. Then they all saw it. A body, and another, and . . . four dead and disfigured girls next to each other as if stacked neatly in a row. Complete, overwhelming horror was postponed, however, as the men heard moans. Amid the rubble was Sarah Collins, alive but with terrible injuries, including a shattered eye; her face had been pierced by about two dozen shards of glass.

Placed in an ambulance, Sarah sobbed and screamed uncontrollably: "Addie . . . Addie!"

D.O.A.

Chris McNair had heard the explosion from St. Paul's. He was familiar with that sound and feared its consequences, knowing the direction it came from. Seeing the plume of smoke in the distance, he raced toward 16th Street.

On arrival, he instinctively snapped a single photo with his ever-present camera, before the sounds of distress and panic alerted him to the likelihood that the damage that morning was not restricted to the church building that he had just photographed.

Maxine McNair's screams were primal. She couldn't find Denise. Her father, M.W. Pippin, who owned the laundromat across 16th Street, having recognized Niecie's leather shoes amid the carnage, broke the news to her.

Dr. Joseph Donald Jr. was the physician on duty at Hillman Hospital (now UAB Medical Center) on Birmingham's Southside when the ambulances arrived with victims. In the end, there were more than twenty injured and the four girls who were pronounced dead on arrival.

Birmingham Coroner J. O. Butler and his deputy, W. L. Allen, had the gruesome task of photographing and identifying the deceased. The negatives were enlarged by the Birmingham police photographer, Don Sharp, and forwarded immediately to the Office of U.S. Attorney General Robert F. Kennedy. As Coroner, Dr. Butler was accustomed to dealing with the bodies of homicide victims, but on this day, September 15, 1963, he had the especially grim duty of leading parents into a makeshift morgue to view the remains of their little girls.

Fourteen-year-olds Carole Robertson, Addie Mae Collins, and Cynthia Morris Wesley and eleven-year-old Carol Denise McNair, all bursting with life, radiant in their Sunday best and filled to the brim with promise earlier that morning, were dead from massive head injuries. Their bodies were horribly burned. Cynthia was only immediately identifiable by her clothes and shoes.

The nightmare image that remains with Chris McNair, now in his ninety-third year, is of his lifeless Niecie with a piece of mortar still piercing her skull.

The Aftermath

The face of Jesus was blown off. Somewhat remarkably, the explosion that destroyed walls, badly damaged buildings in the vicinity, and crushed nearby cars left an image of Christ in a stained-glass window on the 16th Street side of the church intact, except for the face.

The force of the explosion was such that it was surprising anything was left standing in the immediate area and that the death toll wasn't drastically higher. That was, of course, no consolation to anyone, especially Reverend Cross, who would blame himself for the girls' deaths for the rest of his life.

Reverend Cross found it easier to forgive the bombers than he did himself for allowing his church to be used as the assembly point for the spring and summer's protest action, believing it made 16th Street and the children targets for evil. Decades after the attack I watched this fine man repeatedly beat himself up over it. It was heart-wrenching.

Most everyone immediately suspected that the Klan was the culprit. A line had been crossed, shifting the race relations paradigm forever. There had been Klan atrocities for as long as anyone could remember, but usually each event would briefly propel all the pieces of the racism puzzle into the air only to have them come down pretty much where they had been before.

Not this time, however. The bombing and the death of the girls had the capacity to either embolden or break the black community and certainly shook some moderate whites from their complacent Southern stupor. The shock waves rippled through the nation as horrified people everywhere asked how such a thing could happen in the United States.

Politicians in the nation's capital, procrastinating over the proposed civil rights legislation introduced in the wake of the children's marches, faced a new ugly reality.

With the world's attention on Birmingham, what would quickly become a huge, unwieldy, multi-agency investigation was launched.

The Birmingham police force, regardless of the intent of scores of honest cops, was littered with Klan sympathizers who not only had the capacity to hamper inquiries about the bombing but quite possibly had insider knowledge of the crime.

The ranks of the state authority, too, were poisoned by white supremacists and men whose primary allegiance was to George Wallace and a segregated way of life. Prominent among them was Alabama Department of Safety Director Al Lingo.

FBI agents, while certainly not untouchable, were less wedded to the mores of the South. In fact, J. Edgar Hoover, the agency's iron-willed boss, used to insist on stationing G-men in areas where they had no real roots. With their expert resources and personnel, the Feds were the best chance to uncover evidence in Birmingham that could be used effectively in a court of law. Their presence, however, would infuriate local authorities.

Some potential conflicts between city, state, and federal authorities were bypassed when President Kennedy quickly anointed the FBI with control of the investigation. But the immediate challenge of stopping the city from descending into civil unrest and potentially going up in flames rested with local authorities.

In the aftermath, there was a swift eruption of violent protest, and by the end of that terrible day, further fatal violence. Enraged African Americans in and around the city threw rocks at police and bystanders. Passersby were attacked, cars overturned, and several abandoned buildings near the church damaged. One white boy, sixteen-year-old Dennis Robertson, was heading home from work at the farmers market when he was struck by a rock to the face, putting him in a coma for several days.

In the suburbs, whites carried on as normal. The segregationists gathered to have group tantrums about integrating schools and denounce the influence of outsiders and the federal government.

Around the church, a crowd of black folks quickly gathered. Most were there to assist, but many could not contain their anger when they learned of the children's deaths. A riot threatened to break out as police and other officials converged on the scene.

Reverend Cross likely saved a few lives when he pleaded for calm. At one point he grabbed a bullhorn from James Lay, a postal worker and member of the volunteer team that tried to protect the homes and churches of the civil rights leaders from bombers.

Lay, one of the first on the scene to help that day, would play a crucial—though reluctant—role in the investigation and prosecution of the case until he died thirty-eight years later.

Reverend Cross, seemingly powerless to stop the protests, stood surrounded by rubble outside the church. Battling an overwhelming, acrid odor and with ghastly images of disfigured dead girls planted in his head, he used the bullhorn to beseech the crowd for calm, offering some of the prayers that would have been used in the Sunday School lesson earlier that morning: "A Love That Forgives."

More Death

In neighborhoods around the city, people tumbled into the streets to talk and comfort one another. But this was Birmingham. The Chevys with rebel flags continued to prowl the suburbs, their symbolic ammunition more repellant than ever, and at least one community went ahead with a plan for a mass rally to protest school integration.

A bunch of white kids drove by sixteen-year-old African American Johnny Robinson and his friends, who were hanging out near 26th Street. Soda pop bottles and racial slurs spewed out of the Confederate flag–emblazoned car, witnesses said. The teens hurled abuse and rocks in response.

One projectile struck an unintended target, a police cruiser. In the backseat was Officer Jack Parker with a shotgun. The kids scattered. As they ran away, one, perhaps two shotgun blasts erupted. Johnny Robinson was shot in the back and killed.

The cops, who had blocked the alley and the obvious escape route, suggested it was an accident—maybe the police car had hit a bump, and Officer Parker's shotgun went off—or maybe they had stopped too suddenly.

A more credible account came from other witnesses, who said police deliberately shot twice without any verbal warning and hit the fleeing, unarmed teenager, who had done nothing to the officers except run from them.

An inquiry was held, and both a local and, later, federal grand jury found no reason to prosecute Parker. As several high-profile cases have shown again in recent years, taking action for "excessive force" incidents involving white officers and young black males, no matter how apparently clear-cut the case, is a special challenge. It was damn near impossible in 1963.

The same afternoon across town at the Dixie Speedway in suburban Midfield, several thousand white protesters, including many of the Klan's most obnoxious, had gathered for a rally decrying the integration of West End High School.

Even though rally leader Reverend Ferrell Griswold canceled a planned march into the city, tension at the rally was high, anger immense. The federal government, as usual, was blamed for pushing unwanted change, and an effigy of Attorney General Kennedy was burned.

A couple of attendees, sixteen-year-olds Michael Lee Farley and Larry Joe Sims, no doubt fired up by the rally, went off to buy a rebel flag that they mounted on Michael's red motorcycle.

Around the same time, African-American brothers Virgil and James Ware, unaware of the bombing downtown, hopped on James's bicycle. Farley and Sims, apparently aware that white teen Dennis Robertson had been seriously injured in a rock-throwing incident earlier in the day, spotted the boys.

Thirteen-year-old Virgil was on top of the handlebars while his sixteen-year-old brother pedaled toward their home in Pratt City. As the red motorcycle, driven by Farley, drew close, Farley handed his .22 revolver to Sims.

Passing the kids on the bicycle, Sims fired. Bullets from the gun hit Virgil in the chest and cheek. The Sandusky Elementary School student was pronounced dead at 5:05 p.m.

Farley and Sims would ultimately confess. Sims told authorities that he was just trying to scare the boys. Both were prosecuted in juvenile court, but neither was sent to prison, and their suspended sentences carried only a two-year probation.

King Arrives

Grief and rage hung heavy in the air when Dr. King arrived in Birmingham that Sunday night.

Confrontations flared all over the city as the grieving families began the seemingly impossible task of finishing one day and contemplating starting another without their children.

Alpha and Alvin Robertson and their two remaining kids sought solace and strength from prayer, not only for their beloved Carole and the other girls but also for their assailants. They promptly decided that Reverend Cross should memorialize Carole at Alvin's church, St. John's African Methodist Episcopal Church, on Tuesday. Their daughter's fellow choir members from 16th Street would sing hymns in her memory.

Dr. King and other movement leaders wanted to have a single, combined memorial for the four girls to ensure maximum attendance and media exposure to highlight the tragedy. The leaders met with each family, but even with Dr. King's remarkable powers of persuasion, he could only convince three of the four families to participate. The Robertsons stuck with their plan for a separate memorial for Carole.

There has been speculation their decision was influenced by comments Dr. King made criticizing the "apathy" and "complacency" of black people in Alabama, suggesting it contributed to a mindset that made the bombing possible. However, in my dealings with Alpha, who became a close friend years later and a person I admired greatly, that notion was never discussed. She told me pointedly the funeral arrangement was a decision made very soon after Carole's death and the family simply preferred not to change it.

The Blame Game

Some bombing suspects were identified within twenty-four hours. Everyone quickly recognized the Klan was the likely culprit, and before long evidence started pointing at a group of the KKK's most violent, who had a long history of terrorism in Birmingham.

A consensus was forming that, after years of terrorizing black communities in the city, the Klan had gone several steps too far. The city's new mayor, Albert Boutwell, broke down and cried in reaction to the horror and vowed to get "the few" responsible. But a young lawyer, disgusted by the bombing and the destructive culture of accusation, denial, and venality, let Birmingham know the blame should be widely spread.

In a speech of brilliance and bravery on par with the best of the civil rights era, Charles Morgan Jr. homed in on broad truths about the bombing, the murders, and the South, so much of which we still avoid facing today.

On Monday, September 16, Morgan addressed a lunch meeting of the city's white establishment, the Birmingham Young Men's Business Club, at the Redmont Hotel. He didn't need to focus on the Klan. Morgan's righteous attention was on his own people, white moderates who had done nothing to change the oppression of their black neighbors and had perpetuated an apartheid-like culture generation after generation by encouraging or tolerating blatant racial and social injustice.

Morgan was brilliantly indelicate in laying responsibility for the catastrophe at the feet of the people he was looking in the eye at that moment—the people who lived "in a leaderless city where no one accepts responsibility, where everybody wants to blame everybody else."

"Who did it?" he asked.

The "who" is every little individual who talks about the "niggers" and spreads the seeds of his hate to his neighbor and his son. The jokester, the crude oaf whose racial jokes rock the party with laughter. The "who" is every governor who ever shouted for lawlessness and became a law violator. It is every senator and every representative who in the halls of Congress stands and with mock humility tells the world that things back home aren't really like they are. It is courts that move ever so slowly, and newspapers that timorously defend the law.

Morgan's overriding message was that inaction over the city's moral flaws—by people in a position to do something about them—had created and preserved the dysfunction that culminated in the church bombing.

"We all did it," he told Birmingham's most powerful whites.

Eventually, death threats against Morgan and his young family resulted in his relocation out of Alabama.

The Funerals

On Tuesday, about two thousand people attended Carole's funeral, including an estimated one hundred white citizens.

Reverend Cross called it "the most painful eulogy I ever gave," and the choir sobbed as much as sang in honor of their gentle friend. St. John's minister, C. E. Thomas, beseeched the assembled mourners not to resort to violence. Standing by Carole's flower-laden casket, he closed the memorial with a brief prayer: "Grant that her blood may be a symbol of Crispus Attucks," a reference to the first person killed by the Redcoats at the Boston Massacre in 1770, an African American who became an anti-slavery icon.

The following day, in steamy September heat, Dr. King eulogized Cynthia, Denise, and Addie Mae at the Sixth Avenue Baptist Church.

No city officials were among the overflow crowd of an estimated seven thousand mourners, including hundreds of clergy, white and black, from a variety of religions.

"This afternoon we gather in the quiet of this sanctuary to pay our last tribute of respect to these beautiful children of God," King told the mourners.

These children—unoffending, innocent, and beautiful—were the victims of one of the most vicious and tragic crimes ever perpetrated against humanity.

And yet they died nobly. They are the martyred heroines of a holy crusade for freedom and human dignity. And so this afternoon in a real sense they have something to say to each of us in their death. They have something to say to every minister of the gospel who has remained silent behind the safe security of stained-glass windows.

They have something to say to every politician who has fed his constituents with the stale bread of hatred and the spoiled meat of racism. They have something to say to a federal government that has compromised with the undemocratic practices of southern Dixiecrats and the blatant hypocrisy of right-wing northern Republicans.

They have something to say to every Negro who has passively accepted the evil system of segregation and who has stood on the sidelines in a mighty struggle for justice. They say to each of us, black and white alike, that we must substitute courage for caution. They say to us that we must be concerned not merely about who murdered them, but about the system, the way of life, the philosophy which produced the murderers.

Their death says to us that we must work passionately and unrelentingly for the realization of the American dream.

And so my friends, they did not die in vain. God still has a way of wringing good out of evil. And history has proven over and over again that unmerited suffering is redemptive. The innocent blood of these little girls may well serve as a redemptive force that will bring new light to this dark city.

That night after the funerals, Diane Nash, the brilliant civil rights strategist and activist, took an idea she had developed with her husband, James Bevel, to Dr. King and the SCLC leadership.

Nash, like most prominent figures in the movement, had been rocked to the core by the church bombing and the deaths of those children. Decisive action was required to initiate change in Alabama, and she enthusiastically proposed a nonviolent group march on the state capital of Montgomery.

In her passionate pitch, Nash advocated making it a nonviolent "siege"—a concept that King wasn't quick to embrace. Eventually, however, the proposal would be acted on when King led the march from Selma to Montgomery, one of the pivotal events in civil rights history.

The Investigation

It's not only with the benefit of hindsight that we can see how the challenge of carrying out a thorough, focused, and unbiased investigation of the bombing was a monumental task in Birmingham.

It was certainly obvious in 1963, when the President quickly appointed the FBI as lead investigative authority. Local law enforcement was a snake pit and despite the Feds' apparent detachment from local influences, J. Edgar Hoover believed Dr. King to be a dangerous "communist" and was anything but sympathetic to the civil rights movement.

That has prompted speculation that Hoover and the FBI did not put sufficient effort into the investigation. What I found in my review of the files, some thirty-five years later, however, was just the opposite.

Granted, to this day, I don't believe that Hoover went the extra yard because the victims were African-American girls, and he certainly didn't demand a painstaking investigation to placate the civil rights movement, but he did care about himself and the FBI. He knew full well—indeed, he was on record as saying—that "the reputation of the Bureau" was at stake.

Hoover and the organization he shaped knew the danger the Klan presented to the wider community throughout the South and beyond. They were prolific bombers, thugs, and murderers, bound by secrecy, prompting extensive federal law enforcement efforts to infiltrate their ranks. The Bureau had a well-established practice of paying informants inside the KKK monthly sums for information.

The FBI chief duly directed as many resources at the bombing investigation as he could. And crucially, the focus and resolve of the forty or so agents assigned to the case—the "boots on the ground"—were extraordinary. Without their quality work, no resolution of the case would ever have been possible.

The investigation was conducted in a testing atmosphere. The local authorities didn't want Feds there, and even though federal agents could approach Birmingham's African-American population with more hope of securing cooperation than local cops could, they still met with resistance. Additionally, the Klan hated the Feds, viewing them as some sort of Yankee invading force when they descended on Birmingham in the days after the bombing.

Birmingham's blacks at the time understandably had little faith in their police force. There were even whispers that Bull Connor and his goons had initiated the entire incident.

Before the Feds arrived, the vast number of honest local authorities tried to launch the investigation but faced the outrage of the community. Rocks and bricks were launched at official vehicles. A police car bore the brunt of the anger, and was pummeled with missiles on approach to the church. Richard Harris, of the Alabama Gas Company, was aboard.

Harris was there to evaluate if the explosion could have been the result of a natural gas leak rather than a bomb. He quickly dismissed the possibility, insisting there was zero chance any malfunctioning gas line could have been the culprit.

Other local authorities made swift, informed assessments of the scene, including Fire Marshal Aaron Rosenfeld. A bombing expert, no doubt with a lot of fieldwork experience in Birmingham, he evaluated the blast as having been caused by at least ten sticks of dynamite. He suggested that the bomb had been detonated by a fuse-type device, making it easy for an individual to quickly drop the package and depart.

The crater created by the explosion was five-and-a-half-feet wide and two-and-a-half deep. Digging through the debris of brick, stone, concrete, glass, mortar, plaster, and wood lath, firemen and police packaged significant items and samples to ship to the FBI labs. Yet even utilizing the best forensic facilities available, the FBI was unable to determine the exact explosive used.

No fragments of a mechanical timing device fuse or blasting caps were found. However, a small red plastic and wire piece was located near the site and identified as part of a fishing bobber, which didn't seem like much at the time.

As city officials carried out their necessary work straight after the attack, the FBI did what local white cops with a poor reputation in African-American communities couldn't hope to do and canvased accounts from black folks who had been at the church and in the surrounding area. They also drew on contacts, some paid informants, within the Klan's ranks.

There was immense pressure to find the culprits, to be at least seen as doing the right thing in reaction to this horrific act. Even the Klan carried out an "investigation," primarily to establish whether there was any conceivable way to blame anyone but the Klan. Such an investigation also had the possible benefit of being able to hand over a sacrificial lamb from within its ranks to save the organization, if necessary.

A reward, initiated by Mayor Boutwell to find the culprits in residential bombings, such as the attacks on the home of leading civil rights attorney and activist Arthur Shores in August and September, was broadened to include an appeal for information on the church bombing. Donations streamed in from around the country, and the reward ballooned to nearly $80,000. Police believed Klan leaders worried that such riches might tempt one of their many poor members to go to the authorities.

State authorities, anxious to prove they were in control and to keep the Feds at arm's length, made plenty of noise about investigating the tragedy. Colonel Al Lingo, the Director of the Alabama Department of Public Safety, a Wallace appointee who had been the Governor's pilot during the 1962 gubernatorial campaign, clearly wanted to get one up on the FBI. Word trickled out that Dynamite Bob Chambliss, long suspected as the brains behind most of the explosive destruction in "Bombingham," was the State's immediate suspect.

When Lingo announced the arrest of Chambliss, Charles Cagle, and John Wesley Hall on possession of dynamite charges just weeks after the bombing, some believed the case had been solved (and that the FBI had been scooped by the state of Alabama, taking some of the growing pressure off segregationist Governor Wallace).

It was not to be. While the Alabama authorities may have wanted to beat the Feds to the punch, the Klan's vow of silence and the lack of concrete evidence ensured that any attempt at prosecution was premature.

Eventually, the three were charged with a misdemeanor for dynamite possession, fined one hundred dollars, and let go. The $80,000 reward went unclaimed. Nobody from the KKK was talking. The FBI, however, remained convinced that Chambliss was one of their targets.

At first there was a list of thirty-eight possible suspects, all either members of the KKK or the White Citizens' Council. That was quickly whittled down to eleven, most of them Cahaba River Bridge Boys. Chambliss and Tommy Blanton were on top of every legitimate investigator's list, with Bobby Frank Cherry, Herman Cash, and Troy Ingram right behind.

Various sources and witnesses had offered snippets of information about the men's involvement; lie detector tests were routinely failed by the suspects and their associates; and there were numerous reports pointing to the likely use of Blanton's car in transporting the bomb to the church. The alibis of Chambliss, Blanton, and Cherry for September 13, 14, and 15 also lacked consistency, changing as the FBI's questioning became more intense.

One Klansman, Mitch Burns, was so moved by the morgue photographs of the murdered girls that he was willing to risk his life by making secret tape recordings of the suspects boasting about their hateful acts.

Other promising recordings of Klan-related conversations were made, specifically of Tommy Blanton, but the FBI, probably correctly at the time, believed the method of recording would make them inadmissible in the increasingly unlikely event the case made it to trial.

Weeks of investigation turned into months, then years. The outrage over the bombing remained acute while the national news media kept tabs on the FBI's inquiries, but when the Feds' leads dried up, so too did the widespread coverage. As civil rights protests and incidents flared elsewhere in the South and throughout the country, the spotlight gradually faded on Birmingham, whose boosters were anxious to put the ugliness behind the city.

The African-American community, so used to disappointment and lacking faith in any authority, began speculating that the killers would walk free. However, the FBI made a furious push to solidify their case against the Klansmen. The Klan's wall of silence had stayed relatively firm, but there were three outside witnesses—reluctant ones, fearful for their safety—who could possibly help crack the case.

One was James Lay, who was part of a volunteer group keeping an eye on churches and homes of civil rights leaders that were potential bombing targets. At about 1:00 a.m. on September 2, Lay was finishing his rounds, driving down 16th Street. As he approached the church, he noticed two white men, one standing near a car while the other was close to the steps that led to the ladies' lounge.

The suspicious man near the stairs was holding a "grip" or satchel. When Lay hit the bright lights of his car, the two jumped into their vehicle and sped away. He dutifully reported the incident to the police, but officers told Lay, a black man, to "just go on home, boy. You didn't see a damn thing." After the church was bombed, Lay again told the authorities about the car and the men he had seen that night. He would later identify Blanton and Chambliss as those men.

Disc jockey "Tall Paul" White, who lived in a boardinghouse behind the church, confirmed that Lay had told him what he had seen and had asked him to keep searching the area for signs of trouble.

At 2:10 a.m. on September 15, a Detroit visitor, Kirthus Glenn, was looking for a parking spot near her friend's house on 7th Avenue North when she glimpsed the interior light of a car parked in front of Poole's Funeral Chapel, behind the 16th Street Baptist Church. She saw three white men in the car and got a good look at one of them in the backseat. She would eventually identify him as Chambliss.

At the time, she described the car as a Chevy similar to Blanton's; later she identified a model and color for the vehicle that was an exact match. She may have even given police the license plate number, but there was no official record of that information having been handed over.

What Glenn saw that night was similar to a story recorded by the FBI from Mary Frances Cunningham, Chambliss's sister-in-law. Cunningham hated her sister's husband and provided law enforcement with accounts of Chambliss frequently boasting about his nefarious activities. The night before the bombing she was at the Chambliss house as the phone rang off the hook; clearly, something was up. In a statement to an investigator more than a year after the bombing, Cunningham said that she and her sister Flora, also known as Tee, tracked Dynamite Bob to the church. They allegedly watched as Chambliss and his cohorts, including satchel-carrying Bobby Frank Cherry, went about their business under cover of darkness.

Cunningham tried to warn police, calling a sheriff's deputy, James Hancock, with whom she had a relationship of information sharing, and perhaps something more, to let him know she suspected Chambliss had set a bomb. Hancock slammed the phone down on her. In the morning, hours before the bomb went off, she repeated the warning, but he failed to report it.

Cunningham was potentially a game-changing witness, but she had let investigators know, in no uncertain terms, she would not testify. She was terrified. Later, she repeatedly recanted the story that she had followed the Klansmen to the church. In fact, she would protest decades later that she never made such a statement to the FBI.

Both Glenn and Lay would also prove to be recalcitrant.

After four years of investigation, the FBI had a great deal of circumstantial evidence and some solid accounts of the involvement of Chambliss and Blanton, and to a lesser extent Cherry and probably Cash. But no smoking gun was identified. There wasn't even absolute proof a dynamite bomb had killed the girls.

Conviction of white men in the South by all-white, all-male juries was the exception rather than the rule in the mid-sixties, and that was when there was concrete evidence and multiple eyewitness accounts.

The FBI boss, Hoover, no friend to black America, decided with some justification that proceeding with the case and trying to prepare it for trial was a fruitless endeavor. In a confidential internal memo, Hoover shut down the so-called BAPBOMB investigation in 1968 without any charges laid.

TWO

BAXLEY

I was told that in some classes at my elementary school, and across the South, students applauded, although I just recall a stunned silence when we got news of President Kennedy's assassination on November 22, 1963.

Our teachers at Glen Oaks Elementary—apparently attuned to the psychological impact—asked us to write about it. I finally got to openly express my admiration for our young President, and remember, quite distinctly, feeling a strong desire to declare my intention to do something important with my own life.

Perhaps I would work toward being the Governor of Alabama or a senator, and then President of the United States, I wrote.

I secretly wanted to be an astronaut, a baseball player like Mickey Mantle, or a footballer like Joe Namath, but you had to shoot for something more realistic.

With the best of intentions, my parents had tried to "protect" me from the ugliness of the church bombing and the racial animus that flared in response. JFK's assassination, however, was an event covered like no other by news outlets.

The outside world arrived in Glen Oaks on the back of tragedy, and from that point on, my suburban cocoon would frequently be penetrated: from Jack Ruby gunning down Lee Harvey Oswald nine weeks to the day after the church bombing, to Viola Liuzzo's death at the hands of the Klan, to Bloody Sunday in Selma.

When Hoover made the decision to shut the FBI book on the Birmingham bombing, the country had already started averting its damning gaze from the South as civil unrest flared elsewhere. The nation had much on its mind in 1968: the Vietnam War; housing discrimination; the rise of black consciousness, especially in urban centers; and the assassinations of Martin Luther King Jr. and Bobby Kennedy.

The change and tumult were filtered by my increasingly anxious, still white, neighborhood, but they were upon us. All schools were finally integrating.

It happened in fits and starts, but integration was profoundly impactful for me. Rather than routinely seeing African-American kids as "other," we eventually got to share space, ambitions, frustrations, and achievements.

There was widespread community opposition at every step, but the decisive battles to desegregate were fought in the courts, not the streets, including the intended unification of my all-white high school, Fairfield, with the black institution, E.J. Oliver High.

I got the chance to sit in and watch lawyers debate the best way to complete the desegregation process for Fairfield City schools. It was my first experience in a courtroom and I marveled at the rhythm of the process, how waves of information would develop a fuller picture of facts and possibilities with each session.

In the end, the court system, with the best of intentions, ordered a split of school facilities, with white kids in Fairfield (including me) instructed to attend the formerly all-black school for ninth and tenth grades. Older kids, in grades eleven and twelve, black and white, were to squeeze into Fairfield High.

There was a "hell no, we won't go" reaction from the white community to sending their kids to E.J. Oliver. Many fled the district or headed to private schools. My parents shared the anxiety and sent me to an already integrated school in nearby Bessemer for a semester. With so many kids leaving the school system, however, the plan was unworkable, and the judge ordered the closing of E.J. Oliver. Ninth- through twelfth-graders were to attend Fairfield.

On return to Fairfield for my junior year, the school was absurdly crowded. It was challenging, but there was an unmistakable sense that we were all in it together, and I was mature enough by that stage to realize integration was something that had to be made to work regardless of entrenched preconceptions, fears, and prejudices.

I'd always been an involved member of the school community—there wasn't an activity I hadn't tried at least once—and I relished the challenge of contributing to the integration effort. My education on racial issues was fast-tracked—I learned more in one day from a black student's distress at the Confederate flag on our school band uniforms than I had from years of discussions with adults. I also developed a growing political awareness.

In the spring of 1970, around the country there had been vigorous protests about the Vietnam War and specifically the brutal Cambodian campaign. On May 4, 1970, students at Kent State University in Kent, Ohio, were demonstrating when all hell broke loose. The Ohio National Guard, called in to disperse the crowd, fired sixty-seven rounds over thirteen seconds, killing four and injuring nine students, permanently paralyzing one.

The victims were basically kids, just a few years older than me. I was, like most young white people in the South, fundamentally conservative and uneasy about any protest that seemed to disrespect the troops in Southeast Asia, but the Kent State incident stuck in my craw.

At overcrowded Fairfield High months later, my teacher decided we were going to debate the shootings. Not a single student wanted to take the side of the Kent State students. Like the rest of the class, I perceived them as unpatriotic hippies, even though the deaths were terrible tragedies.

Nevertheless, when no one else would do it, I acquiesced and agreed to be the "spokesman" for the assaulted students. As I investigated, I felt a grinding sadness and quiet rage, realizing it was indeed a massacre and the students, these kids, had been murdered for exercising their First Amendment right of free speech. What's more, the principles they stood for were just and reasoned.

A lightbulb went on somewhere in my head (not for the last time, fortunately). I still supported the war effort, but never again would I take as gospel what a government or powerful organization said without fully examining the incident or issue. And I made a vow that I try to uphold to this day—I will always imagine walking in the shoes of others before sitting in judgment.

In my senior year at Fairfield, I had a leadership role as president of the student council, and we stepped up efforts to fully integrate all student activities: football, theater, band, and choir. We even revived the Miss Fairfield Pageant, which, to the horror of some, was won by a black freshman.

Just prior to graduation that spring, I was flattered to be nominated Fairfield High School's Youth of the Year. One of my mentors, Don Byrd, the former principal of Glen Oaks Elementary and Fairfield High School during its transition period, had written a letter to the Kiwanis Club putting my name forward.

It had all the signs of an inside job, my friends ribbed me, as Don, by then the superintendent of the Fairfield City School System, had a lovely daughter, Donna, whom I was dating. But make no mistake, he knew me well, as I'd worked with him to help the integration cause.

In a glowing letter of recommendation focusing on school integration, Don kindly wrote: "Doug's leadership between races and amongst students has been most significant."

I didn't know it at the time, but that recommendation not only made me Fairfield Youth of the Year but also placed me in a larger competition with seniors from school systems across the county. As a result, much to my surprise, I won the award as the Jefferson County Youth of the Year.

That night, Donna and I rode downtown to stare at the giant electronic sign atop the Bank for Savings building overlooking the city announcing that Doug Jones of Fairfield had been chosen as the Jefferson County Youth of the Year. Amazing what a motivation seeing your name in lights in the company of your teen girlfriend can be. I didn't know what I'd be doing in the future, but with my proud dad's counsel that now much was expected of me ringing in my ears, I knew it would involve trying to make a difference.

College

I'd done well academically at high school, opening the door to a vast array of options for future study. My family, however, didn't have any experience when it came to college. I would be the first to attend, so I didn't have insight to draw on when it came to figuring out what field to pursue. In the end, I made a decision that was a prescription for failure.

I was kidding myself when I decided medicine was to be my career. Being a doctor is what bright kids did, right? It didn't matter that I couldn't walk by a hospital without feeling uneasy (the product of a childhood hospital spell while being tested for a heart condition) or that the sight of blood made me dizzy; I would learn to love it.

However, I fairly swiftly realized it wasn't for me. I got through my first year before I broke the news to my parents that I would be continuing at the University of Alabama but studying law instead.

In retrospect, my career fate was probably sealed during those sophomore-year hearings on the school integration process. Also, at college I'd become engaged in campus politics and a push to change the Alabama Constitution and modernize the court system, which hooked me up with the legal fraternity.

A career seemed a long way off, anyway. College life was pregnant with possibilities: politics, fraternity life, sports, clubs. Bottom line: I was determined not to be a spectator.

Extracurricular activities did sometimes threaten to interfere with my study routine, but one summer I got an impactful reminder of why it was wise not to blow the chance I'd been given.

Dad got me a job working the cotton tie mill at U.S. Steel six days a week, ten hours a day. I was young, fit, and hungry to make a few dollars while college was in recess. It would be boring, sure, but think of the beer money!

An hour on the floor of that facility and I wasn't thinking of anything but the possibility I might not survive the second hour. It was beyond exhausting. If I'd been able to breathe properly, I would have told someone I was worried about dying from heat stroke, but I'm pretty sure they wouldn't have been able to hear me anyway in the unceasing, clangorous bedlam.

If you allowed yourself to think about it too much, you would realize an accident was inevitable. And that's what happened. A piece of steel catapulted out of a scrap baller—one of those machines that bind metal together for salvage purposes—and hit me right between my eyes. An inch either way, I would have lost an eye—and probably worse.

Fortunately, the only thing lost that day was any chance I'd falter in my studies.

"You weren't ever going back there," my father said. "I knew you'd do well at college then."

The biggest long-term distraction to study at Alabama was the Watergate hearings. Like millions of other Americans, I was consumed by those events. Public opinion and expectations about our politicians and Washington these days are so low it's hard to convey how shocking it was when it became clear the Nixon administration had been burglarizing, bugging, and intimidating activists and opponents.

Whatever moral high ground we had been standing on internationally gave way like a sinkhole.

When, on February 6, 1974, the U.S. House of Representatives voted 410–4 to authorize the House Judiciary Committee to investigate whether or not Nixon should be impeached, it was the beginning of a purge that had to happen.

Politics had long been a great passion of mine, but it felt far less noble in the wake of Watergate. Nevertheless, I was active in student affairs. As one of the Beta Theta Pi fraternity representatives in "The Machine," a not-so-secret political group composed of the fraternities on campus, I ended up being a two-term Student Government Association Senator.

In the spring of 1974, while an SGA Senator, we appropriated funds for the law student association to bring U.S. Supreme Court Justice William O. Douglas to speak at the university law school, as part of the program commemorating the twentieth anniversary of the *Brown v. Board of Education* decision. The judge had been a Beta himself and graciously accepted an invitation to address our fraternity.

I took advantage of my proximity to one of the country's great jurists to seek a little advice, specifically what suggestions he had for a law student who wanted to be a trial lawyer. Above all, he advocated watching good lawyers ply their trade. It wasn't just about the words they used but how they physically expressed themselves: their mannerisms and the way they represented their clients before the court and a jury. Don't mimic, just watch and learn, he said.

I took his advice with me to Cumberland School of Law at Samford University and acted on it when Alabama's young Attorney General barreled into Birmingham with an ambitious if unlikely plan to get a conviction in the fourteen-year-old 16th Street Baptist Church bombing case.

I'd first been struck by the rise of that young prosecutor from Dothan, Alabama, when I was a teen. Like the students at Kent State, he didn't look much older than me, yet at the time, twenty-eight-year-old Bill Baxley was the District Attorney in Houston County and running for the office of State Attorney General.

He was a political moderate with a progressive outlook at a time when that approach to public life got you trouble rather than a promising career in the South. But in January 1971 Baxley, a 1964 graduate of the University of Alabama Law School, became the youngest State Attorney General in the United States.

Alabama was a one-party state. Democrats controlled everything. In 1970, George Wallace, fresh off his third-party run for the presidency, narrowly edged gubernatorial incumbent Albert Brewer in the Democratic runoff.

Wallace had done what he did best, and conducted a brutal, race-baiting campaign. And once again, a majority of Alabamians casting ballots bought into it. It was, however, an election chock-full of ironies.

Alabama had reempowered the veteran, cynical, pragmatic, win-at-any-cost governor—but just behind him was Jere Beasley, elected as Lieutenant Governor, and the new Attorney General, Bill Baxley. Both were young and energetic rising stars. On the judicial side of the ballot, Howell Heflin was elected Chief Justice on the promise of modernizing Alabama's court system. All three were about as far away from Wallace as you could be and still get elected. Even with the segregation-supporting Governor back, surely the future looked bright to those hoping for change in Alabama.

Baxley, in particular, had an advantage Wallace and countless others from either side of politics could not suppress or hijack; his whole reason for being was shaped by truths learned and instilled in him as a young boy. He never saw a reason to relinquish those beliefs, and with every day that goes by, his commitment is vindicated.

Deep Roots

Baxley can trace his Alabama lineage back to the late 1700s, when his people decided to leave South Carolina and settle in a southeast portion of the state wedged between the Georgia and Florida border. The town of Dothan, Bill's birthplace, grew up around them. All four of his great-grandfathers were Confederate soldiers in the Civil War. His granddaddy was Dothan's mayor, and his father, Keener Baxley, a respected circuit court judge.

The Baxleys were Southern gentlefolk in a region that became best known for peanut production. It was, however, never part of the plantation belt, so some of the plantation mentality that evolved from slave ownership wasn't automatically handed down to prominent white families in that corner of southeastern Alabama, even if the local black population still battled racism and endured Jim Crow. "Dothan, relative to the rest of Alabama, was an oasis of moderation on racism," Baxley said. "But it was still a daily reality for the black population as I grew up."

Born June 27, 1941, Bill was a precocious child in an extraordinary family deeply attached to the South. Indeed, he didn't feel the need to go any further north than Chattanooga, Tennessee, or beyond Memphis to the west until he was twenty-one. Additionally, all his schooling was spent in all-white public schools, including college and law school, until his last year at the University of Alabama, which was integrated in 1963. Yet the Baxleys, unlike many Southern establishment families, were not encumbered with a perceived need to perpetuate a strict color line.

Young Bill, from a tender age, entertained the idea of being a politician. He was also outspoken. Attending the local Methodist church, he noted the inconsistency of what was preached with the reality of what was going on in the streets. "From my earliest memory, I just felt it was inherently wrong the way blacks were treated in my hometown and in my home state," he said. "I just wasn't comfortable with it and no one ever adequately explained," he said. "[So] I kept asking."

His parents, concerned for his prospects and safety, would gently encourage him to "tone it down." "My dad, who was a good person, would say 'son, I'm glad you feel that way, and I always want you to treat people fairly, but you need to watch what you are saying because there is absolutely nothing you can do about it and you are just going to ruin yourself.'"

Baxley and his younger brother, Wade, were often cared for during the day by James Owens, a black man hired by their busy parents. The three developed a close bond. The Baxley boys were confounded and incensed when they'd take a trip downtown and Owens would be made to wait outside a store because of his color. "It didn't make sense," Baxley said. "I let people know." When Owens eventually moved to Detroit, where he expected a little decency, it was a firm signal to Bill that his questioning of local attitudes was justified.

As a teen in the mid-1950s, television reports alluding to how blacks were being treated across Alabama stoked Bill's outrage. When he learned about Rosa Parks, Dr. King, and the bus boycott in Montgomery, it confirmed something could and was being done. While studying at the University of Alabama, he became politically active, supporting the national Democratic Party cause in Alabama with work on John F. Kennedy's successful 1960 presidential tilt.

He also got behind local moderate and reformist politicians such as Tom King of Birmingham.

In 1961, King ran for mayor of Birmingham with the support of Baxley and others at the university, including student leader Julian Butler, only to be defeated by hardline segregationist Art Hanes. King's son, Tom King Jr., recently noted that Hanes was "out front, but the man behind the curtain was Bull Connor."

The Kings were anything but friends of the Klan. According to Tom King Jr., the animosity, actually hatred, stemmed mainly from family patriarch Judge Alta King's decision in 1957 to jail four Klansmen for maximum sentences of twenty years for kidnapping and castrating a black man named Judge Edward Aaron.

When Alta's son Tom stood for mayor, segregationists acted to ensure his chance was over before polling began. Before the election, King, as a courtesy, met with Connor, the incumbent Commissioner of Public Safety.

As King left the brief meeting, someone called out to him. He turned, and a black man reached out to shake his hand. King naturally obliged. It was a setup.

Diane McWhorter detailed "the black-hand treatment" in her book *Carry Me Home*. She wrote that supporters of King's political opponent, Art Hanes, had staged the encounter.

As Tom King explained: "They fixed him up and put him out there to shake Dad's hand." As he did, a photographer in a nearby office snapped shots. It was a career killer in the country's most segregated city. King, who according to his son had been painted by the fear-mongering Klan as a man "sent by JFK and Dr. King to integrate the schools," became a dead man walking, politically speaking. Such was the tenor of politics in Birmingham in the sixties.

On June 11, 1963, from a window at the University of Alabama law school, Baxley watched George Wallace's dog and pony show at the entrance to Foster Auditorium—the infamous Stand in the Schoolhouse Door. As the Governor symbolically tried to block two African-American students from entering the university, Baxley quietly vowed to make Wallace eat his infamous words, uttered at his inaugural months before: "segregation now, segregation tomorrow, segregation forever."

Baxley recognized that Jim Crow laws and mores should have been left behind decades before in the South, but blatant injustices not only continued to be tolerated, they were touted as "normal." He knew then, on the threshold of a law career, what his purpose would be.

Sundays in college were for reflection and relaxation, and on September 15, 1963, the only thing on Baxley's schedule was a leisurely lunch at the fraternity house and an afternoon watching the National Football League. Then the news flash: a bomb in a Birmingham church . . . children . . . death.

Baxley was reeling. He felt sick to his stomach. His first impulse was to head to the scene, if only to provide sodas for rescuers, but that was pointless. Perhaps he would take a sabbatical from law school and volunteer his help to U.S. Attorney Macon Weaver, whom he had met on the Kennedy campaign and had seen standing alongside Deputy Attorney General Nicholas Katzenbach during the Wallace schoolhouse circus.

In the end, he resisted any knee-jerk reaction, though later that same day he made a promise to himself to do whatever he could to ensure the bombers were caught and held accountable. Over time, he monitored the investigation closely. The authorities' inability to bring anyone to justice by the time he graduated law school in 1964 meant the case would haunt him for a long time to come.

Out of law school, he spent a year working as a law clerk at the Alabama Supreme Court. But it was in federal court where the real action was taking place. Many of these federal cases were pivotal civil rights matters involving attorneys such as Charles Morgan Jr., and Baxley was a keen observer. "I was seeing the legal walls of segregation crumble," Baxley said. "I've named three of my children for federal judges."

After his clerkship, Baxley headed off for military service before taking up a position with a firm in Dothan. In 1968 he jumped at the chance to become District Attorney for Houston and Henry Counties, and at the age of twenty-five, he became the youngest DA in the state. A serious young man, he had a deep voice that he regularly activated to argue forcefully about the things that mattered most. He didn't shy away from a fight.

In 1970 Baxley ran for State Attorney General despite his youth (he was twenty-eight years old) and the opposition of powerful conservative forces. He swept into office like a hurricane, pursuing corruption issues and curtailing excess. He moved swiftly to ensure courtroom challenges to block black voting rights were run out of the system.

"First thing I did was dismiss all these cases that were pending to stop blacks from voting and stopping blacks from being on juries . . . segregation cases. I dismissed them all," he said. But before he did, Baxley let Governor George Wallace know what he planned.

Wallace had great respect for Baxley, and despite the Governor's outrageous public persona and reprehensible policies, the young AG got to know him as a man who was surprisingly amenable in private consultation. "He was charming," Baxley said. "I told Wallace I was going to do it—he just said 'do whatever you think you've got to do.'"

After Baxley stirred controversy in 1972 by appointing Alabama's first black Assistant Attorney General, Myron Thompson, Wallace was quietly supportive and curious, leading Baxley to conclude that he was never fully comfortable as a hardline segregationist and may have been thinking about changing his attitude.

Still, Wallace knew that bigotry and segregationist grandstanding were the keys to longevity in Alabama. Baxley equally understood his progressive agenda probably wouldn't buy him a lot of time as a public official. "My attitude was, 'you're here, you may not be here long, so you better do what you can,'" he said. And his number one priority was the girls who died at 16th Street Baptist.

The FBI had ended its investigation into the church bombing without bringing charges in 1968. But the desire for justice never grew dim for Baxley. He wrote the names of the bombing victims on each corner of his government-issued phone card, and he carried it everywhere. Within a couple of weeks of being appointed, he had the files on the case from the police and sheriff's offices. They were full of potholes.

"The first ones I looked at were the state troopers in Montgomery, and I got copies of [the] Birmingham police file and Jefferson County Sheriff file," Baxley said. "They weren't much help. They'd spent most of their man hours on this crazy theory that the blacks themselves had done the bombing in order to gain sympathy for their cause."

Local law enforcement had the challenge of dealing with significant numbers of Klan sympathizers in their ranks, which stunted some inquiries. Also, the FBI took over the investigation early in the process, prematurely curtailing other inquiries. Without access to FBI files—Baxley and his team were repeatedly denied—Baxley's investigators, headed by Jack Shows, were left to piece together leads from the compromised police and sheriff documents.

The FBI had plenty of reasons to be sensitive about opening its files. Sources and informants within the ranks of the Klan, for example, were still threatened by the "kiss of death." Even the hint that someone had talked to the Feds could have lethal consequences.

There was also a lot to cover up. The FBI had used people like Klansman Gary Thomas Rowe as a prime paid informant and in doing so effectively gave him a pass to engage in, even initiate, some of the organization's most violent attacks, including the beating of the Freedom Riders at the bus station in Birmingham in May 1961. He also played a role—indeed, a murderous role—in the death of Viola Liuzzo, the civil rights volunteer shot dead by Klansmen after the Selma to Montgomery marches.

Using a plethora of incomplete, often inaccurate information, Baxley tried to set about charging those responsible for the deaths of the girls. It was a protracted process, and he was destined to take numerous detours and wrong turns—some that opened other cold cases and led to convictions.

The old Klansmen, as always, felt they had nothing to fear. It had happened years ago, the FBI had dropped the case like a stone off a cliff, and no one had a chance in hell of uncovering what had happened—not now, not tomorrow, not ever.

What a Mess

Baxley's presence in the Alabama capital was a breath of fresh air for some, and he backed up his promise of a new and inclusive approach to refining and enforcing Alabama justice by making radical changes in operations, personnel, and priorities. Yet when it came to his number one goal, he was stumped. There was but a scintilla of useful material in the investigation documents he had at his disposal. Promising investigative work seemed to stop abruptly or go nowhere. Clearly, local determination to solve the crime had been underwhelming in some cases and actively undercut in others.

Baxley stepped up efforts to secure the FBI files, but the agency was stonewalling. J. Edgar Hoover, who had seemingly been FBI Director since Moses was in the bulrushes, had brought down the curtain on the matter, and that was that.

When the FBI boss died in May 1972, the Alabama AG hoped the situation would change. Unfortunately, it did not. Baxley made numerous trips to Washington from 1973 to 1975 to try and convince the FBI to give him access to the investigative file, always coming back empty-handed. The Bureau, then headed by Birmingham Special Agent in Charge Clarence Kelley, was as uncooperative as the Klan, if a little more polite.

Baxley was absolutely on his own in pushing this task forward. It was already a cold case that had years before received more federal attention than virtually any other investigation in the South. To some of the few people aware he was looking into it, his actions were obsessive and borderline reckless.

Even the black community, to a great extent, had internalized the pain of the loss and lack of justice. While it would never be swept under the carpet, it was almost too painful to talk about. After so many hundreds of years of abominable treatment at the hands of the law, lack of resolution in a matter such as this was standard operating procedure (though never acceptable).

The lack of FBI cooperation sent Baxley off on numerous wild-goose chases. While he laments "wasting time" chasing one long-enduring suspect, Georgia's J. B. Stoner, for the 16th Street church bombing, Baxley at least got the satisfaction of nailing him for the 1958 bombing of Reverend

Shuttlesworth's Bethel Baptist Church. Stoner was a man who thought Hitler too moderate, who compared blacks to apes and Jews to vipers.

In a different instance, following another church bombing tip, Baxley looked into Klan members in Montgomery who included murderers, bombers, and lunatics fully as bad as those in Birmingham. In the course of the investigation, Baxley's team established that the Klansmen were responsible for the 1957 murder of African-American Willie Edwards, a driver for the Winn-Dixie supermarket chain. They'd dragged him into a car, beaten him, then forced him to jump to his death off the Tyler-Goodwin Bridge into the Alabama River. The case had gone cold, but Baxley eventually (in 1976) reopened it and charged four men with Edwards's murder.

Sadly, a jury would never get to decide the fate of the defendants. Judge Frank Embry dismissed the charges because the actual cause of death had not been determined. He suggested, rather bizarrely, that "merely forcing" Edwards to jump off the bridge "probably" didn't lead to his death. The investigation into Willie Edwards's killing, like several other key civil rights–related cases, would be reopened in the late nineties (although no one was ever charged).

On yet another frustrating trip to Washington in 1975, Baxley had dinner with Jack Nelson, a distinguished journalist from Alabama working for the *Los Angeles Times*. Born in Talladega, Nelson got his start in Mississippi, at the *Biloxi Daily Herald*. He won a Pulitzer Prize in 1960 for local reporting at the *Atlanta Constitution* and moved to Washington, D.C., in 1965 as the *Los Angeles Times* Bureau Chief.

Nelson's influence was significant enough in 1970 for J. Edgar Hoover to put him on one of his secret watch lists. The FBI supremo's ire was raised when Nelson wrote a story about how the FBI had teamed with Meridian, Mississippi, police in a sting operation against the KKK where two Klan members had been ambushed and killed.

That night over dinner and drinks, Baxley vented about the uncooperative FBI, letting Nelson know he was desperate to find a way to get the agency to at least hand over some files, more than twelve years after the crime and four since the AG had started looking into it. Without access to the FBI files, the investigation would likely go nowhere.

A few days later Nelson let him know that Baxley might be getting a call offering assistance. Apparently, the journalist had cornered Attorney General Edward Levi, recently appointed by President Ford, and told him the *Los Angeles Times* was planning a series of front-page stories about the reopening of the 16th Street Baptist Church bombing case. A major angle in the story would be how the FBI and Justice Department would not co-operate with the Alabama Attorney General, thus allowing the murderers to remain free. Nelson told Levi he planned to bring the children's parents to Washington and hold a press conference to complain that the FBI and the Justice Department were covering up facts about the murders. It was a ruse, but it took only a week for Levi's office to let Nelson know that Baxley would get the cooperation he needed.

As the AG's campaign for justice over the bombing became more widely known, there was an outcry from some community leaders who suggested the case should be "left alone" after so many years. The segregationists had always disliked Baxley, but now they had an excuse to hate him publicly. He was called a "nigger lover" and a "disgrace to his race," among other things. Abuse from whites in restaurants and on the street wasn't uncommon. Threatening letters often came his way, and in his second term, there was concern he was on a KKK hit list.

Not surprising was a letter of hate from Edward Fields, a Georgia chiropractor who along with J. B. Stoner ran the right-wing National States' Rights Party. In a three-page diatribe, Fields called the AG a "traitor" to his race for having the temerity to investigate those "good, white, Christian Anglo-Saxon men." Baxley responded on official State letterhead:

Dear "Dr." Fields,
    My response to your letter of February 19, 1976 is—kiss my ass.
    Sincerely,

                          Bill Baxley
                     Attorney General

Bob Eddy

More than forty years after former Marine Bob Eddy found his calling in law enforcement, he still exhibits many of the qualities that made him a uniquely gifted sleuth. An effervescent eighty-six-year-old today, Eddy is handy with a joke and has a rich trove of tales about Southern justice, but he's also a trained listener with a proven ability to seize on nuggets of truth and insight others might miss.

A Korean War veteran, he was at one point a salesman and department head at Sears, but it was a downturn in the fortunes of Eddy's side interests—a restaurant and construction businesses in Huntsville, Alabama, in the 1970s—that ended up being one of the best things to happen to the church bombing investigation. That's because Eddy, a family man, was seeking to make up for an income shortfall and opted to take up an offer from one of the regulars at his Dixie Belle lunch joint.

Madison County Sheriff Jerry Crabtree suggested Eddy could make a few extra bucks operating as a deputy at night. Eddy hit the ground running and quickly developed into the department's top-gun investigator. In November 1976, Baxley hired him as his prime investigator and a few months later told him that for the next ninety days he had only one assignment: he was to go to Birmingham and read every file on the bombing case.

It was an eleventh-hour push on a thirteen-year-old case, as Baxley's term was coming to an end. He was desperate to make some progress toward an indictment. Eddy was instructed to camp at Birmingham's Holiday Inn and work out of the Bureau's local office.

The assumption was that Eddy would be able to draw the curtain back by delving into all FBI files. But that was not the way the Bureau "cooperated." Instead, he was only allowed to read what he specifically requested. "Unless you knew what to ask for, you didn't get it," Baxley said.

Eddy solicited the help of an old Huntsville friend, FBI agent Ed Kennedy, who was working in Birmingham. Kennedy was able to secure an arrangement to give Eddy better access to the records on the provision that whatever notes he made for Baxley he'd also provide to the local FBI.

It was painstaking work. Eddy would read and reread files, taking handwritten notes. An office worker would help him type the notes up and send a copy to Baxley in Montgomery and preserve one for the FBI bosses in Birmingham.

The puzzle came together relatively quickly. There were three prime suspects: Bob Chambliss, Tommy Blanton, and Bobby Frank Cherry. Troy Ingram, who had died in 1975, was also in the mix, and Herman Cash was likely involved. "It looked as though a few dozen of them [in the KKK] had knowledge of it," Baxley said. Witness interrogation and interviews with former investigators confirmed this belief. Eddy knew Dynamite Bob Chambliss was the principal participant.

It was clear the FBI had known this all along, almost from day one. They even bugged the Chambliss house by placing a microphone in a cuckoo clock, but they picked up frequent, loud cuckoos and not much else.

It was not only Chambliss's movements around the time of the bombing and subsequent statements that put him front and center in the FBI investigation. There were witnesses, too. But as Baxley and his team were to discover, the Klan had extensive reach. Getting people to commit to detailing what they knew about the seventy-three-year-old Chambliss and the others in a court of law would be as difficult in 1977 as it had been when the Cahaba River Bridge Boys had run roughshod over Birmingham in the sixties.

A local civil defense volunteer, a visitor from Detroit, and a close relative of Chambliss held the key. If they committed to testifying, Baxley might very well have a case. If not, the bombing investigation would be stalled again, probably for good.

Chambliss

Robert Edward Chambliss was ornery and odious. Actually, he was far worse than that, but even if you had no idea he was a murderous, racist thug, he came across as a mess of a man. According to some who met him, he was as explosive as one of his many incendiary devices and with a short fuse to boot.

"He was just a weirdo," Eddy said, and having spent almost a year digging into the Klansman's background, the investigator knew what he was talking about. "No one could like him."

He was obviously hell to live with, which, as it turned out, was a rare blessing for the church bombing investigators. Chambliss's wife, sister-in-law, and niece were terrified of him but also repulsed enough by his nefarious activities to seek ways to expose his god-awfulness.

Yet, the records of their risky efforts to get authorities to rid their family and city of this dangerous bigot sat in dusty, dog-eared manila folders and flimsy cardboard containers for more than a dozen years, apparently without being afforded more than a glance. It's likely they would have remained unexplored for at least another quarter century had it not been for the determination of Baxley's team.

By the time Baxley loaded Eddy up with a box of documents in January 1977 and sent him off to Birmingham to read everything he could get his hands on, Chambliss was retired but still an angry old troublemaker. No longer physically imposing, he remained unrepentant for the many bombings and the assorted violence he'd inflicted on Birmingham for nearly a half-century.

He'd offended most everyone he'd met in his capacity as a city employee or truck driver and enjoyed bragging about his arson exploits, such as telling his kin he liked "playing with matches" after the torching of a black family's house.

If he'd lived in a society that gave a damn about crimes against the black community, Dynamite Bob would have lived out most of his years inside a jail cell. But in Birmingham, he'd spent his life free to pistol-whip people, beat his wife, blow stuff up, and drink booze with his unapologetic racist buddies under the Cahaba River Bridge.

He appeared to lack empathy for anyone, even his Klan cohorts, and demonstrated almost childlike impatience, impulsivity, and peculiarities. Before he left the house each day, he would have his long-suffering wife, Tee, carefully comb his thinning hair. In a rare moment of apparent passivity and contentment, he would sit still, like an obedient boy, to be groomed. Eddy was right—he was a weirdo!

Chambliss was the number one suspect when the FBI closed the case in 1968, but you wouldn't have necessarily known that by looking at local law enforcement files. Even when he got wind of Baxley sniffing around the case, Chambliss had reason to feel relatively confident that he would remain out of the clutches of authorities.

Eddy didn't know the FBI had been instructed by Attorney General Levi to help out Baxley's team. Certainly, the local G-men didn't swamp him with information or encouragement when he first started sorting through documents. The FBI's obstinate approach to sharing information still riles Baxley and infuriates and baffles many others associated with the case to this day. The protection of sources and informants, understandably, was a primary concern, but the institutional reluctance to share even innocuous information seemed to go beyond reasonable operational priorities.

Fortunately, even though Eddy was taking a stab in the dark each time he requested a file, those guesses gradually became educated. Also, after initially being ignored or dismissed by the agents, he managed to gain their respect, and there was an occasional unsolicited push in an interesting direction. "I found if you promised them it would never see the light of day they'd live by that . . . that's the way they get information. They understand that sort of agreement."

Playing by the FBI's rules and working out of their offices in the 2121 Building in Birmingham made an investigation possible even if it was frequently compromised. Eddy insists the men and women on the ground for the Feds shouldn't be blamed. "They did want it solved. They did want it done. Some of them, when I first went in there, would tell me I'm wasting my time, but after a while, it turned around, and they started being more helpful with everything," Eddy said. "They started making people available."

Gaining access to old FBI agents who had worked the case was particularly valuable.

Despite the obstacles, Eddy confirmed the FBI case led inextricably to Chambliss; Tommy Blanton, an angry, calculating man; and motormouthed Bobby Frank Cherry, who loved to brag and fight, and brag some more. Another suspect, Herman Cash, was less obvious, but the clear indication was that at least three of these men arrived at the church in Blanton's car to place the bomb under the stairs in the early hours of September 15, 1963.

The FBI conclusions had been based, in part, on the results of batteries of polygraph tests with Klan members and their connections in the sixties, observations and finger-pointing from witnesses, and statements from the suspects themselves, whose shaky alibis regularly changed. In Chambliss's case, his purchase and possession of dynamite around the time of the bombing helped place him squarely in Eddy's crosshairs.

But some of the weightiest pieces of evidence that eventually came across Eddy's desk were clumps of insight from a few women who had endured Chambliss at close range for decades. What Chambliss's niece Elizabeth Hood (later Cobbs) and sister-in-law Mary Frances Cunningham told the Feds elevated Eddy's fishing expedition to the status of a focused hunt.

One complication was that the women's cooperation in the sixties had been cloaked in secrecy—Hood was eventually given the code name Abingdon Spaulding, and Cunningham, Gail Tarrant. It made for confusing reading when these names popped up without context amid thousands of pages. Eddy was frustratingly left to work this out for himself over weeks in the offices of an organization full of people who could have simply outlined the puzzle to him over a cup of coffee.

But before he had even contemplated the complicated business of identifying informants, Eddy was stunned by statements attributed to Hood about what she had heard and witnessed in the Chambliss household. Glimpses of her uncle's bomb-making exploits had been a feature of her upbringing, and she came to understand that barking hateful comments sprinkled with racial slurs was pretty much his idea of a conversation.

In front of the family, Chambliss had often stated a desire to oppose integration violently and dwelled on his obsession with bombs. According to Hood, these threats peaked in the days before the church bombing as he warned he had "enough stuff to flatten half of Birmingham." Ominously, he told the household something so big was about to happen that "they'll beg us to segregate."

Chambliss, often riled by family taunts that he and his KKK friends liked to talk up their bombings and bashings, couldn't help himself on that fateful weekend, blurting: "Watch the news tonight and see if this one is big enough."

Hood explained that her mother's side of the family detested Chambliss but lived in fear of Dynamite Bob and his Klan brothers. She, however, was prepared to testify against him if she knew he would be convicted, she had told the FBI.

Eddy could hardly believe it: the Bureau had this incredible witness, then . . . nothing. The document trail suddenly went cold. He knew there had to be more. He consulted Baxley, and they resolved to get to the source—to find Hood.

Birmingham Mayor David Vann assigned two Birmingham policemen to the case, Jack LeGrand and Sergeant Ernest Cantrell. Both had worked on the bombing investigation with dedication and without prejudice in 1963. Called into action by Eddy and Baxley, Cantrell quickly located Hood in Birmingham. She was married and went by Elizabeth Cobbs, and had become a Methodist minister, the first woman to be ordained in Alabama history.

In their first conversation, Cobbs assumed Eddy knew more than he did, confirmation for the investigator that there was much more to be learned from the files. "I wasn't there that night. I took Tee's place," she told him. Eddy knew that Tee was Chambliss's wife; but what did she mean by taking her place? He had to let her believe that he knew what she was talking about.

The interview was a strain. Cobbs obviously feared retribution from her uncle and the Klan, and repeatedly said she would not testify. She did, however, repeat much of what she'd told the FBI thirteen years before.

Eddy would eventually piece together that Cobbs had faded from the FBI records to protect her as a witness and that Tee Chambliss's sister, Mary Frances Cunningham, was the mysterious Gail Tarrant. Both women had given priceless information to the authorities that went beyond recounting Chambliss's threats.

The extent of their commitment to steer authorities to Chambliss was remarkable. They had cooperated with investigators as best they believed they could. Their personal observations about what went on at the time of the bombing also undoubtedly contained information gleaned from or provided by Tee Chambliss, Dynamite Bob's wife. Indeed, Mary Frances Cunningham and Cobbs once told the FBI that they had been eyewitnesses to the Klansmen, including Chambliss, delivering something, likely the bomb, to the church around two in the morning of September 15. Unsettlingly, though, they did not give their blockbuster stories to the FBI until fifteen months after the bombing.

Why did Cunningham and Cobbs wait so long to report their alleged eyewitness accounts? Eddy wasn't the first and will certainly not be the last investigator to ponder that question, but overriding it was one terrible, verifiable fact: law enforcement had been warned about what was going to happen in the hours *before* the explosion.

Hancock

FBI records indicate that in December 1964, Cobbs told FBI agents that she and Cunningham (referred to as Tarrant in the FBI account) donned wigs and followed Chambliss on the night of September 14, ultimately ending up near the 16th Street Baptist Church in the early morning hours of September 15.

In talking to Eddy thirteen years later, Cobbs explained it was actually Tee, not her, who was with Cunningham. Cobbs had been articulating what the other two women said they had observed.

The women had alleged that they watched Blanton's car carrying Blanton, Chambliss, Cherry, and possibly Cash pull up near the church, just outside Poole's Funeral Chapel. One man, whom they believed to be Cherry, emerged from the car carrying a bag or a satchel and walked down an alley to the church. Once he deposited it, his accomplices drove to him. He got in, and the group departed.

After talking with Cobbs, Eddy immediately tried to track down Cunningham's FBI informant file. It eventually appeared on his desk with a "you've never seen this" understanding. With it, he was able to verify the Cunningham narrative was the same as Cobbs's story.

The investigator convinced a reluctant Cobbs to set up a meeting for him with Cunningham. Clearly terrified, even more than a decade after the bombing, "Gail Tarrant" told him point-blank she would not testify but reiterated how Chambliss would talk about "bombing niggers, including the church."

She also detailed the intensely hostile reaction the children's marches in the spring of 1963 had generated among the Klansmen, who frequently visited the Chambliss home. One night, when Blanton came calling, Cunningham baited them, saying the Klansmen weren't going to do anything, that they were all talk. Blanton flew into a rage and launched into a tirade, saying he'd get his machine gun and "mow down all those niggers" by himself if no one else was going to do anything about them.

Much of what Cunningham said reinforced the picture Eddy had been piecing together from other FBI documents. Both Cunningham and Cobbs were often at Tee's side in the Chambliss house. There was little doubt they had observed much of what they reported while also passing on what the Klansman's wife had told them.

Cunningham felt she could never come out publicly against her brother-in-law in part because that would compromise her sister's safety. Additionally, the woman who became the FBI's mysterious Gail Tarrant would have an immense bounty on her head if it were discovered that she had been an ongoing law enforcement informant since the early 1960s. She had been supplying information to a Birmingham sheriff's deputy, James Hancock. Eddy was staggered when he learned that after her night of alleged surveillance with Tee, Cunningham had called Hancock around 2:30 a.m. to inform him of what they had allegedly seen at the church. She wanted him to know she thought the men were setting a bomb, but he hung up on her.

After the sun came up they talked on the phone again—Cunningham said she repeated her suspicions. They set up a meeting where she repeated the story that her brother-in-law and the other men had planted a bomb at the church. Hancock had not called in the information overnight and did not act immediately after meeting with Cunningham. He later told Eddy that he was driving in the direction of downtown to look into it when he heard about the explosion on the radio. "Just one phone call from Hancock," Eddy said. "It would never have happened."

Ms. Glenn

In interviews with Baxley's team, Cobbs and Cunningham eventually recanted the story they had told the FBI in 1964 of following the Klansmen to the church. Instead, they said, they had deduced at the time that something was going to happen because of Chambliss's strange behavior and the flurry of Klan activity that night.

There was, however, no doubt that Cunningham called Hancock around 2:30 a.m. to warn him and followed up by spelling out her concerns in the morning before the bomb exploded. Hancock confirmed to the FBI during the original investigation and subsequently to Eddy that he'd received that early-morning call and eventually got information about a possible bomb hours before the 10:22 a.m. explosion.

Cobbs said Cunningham had concocted the tale of surveillance because the family had waited fifteen months for Hancock to do something with the information. With no action taken against Chambliss, they decided to present what they knew to the FBI in what they perceived to be the most forceful way, as eyewitnesses to the planting of a bomb at the church.

Over the years, many have speculated that Mrs. Cunningham's relationship with Hancock went beyond information sharing. A romance, perhaps, complicated matters and may be the reason that Hancock did not immediately report her warning. Certainly that would explain, to some degree, why the married cop would slam down his home phone on her at two or three in the morning.

On reviewing the FBI statements of both Cobbs and Cunningham, it's striking how similar they are—almost verbatim. It seems a little odd, and perhaps contributed to why the Feds didn't initially appear to wholeheartedly embrace the eyewitness allegations.

Significantly, though, not a single investigator who worked the case thought Mrs. Cunningham's account of the bomb delivery was pure fantasy, even if she wasn't an eyewitness. She knew what had gone down, possibly by piecing together what the women had heard that Saturday night as they took calls in the Chambliss residence and monitored the movements of the Klansmen. "I still go back and forth on whether she was there," Baxley said recently. "I know she knew exactly what happened—that I don't doubt—but was she there? I don't really know."

Baxley did try to convince Cunningham to consider testifying, but she would not entertain the idea, insisting she would deny everything. It would have been difficult to use her even if she had agreed, as Tee's safety most certainly would have been compromised. Additionally, even though the investigators were (and still are) convinced Cunningham's description of that night was exactly what happened, any decent defense lawyer would have a field day shooting holes in her story and attacking her credibility.

The best Baxley could realistically hope for was valuable testimony from Cobbs detailing the threats uttered by Dynamite Bob and the frantic activity in the house associated with the Klan in the lead-up to the bombing. Despite initially telling Baxley she would not take the stand, Cobbs eventually tentatively agreed.

To ensure they could have a shot at proving to a jury what everyone associated with the investigation already knew, Baxley's team needed someone who could provide a similar eyewitness account of the bomb planting at the church in those early hours of September 15 and would be prepared to stand by it in a court of law.

Eddy finally unearthed the gem the team had been seeking from the mountain of FBI files—a woman who had observed activity around the church during those overnight hours in an account that uncannily matched elements of the original Cobbs/Cunningham story.

Kirthus Glenn was a Detroit seamstress who had been visiting her old hometown of Birmingham that fateful weekend. As she was coming home from a night on the town at about 2:10 a.m., she spotted a car later identified as Blanton's as she was looking for a place to park.

She was with a friend, Henry Smith, when she noticed, parked near the church, a white-over-turquoise Chevrolet with a tall CB radio antenna. The dome light of the car was on, illuminating the presence of three white men in the vehicle. White men loitering in a black neighborhood during the overnight hours was most notable in 1963 Birmingham. She would later identify one of the men as Dynamite Bob Chambliss.

Glenn's companion saw much the same thing, although he admitted to being drunk and thought the car was red.

Glenn had given her account on a number of occasions, yet thirteen years later, despite multiple visits from Baxley's team to her home in Michigan, she steadfastly refused to return to Alabama or commit to testifying in the case. That is, until Baxley himself, over coffee, cookies, and pleasant conversation at her Detroit home, finally found the hook to reel her in.

As he grew more frustrated with Glenn's refusal, he noticed on her coffee table a copy of an old *Jet* magazine featuring a story about the Montgomery bus boycott, including a photograph of Martin Luther King and Rosa Parks with their attorney, a very young Fred Gray. By this time, Gray was a member of the Alabama Legislature, one of the first blacks elected to serve. He and Baxley had become friends.

Baxley showed Glenn the picture: "Dr. King and Mrs. Parks trusted this man to represent them," he said. "If I can get him up here to talk to you, would you consider changing your mind about testifying?"

"Well, I'd consider it," she said.

Sensing what he described as a "sea change" in her attitude, Baxley immediately called Gray at his Tuskegee office and got his agreement for a trip to Detroit. The AG arranged for a state airplane to transport his friend, and a day or so later, the men headed to Glenn's house.

Ms. Glenn sized up the new guest. She placed the *Jet* magazine next to

Gray's face and scrutinized it: the picture in the magazine was twenty years old, but fortunately Fred had aged well. "It is you," she said.

Glenn reluctantly agreed to testify. Baxley and his team had a case.

Cornering Cherry

It was a solid, albeit circumstantial, case against Chambliss, but the investigators wanted more on the other suspected participants. If nobody could say for sure that Cherry was one of the culprits, maybe the notably verbose former ammunitions specialist would do it himself. He was renowned in Klan and law enforcement circles for saying "too much."

Eddy took a trip to Grand Prairie, Texas, to visit Cherry, who had moved to the Lone Star State some years before. The mouthy bigot was reluctant to meet with Eddy, but so loved talking about himself that once the interview got rolling it was hard to shut him up. He came ever so close to at least revealing he had knowledge of what happened the morning of the bombing.

Cherry seemed to delight in walking the fine line, almost teasing his interrogator. Toward the end of the interview, Eddy decided to see if he could knock Cherry off-balance. He let the old windbag know there was an eyewitness who had seen him carrying the bomb satchel to the church. "He immediately knew things weren't looking so good," Eddy said.

Cherry clammed up. Eddy suggested he think over an offer to talk more about the situation, to provide his interpretation of events. Sure enough, the phone rang at Eddy's hotel around midnight, but an angry Cherry wasn't calling to confess anything.

"Chambliss didn't tell you about me," Cherry fumed.

Calmly, Eddy replied, "I never said Chambliss told me anything."

With that, Cherry said he was through talking and slammed the telephone down.

Back in Birmingham, Eddy traced the calls from Cherry's house that night and found the Klansman had called an auto parts store in Birmingham owned by Bob Gafford, a businessman and Klan sympathizer. It wasn't hard to imagine Chambliss being quickly informed of Cherry's presumption that he'd been exposed by Dynamite Bob. Apparently, Gafford had provided the reassurance Cherry needed that Chambliss had done no such thing.

Eddy knew he was on the right trail.

Baxley later traveled to Texas to try his hand with Cherry, but the two firebrands didn't get anything but high blood pressure from their angry exchange.

Baxley, with his term as AG coming to an end, needed to act. He knew, for the moment, that Cherry might be a bridge too far. The other major suspect, Blanton, had laid low since the bombing. He had stuck to an alibi he constructed in consultation with his then girlfriend, later wife, Jean Barnes, that he left her home at 2:30 a.m. on September 15—after the car was spotted by Kirthus Glenn at the church.

Chambliss's case was the most promising, though still circumstantial. Even with Elizabeth Cobbs and Ms. Glenn, there was no smoking gun.

Baxley consulted his friend Chris McNair, father of Denise, about the state of the evidence and their chances for success. "I thought it was going to be an uphill battle, but I thought it was worth making the effort," Baxley said. "Chris said 'you sure you got the right guy,' I said 'yes,' and he said, 'well we should go ahead because if you don't do it, surely nobody else will.'"

Baxley decided he'd prosecute Chambliss for the death of Denise McNair only. If he lost that case, then he could still shoot for a trial for one of the other victims. He knew that double jeopardy might prevent another trial after an acquittal, but it was the strongest plan under the circumstances.

Indeed, there was enough evidence against Chambliss to get what the FBI probably thought impossible in the sixties: a Jefferson County grand jury returned an indictment against Dynamite Bob in October 1977. He would stand trial for the murder of Denise McNair.

The Chambliss Trial

Baxley often says that he and I have very different opinions of James Lay, the volunteer worker who saw the Klansmen conducting what was either a failed bombing attempt or a dry run just two weeks before the fatal Sunday. Merely mentioning the man's name infuriates my old friend, as Lay was less than helpful, even callous, in the countdown to the 1977 trial. However, I got to see a different side to Lay in later life.

Armed with the accounts from Ms. Glenn and evidence of the Chambliss statements from his niece connecting him to the bombing, Baxley knew that the testimony of Lay and radio personality "Tall Paul" White, who had been with Lay that night, would be extremely important. Their accounts reinforced the notion that the same Klansmen identified by Glenn as being at the church in the early hours of September 15 had been targeting the church weeks before. As lawyers would say, that is damn strong circumstantial evidence.

But Lay, a member of the black Civil Defense Unit, steadfastly refused to cooperate with Baxley. There was little doubt he felt threatened by the Klan, but Eddy speculates something else contributed to his reluctance. "He was the kind of fella if you rub him wrong, he ain't going to help you," according to Eddy. Baxley, apparently, rubbed him the wrong way.

It wasn't for want of trying. One morning, Baxley even had Chris McNair cook up a down-home Southern breakfast of eggs, grits, and bacon while they put the hard sell on Lay. "But no and no," Baxley said, referring to Lay's refusal to be involved. (White wasn't as crucial, as he didn't see the car—his usefulness was as a supporting witness to Lay.)

Decades later, an aged and sick James Lay, perhaps seeking to clear his conscience, would be crucial to my efforts to convict Blanton and Cherry, but Baxley had to try and convince a Southern jury of the unquestionable guilt of Chambliss without that important evidence.

The media and public attention given to the Chambliss trial was extensive. However, rather than resounding calls of "about time" in the rundown to the trial, Baxley was widely denounced for stirring unwanted old memories.

That was lost on me at the time, as I was consumed by the legal process itself. As a law school student and aspiring trial lawyer, the Chambliss prosecution brought a unique opportunity to act on Supreme Court Justice William O. Douglas's advice. I resolved to cut classes to watch a great lawyer in action in what would be the biggest trial ever in the state.

On November 14, 1977, Judge Wallace Gibson gaveled the court to order in *State v. Chambliss*. Closest to the jury box were Baxley and his prosecution team: George Beck and John Yung. Opposite sat Chambliss and his legal defense, former Mayor Art Hanes, his son Art Jr., and junior associate Mike Bolin.

The jury consisted of nine whites and three blacks.

They heard from police and other witnesses about the events of that night, including the 1:30 a.m. false alarm of a bomb threat at the Holiday Inn, widely believed to be a deliberate effort to distract law enforcement about the time the bomb was placed at the church. Reverend Cross also presented emotional testimony about the bombing scene, and the court heard survivor Sarah Collins's moving account of how she called out for her sister Addie.

Useful evidence for the prosecution steadily mounted with each witness, though Chambliss displayed little or no emotion, his regular scowl
seemingly frozen in place.

Kirthus Glenn, the reluctant witness from Detroit, was obviously nervous as she testified that the FBI had questioned her about the car she had
seen in the early morning hours of September 15 and showed her pictures
of possible suspects. She assertively identified Chambliss as one of the three
people she saw in the car that night and told the court she had done so on
three separate occasions during the investigation.

Cobbs's turn came soon after. She was terrified when Eddy picked her
up for the trip to court. "I had to be the bodyguard," Eddy said. "She could
hardly talk. I told her that when she was on the stand to look my way and
not to look at [Chambliss]."

The tension was close to unbearable even before she walked into the
courtroom, which was in lockdown. Eddy tried to protect her from prying
eyes and stayed beside her, but a phone call came in that he had to take before he escorted her in.

On the line was Tee Chambliss. "Are they going to convict him?" she
asked Eddy. The investigator had never spoken to Dynamite Bob's wife before, but she had asked for him by name.

"I believe so," he said.

Tee was desperate: "Do you really know?"

"No," Eddy conceded, "but my experience tells me they will."

The defendant's wife, who had carefully and dutifully combed his hair
before the authorities took him into custody, sighed and said, "Oh, I hope so."

Inside the court, anticipating Cobbs's entrance, everyone was looking at
Chambliss to witness his reaction to the appearance of his niece.

Eddy rejoined her as she was led in from the back, walled off from
the gallery by a bunch of sheriff's deputies. All eyes in the room, including mine, fixed on this brave thirty-seven-year-old woman who had been
twenty-three at the time of the bombing. Chambliss shook his head in dis-
approval.

John Yung, Baxley's assistant, handled the questioning. Cobbs stared
relentlessly in Eddy's direction as she answered. She testified that she had
been at the Chambliss home on Saturday, September 14, visiting her Aunt
Tee, who had been ill.

She said that there had been an incident in the city the night before
in which a black youth cut a white woman with a knife. When a report of
the assault came on the TV news, Chambliss became enraged, spewing a

stream of racial epithets and calling Governor Wallace a coward for not doing anything to stop integration. Chambliss, she said, hollered: "It seems like I've been fighting a one-man war since 1942."

Later her uncle railed that he had enough "stuff" to flatten half of Birmingham before warning ominously: "You wait until after Sunday. They'll beg us to let them segregate."

"I asked him what he meant by that," Cobbs told the court. "He responded, 'You just wait and see tomorrow.'"

She later testified that about a week after the bombing, Chambliss was watching TV when a news bulletin said that murder charges would be brought against anyone connected to the crime. Chambliss, she said, looked at the TV and solemnly said: "No one was supposed to die."

Baxley and his team were masterful, linking observations from various witnesses to paint a damning picture of Chambliss. They scrupulously put together the story of how he came to be where Glenn placed him around 2:00 a.m., just hours before the bomb exploded.

The defense team believed that Chambliss's only chance to beat the charge was to take the witness stand. Arthur Hanes Jr. handled most of the case, along with his father, who was a former FBI agent and former Birmingham mayor. Both father and son were lawyers familiar with controversy, having initially been retained to help defend Martin Luther King Jr. assassin James Earl Ray. They had also worked for several prominent Klan clients.

The defense case focused on calling character witnesses and was built around the defendant's expected testimony. Dynamite Bob had been eager to tell his side of the story, but as the trial progressed, Chambliss became uneasy about taking the stand. Baxley had scorched some of the defense witnesses on cross-examination, including the old Klansman's nephew, a Birmingham police officer.

Chambliss was as mesmerized as everyone else in the court by Baxley's evisceration of the credibility of each defense witness. When Hanes Sr. announced that their last witness would be the defendant, Dynamite Bob's cowardice took hold. He sat in his seat and wouldn't move.

As Hanes tried to budge him, Chambliss muttered: "I ain't going up there."

Feigning he didn't hear Chambliss or didn't understand, Baxley asked, "What did he say? What'd he say?"

"I ain't going up there," Chambliss said again, loudly.

At the moment this brief exchange unfolded, it was difficult to see how important it was. But Baxley knew. Had he, as prosecutor, made any reference to the defendant's refusal to testify on his own behalf it would have been an automatic mistrial. Instead, by repeatedly asking, "What'd he say?" within earshot of the jury, Baxley baited Chambliss into declaring loudly what he was doing—refusing to take the stand.

Judge Gibson gaveled the courtroom into silence and recessed for Hanes Sr. to confer with his client. But pleas to Chambliss to reconsider fell on deaf ears. "I swear at that moment his face shimmered with evil, and I knew this is the most evil, unrepentant son of a bitch I have ever met," Hanes Jr. told Al.com's Jon Solomon in 2013.

Indeed, dealing with Chambliss shook the lawyer to his core. His faith in humanity damaged, Art Hanes Jr. opted never to defend a criminal murder case again.

Not only did Baxley's maneuver effectively collapse the defense's strategy; it arguably sealed the fate of not just one killer, but three, as history suggests that without a Chambliss conviction, getting the others would have been even harder decades later.

Before closing arguments, Baxley's assistant Yung drew the AG's attention to Denise McNair's death certificate and the date of her birth. As fate would have it, it was Thursday, November 17, Denise McNair's birthday. She would have been twenty-six years old.

I sat in the balcony, barely moving, locked onto Baxley's argument. As he laid out photos of each girl taken in the morgue, there was not a dry eye in the house, including mine. It was passionate, sincere, and a loud cry for justice—something to behold and exactly why I skipped classes.

"Today," Baxley told the jury, "you can give Denise McNair a birthday present. You can bring her killer to justice." In short order, they did.

When the guilty verdict was read, and Judge Gibson asked Chambliss if he had anything to say, the convicted Klansman said, "I swear to God I didn't bomb that church." Dynamite Bob was then sentenced to life in prison for the murder of Denise McNair and led out of the courtroom in handcuffs.

Baxley had achieved what had been perceived as nearly impossible. Yet, in the end, it all felt so obvious. "Cobbs and Ms. Glenn, they were crucial, but the end with Chambliss saying he wouldn't get up—that was crazy," Baxley reflected. "It just fell in our lap, and that did as much as anything else [to convict him] because the jury could see he was guilty."

After the trial, Art Hanes Jr. was given the task of breaking the news to Chambliss's wife that her husband wouldn't be coming home. Years later

Hanes recounted the scene to Baxley: He arrived at the Chambliss home to find the drapes drawn, the lights out. Tee was lying on a sofa in a dark den with a washcloth on her forehead.

When told that her husband had been convicted and wouldn't be returning, Tee asked Hanes to repeat himself several times. "Are you sure he won't ever be coming home?" she asked. Again, the young lawyer said he would not. Suddenly, apparent despair turned to relief, then elation, as Mrs. Chambliss jumped from the sofa, threw the washcloth away, dashed to the windows, opened the drapes, and exclaimed: "Hallelujah, Hallelujah. Thank you, Jesus."

And thank God for Tee Chambliss, Kirthus Glenn, Elizabeth Cobbs, Bill Baxley, Bob Eddy, and the rest of Baxley's team.

Immediately after Chambliss was convicted, the prosecution team explored the possibilities of building court-ready cases against Blanton and Cherry, but there was not enough time left in Baxley's tenure as Attorney General. In the years that followed, the political will wasn't there to reinspect the festering old wound. The aging former Klansmen once again walked out of the spotlight.

Blanton, who eventually received a law degree but never passed the bar exam, felt safe enough to (again) divorce Jean Casey, his alibi for the night of the bombing. In doing so, he surrendered the protection marriage gave to couples at the time (they did not have an obligation to testify against their partners). Meanwhile, Cherry remained in Texas and continued to talk about himself and who he hated to anyone prepared to listen. He demeaned women and harassed his family. In other words, he continued being his usual obnoxious self.

THREE

LANGFORD

M ost anyone with an interest in the church bombing case knew Chambliss had accomplices who were still walking the streets. But racism, shame, and political maneuvering stymied a few nascent attempts to secure resources to go after them.

At the least, it would have required a broad and sustained political push to walk through the door of opportunity Baxley had kicked open. But the African-American community, despite civil rights advances since the sixties, was still vastly underrepresented in Alabama's political and business communities in the late seventies and eighties.

Black folks were left to fume silently about the case for much of the next twenty years. While citing the Chambliss conviction as justice having been done, the white community turned away from the shame of the bombing, even if the incident was wedged in the psyche of some.

Alabama inched away from the legacy of Jim Crow as reforms from the sixties, including the Civil Rights Act and the Voting Rights Act, gradually impacted the South, but it wasn't until the late eighties that the next generation of black leadership got a genuine opportunity to vie for power throughout the state. By that stage, the national political scene had been transformed.

President Ronald Reagan had made the evangelical vote his own and capitalized on vast white disenchantment with societal change. The celebration for Democrats that would accompany the election of Bill Clinton in 1992 masked the rising tide of conservative influence at the local and state government level around the country.

As the Reagan and George H. W. Bush years came to a close, extreme religious conservatism and scare tactics in the law-and-order debate created an atmosphere in which blacks and minorities were targeted as the cause of societal ills. Fear and loathing were everywhere and were framed as a consequence of liberal (civil rights) policies. The mindset wasn't confined to conservatives; successfully promoted by Reagan and Bush, it impacted the way the incoming Democratic administration chose to deal with crime, drugs, and welfare. The big losers for the next generation would be African Americans, Hispanics, and poor whites.

At the time, there was also a push to identify and challenge public corruption. As noted by academics, including University of Maryland's Professor George Derek Musgrove, African-American leaders had been disproportionately targeted in corruption probes since the civil rights era. By wading through FBI and Department of Justice documents from the civil rights era to the mid-nineties, Musgrove concluded that Alabama's black leaders were about fifty percent more likely to be investigated than whites. One of the most prominent targets, Richard Arrington, was Birmingham's first black mayor. Musgrove said Arrington was the subject of as many as fifteen discredited investigations.

Arrington came to power on the wave of outrage over the fatal police shooting of an unarmed African-American woman, Benita Carter, in Birmingham in 1979. As a black politician, he was very much the exception to the rule but cemented his mayoral status with vast support from the black community as white flight impacted the city throughout the eighties.

Arrington was born in rural Sumter County in the Black Belt of Alabama, a region famed for its rich, dark soil and history of cotton farming. Many former slaves stayed in the area to become sharecroppers and independent farmers.

After moving to my hometown of Fairfield, Arrington built a reputation as a mild-mannered progressive who also worked studiously to win the trust of the Birmingham business community.

When allegations of cronyism and corruption were raised against him in the late eighties, the Mayor didn't take them lying down. He fought back, enlisting the media and the public's support, challenging the legitimacy of the investigation, and claiming it was race based and part of a campaign to diminish the power of black Democrats.

In the early nineties, he was at loggerheads in public with Frank Donaldson, the no-nonsense Northern District of Alabama U.S. Attorney who investigated allegations that Arrington received financial kickbacks from a project that would become the Birmingham Civil Rights Institute.

In 1991, Arrington supporters took to the streets, as relations between federal authorities and the black community nose-dived. The African-American community and the Justice Department, in particular, had been great allies in the fight for civil rights through the late sixties and seventies, but a decade of less-than-stellar relations wiped away much of the goodwill and opened old wounds.

During this unsettled period, a well-meaning, God-fearing FBI agent came to town and quickly recognized the need to renovate the crumbling relationship between the Feds and the black community. Rob Langford let it be known he wanted to initiate talks to build a rapport with black leaders. The response he got to an enthusiastic and heartfelt outreach was about as jaunty as the sound of crickets chirping.

Finding My Place

The first decade or so of my career since graduating from law school in 1979 involved stints as both a federal prosecutor and a defense attorney. When in private practice, I also was active politically, working for several prominent Democratic Party campaigns.

I'd struck up relationships with several significant political figures while at university and law school, among them Chris McNair, the father of bombing victim Denise, and revered Alabama leader Howell Heflin.

In 1973, McNair had been one of the first blacks to take a seat in the legislature since Reconstruction. Widely acknowledged as a voice of reason in race relations, he was instrumental in helping Birmingham improve its image nationally.

Astonishingly, the man who sat next to him in the legislature, Bob Gafford, was a noted Klan sympathizer and friend of the white men who murdered McNair's eleven-year-old daughter.

Only in Alabama.

I maintained a close relationship with Chris as I prepared to enter the workforce. So too with Howell Heflin, an inspiring moderate voice for the state. I'd worked on his successful 1978 Senate campaign alongside another law student, Greg Hawley, a baseball-loving buddy (another misguided Red Sox fan) who would decades later become my law partner.

I also had the good fortune of striking up a relationship with then first-term Delaware Senator Joe Biden. We hit it off when the man who would become Vice President visited Birmingham at the invitation of my law school, where I had a role coordinating events.

Together with my campaign for Senator Heflin, interaction with Biden helped solidify my political views and fuel my interest in public life. A career in law and politics was probably the eventual goal, but I didn't want to get ahead of myself. Straight out of law school, I was anxious to secure a modest legal role.

As I was sending out scores of letters requesting interviews with Alabama firms, I got a call from Senator Heflin's Chief of Staff, Mike House. In his first year as a senator, Heflin wanted to give a recent law graduate a twelve-month "clerkship" as a staff attorney on a Judiciary Committee subcommittee he was chairing. The twelve-month role had a paltry salary of $17,000, but it was mine if I wanted it. Hey, the money didn't matter (when did you last hear a lawyer say that?). I jumped at the chance.

My education in matters legal and political was supercharged that year in the capital. Building on what I'd witnessed with Baxley, I became acutely aware of what could be done to address injustice by using existing political and judicial tools.

In many ways, the move kick-started my adult life, which quickly became more enthralling and complicated than I could have imagined. I saw history being made every day. I was a young man from Birmingham, attached to that city's prospects as I knew I'd be heading back in one year, but suddenly brandishing a kind of twelve-month hall pass, a license to explore ideas and formulate ambitions that just weren't part of the mindset back home.

In the summer of 1979, I was also newly married to a young woman, Faye Mann, whom I met working at the Birmingham law firm Bradley, Arant, Rose & White. It had been a whirlwind romance, a partnership forged in the giddy atmosphere that envelopes young love, obscuring reality and deviously masking the possibility that hardship, disagreement, or foolishness could ever intrude on such a gloriously positive union of two people who knew little of each other.

Our honeymoon was the move to D.C. After we headed back to Birmingham a year later, a divorce (in the spring of 1981) became inevitable. I had jumped into marriage with the same kind of naïvety that made me think medicine would be the right choice for me at college.

Nevertheless, the year in Washington planted a seed in me. It was a unique time in American history. President Jimmy Carter was vastly unpopular, coping with domestic and international terrorism, and an economy featuring double-digit inflation and interest rates that looked poised to collapse.

Yet despite the intense political anxiety, I witnessed a Senate going about its business in a way fitting of its billing as the most deliberative government body in the world. Many of the greatest generation, veterans of World War II and the Korean War, served in Washington politics at the time. For the most part, they did so with distinction, a focus on the greater good overriding partisan political battles.

Social change was painful, especially at a time when the country's self-image was being undermined, but officials continued reforms initiated in the sixties. The mandate had been given, and despite pockets of resistance, mainstream America recognized change was overdue.

It reinforced my belief that for all the noise and impatience on the fringes of any debate, a solution usually comes down to moderates finding common ground with their colleagues to support an issue with enough backing to ensure meaningful and prolonged reform. It also helped grow my desire to find a role in public service.

On return to Birmingham, I had my first stint as a federal prosecutor, as an Assistant U.S. Attorney. I learned on the job and was thrown into a wide array of cases—stolen Treasury checks, illegal guns, small-time drug offenses, counterfeiting, even a cold case stemming from the 1972 hijacking of a Southern Airways flight out of Birmingham that ended in Cuba.

The diversity of experience during my four years as an Assistant U.S. Attorney was invaluable. I loved the workload, and initially it was a distraction from the distress of my marriage breakup. After a while, I felt confident enough about my future prospects and my commitment to Birmingham to start entertaining the idea of spending time doing something other than working, watching the Yankees, supporting Crimson Tide football, and working some more.

I became enamored with a secretary at the U.S. Attorney's office. Barbara Jo (B. J.) Nall and I married in the spring of 1983, buying a little home in Crestline Park in suburban Birmingham. Having laid down roots, a family seemed like a good idea, and we were thrilled when my first child, Courtney, came along in May 1984.

At that time, I took the plunge into private practice. It was a difficult decision to leave a stable government job with benefits to strike out on my own when Courtney was only eight days old, but I was confident enough of my ability. I was fortunate to share office space with a wonderful lawyer and friend, Bob Moorer, who helped guide me through the process of setting up.

It felt like I'd made a fresh start. I knew nothing about business but realized I needed to develop a specialty to set me apart in the legal world, or at least create a little niche for myself.

A recurring message and lesson from all the fine role models I had come across was to do what you knew how to do best. At the time, many lawyers didn't like practicing in the more formal federal courts, which had a different pace and process than state courts. Yet I enjoyed the federal system; it was where I had cut my teeth. So I set about seeking referrals from other lawyers and court-appointed work in that arena.

I had a plan, good experience, and a solid work ethic. However, one thing they don't remind you of enough at law school is that after opening your own practice you have to *make money*.

I had borrowed enough that wasn't going directly to diapers and other baby expenses to buy a desk and computer and pay a month of rent on a tiny office downtown. It quickly became apparent I needed more money for the month that would follow.

I had high hopes. Atticus Finch one day? Maybe. But in those initial months, with family expenses and office costs mounting, I was happy to take any job that came my way, from defending a state court judge in a DUI case to agonizingly sad drug cases—anything available to a willing court-appointed attorney.

If you aren't from the South, you might not be familiar with the range of characters we have in some of our tough towns and cities. I may be a Birmingham boy, but even I didn't have a grasp on just how fascinating the criminal underbelly was in Alabama. Among other memories, I am still visited at unusual times by the distinct vision of being wedged in a jail interview room with Teeny Man West, otherwise known as the "Mayor of Sand Mountain," who at four hundred pounds was someone who must have been hiding in plain sight at various times during his eleven years as a fugitive.

My federal expertise also brought me cases such as Tom Posey's. The founder of the Civilian Military Assistance Organization, he was arrested for violating the Neutrality Act after his group smuggled weapons into Nicaragua to assist the Contras in their fight against Daniel Ortega.

I cultivated my reputation as a go-to guy in federal cases and slowly built my little business. Unfortunately, I wasn't as successful in my family life and my marriage disintegrated. We split custody of Courtney—I eventually did what many parents in the Birmingham region do and moved to the best school district for my kid, Mountain Brook. My daughter's welfare was my top priority, and I shuffled my business arrangements accordingly.

Not long after divorcing, I changed law firms, forming a partnership with Mark Polson and John Robbins.

Robbins was young, but you could tell he was destined to be a very fine defense lawyer, and I got to witness that development up close when, a dozen years later, he defended Tommy Blanton against my federal prosecution team in the bombing case.

While the domestic demands of caring for Courtney were considerable, a few big cases, including several corruption cases against Alabama politicians, helped ensure I wouldn't crash and burn professionally.

A bonus of being in private practice was that I was free to indulge my passion for politics. I had been active in Senator Heflin's first reelection bid in 1984, even playing the role of Heflin's very conservative opponent, Republican Albert Lee Smith, in a mock debate. (To this day I believe I won!) In 1987 I played a role supporting Joe Biden as he pondered a 1988 presidential run. After he dropped out of the race, I took up the baton for Michael Dukakis.

I was behind any Democrat and, in the end, supported Dukakis because of his broad vision. Also, unapologetically, I thought a victory for the Massachusetts Governor might facilitate my return to the Department of Justice as a U.S. Attorney—an ambition I had quietly, somewhat inexplicably, harbored since my four-year stint as an assistant.

In the end it wasn't a debate I needed to have with myself as Dukakis basically snatched defeat from the jaws of victory in losing the election to George H. W. Bush.

As is often the case, it was all for the better personally, though it didn't seem so at the time. I took full custody of Courtney and eyed an opportunity to have another tilt at making my own firm the provider for myself and my girl.

As it turned out, this breakout of relative domestic and career stability opened the door for me to find my true love. Louise New, from Cullman, Alabama, seemed to understand everything about me, except my admittedly peculiar desire to eventually take a pay cut, step away from any Atticus Finch fantasy, and work for the government.

Langford's Breakthrough

In 1992, Arkansas Governor Clinton swept through the country to the soundtrack of Fleetwood Mac's "Don't Stop" to win the presidential election. Clinton's success meant I could realistically speculate about the possibility of securing a U.S. Attorney slot, and I wasted no time in seeking support for a possible appointment. I worked the party faithful at the President's inauguration in Washington, D.C., and was buoyed by promises of backing. But I was also acutely aware of the need for greater diversity in appointments to key positions in the South.

In Alabama, three U.S. Attorneys are appointed to cover the three federal judicial districts. In my mind at least one, likely the Northern District, home to Birmingham's large African-American population, was a prime position for a black candidate. Such an appointment would have been especially timely given the tension created by the investigation into Mayor Arrington.

As I considered whether it was in the community's best interests for me to throw my hat in the ring, former U.S. Representative Claude Harris let it be known that he also was interested. Harris was not an African American but had a long and prestigious career in public service as District Attorney for Tuscaloosa County, a circuit judge, and then a three-term United States congressman. In 1990, while he was representing the Tuscaloosa area in Congress, the state of Alabama lost a congressional seat, and Harris's old district merged into the one held by another Democrat, Ben Erdreich, in Birmingham.

Harris, being the junior, magnanimously decided not to run against Erdreich, setting himself up to be appointed U.S. Attorney. Knowing there was no way I could compete, I let my old boss, Senator Heflin, know I would step back.

In October 1993, Harris took the oath as the U.S. Attorney for the Northern District of Alabama. Once again, I set about building my private law practice, thinking my opportunity had passed.

The U.S. Attorney's job was a daunting challenge in the early nineties. Harris inherited the role from my friend and future law practice partner Jack Selden. His predecessor, my old teacher and former boss Frank Donaldson, had presided over the intense joint investigation with the FBI into corruption allegations against Mayor Arrington.

Selden, the son of a former U.S. congressman and Ambassador to New Zealand, was installed as Donaldson's replacement in Birmingham in 1992. A key part of his job was to handle the erosion of the relationship between the Department of Justice and the African-American community. Jack and I had served together as Assistant U.S. Attorneys in the early 1980s. Although he was an excellent lawyer of great integrity, Selden was largely unknown to the black community. But the Arrington matter had become so polarizing, any change was a welcome development for the Mayor's supporters.

In the fall of 1992, Selden announced the termination of the investigation into the Mayor. The overdue news was welcomed but also proof for some that the allegations had been baseless and motivated only by the color of Arrington's skin.

The FBI's new regional Special Agent in Charge (SAC), Rob Langford, was no stranger to environments where strained racial relations were a fact of life. He had grown up in Tuscaloosa, "Hometown of the KKK," as an infamous roadside sign declared. In 1962, after graduating from Auburn University, he joined the Marines. He was engaged in some of the fiercest battles of the Vietnam War, winning a Bronze Star during deployment.

Returning to the United States, Langford joined the FBI. During stints in Detroit and Buffalo, he noticed there was a pronounced dislike and suspicion among blacks toward the Bureau, which had a conspicuous shortage of African-American agents.

In Buffalo, Langford and his wife, Martha, decided to reach out to minority communities, regularly visiting local black churches and, in the process, slowly dismantling the adversarial relationship between blacks and the FBI. Transferred to volatile Birmingham in 1993, he employed a similar approach, regularly visiting black churches. He also reached out to the community leadership, consulting Johnnie Johnson, the city's black police chief, for guidance.

Johnson supplied Langford with the names of thirty prominent African-American leaders, and the FBI's head man wrote a personal letter inviting them to join him at a special "meet and greet session." Not one responded. No one came.

He called to follow up. No one called back.

But Langford persevered, independently linking with a few prominent folks. Lemarse Washington, a leader in the local National Conference of Christians and Jews, an organization Langford would eventually join, was impressed by the agent's genuine concern over race relations in the city. So too were the then minister at 16th Street Baptist Church, Chris Hamlin, and Powell Junior High School principal Eva Jones. They helped Langford set up a meeting with the black Birmingham leadership, many of them ministers, in the conference room at the FBI's Birmingham offices.

A tense, somewhat hostile atmosphere prevailed, with Reverend Abraham Woods, never a shrinking violet and an unwavering Arrington supporter, alerting the newcomer to the depth of the problem. "They felt black leaders had been targeted by the FBI office, including the Mayor Richard Arrington situation, which had been resolved before I got to Birmingham. I really wasn't aware of the details since it had been settled," Langford recalled.

There was one other elephant in the room at the meeting, and when it was acknowledged, the FBI agent knew the issue was at the core of Birmingham's problems.

"Reverend Woods finally asked, 'Why hasn't the FBI done anything about the church bombing in 1963?' I admittedly knew very little about the situation, which obviously stirred his emotions."

Langford, proudly a man of his word (he was an active member of an organization called Promise Keepers), told the doubting clergy he would look into it. Shortly thereafter he started perusing the files from the cold case, code-named BAPBOMB.

Evaluating the documents, Langford was struck by the high quality of the FBI's investigation. But he could clearly see why there was animosity toward the agency over the case. All that effort, but no FBI-initiated prosecutions to show for it. Why?

A fresh, detailed look at the case might lead Langford to the same legal cul-de-sac apparently encountered previously by the FBI, but if he achieved that, at least he could provide the black community with an informed assessment.

It was an old case but one not burdened by a lack of effort from investigators or, indeed, an absence of prime suspects. He needed a pair of experienced eyes to take a good look and evaluate the possibility of building on what had been constructed three decades before. The challenge also came down to finding witnesses who were still alive and lucid enough to reliably recall facts from so long ago.

Langford's choice was Special Agent Bill Fleming, a veteran investigator, civil rights case specialist, and remarkably astute individual with an odd, intense interest in photographing the graves of Confederate generals. Langford got the ball rolling by calling David Barber, the District Attorney for Jefferson County. If a state offense rather than a federal crime were adjudged to have been committed all those years ago, then it would be Alabama's responsibility to help prosecute it. Barber told Langford what he wanted to hear: "If you have the evidence, then we will prosecute them."

Stopping injustice from poisoning a community is not best achieved by waving a gun, bullying, or blindly imposing the rule of law. Langford used the expertise and resources he had at his disposal to carefully assess the issue and identify the underlying causes of the Birmingham problem. There could not have been a better use of law enforcement structures.

More than thirty years after the bombing, Langford initiated a process that would bring together a group of investigators and prosecutors who would pour their hearts, souls, and minds into the case. The Klansmen's vile act in 1963 prematurely ended the lives of four girls, but the belated process of holding them accountable added unexpected meaning, purpose, and depth to scores of others'.

Initially, not a lot more new information was learned about the bombing. But even in those early stages, when Langford's investigators were just looking to see if a full-blown inquiry was worth pursuing, it was clear there would be no loose ends. A certain kind of indomitability characterized the process and the people associated with the new effort.

That was a common thread after the investigation came to the attention of the public in the summer of 1997, raising the hopes of many in the African-American community in Birmingham and beyond. In any investigative process, it's important for all parties to be on the same page. The case had that professional quality, but there was also an unspoken bond between those involved. For one thing, it was clear to everyone that the Langford-launched re-examination of one of the South's most shameful events would be the last. Secrets were already going to the grave and lessons from history were being compromised.

Those involved in the final effort knew what was at stake, and, crucially, almost everyone recalled how good people—families, friends, and neighbors—had failed to counter the toxicity that filtered into every corner of society in the fifties and sixties. If not guilt, then intense regret had lingered latently in many of us. Indeed, most everyone who would become associated with the reopened case was white, from Alabama, and of an age to remember Birmingham "back then." Despite Langford's best intentions, however, the crusade almost evaporated before it started.

A decorated local cop, Ben Herren, joined Bill Fleming in evaluating the case. They were brilliant investigators, but they struggled to make headway, forced to sort through tens of thousands of documents housed by the FBI, a bureaucracy not used to sharing its archived secrets. But with perseverance, what seemed at first to be an investigative carousel for the two old hands eventually became the ride of their lives and took Southern justice on a journey it should have taken decades before.

The Coldest Case

Even before the renewed interest in the case was made public, Fleming wanted to quit. The veteran FBI man wrote a letter of resignation and kept it close in case he needed swift access. He was nearing retirement and felt Langford had dumped an impossible cold case on him.

The Feds had done a thorough job thirty years before, and Bob Eddy, the best in the business, had revisited it in the seventies, so what was the point of doing it all again? The workload was enormous, and Fleming was not one to take shortcuts. So it was always going to be a long haul—so long, he felt certain he would be spending the last days of his career filing dog-eared documents rather than solving fresh crimes.

At least they had brought in another sucker to put another set of eyes on the contents of thousands of stained files. Herren, on loan from the Birmingham police force, was allowed access to a tiny, windowless room in the FBI building to go over the case documentation (although the Bureau's staff toilet was off-limits). A fussy note-taker, he embraced the challenge, jumping through every procedural hoop the Feds presented and, just like Bob Eddy twenty years before, eventually won the admiration of doubters within the organization.

Eddy was the man Langford and Jefferson County DA Barber approached at the genesis of the new process to see if it was even worth getting a professional of Fleming's standing to look at the case in greater detail. Not a soul had talked in earnest to the long-retired Eddy for a decade or so about the bombing, so to hear from officials in 1995 was, as he later put it, "a bit of a surprise." Langford and Barber asked if he thought it was still worth pursuing and Eddy suggested it was never too late. With that, the lawmen pushed ahead, convincing the old investigator to attend a meeting in Birmingham.

There was some discussion at the meeting about potential strategies and the need to check how many witnesses were still alive thirty-two years after the tragedy. But following the meeting, neither Fleming nor Herren heard anything else for at least six months. They continued looking into the matter; Police Sergeant Herren squeezing it in between his duties as head of Birmingham's burglary unit. Fleming, meanwhile, read every published item about the bombing and perused the impressive BAPBOMB files.

Through meetings and consultations, Langford became even more intensely aware of what the case meant to the black community. He concluded a full multi-agency assault would be the best way to crack it open if a genuine investigation was ever endorsed. "We started having meetings with black dignitaries, the Chief of Police and the District Attorney," Fleming said. "In one of our final meetings [in the summer of 1996], that's when it was decided that the FBI would collaborate with the police department in re-investigating the case."

Fleming, closing in on retirement, wasn't happy. "I told him the chances of us finding success after all these years was totally unrealistic. I'll never forget how Langford responded. He said, 'Well Bill, the people of the state of Alabama need another look at this.'"

Herren, though less willing to concede the case looked hopeless, let Chief Johnnie Johnson and Deputy Chief Bob Berry know his concerns when they summoned the seventeen-year police veteran to HQ for an update. "I told [them] honestly that I didn't think there would be a whole lot of success in a prosecution, but if we were going to try to get enough evidence, then let's do it right. I knew it would be the last time it would ever be investigated, and we needed to at least show the public that we gave it our best shot."

It would mean appointing Herren full time to the case, making him answerable only to Johnson and Berry, and giving him a car so he could be on call at all times. "I didn't have to go into my office, I didn't have supervision responsibility for thirteen guys, and I would be able to do what I enjoyed most, investigate a case, even one with more questions than answers," he said.

Perhaps if he'd known what his working conditions would be like, Herren might have reconsidered before completely throwing himself into the case. The "man-trap" assigned to him in the FBI building was oppressive. There were two padlocked doors leading to the man-trap, usually the scene of intense FBI interrogations. An FBI secretary was Herren's source of entry to the stark, neatly furnished area with a World War II metal surplus desk and three chairs. There wasn't a lot to do there except research, so that's what he did, relentlessly poring over thousands of BAPBOMB and related files. Occasionally he'd get a perfunctory visit from an agitated Fleming.

"Sometimes I wondered, 'Who did I piss off to get this assignment?'" Herren said.

Progress was slow, and just as Eddy found in the seventies, even when a "fresh" lead appeared it would almost always prove to be a dead end. Nevertheless, everything required checking.

Gradually Herren's meticulous investigative efforts earned Fleming's respect, and the pair slotted into a familiar routine. Fleming, having done his research, would bring files for Herren to read closely. For nearly six months, it was the same process almost every day, including most Saturdays and Sundays. They read ninety-one volumes of files, totaling 200,000 pages. Many of the reports were typed on colored onionskin, and the words had faded over the years, often forcing the investigators to hold the document to the light to read the copy.

A major challenge was to correctly weigh the importance of the reams of recorded observations, statements, law enforcement notes, and other items, including lie detector test results and the impressions of secret informants. There were memos of interviews with suspects and witnesses, and transcripts, often incomplete, of recorded conversations between Klansmen. They all had to be matched with other material, including the written observations of FBI agents. Even when the investigators matched one hard-to-read page with another, it was difficult to evaluate what would be usable in a court of law. Slowly, though, it became obvious that previous investigative efforts kept coming back to a small circle of suspects connected with the Eastview Klavern #13.

Plainly, the plan and the perpetrators belonged to this group of misfits whom even the regular Klan was reluctant to acknowledge as its own. The greater Klan organization and its leaders may have had knowledge—perhaps even promoted the idea—of the bombing, but decades later it was obvious that Chambliss's criminal associates, the group of renegades who met under the Cahaba River Bridge, were behind it.

Chambliss had died in prison in 1985, and many of his fellow Klansmen had passed, but at least two of the killers still walked free.

With the groundwork in place to launch a full investigation, Langford decided to seek the necessary approval of interim U.S. Attorney Caryl Privett to reopen the case officially. Wanting to get it underway before retiring in 1996, Langford contacted John Ott, the Criminal Section Chief in Privett's office, to arrange a meeting. Langford and Fleming attended, as did Privett's First Assistant, Bud Henry. The SAC insisted to the gathering that there were enough leads in the files to justify reopening the bombing case. In his gut, he told them, he believed justice could be delivered.

It was a bolt out of the blue for Privett and Henry. Throughout their respective careers, both had taken hard decisions that many others would have passed on, and they were acutely aware of the intensity of feeling about the case within the black community. Moreover, Privett, like me, had been profoundly impacted on a personal level by Baxley's work to convict Chambliss in 1977.

"But you don't make a decision of this magnitude based on emotions," Henry said. This wasn't just a cold case but, as Privett said, "a cold, cold, cold case," already thoroughly investigated twice.

Since the last inquiry, which only managed to nab Chambliss, scores of potential leads and evidence would have dissolved. "Memories fade of the witnesses still alive," Privett said. "Many witnesses were already deceased, and there wasn't much physical evidence, and there just wasn't much forensic evidence." She also questioned whether federal authorities had jurisdiction over the issue. The assumption was the case closed because the federal statute of limitations expired in 1968. There was a question in her mind as to whether they had the authority to grant permission to delve back into a case from 1963.

An overwhelming concern was how the city's black leaders and community would react if the case were reopened but nothing came of it. Would the effort be appreciated, or would it simply reinforce the belief that the Feds didn't care and had only been patronizing the black community?

Fleming, despite his personal doubts, had seen enough of the quality of Herren's efforts to know that if there were something useful in those files they would find it. No guarantees, he told the U.S. Attorney, but she could rest assured every lead would be followed and exhausted.

Privett was impressed by their commitment and satisfied herself on the jurisdiction issue by considering the possibility that the dynamite used to bomb the church had been made across state lines and transported to Birmingham. If that proved to be the case, then there was no statute of limitations.

She remained unsettled about the potential for an adverse reaction from the African-American community until Langford told her of his meetings with community leaders and their support for an attempt to bring a delayed justice. Within an hour, Privett, Henry, and Ott gave Langford the green light. "Some cases, no matter how hard they are to win, you just have to do it," said Henry.

Fleming and Herren's professional partnership had been officially "blessed," although the investigation continued in secrecy to avoid raising public expectations.

"By the time I had finished reading the files [including the Chambliss trial documents], I was convinced that the FBI had missed nothing in the original investigation. Every rock had been turned over," Herren said. He also was convinced he knew the identities of the two men, still alive, who aided Chambliss.

"A good investigator lets the case lead them. You don't lead the case. I went in thinking that possibly it wasn't them, but by the time I had finished with the files, I was convinced it had to be them. There was no other possible conclusion."

Fleming agreed. They knew who did it, without a shadow of a doubt. Bobby Frank Cherry and Tommy Blanton were about to get a lot of unwanted attention.

Petric Smith

The potential witness list was getting shorter by the day. Old Klansmen, their wives and girlfriends, cops, G-men from the fifties and sixties, residents, and victims' family members were rapidly disappearing. Age catches up with all of us, and it was overtaking many associated with the original investigation.

Chambliss's niece, Elizabeth Cobbs, Baxley's stellar witness, was barely recognizable, but not due to the ravages of age. She was now he. The formerly female minister had undergone a dramatic personal remake courtesy of the miracle of modern medicine and was now Petric Smith, author of *Long Time Coming*, which told the story of the bombing and its aftermath in his words.

"Now, there was a surprise," said veteran investigator Eddy, who was Cobbs's escort to court in 1977. She had been chased out of town by threats in the wake of her brave testimony.

By the time Fleming and Herren got the chance to meet Petric Smith, he was suffering from what would become terminal lung cancer. It wasn't long after their meeting that Smith died, aged fifty-seven.

During his exchange with the investigators, Smith had confirmed Herren's belief that Cherry and Blanton assisted Chambliss in planting the bomb.

Flushing the truth from the two primary suspects became an intense focus. Before talking directly to the men, Fleming and Herren read everything they could about them and talked to family and associates. There were a few wild-goose chases, including an anonymous tipster who alleged he'd heard Cherry admit to the crime. It took six months to locate the man and about six minutes into a phone call for Herren to question his credibility. Before the investigator could hang up, the source was offering insight into who "really" murdered JFK.

False leads were a distraction, but everything had to be looked at, especially as the verbose, ever-boastful Cherry seemed to be the kind of person who would incriminate himself. According to Eddy, the bulbous-nosed old thug came very close to confessing to him during the Baxley era. Maybe he'd do it again given the opportunity. At the very least, the inquiry needed some indication of fresh hope. If the suspects continued to stonewall, it would be difficult to justify taking the investigation to the next level.

Meanwhile, momentum was building. The inquiry involving the U.S. Attorney's Office, the FBI, the Jefferson County District Attorney's Office, and the Birmingham city police expanded. Robert Posey, an outstanding Assistant U.S. Attorney, and Jeff Wallace, a vastly experienced Deputy District Attorney for Jefferson County, added prosecutorial muscle to the cause. From Washington, D.C., Attorney General Janet Reno added experienced Civil Rights Division prosecutors Roy Austin and David Allred to the team.

The investigators did the math: as many as 200 of about 300 potential witnesses had died or disappeared, so there was no time to waste. After eighteen months of preparing and assembling the basics of a circumstantial case, it was time to test the viability of the investigation's theories and get a few more witnesses on the record.

Cherry was the number one target, so Fleming and Herren decided to take a shot with a visit to the former Klansman, now living in Texas. Posey and Wallace would remain in Birmingham, waiting for a phone call, hopefully with news of a confession.

"The strategy was simple," Herren said. "We wanted to catch him off guard, take him by surprise. It had been twenty years since the Chambliss conviction, and he had to feel comfortable that he had escaped ever paying for this crime."

To add to the surprise, Eddy, who had started farming in Chilton County, Alabama, after retiring in 1995, had agreed to go to Mabank, Texas, for a reunion of sorts with Cherry. His presence in the interview would be the wild card.

Herren would probably do the talking. As a member of the police department, he wouldn't be immediately viewed as the devil incarnate by Cherry, who, like most Klansmen, old and new, hated the Feds.

Keeping the visit under wraps proved a little tricky, as a Dallas television station had gotten wind of the interview plans. Fortunately, Joe Lewis, who had replaced the retiring Rob Langford as the Special Agent in Charge of the Birmingham bureau in 1996, worked a bit of magic by persuading the station not to air a piece about the imminent arrival of the investigators in Texas.

Fleming, Herren, and Eddy boarded an airplane in Birmingham and headed to Dallas on July 8, 1997. Civil Rights Division lawyers Roy Austin and David Allred also flew to Texas to be on hand.

The local police contacted Cherry, asking him if he would come downtown for an interview, hinting it had something to do with one of his children. His sons had a history of run-ins with law enforcement. However, when deputies picked him up for the drive to town, Cherry knew something was up. When he asked if this had anything to do with Birmingham, the officers in the car didn't respond, eliciting an "I ain't talking to no one from Birmingham" declaration from Cherry.

It should be noted that the old Klansman had been away from Birmingham for decades, yet he immediately jumped to the conclusion that his ride downtown had something to do with the city and, no doubt, the bombing, even though the investigation was not yet public knowledge.

Eddy and Herren handled the Cherry interview while Fleming was in another interrogation room conversing with the suspect's son, Tommy Frank.

"I'm expecting . . . that once he sees Bob Eddy, he will grab his chest, have a heart attack and die right there," Herren quipped. "Amazingly, that wasn't the case at all.

"He tells Bob Eddy, 'I thought you had retired and was farming.' He told me that I looked familiar and might have seen me around. He acts like we're all friends and was actually happy to see Eddy, a man he had almost confessed to some twenty years earlier."

For the next four and a half hours, Herren and Eddy asked questions, but for the most part, Cherry just talked and talked and talked and . . .

At one stage he said he needed to take his wife to the doctor. Since he was an inveterate liar, neither Herren nor Eddy knew what to make of it. The problem was solved when Cherry, apparently enjoying the attention, told them that he'd just get one of his sons to take her if necessary.

Herren desperately wanted to record the Cherry interview, but that was not the FBI way. Instead, he wrote notes for four hours on thirty-two pages of legal pads and later transferred the transcript to official FD 302 forms. Most of what Cherry had to say was nonsense, so it wasn't an efficient process, but you never knew what could eventually be relevant.

Herren remembered: "At one point in the interview, all of a sudden, he just blurts out, bragging, 'Hey, did you know that one time I busted old Shuttlesworth right in the nose and busted his head open with my brass knuckles?'"

Until that time no one had any idea that Cherry had assaulted Reverend

Shuttlesworth. (Later, with the help of an excellent reporter from Mississippi, Jerry Mitchell of the Jackson *Clarion-Ledger*, we would find film that showed Cherry assaulting Shuttlesworth outside Birmingham's Phillips High School in 1957.)

Amid the rambling, Cherry reiterated what he'd told Eddy twenty years earlier about his movements that fatal weekend. "On the Saturday night before the bombing, I had been at home all night watching my favorite television show, professional wrestling." Aged thirty-three at the time of the bombing, he had conceded he was at the sign shop (with Blanton and Chambliss) until ten o'clock, but said he went home immediately to watch the wrestling and take care of his wife, Virginia, who was terminally ill with cancer.

Herren had gone into the interview trying to keep an open mind. He wanted to get the story—the whole story—from the horse's mouth.

"We had narrowed the suspects down to a few individuals," he said. "But I wanted the smoking gun. I wanted him to say he did it, but he never did.

"I'll use every technique you can think of. I'll cry with a suspect, I'll be their buddy, and I will give them enough rope to hang themselves. Anyway, I told him that I understood the times, and knew all about the Klan, [and] I knew the Klan did things people approved of at the time.

"I was really pressing and went into a monologue with Cherry trying to get him to confess. I told him there must have been a malfunction on the time device, that it wasn't supposed to go off at the time that there were people at the church."

Cherry finally responded: "Well, you know, it's like pulling a trigger on a gun. Once that bullet leaves the barrel, you can't call it back."

That was enough to put the matter beyond question for Herren. "I was sitting there saying to myself, he did it. I knew without a shadow of a doubt."

But there was no overt confession. Cherry signed off at the end of the interview with "Birmingham ain't nothing but a fucking little Africa."

Despite their efforts and further confirmation of their personal belief that Cherry was involved, the team headed back to Birmingham disappointed. The interview was the pivot on which the investigation either went forward or slumped back toward the archives. Getting a case against Cherry that could be proved beyond a reasonable doubt looked, well, doubtful.

"I went in to to see [SAC] Joe Lewis," Fleming said. "I told him this case is dead. It can't go anywhere. We have no evidence. We have no witnesses. We know he did it, but we can't prove it."

Cherry's Press Conference

A few days after the interview, on July 11, 1997, while investigators mulled how, and even if, they should press on, Cherry cut them a break. He opened his mouth in public.

The motormouthed old bigot decided to hold a press conference to complain about the FBI, saying the agency had been harassing and hounding him for thirty years about the church bombing.

Clearly Cherry thought that by publicly complaining, he would get authorities off his back. But at the FBI office in Birmingham, phones started ringing. As the story made its way around the country, memories were stirred, consciences pricked, and people let the right folks know more about Cherry.

"People were calling from all around, telling us that they had heard Cherry brag about bombing the church," Herren said. "If he had kept his big mouth shut, it's highly unlikely we would have ever had a case against him."

While Cherry was unwittingly assisting authorities with their inquiries, Blanton, as had long been his way, wasn't saying much of anything. However, when Cherry's press conference made the news, and it was clear Blanton was the other main person of interest, he felt compelled to write to the *Birmingham News* denying his involvement and accusing the FBI of harassment.

On the strength of the evidence presented at the Chambliss trial, Blanton had been the more likely of the two to be next in line for prosecution, but the less erudite though equally heinous Cherry had now managed to make himself the focus of attention. He was the front-runner for prosecution, although his public tirade would prove invaluable in bringing the house of cards crashing down on fellow troll Blanton.

In the wake of Cherry's public comments, Fleming and Herren, released from the bondage of research and routine, hit the road to check out new leads. Road trips were even more enlightening and entertaining than their lunch dates, which offered a welcome respite from the cluttered FBI offices.

After a particularly intriguing phone tip, the pair headed down to the tiny town of Randolph, Alabama, population about 1,500, an hour south of Birmingham. On arrival, Fleming insisted on stopping at the local post office for directions to a residence.

"Bill will use the post office any day of the week before he'll ever get a GPS," Herren said.

A large, elderly woman greeted Fleming.

"Are you the postmistress?" he asked.

"Mister," she said, "the government doesn't pay me enough to be anybody's mistress."

She sent them on their way with detailed instructions, although there weren't too many streets to confuse a traveler in Randolph. The pair was visiting Michael Gowins, a man suffering from chronic obstructive pulmonary disease and close to the end of his life. Confined to his residence, Gowins was watching a newscast on Friday, July 11, and up popped Cherry in all his unmistakable, bulbous-nosed glory.

Gowins was bemused as he watched the man he had known from his days in Dallas, Texas, pronouncing his innocence in relation to the church bombing in 1963; after all, Cherry had bragged to him about his involvement.

Gowins called the Birmingham FBI office and told Fleming he'd never forgotten Cherry's bragging about the church bombing when the two had met in the Dallas area in 1982. Fleming quickly scheduled an in-person meeting.

On arrival, the investigators encountered a man gasping for breath and relying on an oxygen mask to help sustain him. It was a physical struggle, but there was nothing wrong with the man's memory as he spelled out his story in detail. Herren pulled out his pen and pad.

In 1982 Gowins was living in the suburbs of Dallas, where his mother managed the Munger Apartments. While his principal job was security agent, he assisted with maintenance work and cleaning the apartments.

The man in charge of cleaning the carpets was Bobby Frank Cherry, who had his own cleaning business at the time. Both men were natives of Birmingham, which apparently prompted Cherry to tell Gowins and his mother that he had to leave the Magic City because he bombed the 16th Street Baptist Church.

It's not the sort of thing easily forgotten. Nor was the depth of hatred Cherry spewed. He suggested to Gowins that present-day "Mexicans" should meet the same fate as "niggers" did back in the sixties in Birmingham.

At least two other important calls came into the Birmingham FBI the day Cherry adorned television screens to protest his innocence. On a swelteringly hot afternoon in Keller, Texas, twenty-four-year-old Teresa Stacy had just put her ten-month-old down for a nap when she heard an unwelcome but familiar drawl: "I feel sorry for those girls who got killed back in Birmingham, but I didn't have nothing to do with their killing."

Stacy dropped her dish rag and checked the TV to confirm who was lying to the camera: the nose, the hat, the big glasses—it was her paternal grandfather, Bobby Frank Cherry (she was his eldest son Tommy's daughter).

Stacy had never lived in Alabama and wasn't born until more than a decade after the bombing, but she recalled Cherry's bragging at family functions about bombing the church and killing the girls. That wasn't the only reason she hated the man. He had sexually molested her, cementing her estrangement from the family for some time.

Around the time she was going through puberty, she moved with her divorced father, Tommy Frank Cherry, next door to her grandfather, who took to touching her inappropriately. She ran away from her abusive family at the age of sixteen and stumbled into a nightly routine of exotic dancing in a haze of drug abuse that led to cocaine addiction. It is a sadly familiar trail for abused kids, but by 1997 Stacy had steered clear of that destructive existence and was rebuilding her life with a new family.

Hearing Cherry's voice again brought back some terrible memories about a part of her life she preferred to forget. But Stacy had grown. She would no longer avoid the source of her pain. It was time to deal with it.

Without hesitation, she picked up the telephone and called the local FBI office in Dallas, telling them unequivocally that she knew Cherry was lying. An agent in Dallas sent her call on to Fleming in Birmingham.

"Thank God, somebody is looking into the church bombing," were the first words out of Stacy's mouth to Fleming, who swiftly arranged to fly to Dallas with Robert Posey to interview her.

"One of the most impressive things about her was her readiness to admit to her own shortcomings," Posey said. "She was rock solid and her convictions unyielding. She had straightened her life out, had one child at the time, and was happily married living in an upscale neighborhood."

Calm and collected, Stacy told the men about the abuse and how Cherry had boasted about bombing the church. Posey knew she would be an excellent witness, even if she would likely have to endure a courtroom attack on her character, given her rocky teen years.

Another person haunted by a childhood memory of Cherry was Bobby Birdwell, a friend of Tommy Frank Cherry when they were kids. A neighbor in suburban Ensley back in 1963, eleven-year-old Bobby had been playing with Tommy in the Cherrys' front yard on a hot September day in 1963 when he overheard an adult say "the dynamite is there."

Fleming and Herren headed south down Highway 280 on July 24, 1997, crossing the infamous Cahaba River Bridge en route to Shelby County to get more of the story from Birdwell.

A commercial plumber, the Vietnam veteran recounted his stark memories of that day, including seeing Cherry's Klan suit and hearing four men, including Tommy Frank's father, sitting around a table in Cherry's kitchen discussing methods of stopping integration. They resolved that one form of deterrence would be to bomb the 16th Street Baptist Church.

When asked why he didn't report what he'd heard back in 1963, Birdwell reminded the investigators he was only a boy at the time and had feared for his life.

After hearing Cherry proclaim his innocence, however, Birdwell had decided to reveal the awful secret he'd carried around for decades. He said he was prepared to testify against the old man. Like the other callers that day, Birdwell did not ask for anything in return for his cooperation.

"They were heroes," Fleming said. "They were mad that Bobby Frank Cherry had gotten away with murder for all these years.

"Without them, the case against Cherry wouldn't have gotten off the ground."

None of the trio had played a part in previous inquiries.

"They didn't show up in any of the FBI files," Herren said. "They had never been interviewed at any time. They just wanted to right an awful wrong."

PART
TWO

FOUR

THE JOB

Maybe it was the influence of Bill Baxley, the unique blend of judicial gravitas and public service that accompanied the job, or a naïve desire to be some sort of prosecutorial Atticus Finch, but I couldn't quell my desire to be appointed a U.S. Attorney.

After Claude Harris slipped into the position I had been coveting in 1994, I was forced to focus again on a career in private practice and set about rebuilding my little firm. Tragically, though, Harris contracted lung cancer and died only one year after taking office, reopening the door to a possibility I had thought was closed.

When it came to nominating a replacement, Senator Heflin called me to ask if I was still interested. I was, of course, but we both knew any move to replace Claude was likely some way off. And with President Clinton experiencing sagging approval ratings, there was a real chance the next U.S. Attorney might only be in place for a relatively brief time before a new President ushered in a new appointee.

I couldn't afford to risk becoming unemployed after only a year or so in office, so I turned down the opportunity to throw my hat in the ring. Instead, it looked as though either the interim U.S. Attorney, Caryl Privett, or my old buddy and baseball adversary, Greg Hawley, were front-runners for the job.

Both would have been excellent choices, but I backed Hawley, believing he had the political clout and an ongoing connection with Heflin that would help him be most effective. Hawley was in the driver's seat when President Clinton's poll numbers started to climb again. But the process dragged on for over eighteen months. When Heflin's Chief of Staff, Steve Raby, finally called in May 1996 to advise that the President was ready to go forward, Greg opted to take the safe route, waiting to ensure Clinton was reelected before being appointed.

Over the course of the summer, however, Hawley's private practice had taken off. He had a young family and was suddenly earning a very good living. He called me for lunch to deliver the news that being a federal prosecutor wasn't for him.

"Doesn't this open the door for you again?" he asked.

It did, but the last few years had been tough on those around me. Our baby boy, Carson, had arrived in March 1995, ensuring a full night's sleep had become a luxury, and we'd moved several times as a contractor took about as long to finish our house renovation as the Clinton administration took to make an appointment. Eventually, Louise and I finished the renovation ourselves, working through bouts of sleep deprivation to rebuild a home at night and my little firm by day. My marriage was blissful, although we had teetered on the brink of bankruptcy.

My firm was on the way up again, and this was my dream job that also offered some much-desired financial stability. Hawley and I devised a plan.

We waited until after the election to officially announce he was withdrawing. On the day of the announcement, I called my friend Peggy Sanford, who covered the federal courts at the *Birmingham News* to discuss Hawley's decision. Not unexpectedly, she asked if I was interested in the position. "Why, yes I am," I told her, adding that I had been approached by several people about taking up the opportunity. Soon after, I was in Washington discussing the possibility of seeking the appointment with soon-to-retire Senator Heflin and Steve Raby.

The Senator gave me his backing but told me that he would only send my name over to the White House if I could garner the support of the Democratic faithful. Fortunately, I had made enough friends in the world of politics and had a good enough reputation that I was able to get the support needed.

The next hurdle was the Republicans. On Heflin's retirement, Republican Jeff Sessions defeated Democrat Roger Bedford to win the vacant Senate seat. I had to convince two Republicans, Sessions and the other Alabama

Senator, Richard Shelby, to back me. Somehow, with the help of a slew of friends and professional acquaintances, I did.

The nomination process during the spring and summer of 1997 was grueling. Background checks, interviews, seemingly endless delays. It was a full seven months before I was confident that my nomination was actually going to happen.

My last interview was with Attorney General Janet Reno. When you reach the point of speaking with the AG, you are pretty much assured of having your name submitted and being nominated by the President, so my main goal at that stage was to avoid doing something really stupid.

In her office, I braced myself for the tough questions. "I see you have gotten the support of everybody in Alabama. How in the world did you do that?" she asked. I immediately relaxed.

We enjoyed a great conversation. I was to be nominated, although it would not be until after Labor Day 1997. The Department broke the news to Caryl Privett, who I am sure still held out hope that she would get the nod. Graciously, my old friend called to congratulate me. Invaluably, she also invited me to be her guest at an upcoming statewide law enforcement conference where I would meet all the major players with whom I'd be dealing.

Amid the excitement, it dawned on me that confirmation of the appointment could be up to three months away. I had been winding down my caseload and wouldn't be able to take on any new clients, knowing I couldn't commit to them in the future, so my income was close to drying up.

I needed to get in office before my Senate confirmation—an option, if official approval could be secured—but that would mean displacing Caryl earlier than expected. My motivation was not entirely selfish: I would be the sixth U.S. Attorney for the office in just about as many years and everyone, including the Court, was looking for some certainty and stability in the office.

I sought the advice of Judge Sharon Blackburn, another friend and colleague from our days in the U.S. Attorney's Office and Caryl's close friend. Soon after, Privett graciously stepped aside earlier than required and I was temporarily named the interim U.S. Attorney (her position) before my official confirmation. It was the selfless act of a friend and professional whose ongoing contribution to the justice process in Alabama ranks her as one of the greats.

It was a tribute to the tight ship Privett ran that the Langford-initiated effort to carefully examine the church bombing case had stayed out of the headlines. Like me, she knew how much the case meant to the black community, and also like me, she had had her legal career steered in a significant way when she watched Bill Baxley haul Southern justice to new heights in 1977.

Any hint that authorities were re-examining the case could have prematurely raised African-American hopes and likely induced widespread amnesia among the scores of people with any old connection to the Klan. Not only were the initial stages of the investigation conducted with stealth and the process never revealed to the public, but it was also a successfully maintained secret in legal circles.

Even when I looked certain to get the nod as U.S. Attorney, I was as oblivious as the next Alabamian that Langford had his man Fleming and the exceptional Birmingham cop Ben Herren scouring FBI files on the bombing and rustling a few Klan feathers with their inquiries. Until, that is, one warm summer's day in July 1997, before I needed to fully rearrange my life and impose on Privett to take on the new job.

With my nomination all but set, I was feeling especially positive and enjoyed pondering what caseload I would inherit and the priorities I would bring. Then, early one morning, I walked down my driveway and unrolled the morning paper. There on the front page was confirmation that authorities had officially reopened the cold case of the fatal 1963 bombing of the 16th Street Baptist Church.

Planting myself on the stone wall at the end of the driveway, I stared at the story. It had influenced my whole life. This was a chance to get answers to questions the city needed resolved in order to move on assertively—to stop shuffling about in latent shame.

Sitting on that rock wall, amid a flurry of thoughts about Baxley; Chris McNair, whom I had come to know well; his daughter and the other girls; and Birmingham past and present, it occurred to me that this was why I wanted to be a U.S. Attorney. To envisage the chance to grab this thing by the scruff of the neck was invigorating and in some ways liberating. I was thrilled and strangely relieved, as if I'd suddenly discovered what had been ailing me all these years.

I raced back to the house, bursting to tell Louise. As she made the kids breakfast, I showed her the headlines.

"Wonderful," she said while busily making toast. "I hope they get them."

"But you don't understand," I said. "This is a federal case, so it's now my case. This is why I wanted to become a U.S. Attorney." It was a turning point in my life, and Privett had made that moment possible. She had opened the door to redemption for the whole city, and thankfully when I got the nod to take over, she stayed on as my Executive Assistant U.S. Attorney for a year. With Bud Henry on board as my First Assistant, I was able to slot straight into the role. As I took the reins as U.S. Attorney, the investigators were still saddled with understandable doubts about the strength of the case. I knew we had a great team; but witnesses were dying, memories were fading. If you spent too much time thinking about what we lacked, it would be hard to move forward, but we were at least heading in the right direction. Certainly, a chance like this wouldn't come around again.

The Team

Call it fortuitous or divine intervention: the release of Spike Lee's documentary film about the bombing, *4 Little Girls*, coincided with my assuming the U.S Attorney role. Birmingham's conscience and mine were tugged by the movie, which was the first comprehensive, mass market review of the bombing and the impact on the families and greater community. It seemed to aid the momentum that was building in the prosecution of the case.

Chris McNair figured prominently in the film, which cut the Magic City little slack. The ugliness of the Klan, segregation, and the injustices imposed on those struggling for civil rights were spelled out, generating national attention.

Until the meeting with Rob Langford, the African-American community had been relatively silent on the case as Baxley's 1977 conviction of Chambliss drifted into history, but media focus, especially for a major film, helped build renewed hope that action would be taken. As my prosecution team began to gel, discontent about the injustice that several killers still walked free became more audible.

The calls for action grew a little louder with an official Birmingham premiere for *4 Little Girls* in September. I thought it prudent not to attend, although I welcomed Spike Lee's commitment to confronting the city with his Academy Award–nominated documentary.

Our prosecution team, meanwhile, continued turning dog-eared pages and dipping into the bizarre world of the KKK to try and unearth something new in the case.

By October 13, 1997, Ben Herren had been on loan from the Birmingham Police Department to the FBI for 550 work days, most of them at least twelve-hour shifts. Eventually, he'd been allowed into the FBI parking area, been given access to the staff bathroom, and received encouraging backslaps he richly deserved from the G-men.

At a relatively innocuous cost to the FBI—a substantial proportion for legal pads and ballpoint pens—he had meticulously documented the circumstantial case he and veteran Bill Fleming were assembling.

Finally, this small man with a big heart and the patience of a saint retired from the Birmingham Police Department. Sixteen hours later he officially took the oath as a member of the Federal Bureau of Investigation.

For Bill and Ben, that was confirmation that they were collectively committed for the foreseeable future to nothing else but this frustrating, though immeasurably meaningful, case. It was a destiny that would include too many interviews with old Klansmen in the backwoods of Alabama, many lunches, the occasional chance for Fleming to snap a shot of a Confederate general's grave, and regular episodes of the "Doug Jones hour"— the affectionate (I hope) term they gave to our gatherings to strategize.

I didn't have to tell anyone how to do their job, as experts surrounded me, but a major task on a cold case that had been dissected and put back together several times was to ensure our effort remained energized and positive.

It was important to let these talented people do what they do their way, but I wanted to be involved in every aspect of the case and was probably as irritating as a swarm of gnats at a ball game. It was up to me to maintain the momentum and, together with experienced attorneys such as Robert Posey and Jeff Wallace, fully cultivate the fine investigative work by effectively blending it with the judicial process.

Fleming had been right to lament the apparent hopelessness of the situation when he first looked into the case. But it wasn't the quality of the investigation that had let down the community. The lack of institutional commitment to seeing the prosecution through to the death had shortchanged the families and the justice system. That was my job: to stand on Baxley's shoulders and push hard—and push back when necessary; to ensure the system didn't act defensively by refusing to face facts because mistakes and institutional stumbles had tarnished our judiciary at times in the past.

The U.S. Attorney's Office would be hands-on. I wanted to ensure that the dignified authority it represented was obvious to all these old Klansmen and their cronies who had been able to tumble through life with little or no regard for others.

The low-hanging fruit had already been picked, but there was more there for the taking when you looked closely. Somebody with the opportunity just had to shake the tree hard enough. At least, that's what I told myself.

Inside Agitators

Nearly everyone who grew up in the South in the fifties and sixties would have heard it from their parents and community leaders. In the media, at school, in church, adults reaching for something to adequately explain (or dismiss) the cause of civil unrest would blame it on "outside agitators."

It was their way of saying no one in our community would dare be so disruptive to our Southern way of life. It must be the work of others. Of course, this ignored the dissatisfaction and understandable anger of vast numbers of the population. If you were a local who was critical of racism and discrimination you ran the risk of being labeled a radical.

But that was the big lie segregation could never sell effectively, because, no matter how sheltered your childhood, you gradually came across instances of injustice that just couldn't be easily explained away. And that exposure increased as integration accelerated.

There wasn't a radical notion among any of the team looking into the church bombing case. But as white kids growing up in Alabama, we all shared that experience of eventually realizing that there was something fundamentally wrong with our way of life. The disharmony it generated wasn't the work of outsiders or radicals. It was the inevitable consequence of oppression. For some, this came as a swift epiphany, for others a slow burn. For all of us, it was profoundly informative when dealing with the bombing case.

The attack at the church was a peak example of the dysfunction of the era. The failure over decades to fully prosecute the case related to the ugly truths we learned as kids. It wasn't guilt that drove us to see it through this time; rather we were empowered by the kind of knowledge our parents' generation did not access because of the great lie.

Privett, like me, was largely oblivious to anything civil rights–related as a young child growing up in the fifties amid the dignified surrounds of Mountain Brook, in suburban Birmingham. But during her high school years, she was horrified by the violence imposed on the 1965 Selma-to-Montgomery marchers and outraged by newspaper letters and editorials criticizing the protesters. So many had a common refrain, blaming "outside agitators for stirring things up," Privett recalled recently.

She was a student at Vanderbilt University when, hit with the flu and bed-bound on April 4, 1968, she watched her tiny black-and-white television as news broke of Martin Luther King Jr.'s assassination in Memphis. "I just felt horror for the entire country," she said. When an assassin took the life of Senator Kennedy two months later, it solidified her commitment to become a civil rights attorney and return to Alabama.

There she would aspire to be a self-described "inside agitator"—a local initiating real civil rights change in the state where it was needed most.

Having earned her law degree at New York University, she returned home and began her law practice with the law firm Adams, Baker & Clemon. Privett, a white woman in a black firm, was working in legendary company. Each of the named partners made history: Oscar Adams was the first African American on the Alabama Supreme Court; Jim Baker was Birmingham's first black City Attorney; and U. W. Clemon was Alabama's first black federal judge.

Privett quickly cemented a reputation as an innovator and a changemaker and later in her career made a hugely positive impact as an Assistant U.S. Attorney before becoming the first female U.S. Attorney in Alabama. She went on to claim a spot in history as one of the first female state court judges in Jefferson County.

The other professionals on my team held a similar no-nonsense commitment to ignoring the noise around an issue and paying suitable reverence to the truth.

Both Bill and Ben were investigators' investigators, while Robert Posey and Jeff Wallace were, like all great prosecutors, able to recognize the often incremental but positive potential every case held for the greater good. It was not about exercising vengeance or asserting power but striving for accountability in behalf of the community.

That isn't a grand ideal or empty rhetoric; it's the mindset that allows you the freedom to do the job as it needs to be done. In a sense, it takes some of the emotion out of the process—something that in a case as overwhelmingly affecting as the church bombing was essential. The goal of obtaining "justice" for the families and their communities is a given, but you're striving to redress an imbalance, to restore the natural order of things that the failure to fully prosecute, in this case, had distorted in Alabama. To bend that arc in the right direction.

Inaction is as damaging as the imposition of a biased law or the willful misuse of the law. The children's deaths could never be avenged. However, the lack of respect shown for the victims, the abuse of the sanctity of the space the killers attacked, and the morally decrepit image that plagued Birmingham after the event could be, in part, redressed.

Good People

The son of a Methodist minister, Jeff Wallace is the same age as me. As a nine-year-old, living in Childersburg, Alabama, a good lake-fishing town of fewer than 5,000 on the Coosa River, less than an hour's drive from Birmingham, he experienced the bombing as yet another terrible deed carried out in the Magic City—so close, yet so far—by the ruthless Klan.

He grew up wanting to become a police officer, but he listened to his father, who urged him to complete a law degree. Being a prosecuting attorney combined some of the appeal of both law enforcement roles. Through the years, Wallace would be on the scene of more than two hundred homicides and lead the prosecution in more than fifty trials associated with those deaths.

Not unlike Bill Baxley, who had the names of the four victims from 16th Street etched onto his phone card, Wallace, the Deputy District Attorney for Jefferson County, kept a map of the area and used an electronic pin to identify the locations of those two hundred homicides.

Robert Posey, like Wallace, had endured more capital cases than was sensible in his career—first as an Assistant District Attorney in Jefferson and Shelby Counties, then as an Assistant United States Attorney.

A twelve-year-old in 1963, Posey would have been a near neighbor at some stage to Caryl Privett in the leafy Birmingham enclave where the events of downtown were even further away in the mind than the perspective from my childhood spot in working-class Fairfield.

Not much would get to the studious Posey, but sitting in his seventh-grade math class, Posey was rattled to the core by the shooting of JFK that afternoon in Dealey Plaza, west of downtown Dallas.

Posey's response to troubling times was to focus on his work, a habit I was privileged to witness many years later, when his intellect and poise were the foundations of one of the best closing arguments I've ever witnessed in a criminal court.

Fleming, like Posey, was old enough to have experienced the remnants of Jim Crow as a teen and is very much a man who represents the best of a previous generation. Being a kid in Albany, Georgia, in the fifties was no cakewalk. It was a tough town, with more than its share of racial tension.

He was eighteen when the Birmingham church was bombed, but the case that is imprinted on Fleming's mind is the 1964 Klan murder of decorated U.S. Army Reserve Lieutenant Colonel Lemuel Penn.

Colonel Penn was driving straight through Georgia to Washington with two fellow reserve officers because he couldn't find a hotel that would allow blacks to spend the night. Near Athens, Georgia, a car filled with Klansmen drove past the military men. Shots were fired, and a bullet hit Penn, instantly killing him. Two of the Klansmen were arrested for the murder, but both—Cecil Myers and Howard Sims—were acquitted by an all-white, all-male jury.

"I was eighteen years old when that happened," Fleming said. "My next-door neighbors were like a second father and mother to me. I'll never forget telling them how awful this was about Colonel Penn and the response I got from them just saddened me.

"Basically, they said he got what he deserved for being down here trying to stir up things.

"That really shook me up."

After serving his country in Korea, Fleming returned home and was faced with a choice—starting a career in retail or joining the FBI. Happily, the Bureau edged out Kmart. His fastidious approach gained him a level of notoriety in the Bureau, and his extracurricular interests, specifically his intense interest in the Civil War, enhanced his reputation as a true original.

To date, Fleming has visited the graves of 339 of the more than 400 Confederate generals. He'll do his best to attend to the rest, although one, buried in Egypt, might be an ocean or two too far.

His last partner in the Bureau, the former cop Ben Herren, quickly got to know Fleming's quirks on their road trips. A daily trip might be an interview with an angry, uncooperative old Klansmen, lunch at the local greasy spoon, and a detour to a cemetery before heading home.

Even if the routine was a little unusual, working with Fleming was refreshing. Herren had enjoyed his time as one of Birmingham's top cops, leading the law enforcement effort against burglars and drug suppliers, but there was something personally challenging about taking on the bombing cold case that he hadn't experienced before.

Unlike Fleming, Herren had long known he wanted to be in law enforcement before he took the plunge. Standing just five foot two and weighing in at around one hundred pounds as a young man, he fudged his way onto the force. He was about seven pounds under the required weight, so he taped rolls of quarters to his legs and carried three guns, "but they found two of them," he said.

He was nine at the time of the bombing of the church and remembers adults talking about the rioting downtown. Watching the six o'clock news daily heightened his understanding that the Klan was "no good."

The Klan's influence within the Birmingham Police Department had been largely cleaned out by the time Herren joined. It was vastly different from the corrupt and racially biased law enforcement body that he was amazed to read about in researching the church bombing case.

"It's hard to imagine today, but you could see how it could influence the city," he said. "I was proud of the Birmingham Police. Making sure we made good on the work years before was something that needed to be done for them too."

Persons of Interest

To everyone associated with the case in the second half of 1997, Blanton's close connection to the crime was rarely, if ever, in doubt. While Dynamite Bob Chambliss was always spotlighted by law enforcement as the prime suspect, the next most likely over the decades had been Blanton.

However, over the years he had remained relatively quiet about the bombing. Cherry, on the other hand, had opened the door to exposure with his public statements. The case against him had grown accordingly.

To Baxley's frustration, in the seventies, Eddy was fed evidence piecemeal by the FBI. He always suspected there was more he could have used if he and his team had open and easy access to all material related to the case. Twenty years later, Fleming had that access, although knowing what to look for was a different matter. Matching evidence sheets with statements and relevant stored materials was more art than science amid the clutter of the seventh floor of the 2121 Building.

During the summer of 1997, Fleming, plowing through boxes, bags, cabinets, containers, file folders, and other aged office supplies, found himself staring at an evidence sheet. It was dated 1981, four years after Chambliss's conviction. Included in the FBI document was a note that audiotapes of Blanton were made in 1964 with the help of an informant named Mitchell Burns. Working back through evidence from the sixties, the investigators established that Burns, a former World War II Marine, had risked his life to allow a reel-to-reel recording device to be planted in the trunk of his car. It produced hours of conversations between himself and Klansmen.

Baxley's team in the seventies didn't have a clue about the tapes or Burns's role as an agent provocateur.

Investigator Eddy, of course, had to know what to ask for or rely on the largesse of Bureau agents when seeking material related to BAPBOMB. Even as we got down to business in our investigation, the FBI was extremely protective of anything associated with informants. Burns's FBI codename was Tom Dooley.

That's possibly why the agents Eddy was dealing with failed to pass the recordings on in 1976 and 1977, though it is quite likely most of the G-men feeding him material just didn't know about them, even if someone higher up the chain most certainly did.

All the way into the late nineties, the perception among a few old FBI agents was that while there were recordings made of Klansmen during the bombing investigation, they had proved to be relatively useless. Additionally, most were thought to be illegally obtained, rendering them unusable in a court of law.

The tapes made of Burns and his Klan cohorts were legal—if one party gives approval for a recording to be made, they are lawful. However, they appear to have been assessed by the Bureau at the time as having produced very little useful material and were treated as such in storage. Yet there were spotty transcripts of some of the FBI tapes, including those made by Burns, and even on paper they were quite stunning, despite the absence of an obvious smoking gun.

A search through more clutter located the Mitch Burns tapes—boxes of them. They would have to be carefully listened to and assessed, and matched with transcripts where possible and written observations from the Feds who were monitoring the process at the time.

Initially, Fleming and Herren focused on talking to Burns himself. The man was very much alive and well, living just north of Birmingham in Warrior. Using the partial transcripts as their reference material, the investigators hoped to get Burns to fill in a few of the gaps and expand on his experiences. He would prove most obliging.

Back in 1964, Burns had pursued a romantic interest in a young waitress, Marie Aldridge, who knew Pops Blanton and his son Tommy. Pops was a Klan legend, a conniving, cruel man. Back in the day, his boy was a rising figure in the movement. Known for his willingness to engage in physical intimidation and for taking chances, Tommy had avoided charges over the bombing despite an expanding file of circumstantial evidence.

The FBI tried to enlist Burns's help as an informant, but he resisted until one day an agent, Brook Blake, showed him graphic photos of the mutilated bodies of the girls killed in the 16th Street Baptist Church bombing. Shaken to the core, he told Blake he would do anything to put the guilty parties behind bars. The FBI rigged Burns's car with a cumbersome seven-inch reel-to-reel recorder, squeezing it into the trunk and planting a microphone behind a disabled car radio.

Burns struck up a friendship with Blanton courtesy of their mutual connection, the waitress, and the pair would go "catting around town." Like all Klansmen in Birmingham, Blanton was paranoid about the FBI placing wiretaps on his phones and bugs in his house. He was convinced that his car was being bugged, so when the two men went cruising, Blanton insisted on riding in Burns's automobile.

There was no music on the ride courtesy of the "broken" radio, and fortunately, there was no reason to open the trunk, which would have obviously killed the scheme and probably ended Burns's life.

Blanton introduced Burns to his buddy Bobby Frank Cherry. On the drive to a friend's house in Burns's car, Cherry opened up about how much he hated the FBI, sharing that he'd like to blow up the 2121 Building and revealing how he had lied to the agency every time they had interviewed him. Blanton, at one stage, felt compelled to admonish Cherry about talking too much around Burns. "He doesn't know too much," Blanton said, "and we need to keep it that way."

There was no recording of another moment, reported to the FBI by Burns—a conversation inside Cherry's house when Blanton talked about the night of the bombing and how he'd "missed the alley" on his way to pick up Cherry. According to Burns, in the same conversation Cherry offered: "Yeah, the FBI thinks they know where the bomb was made, and they ain't got a clue where it was made."

On the tapes, there were hours of racial slurs, sexual references, dialogue about people they hated, taunts to the Feds ("hear that FBI?"), and awkward discussions that hinted at nefarious deeds, but no point-blank admission of guilt in the church bombing. Nevertheless, when we eventually got the chance to listen to many of the tapes, it was clear they and Burns could be very useful at a trial, should it ever come to that.

Herren had struck up a relationship with Burns, driving to Warrior to talk with the old man at his meticulously cared for home. Later, Fleming would return with his partner for multiple visits, and I ensured I got the chance to meet with him in Warrior too. We got to know a principled but flawed man. Burns had followed family tradition by joining the Klan back in the day and never relinquished his opposition to integration, but his disgust at the violence of his peers was a testament to his humanity.

I was thrilled by news of the Burns tapes and elated he was cooperating with the team. When I met him, it was clear he would be a forthright and believable witness. His potential testimony certainly improved Blanton's odds of being the next to face trial.

As Fleming consumed the information piece by piece in the cluttered evidence room, he saw references to other tape evidence, including intriguing notes about recordings obtained by bugging Blanton's kitchen and the cuckoo clock at the Chambliss residence. The word from old agents and notes in the evidence stash indicated they mainly consisted of dishes clanging in the sink, a cuckoo clock signaling the arrival of each hour, and the sound of men playing games of checkers.

The recordings were produced via an electronic bug and perceived to be of little legal use. According to the records, one FBI agent in 1964 said tersely: "We ain't got shit on these tapes."

They had been filed away, somewhere among thousands of documents, and largely forgotten. To find them would be an arduous, time-consuming task, but it was high on the very long list of "to-dos."

Every old lead and every possible new lead had to be evaluated. In addition to checking out the people and information that flowed from Cherry's press conference, we focused toward the end of 1997 on two other potential witnesses.

We believed that both Klan associate Mary Lou Holt and FBI informant Gary Thomas Rowe had important knowledge of the bombing and, after all those years, perhaps would have a change of heart about revealing exactly what they knew.

Holt, an exceptionally attractive woman, had been married to two Klan leaders in the 1960s and regularly attended meetings where the likes of Chambliss, Cherry, and Blanton were present. She was also rumored to be "friendly" with Rowe and had often turned the heads of prominent Southerners, including politicians.

Holt was unusually powerful for a woman in Klan circles. Klan women were treated dismissively at best. Often they were treated brutally. But they remained inexplicably loyal to their partners and Klan associates.

Fleming and Herren had been expecting the old Klansmen who were still around to be reluctant interviewees but had not counted on the recalcitrance of the former wives and partners after so many years. "One thing you need to realize about these Klan wives," Fleming said. "Some of them were tough nuts to crack. Many of them were tougher than the men, close-mouthed, and in many cases, just mean." According to Herren, it wasn't un-

Children marching away from the 16th Street Baptist Church, the meeting point to protest segregation in Birmingham, May 1963.

There was a surge in KKK numbers in the 1950s and '60s as the last pillars of Jim Crow laws crumbled in the South.

Reverend Fred Shuttlesworth (*front, right*) and attorney Oscar Adams (*front, left*) accompany James Armstrong and his two sons, Dwight and Floyd, as they become the first black students to attend Graymont Elementary School, November 9, 1963.

Parker High School student Walter Gadsden after he was attacked by police dogs. Images of young people protesting racial segregation and being attacked by Birmingham's police and fire departments shocked the world. Photo credit: Alabama Department of Archives and History. Donated by Alabama Media Group. Unknown photographer, *Birmingham News*.

Children being detained by police during the Children's Crusade marches. Photo credit: Alabama Department of Archives and History. Donated by Alabama Media Group. Photo by Norman Dean, *Birmingham News*.

Cars parked on 16th Street near the explosion were destroyed by the force of the blast. Photo credit: Alabama Department of Archives and History. Donated by Alabama Media Group. Photo by Tom Self, *Birmingham News*.

The explosion caused extensive structural damage to the church and other buildings nearby, but a stained-glass image of Jesus remained intact with only the face of Christ blown out.

Bombing survivor Sarah Collins's last memory before the explosion is standing at the ladies' lounge sink and turning to see her sister Addie tying the sash of her friend Denise McNair's dress.

The bomb obliterated the ladies' lounge where the victims were preparing for a special youth service.

Bombing victim Carole Robertson. Died age 14. Pronounced dead at Hillman Hospital, September 15, 1963.

Bombing victim Cynthia Morris Wesley. Died age 14. Pronounced dead at Hillman Hospital, September 15, 1963.

Bombing victim Denise McNair. Died age 11. Pronounced dead at Hillman Hospital, September 15, 1963.

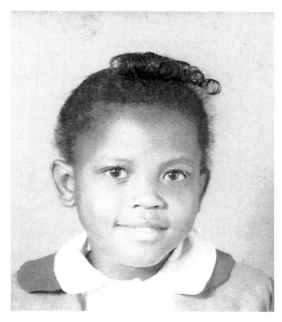

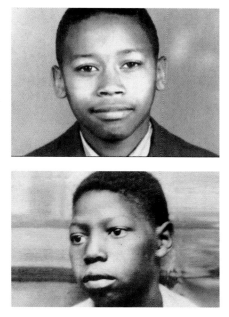

Bombing victim Addie Mae Collins. Died age 14. Pronounced dead at Hillman Hospital, September 15, 1963.

Virgil Ware and Johnny Robinson both died on the same day as the bombing. Ware was fatally shot by a white teen while riding his bicycle with his brother, and Robinson was shot in the back by a police officer.

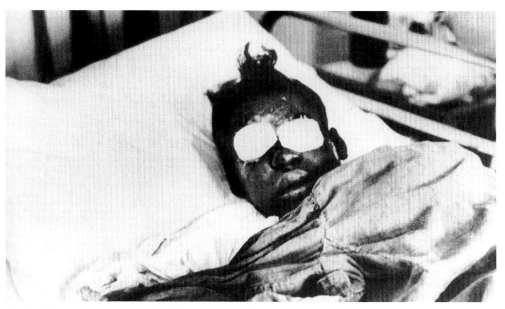

Sarah Collins, younger sister of Addie Mae, survived the bombing but had extensive injuries.

Tom Blanton. In the 1960s, Blanton had a reputation of being a particularly violent Klan figure.

Bobby Frank Cherry, a volatile and verbose Klansman, let it be known that he had extensive experience in developing and preparing bombs.

Bill Baxley (*left*) during the Robert Chambliss trial. Alabama's youngest Attorney General, Baxley gave a courtroom master class and ultimately secured a conviction against the former Klansman.

common for law officers to have doors slammed in their faces by the women. Some feared reprisals from the Klan or beatings from their husbands. Many were just awful people.

Holt was a case apart. She was a trusted insider in the fifties and sixties and a celebrated figure in the movement. As I reviewed the investigation documents from the period, it seemed to me that she probably knew as much or more than most Klansmen about the bombing. That was even more true decades later, with most of the scoundrels having taken knowledge of the sin to their graves.

She had been identified in Blanton's and his then girlfriend Jean Casey's alibi as someone they saw at the drive-in on the night of Saturday, September 14. Additionally, it was widely speculated that a test of the unique fuse likely used on the church bomb had been performed at her house (it allegedly flared out in a flower bed). Scuttlebutt over the years surrounding the case was immense and obviously not all true, but Holt was a recurring figure in many stories.

We had to get to Holt before she joined her colleagues in whatever afterlife old Klansmen went to. We had been refused access to her in a nursing home by her family but hoped her nephew Don Luna, a strange Klan figure himself, would help us make contact.

Luna was a huge man, over four hundred pounds, and battling diabetes. He had been convicted of fraud and was looking for a deal to blunt a new federal indictment in South Carolina when we interviewed him on November 26, 1997. A con man from early in life, he had famously decided to build a gated community on Lake Purdy, just south of Birmingham, for Klan members only. Unfortunately, the land he was trying to sell to his hooded friends was owned by the Birmingham Water Works.

The more familiar we became with the hierarchy and pockets of power in the Klan from the sixties, the more we came to believe that Holt had the knowledge to blow the case open. But before Fleming and Herren had the opportunity to interrogate her, she passed away.

It was a salient lesson. Time had essentially expired for most of the people with whom we needed to talk. Those still on this earth were hanging by a thread. Without ceremony or looking for the best introduction, we just had to locate as many of these folks as possible right now.

With a fresh sense of urgency, we turned our attention to Rowe, though we knew he wouldn't be the easiest to find—and we certainly weren't the first group to go looking for him. Every Klansman in the South wanted to get their hands on the ex–FBI informant.

He'd been suspected of being, and was occasionally treated like, a potential informant by some of his fellow KKK members as far back as 1962. On one occasion, Dynamite Bob had even stopped a meeting of the Eastview Klavern, saying there was a Judas among the group, a possible member of the CIA or, even worse, an FBI operative.

Eventually, Rowe was exposed as an FBI informant and wrote a book, *My Undercover Years with the Ku Klux Klan*, in which he admitted participating in the 1961 beatings of the Freedom Riders in Birmingham. He was also suspected of murdering a black man in 1963, which helped make him a suspect in the church bombing. Interrogated in 1963, Rowe took a lie detector test, which proved inconclusive.

What was conclusive, however, was that he was in the car when fatal shots were fired killing Viola Liuzzo, a civil rights volunteer from Detroit who had come to Selma in 1965. Testifying for the prosecution, Rowe helped convict his KKK buddy Collie Leroy Wilkins. It was during this time that he was given the new name Thomas Neal Moore as a member of the Witness Protection Program. In 1975, he made an appearance before the U.S. Senate Select Committee on Intelligence, where he testified he had been in the Klan and had participated in the beatings of blacks. Ironically, to protect his identity he wore what resembled a white KKK hood when testifying. By 1978, he was indicted for the murder of Liuzzo, but a federal judge refused to extradite him to Alabama for trial.

During his waning years, Rowe went bankrupt, divorced his wife, and had no contact with his five children. While Fleming and Herren were preparing to visit Rowe in Savannah, they got word that the controversial FBI informer had died.

To this day, Rowe is routinely blamed by former Klan members for just about every instance of violence in the South. He is the Klan's scapegoat. As a confirmed turncoat, he is the go-to explanation for any KKK involvement in the 1963 church bombing, among many other atrocities. Rowe may have had some knowledge of the terrorist plot, but there is no reason to believe he was an active participant, if for no other reason than the Eastview Klavern did not trust him enough to involve him.

FIVE

RUDOLPH

I had friends whispering advice in my ear even before I took the oath as U.S. Attorney that the bombing investigation was folly. They had my best interests at heart. There was not a lot of political or career upside in re-evaluating what had already been tirelessly investigated. Even in the unlikely event that we got to take someone to trial, the prospect of getting a conviction was remote. And as Caryl Privett had warned, reopening the case only for it to go nowhere would be another devastating blow for the African-American community. So, as was suggested to me more than once, "what's the point?"

Of course, the point was that there were at least two men walking around free who had murdered four girls in 1963. Sure, we were regularly losing witnesses; but unbeknown to the public, parts were falling into place as potentially helpful individuals came forward and a few pieces of useful archived material, such as the Burns tapes, surfaced.

The black community remained, at best, cautiously optimistic, which suited me just fine. I didn't want to build unachievable expectations and was buoyed by the restraint and common sense shown and shared by African-American leaders. They, more than anyone, knew disappointment in this matter but, like my team, had been heartened by the success of a few cold case investigations in the nineties, most notably the conviction of Byron De La Beckwith for the 1963 murder of Medgar Evers. If a jury in Jackson,

Mississippi, could convict De La Beckwith for the Evers murder, a panel of citizens in contemporary Birmingham should be able to consider a church bombing case without bias.

We were throwing everything we had at the case, and word seemed to be spreading that this was no token reevaluation of an old crime, which, perhaps, helped prick the consciences of a few people who may not have been expected to help us.

With Robert Posey and Jeff Wallace in Birmingham and Roy Austin and David Allred in Washington, we contemplated commencing a grand jury to secure sworn statements from witnesses around February 1998. But that plan had to be put on hold, as Birmingham again experienced a bombing.

Sergeant Sanderson and Emily Lyons

On January 29, 1998, Birmingham police officer Robert "Sande" Sanderson was a last-minute fill-in as security at a Birmingham woman's clinic. Such facilities followed strict protocols in response to frequent threats and protests over abortions, employing off-duty cops as much-needed eyes and muscle. On this Thursday morning at around 7:30 at the New Woman, All Women Health Clinic, Sanderson noticed something suspicious in the shrubbery near the front door.

He tried to prevent Emily Lyons, a nurse who had just arrived for work, from getting too close and quickly attempted to move the object. A bomber, watching nearby, pushed a remote detonator, exploding a device loaded with hundreds of nails and shrapnel. Sanderson and Lyons lay mangled amid broken glass, blood, and burning debris. Thirty-five-year-old officer Sanderson died instantly, while forty-one-year-old Lyons sustained horrific injuries requiring months of hospitalization.

It was the first fatal bombing of an American abortion clinic (shootings had taken other lives) and shook Birmingham, literally and figuratively. Terrorism was visiting Birmingham again. This time it was on my watch.

The clinic was adjacent to the University of Alabama in the city. The explosion shattered windows blocks away. Thirty minutes later the area would have been crowded with workers and passing students. The scent of smoke and scorched steel drifted through the city all day. It was a consuming sensory experience, especially for old-timers who recalled the days of Bombingham. Helplessness, fear, and anger were expressed in the immediate aftermath. Why our city? Could this be the start of another wave of bomb attacks?

I felt a weighty responsibility to act immediately and decisively, to marshal whatever resources we had to hunt down the perpetrator and ensure there were no further attacks, which we rightly feared were a distinct possibility. It was an all-hands-on-deck event.

I had been driving to breakfast to meet with *Birmingham News* reporter Peggy Sanford to reflect on the first months of my tenure as U.S. Attorney when I got word of the explosion. I was mere minutes away from the site on Birmingham's Southside and headed straight to the clinic.

On the way I called First Assistant Bud Henry and instructed him to notify Attorney General Reno. On arrival, I encountered an old friend, Birmingham police officer Lionel Wilson, who told me there had been a bombing. An officer was dead and a nurse critically injured. "We just got her out. I don't know if she will make it," he said.

He pointed to the scene. I noticed Sanderson's body on the ground, and my immediate instinct was to run toward him. But an FBI agent stopped me. There was concern a second bomb could be triggered as people converged.

While the injured nurse had been hurriedly (and bravely) removed, the officer's body remained in a crumpled heap near the entrance for some time. His injuries were devastating. It was a horrid scene.

Law enforcement flew into action. Birmingham police and multiple federal agencies poured into the area. We set up a command post on the grounds of the nearby University of Alabama campus as more than one hundred investigators converged. There was an immediate, palpable sense that acting swiftly was the key not only to cornering the culprit but to shutting down the possibility of it happening elsewhere.

Local cops were understandably shaken by the murder, and there was a pronounced, all-in effort to track down the bomber. It was a grim and exhaustingly emotional day. I have rarely seen greater singular focus from a law enforcement group.

When the afternoon newspaper the *Post-Herald* made the callous and unnecessary decision to put an aerial shot of Officer Sanderson's crumpled body on the front page, it generated outrage. Soon after it hit the newsstands, the papers mysteriously disappeared. Although perhaps not an organized effort, cops fanned out across the region and "bought" every available copy.

Despite immediate cooperation among everyone on the ground, it became apparent the FBI wanted to take control of the investigative process. But Sanderson was one of Birmingham's own. There was no way local authorities would settle for anything but a key role in tackling the case.

It was clear to me we quickly needed to settle on a multi-agency process:

the expertise of the Bureau of Alcohol, Tobacco, Firearms, and Explosives (ATF) was in assessing the bomb and explosion; the FBI was best to chase down leads and take care of other crime scene details such as fingerprints; while local authorities knew the area and people impacted. As with the church bombing, ultimately the case could result in state murder and attempted murder charges. Birmingham input was crucial.

At the command center, I had a conversation with ATF boss Jim Cavanagh and the FBI's Joe Lewis, and we quickly resolved to work together with local police. Police Chief Mike Coppage was brought into the discussions.

It would not be as easy a road, however, with the Washington office of the FBI, which over the course of what became a very long investigation regularly sought to impose its will. But with each law enforcement body bringing its unique talents to the case, it was astonishing what was achieved in a short time, including a detailed mock-up of the bomb that revealed some of the material used for its construction could only have been purchased from Walmart.

The investigation moved at a frantic pace, and it wasn't long before a prime suspect emerged. UAB student Jermaine Hughes had heard the nearby explosion as he was doing his laundry and looked outside to see a man walking away from the devastation as everyone else ran toward it. At considerable personal risk, Hughes tracked the man, who wore a blond wig, as he took a circuitous route to a Nissan pickup.

Along the way, lawyer Jeffrey Tickal, while breakfasting at McDonald's, overheard Hughes relating the sighting to authorities on a 911 call. Seeing the suspect in the distance, they both set off after him. They got the license tag of the man's truck, and both looked the murderer in the eye.

Even though authorities couldn't immediately corner the suspect after Hughes and Tickal lost sight of the Nissan pickup, we now had a name, Eric Robert Rudolph, associated with the vehicle and the case. The listed address for him, however, was an old one, and we had no idea of his whereabouts.

In a news conference, I revealed we were interested in talking to Rudolph, the owner of the Nissan. We had a material witness warrant for his arrest. The decision to release his name wasn't straightforward. We didn't know at the time whether or not Rudolph was, in fact, driving the truck, but we knew that the media had been monitoring law enforcement radio and it was only a matter of time before Rudolph would be identified publicly. The injustice and embarrassment that followed the media identifying security guard Richard Jewell as a potential suspect in the Atlanta Olympic

Park bombing in 1996 were fresh in our minds. Jewell, who died of natural causes in 2007 aged forty-four, was mercilessly maligned in the public eye before finally being recognized as a hero in the fatal bombing.

In the immediate wake of the Birmingham bombing, we had no idea that Rudolph was behind a series of sophisticated attacks, including the deadly explosion at Olympic Park.

The device used there was the largest pipe bomb ever detonated in the United States. Weighing forty pounds and filled with nails, the bomb was hidden in an army backpack. Jewell had spotted the knapsack, informed police, and begun moving people out of the area when it exploded. The massive blast killed Alice Hawthorne of Albany, Georgia, and injured 111 others. A man died of a heart attack as he ran to the scene.

The Birmingham bomb was also huge and designed to inflict awful injury and death.

The investigative team swiftly tracked Rudolph to a residence in North Carolina. When they burst in, the television was on, and there was evidence the former U.S. Army specialist had fled, perhaps only moments before. It was the beginning of a five-year manhunt for Rudolph. It soon became evident he was behind multiple terrorist attacks. He lingered on the FBI's Ten Most Wanted list as he hid in the Appalachians until a rookie cop came across him in a dumpster diving for food behind a store in Murphy, North Carolina, at 4:00 a.m. on May 31, 2003.

Rudolph was a religious extremist who later tried to justify bombing Olympic Park, the Birmingham health clinic, a clinic in Atlanta, and a gay and lesbian bar in the Georgia capital by citing his fundamentalist beliefs. He was finally returned to Birmingham in April 2005 to face trial, having agreed to a plea bargain that avoided an execution order but imposed a sentence of four consecutive life terms.

In my dealings over the years with various nefarious groups and individuals—the Klan, drug rings, corrupt public officials, and violent thugs and thieves—I have been occasionally repulsed, angered, and saddled with a deep sense of concern for the community, but I have never felt significantly personally threatened. However, such was the fanaticism of some of Rudolph's supporters, I became concerned for my personal welfare and quickly got into the habit of double-checking my mail for fear of a harmful device or substance and inspecting the perimeter of my home each day for any evidence of intrusion. I was genuinely scared for my young family for a long time.

Rudolph's family was especially volatile. His brother Daniel videotaped himself cutting off his own hand with an electric saw in protest against the agency's hunt for Eric.

While Rudolph's survival skills allowed him to thwart authorities for years, I was proud of the Birmingham-based effort. We threw manpower and resources at the bombing investigation and quickly established the extreme threat the suspect posed. The courage and foresight of the witnesses and responding officers who tracked him in a well-drilled pursuit, in my opinion, prevented many more bombings. As part of his plea deal, Rudolph revealed the location of more than 250 pounds of dynamite he'd hidden in the forests of North Carolina.

Over the years, the tension between our investigation and the FBI never really subsided. Even though the local agents knew our efforts were effective and inclusive, the FBI bosses didn't get it. Occasionally they demonstrated the kind of arrogance and narrow-mindedness that was evident in their dealings over the years in other cases, such as the Baxley investigation of the church bombing. Our approach was to avoid the internal politics and create an investigative group committed to every task. It meant an enormous workload: seven-day-a-week obligations for months on end.

The case threw me into the national spotlight and the attention was intense, especially in the early months. I was constantly giving the media updates to the point that my boy Carson thought I had an office at a local television station. He took to watching news updates with me, including one morning over breakfast when Rudolph was thought to have been spotted in north Georgia.

As the screen showed automatic weapon–carrying law enforcement officers descending on a small town, Carson turned to me with a puzzled look. "They're looking for Rudolph?" he asked.

I explained that they just wanted to talk to him. Carson, his face collapsing, responded, "But he's just a tiny reindeer with a shiny nose." I was a little late to the office that morning.

Despite the fine work by my team and other law enforcement groups, Rudolph escaped the net. There would be no swift arrest as tense weeks turned into frustrating months. At home, at least, there was much to celebrate in March 1998, as our youngest, Christopher Gordon, named after my dad, was born.

It was clear when the Rudolph case broke that our primary attention had to shift from the church bombing cold case to the devastating crime of the day, frustrating the long-suffering African-American community. Certainly, many thought the best and last chance to nab the killers from 1963 might have become a victim of the Rudolph bombing too. But for the most part, black leaders remained patient and positive.

James Lay

Ben Herren applied his skills full time to the Rudolph case for several months and would end up spending a total of the better part of eighteen months on the investigation. But his knowledge about the church bombing was invaluable, so he split his time between the cases when required.

Everyone lamented dialing down the focus on the church bombing, but in some ways that was a positive for us. We still had a stellar team, including Robert Posey focusing on unearthing witnesses. Plus, operating a little more under the radar, we decided to approach a man who had been less than helpful to Baxley's team.

On July 9, 1998, exactly one year after the interrogation of Cherry in Texas, Bill Fleming, teaming with agent Jimmie Brown, walked into the main post office in downtown Birmingham for an interview they expected would yield little.

They were visiting with James Edward Lay, the "watchdog" who had reported seeing Blanton at the scene of the crime just two weeks before the bombing but had refused to testify at the Chambliss trial. Now seventy years old and in failing health, Lay was enjoying a retirement party staged for him by co-workers. Surprisingly, he was willing to talk to the agents. His memory of the bombing and the weeks leading up to it had not diminished. He again recalled seeing someone he believed to be Blanton with an overnight bag approaching the church two weeks before the bombing. When the Klansman spotted Lay, he returned to a car where Chambliss was waiting and sped away.

Lay's potential testimony was golden. It expanded our understanding of the threat the Klan posed and spotlighted how the church had become a very specific target. The image of white men of ill will circling their prey in a black neighborhood under cover of darkness only to be thwarted by a vigilant African American was powerful. Together with the Burns tapes, and the information generated by Cherry's press conference, Lay's commitment gave us significant forward momentum.

The first step in moving the case through the courts was to put evidence before a grand jury. Rather than cajoling or negotiating with potential witnesses to get them to share what they knew, we would send out as many subpoenas as possible to those with information that could be helpful, including surviving members of the Eastview Klavern.

It would be an opportunity for people who'd spent decades sitting on material relevant to the murder of four girls to come clean. If that weren't enough, by placing them under oath, they would be subject to perjury charges. A grand jury represented their last best chance to tell what they knew without being "exposed," as the courtroom gathering is a meeting held in relative secrecy. We could assure them of protection if they needed it, a promise we could not make if the matter went to trial. Heightening the pressure, FBI agents would be showing up at their house to deliver the subpoena papers.

There are no defense lawyers in a grand jury room, only prosecutors. The evidence is unfurled before a panel of up to twenty-three citizens, and the material they consider is confidential. Even investigators, Ben and Bill included, would be excluded from the process unless called as witnesses. In this environment, people would swear under oath to what they knew or didn't know. Changing testimony later would mean perjuring themselves.

Ultimately, a prosecution, having established "probable cause," might seek indictments for individuals to face charges. But initially, at least, we simply wanted a grand jury to be an investigative tool.

As part of this intense campaign to get witnesses on the record, I felt it important to highlight the absolute commitment of the DOJ to the case by sitting in on as much of the testimony as possible and, when it was an option, bringing witnesses into my office. I ended up hosting more old Klansmen than Cash's BBQ Restaurant on a Friday night.

I suspected, rightly as it turned out, that I probably wouldn't get much out of them. But I did not want the bigots to be in a position to turn around later and suggest they had "just remembered" something that might be of assistance to the suspects.

While a grand jury is held in a closed environment, there is no hiding the fact that it is being staged, especially in a town the size of Birmingham. Sure enough, on the first day of the grand jury session, October 10, 1998, we were besieged by media. The *Birmingham News* ran a photo of Reverend Cross walking across the street with me to the courthouse. I couldn't answer questions about proceedings, but it was obvious what was going on. There was also a shot of Robert Shelton, the former Klan Grand Dragon, getting in a car after his appearance.

All the usual suspects were summoned, as well as a few individuals who hadn't been out of the backwoods of Alabama for decades. Thirty-six years after the crime, the waiting room looked like a geriatric clinic. Many of the aged Klansmen and their wives were on their last legs, but lifelong habits of keeping secrets were hard to break. Selective memory was common. There was never an admission of "personal" involvement, but snippets of information helped us build a fuller picture and confirmed again what had been presented at the Chambliss trial.

As public knowledge of the investigation expanded, national media outlets began to sniff around. News of what we were doing eventually reached even the remotest parts of the country and stirred the memory and conscience of a significant and colorful witness.

Willadean Brogdon

During my early briefings about the case, a common question in discussions was "where is Willadean?" Cherry had relationships with a bafflingly large number of women, including Willadean—they were married in the early 1970s—but no one had a clue what had happened to her.

Baxley and Eddy tried to locate her in 1977 but had no luck, and our search for Cherry's third of five wives kept coming up blank too. Fascinatingly, she was described in old documents as having "Bozo" hair. Hard to miss, you would think. Finally, as it did more than once in this strangest of cases, the planets aligned for us.

Like many people in the Big Sky State of Montana, Willadean Brogdon had been busily preparing for the oncoming winter, even though it was only October. On the morning of October 11, 1998, Willadean was sitting in her house glancing through the local paper when she came across a story by Jerry Mitchell first published in the Jackson *Clarion-Ledger*. It detailed that a grand jury was convening in Birmingham to hear witness statements about the bombing of the 16th Street Baptist Church. Bobby Frank Cherry, the piece noted, was a prime suspect in the case.

Willadean had vowed never to see the nasty old brute again and had rarely given him a second thought unless she had to. This was one of those times. She called the nearest FBI office, in Billings, a mere 221 miles away.

It may have been a strange conversation with the two local agents, who knew nothing of the church bombing case. The FBI gets more than its fair share of weird calls in remote locations, and Willadean had a unique way of conversing. Perhaps sensing her call had fallen on deaf ears, she drove for three hours to talk to the agents face-to-face. There she proceeded to detail what she had heard Bobby Frank Cherry explicitly say about the 1963 church bombing. When she left the FBI office, the agents followed protocol and immediately called their colleagues in Birmingham.

Fleming and Herren were so excited that literally an hour after receiving the call from Billings, and without my knowledge, they were on a plane to Montana.

As a Klan spouse, albeit relatively briefly, she had likely endured much. Many Klan women still feared their husbands after they managed to escape the relationship. Even deceased Klansmen were threats to some who believed they were haunted by their violent ghosts. On the other hand, some spouses were just as repulsive and intimidating as their partners. Where would the former Mrs. Cherry fall on the spectrum?

"We found her to be a nice lady," Fleming said. "She told us of how Cherry had often bragged about being part of the bombing. She also told of the times he would have nightmares and say things about the bombing like it shouldn't have gone down that way." Brogdon recalled how her car broke down near the 16th Street Baptist Church one day. Cherry was with her and pointed to the steps where he said they planted the bomb. Fleming and Herren knew they had a winner.

Cherry's ex-wife opened up to the investigators, sparing no details. She confirmed she had been a truck driver when they first met in 1969 and married in 1970. It was a union littered with beatings and threats. Cherry slept with a butcher knife near his bed. His message was if she ever attempted to end the marriage, he'd use the weapon on her. He told her that he had killed before and he'd kill again. She believed him.

On a trip through Alabama in 1973, with five kids and Cherry on board, Brogdon stopped her car in Mount Olive, a small town about twelve miles from Birmingham. Bobby Frank got out and stretched his legs. That was the opening she needed. She slammed on the gas, sending the kids tumbling around in the car, dust flying, and looked back for what she hoped would be the last glimpse of her husband.

But the curse of the KKK visited Brogdon in the worst possible way. One of her children, Rebecca, died in a fire at the age of nine, only weeks after Cherry was left choking on the dust from her spinning tires. Although she could not prove it, she was convinced it had been Klan retaliation. Another daughter, Gloria LaDow, who was with Brogdon at the time of the agents' visit, revealed how Cherry had molested her as a little girl. As part of the abuse, Cherry watched as he forced her to have sex with one of his sons. A lifelong battle with drug abuse and destructive behavior that included numerous run-ins with the law ensued.

SIX

GRAND JURIES

The scores of statements investigators compiled and the evidence we were presenting to the grand jury nudged the case in the right direction. However, jurisdictional and statute of limitations issues raised doubts about whether we could ultimately hold people accountable via the federal system. Proving that explosives used in the bombing had been moved across state lines, thus ensuring a case covered by federal law, was looking increasingly unlikely. Fortunately, there was legal precedent to move evidence compiled in a federal grand jury to a state investigation if that became necessary.

While the statements delivered to the grand jury contained few new revelations, the circle was closing around Blanton and Cherry. They knew we were coming for them. Feedback from witnesses—and Jerry Mitchell of the *Clarion-Ledger,* who had been in contact with Cherry—indicated it might be time to rattle the old Klansmen's cages. I wanted to confront the men and see if we could wrestle an iota of honesty and compassion out of them. It was likely that would fail, but I wanted to at least explore the possibility that one of them might choose to point the finger at the other.

Creep Show

In the summer of 1999, the federal grand jury was in full swing, with a stream of old Klansmen limping, shuffling, and grumbling their way into the Hugo L. Black Courthouse in Birmingham. The investigative team worked tirelessly to connect with every potential living witness, meaning we were reaching out to a cast of characters that included a few who belonged in the stranger-than-fiction category.

Willadean's brother Wayne Brogdon, perhaps not surprisingly, was one of these. A man who struggled with the bottle—he had fifty-five alcohol-related legal incidents to prove it—he had told agents how, decades ago, his former brother-in-law "bragged" about making the bomb. Cherry had also once said that the bomb wasn't meant to kill the girls, though the old Klansman had added: "at least they can't breed."

We needed to get that before the grand jury, so we arranged a bus ticket to Birmingham for him. Fleming was at the terminal to greet the witness but no one remotely Wayne Brogdon–like alighted. We tracked him down again with the assistance of Florida authorities, and found him naked and drunk in his backyard. Somehow local officials poured Brogdon into a seersucker suit and onto a plane to Birmingham. After it landed, Fleming watched all the passengers disembark. The last one to stumble out was dressed in a Hawaiian shirt and calypso pants. Mr. Brogdon had just enjoyed his first-ever ride in an aircraft.

The always gentlemanly and handsomely attired Robert Posey was somewhat taken aback when Fleming hauled the disheveled witness into the courtroom. But Brogdon did his piece, and we got some valuable testimony on file.

Sometimes the weirdness factor was trumped by pure creepiness. The "Klan Barber" Bill Jackson made my skin crawl. A wannabe Klansman and Eastview Klavern loiterer, his presence was somehow tolerated by the KKK despite the fact he was a Catholic and as unpredictable as a cut snake. Over the years he had told more than one person he'd been at the Cahaba River Bridge drinking beer the night they had decided to bomb the church, even though he was routinely exiled when Klan "business" came up.

Our inquiries confirmed that he was an unapologetic perversion, even in the eyes of his family. His brutality was unfathomable. On one occasion he allegedly unstrapped his belt to beat his infant son in his crib.

Jackson, the investigators learned, had been treated for his violent rages. He found the electric shock treatment so much to his liking that he reproduced its effects by using a homemade mechanism powered by jumper cables on his car battery.

Regardless of how repulsive he was, we knew Jackson could place

Blanton and Cherry, along with convicted bomber Chambliss, at meetings under the bridge and could link all three during those critical days leading up to the bombing of the church. Jackson had boasted through the years about having been at the Modern Sign Company along with his underage girlfriend on the nights leading up to the bombing. He had testified in the Chambliss trial about being there on the night of Friday, September 13, 1963.

We got him on the record and immediately felt a need to wash.

A stream of high-profile witnesses appeared before the grand jury the week of July 20, 1999. The press wasn't able to access the proceedings, as specific evidence was, and remains, secret, but the pre- and post-hearing media scrums were a spectacle.

The courthouse gatherings of Klansmen and associates were something to behold. Many of the aging white supremacists had not seen each other for years, and we speculated what it might be like to be a fly on the wall as they bided their time waiting for their turn to provide testimony. That's why, when the oddball Klansman and con artist Don Luna offered to wear a wire in the waiting area, we took a chance on him.

Luna was (pointlessly) seeking to ingratiate himself with the Feds because he was facing fraud charges in South Carolina. We knew there would be no lawyers in the room with the Klansmen, alleviating concerns that their discussions might be privileged, so we pressed ahead, calling a bunch of them at the same time when possible.

We hoped as they milled about together, a secret or two might slip from their lips and be captured courtesy of Luna's wire. In the end, however, we got nothing except an insight into how much each old white supremacist resented being called and made to wait. Between greetings, they grumbled rather than colluded.

When she was called into the grand jury hearing, Jean Barnes, formerly (twice) Jean Blanton, closed her Bible and walked in oozing solemnity. Over the years, Barnes had stuck to a story, for which she had consulted Blanton, about her whereabouts on the night of September 14, 1963. It was her former partner's alibi.

Despite decades away from Blanton and a new marriage, Barnes (Carolyn Jean Casey when she was Blanton's teen girlfriend in 1963) was still standing by her Klansman in interviews with my team. She was an immeasurably frustrating individual, intensely dedicated to someone we believed to be a bigot and a killer. She blatantly stonewalled the investigation whenever the bombing was discussed. On exiting the grand jury, she told the press she wouldn't discuss her testimony and that she had no information on her ex-husband anyway.

Although testimonies are confidential, Willadean Brogdon wasn't shy with the media on the front steps of the Birmingham courthouse after her appearance. Having stuck to her word and driven from Montana to Alabama for the grand jury appointment, she was willing to talk to anyone who asked about Cherry. She was quoted in the *Boston Herald* on July 22 as telling the grand jury panel: "[Cherry] admitted it. He bragged about it."

Openly hostile toward her former stepfather, Gloria LaDow, Willadean's daughter, added: "In some circles, he openly bragged that he had lit the fuse to the bomb and was a big leader in the Klan."

One of the clunky tasks of the grand jury process had been getting LaDow to Birmingham to testify, as she'd been incarcerated in Florida at the time. Federal marshals were supposed to transport her to Birmingham, but she somehow ended up in an airport in Oklahoma before they finally got her to Alabama. Thinking she'd only be in Birmingham for a few hours and then be taken back to Florida, she didn't even bring a toothbrush.

Forty-two-year-old Thomas Cherry, nearly two years to the day after he met with me, Fleming, and Herren in Austin, Texas, told the media he testified that his father had mentioned to him names of other people involved in the bombing. Importantly, Thomas said he had been with Bobby Frank Cherry at the Modern Sign Company on the morning of September 15 when the bomb went off. He recalled the building shaking at the time the explosion ripped through the church.

Taking stock, we were making progress but lacked specific detailed evidence about the bombing itself. We did not have the key witnesses Elizabeth Cobbs or Kirthus Glenn, both deceased, but potentially we could call on two significant figures who had not played a role in Chambliss's conviction: Mitch Burns and James Lay.

Cherry's ex-wife and family outlined what kind of a mess of a man he was in the decades after the bombing, but we needed to assemble testimonies from people who could explain what kind of people Blanton and Cherry were in the sixties.

Waylene Vaughn, a Blanton love interest at the same time he was dating Jean Casey, was someone who had spelled out to the Feds years ago just what a malicious individual the Klansman proved to be. We tracked her down to the backwoods of southern Alabama, where she lived in a small mobile home with a porch. It was beyond sad. Walking with a cane, she looked like a broken woman. Years of service to her country—she had joined the military to escape Blanton—had not set her up for later life.

Despite her surroundings and her obvious, understandable trepidation at our presence, Vaughn tried to answer our questions. She said that she deeply regretted the relationship with Blanton back in 1963, when she would ride around town with the Klansman between her shifts working a lunch counter at the bus station.

As she had nearly four decades earlier with the FBI, Vaughn detailed some of Blanton's less appealing traits, such as the fact that he had been almost giddy and gleeful after the bombing. She also related how he had driven his Chevy right at a man who had to jump to escape being splattered. "I screamed, and the black man jumped to the curb, just avoiding being hit," she said. Blanton also enjoyed pouring an acidic substance into the cars driven by blacks or men he knew to be Catholics or Jews. This was his idea of fun.

Vaughn was expansive. She could not provide evidence that Blanton had admitted to the bombing. But she could make important contributions, explaining to a jury how this now crumpled, rapidly aging man was once a relentlessly violent, physically imposing, hateful young Klansman.

Initially, she refused to agree to testify. I fully understood. Vaughn had endured more than enough over the years and had been shadowed for four decades by the specter of her association with a man she knew in her heart to be unapologetically evil. Even now she was scared, having seen firsthand what Blanton was capable of. But she was a brave soul. You could sense it, and her regret about having indulged in that relationship was profound.

I appealed to her, pointing out this was her chance to put that time behind her for good. She took in my request without directly answering my repeated pleas for her continued cooperation. I could do little more than ask and hope that if and when the time came for a trial, she would make herself available.

I also wanted to explore the enigma that was Mary Frances Cunningham—Chambliss's sister-in-law, who at one stage alleged she had witnessed the Klansmen carrying something to the church in the early hours of September 15, before retracting that story. I did not anticipate using her tale should we make it to trial—she would be ripped to shreds by the defense. But there was no doubt she had knowledge that the bombing was about to take place. She may have concocted the tale of following Chambliss and the other bombers. However, there was no disputing the fact she had tried to warn police officer Hancock about what was going on.

Mary Frances Cunningham

The question of whether she was there at the church as the bomb was placed under the stairs kept cropping up despite her frequent denials and refusal decades before to testify. There was an uncanny level of detail in her original account that matched many of the late Ms. Glenn's eyewitness observations, including who was present, where the Klansmen parked near the church, and the time of morning (shortly after 2:00). We could not contemplate using that as part of the prosecution's case, even though the 2:30 a.m. call to Hancock from the Chambliss residence alerting him to the possibility a bomb had been planted was proof she knew what was going on.

Bill and Ben had talked to Cunningham on several occasions. None of the meetings had gone terribly well. In their first encounter, at her house, they had swiftly tried to get clarity on a few important questions, including the nature of her relationship with Officer Hancock. In the records, there were details missing about what happened during that four-hour or so period on Sunday morning, September 15, when the cop picked her up and discussed her story.

The theory among investigators for decades was that the pair was having an affair. So Fleming delicately asked her. Cunningham, a wife, mother, and grandmother in her seventies by that stage, didn't answer. Instead she wailed and rolled around on her couch. The mortified agent left the room, surrendering the scene to his partner, who tried to redeem the situation, to no avail.

Soon after, I wanted to delicately broach the issues again, so I asked Cunningham's daughter to come into my office for a discussion. To my surprise, she brought her mother. Ms. Cunningham, reportedly a woman of considerable beauty in her youth, and of a certain winsomeness in later life, was courteous and talkative. But the discussion went in circles. She gave us nothing.

We tried again, once more at her house. Fleming, Herren, and Posey joined me opposite the elderly lady in her tidy lounge area. We inched toward the tough questions rather than being confrontational. Without any prompting, Ms. Cunningham startled everyone when she suddenly fell to her knees and crawled toward Herren. The veteran cop's look of mild terror was something to behold. When she started referring to him repeatedly as her "angel," it was pretty clear it was time to end the discussion.

Ben is a fine man, but he certainly isn't a celestial being. I'm sure he appreciated it a few days later when the gift from Fleming of an angelic statue turned up at his desk.

The remote chance that Cunningham could be of use in a trial was quashed. At least we had Lay and Burns. Or did we?

My friend Bill Baxley still flinches when Lay's name is mentioned. The memory of the angst he caused the prosecution by refusing to testify at Chambliss's trial hasn't disappeared forty years later.

For us, Lay had been more than helpful, and I couldn't work out how he could be the same man who turned down a point-blank request to testify from victim Denise McNair's father. But something changed as word got out we were moving the church bombing case through the judicial system. "He's getting cold feet," Fleming warned me. There were no guarantees he'd repeat his story under oath.

Mitch Burns, a man who had risked his life daily to help nab Blanton, was also hedging. It wasn't clear what the issue was, although Burns was perturbed that his family would have to listen to him indulging in vile conversations with murderous Klansmen if tapes were played in court. He also had a bee in his bonnet about, well, me.

"What did I do?" I asked Jeff Wallace, who let me know I wasn't on Burns's Christmas card list.

"I don't know, but he doesn't like you," Wallace said, with no compunction. "You might want to back off a bit." Along with Ben Herren, Wallace continued to liaise with Burns, ensuring a potential gem of a witness didn't completely rule out cooperating.

I knew I had to get both Lay and Burns on the record in the grand jury, one way or another. Without them, we simply didn't have a shot at getting a positive courtroom result.

It was time to step it up another gear. Blanton and Cherry knew the noose was tightening. I planned to urge them to plead guilty to spare everyone a trial (and give them the chance to blame each other). It would mean jail time, but we could probably find a way for them not to die in incarceration if they took a plea.

Blanton all but gave me the finger. Such was his arrogance, he barely bothered to answer my questions when I brought him into my office with his lawyer, Bill Brower. It was an attitude that had been honed during thirty-seven years of undeserved and largely unchallenged freedom. He'd been shrewd enough to keep his mouth shut for much of the last few decades and wasn't going to start talking about the bombing anytime soon. He smirked dismissively and calmly feigned disinterest.

"Suit yourself, Tommy, but I'm going to get you," I said. "I want you to remember that."

Herren and Fleming then flew with me to Texas, where we met with the then sixty-nine-year-old Bobby Frank Cherry, his wife Myrtle, and his lawyer Ronnie Van Baugh.

There were no pleasantries. Cherry knew we had him in our sights, and the fallout from his press conference after the team had interviewed him back in 1997 ensured he wouldn't be able to wriggle free easily this time. He protested his innocence, and you could see him trying to stop himself from saying anything stupid, which was obviously an epic battle. He was jittery. He looked vulnerable. I was quietly willing him to sell out Blanton.

"I know you were involved, and we will prove that," I told him. "It's up to you to let us know the level of your involvement. If you can detail what the others did, perhaps we'll have a better understanding of your situation."

He dismissed the idea, but you could see the wheels turning in his mind. I squeezed tighter, letting him know we would be filing rape charges against him in Shelby County, Alabama, for sexually assaulting his stepdaughter Gloria LaDow back in 1971.

He was struck dumb. His wife's face was ashen. Cherry tried to summon defiance, but I knew he was on the back foot and we went outside so he could discuss the situation with his attorney.

His lawyer knew I was angling to trade information, as lawyers do. Van Baugh initiated the delicate process of proposing cooperation in exchange for something without being locked into a bartering situation. Periodically, after consulting with Cherry, he would wander out to us and say something to the effect of, "If, in theory, my client was to talk about . . ."

At one stage, the "theory" was he might be able to discuss the rumored trial of the detonation device at a Klan couple's home—which we obviously took to mean Klan queen Mary Lou Holt and her husband Bill. Van Baugh also asked me in general terms about transportation of explosives across state lines and whether it would be worthwhile if Cherry could shed light on that situation. Indeed it would, as we wanted proof of interstate transportation of explosives to solidify the federal case.

It was a tense situation. If Cherry started talking, we all suspected he probably wouldn't stop. Just as Bob Eddy thought he was on the verge of getting a confession or concession from Cherry all those years ago, we thought we were moving steadily toward getting him to roll over.

I have no doubt Cherry was weighing whether to try to cut himself a deal. For a few hours, we were close to opening the floodgates on a stream of Klan information that could have ended decades of angst, despair, and frustration for the community.

We tried not to get our hopes up. It was the right decision, as it turned out, since Cherry, in the end, gave us nothing but a miserable flight back to Alabama.

Not only had Cherry's reaction in the interview somewhat echoed the one Eddy had encountered years before, but the old Klansman, just as he had in 1977, called his Klan network after being interviewed. Eddy had snagged him telephoning Chambliss via businessman Bob Gafford; this time, we discovered through phone records, he made contact with Wyman Lee, a small-business owner, Klan friend, and buddy of Blanton.

Soon after, both Cherry and Blanton blurted inaccurately to the media that we had proposed a deal. Van Baugh reportedly said we offered Cherry probation in exchange for information about interstate transportation of explosives. Of course, we made no such offer. But we did make good on my intention to bring charges against Cherry for the statutory rape. He was taken into custody in May 2000. This signaled our intention to use whatever means necessary to hold the Klansmen accountable, even as the judicial structures we had hoped to use to bring them before the courts were crumbling around us.

It was becoming increasingly clear that the case was unlikely to pass muster as a federal concern so many years after the bombing. Proving the dynamite used had crossed state lines looked highly unlikely (especially as we had no traces of the actual explosive). And even if we could secure evidence of that, it alone did not necessarily guarantee a murder case could move through the federal system. Reluctantly, therefore, I accepted the fact that we would have to attempt to shift the prosecution effort to the state.

My discussions with all parties, including Jefferson County DA David Barber, indicated we would have official support to do so, but there was a chance my contribution and that of my fellow federal employee Robert Posey could be coming to an end.

I was desperate to ensure we could somehow continue. While we still lacked any significant physical evidence, the investigation had positive momentum at that point. I set up a meeting with Barber over lunch at Ted's, an unassuming but revered "meat and three" restaurant in Birmingham, to plead my case. Perhaps the freshly cooked vegetables helped. Barber embraced the idea of finding a way for our team to continue with the case and promised to discuss the matter with Alabama Attorney General Bill Pryor.

I later had a phone conversation with Pryor, who emphatically supported keeping the team together and transferring the case from federal to state jurisdiction.

Fortunately, too, Federal AG Janet Reno agreed Washington would continue funding the process, which would resume as a state grand jury on May 16, 2000. Posey and I would be appointed to special state roles for the duration of the prosecution process. With that green light, we surged ahead, aiming to lock in Burns and Lay, the crucial components in our case.

I left Burns to Jeff Wallace while our law clerk, Robin Beardsley, had the intense and spiritually eviscerating duty of listening to every second of the hours of tape made of Burns's discussions with the killers from the Klan. She learned a few new words and got a glimpse of a side of a peculiar kind of Southern man no one should have to endure.

As we prepared to go to the state grand jury, Lay was a growing concern. As with numerous other witnesses, I arranged for him to come to my office. I wanted him to experience the formality of our approach. Taking no chances, I also had a subpoena for him to appear at the state grand jury.

Frail, very quiet, and looking decidedly uncomfortable, he was nothing like the intelligent and assertive individual who had been assisting our inquiry. I felt for him. He was obviously concerned for his safety. I opted not to discuss his previous statements for fear he might backtrack or soften his allegations. At one stage, he became emotional as he expressed his concerns. Tears welled in the old man's eyes. I was losing him.

"Mr. Lay," I said. "All I want you to do is tell the truth. We need your help." I pulled out the subpoena and explained it required his presence at the grand jury. "Mr. Lay, I am going to call you to testify. I will go through everything with you there. It will be just us, no defendants.

"You will be under oath and I have confidence that whatever you tell that grand jury is going to be the truth.

"Is that fair?"

He looked at me solemnly. "That's fair," he agreed.

I didn't know exactly what he would do, but I was pretty sure there was no limit to the fear the KKK instilled in so many people in the sixties and was resigned to the fact that it would be this quiet old man's decision whether to help or perhaps fatally hinder our cause.

Lay Takes the Stand

We successfully applied to introduce the testimony that we had entered into the record during the federal grand jury to the state panel of twenty-three men and women.

It was now or never. The preseason was over. Preparations had been made, and we had to test the system to see if we could secure judgments of "probable cause" needed for indictments.

Burns was a great witness at the state grand jury. Plumber Bobby Birdwell, the seriously ill Gowins, a nervous Tom Cherry, and the investigators Bill and Ben also gave evidence.

When Lay's time came, I did not know which way his testimony would go. He looked ill and nervous. I had prepared for the worst—now I knew what Baxley was talking about—but the former postal worker was superb, the kind of softly spoken witness that makes a jury want to lean in to listen attentively to every word. His statements to the FBI all those years ago about what happened on the night of September 2 didn't make it into the Chambliss trial but now they were part of the official record in the case.

His secret testimony to the grand jury in 2000 was stunningly effective not only because of the content but because of his obvious humility on the stand. Baxley was right to be angry about Lay's lack of cooperation in 1977; Lay was an invaluable prosecutorial presence. I was elated and told the team, without in any way exaggerating, that Lay might just be the one to "get us over the line."

Free on Bail

On May 16, 2000, just a day after convening in the Jefferson County Courthouse, the grand jury indicted Bobby Frank Cherry and Thomas Blanton Jr., each on four counts of murder, one for each girl. Blanton, aged sixty-one, turned himself in the next day, while the sixty-nine-year-old Cherry, already in custody on the felony charge out in Shelby County, joined his former Klan cohort in a brief appearance before District Judge Pete Johnson.

The sight of the ragged pair in pink-and-white prison garb was the only "victory" I allowed myself to celebrate. Those tough old birds looked suitably trivial, sunken, and, at least temporarily, defeated. Blanton's smirk gave way to an unrelenting glower, his thinning hair and droopy jowls adding to a sad clown-like countenance, making the striped outfit mildly comical.

Cherry's macho posturing added to the absurdity as he rambled pointlessly, apparently telling the nonplussed Blanton not to worry as he'd "called headquarters." While Blanton frowned, I couldn't suppress my grin. I was bursting with pride and thrilled for the victims' families and my colleagues.

Charlene Thornton (who had replaced Joe Lewis as the Special Agent in Charge of the FBI office in the city), David Barber, and I met with the media. Barber, the county DA, spelled out where we were with the case.

"The Jefferson County grand jury convened specially to hear testimony relative to the September 1963 fatal church bombing at 16th Street Baptist Church, returned indictments against two individuals, Thomas Edwin Blanton Jr. and Bobby Frank Cherry, charging each of those individuals with four counts of murder in the first degree; murder in the first degree being under 1958 recompilation of the Alabama criminal code, which is the law that was in effect at that time.

"These indictments are the result of the ongoing, continuing investigation by the United States Attorney's Office in cooperation with our office as a joint and federal investigation. I must also tell you that an indictment is merely a charge, an allegation against these two individuals, and there is a presumption of innocence in these cases until there is a trial and a finding of guilty in these matters."

When Barber turned it over to me, I took the opportunity to outline briefly to the media how we had shifted the matter from a federal grand jury to the state and what would be the next step in the process. "At this time, we have no idea when the court may hear any of that or when this case will be set for trial," I said.

The African-American community, understandably, was elated by the indictments. So many times hopes had been raised only to be dashed; but now, following the lead of Mississippi in prosecuting Byron De La Beckwith and another lethally violent white supremacist, Sam Bowers, Alabama was about to get its chance to atone a little for a past sin.

Black leaders had worked overtime to play down expectations, but the order to stand trial swiftly lifted hopes that justice would finally be done. Unfortunately, excitement quickly gave way to outrage when the old Klansmen were released from custody pending trial after their bonds were reduced to $200,000 each. Many of the good people of Birmingham were dangerously angry and expressed it publicly.

Secret Meeting

Fifty-eight-year-old Circuit Judge Jim Garrett was assigned to preside over the trial. Familiar to all lawyers in the case, he had a great reputation as tough but fair. It was clear from the outset he would have his hands full with this one.

Cherry's attorney, Mickey Johnson, a vastly experienced, no-nonsense defense counsel, and Blanton's lawyer, former cop David Luker, immediately filed motions to dismiss the case, alleging that their clients had been denied their constitutional right to a speedy trial. They argued the state had been in possession of the evidence for decades, so their clients should have been brought to court years ago. I didn't think there was much of a chance for dismissal because the defense had to prove both prejudice and that the delay had been intentional in order to gain a tactical advantage, a very tall order. However, they also filed for a change of venue, alleging that their clients could not get a fair trial in Jefferson County because of extensive publicity. Frankly, that one concerned me. For the sake of the families, the community, and the greater good, the case needed to be tried in Birmingham.

I knew from experience the old Klansmen would probably be granted bail, with a bond set at a level that wasn't completely out of reach for each of them. Given their advancing ages and the perception that they were neither a flight risk nor a present danger to the community, I expected the court to give them the option. But the howl of indignation was deafening, and the community was inching toward throwing the presumption of innocence out the window. If that perception was to permeate the potential jury pool before trial, it could very well give the judge no choice but to change the venue.

It was certainly not my place to tell the community how to act, but I did have an obligation to make sure they were fully aware of the potential consequences of publicly "convicting" Blanton and Cherry. Reverend Chris Hamlin, the 16th Street pastor at the time, helped organize an off-the-record meeting between myself, FBI SAC Thornton, and prominent African-American clergy, the most powerful leaders in the black community. We gathered in the Board of Directors conference room at the Birmingham Civil Rights Institute, the city's museum and learning center dedicated to the movement. Opened in 1992, it has rightly assumed a role as a key cultural landmark in the South. It sits across from 16th Street Baptist and Kelly Ingram Park. I'm proud that, years later, I would serve as its Chairman.

The Civil Rights Institute is promoted as a living history museum. It certainly measured up to that billing when the most prominent black clergymen in the city arrived to discuss the anxiety induced by the release of Blanton and Cherry. While the cool quiet of the institute and its high domed entrance give it a reverential feel, the angry tone I encountered as we convened made it clear no one was going to hold back.

I had to fight the urge to spell out that we were running the risk of undermining years of work by insisting on the defendants' guilt before trial. But I knew better than to lecture the clergymen. A few, such as Reverend Woods and Reverend Nelson "Fireball" Smith, had been on the front lines in the struggle in Birmingham decades earlier and weren't going to be instructed to do anything. Instead, I simply explained that under Alabama law every defendant, as long as they're not a flight risk, is entitled to have a bond set that they have a chance of paying.

"The more the media makes it look like these men are guilty, it is going to make it look like they can't get a fair trial in Birmingham, and that's the one thing that we don't want to happen," I said. "We don't want this case moved from Birmingham to Mobile or anywhere else."

The ministers listened politely; some asked questions. In the end, they took it on board without making any promises of muzzling themselves or their communities. Most indicated they would let the spirit of the Lord move them with each and every word they spoke. I sincerely hoped Heaven was listening.

It may not have been divine intervention, but I did take away something valuable from the gathering, courtesy of one of the strongest, proudest, and most insightful voices for civil rights in Birmingham. Reverend Woods, the former leader of the Southern Christian Leadership Conference and Martin Luther King's friend and confidant, was the man who had let Langford know years before, in no uncertain terms, that inaction over the church bombing was an ongoing barrier to better relations with federal law enforcement in the city.

A civil rights doyen who had never strayed from the MLK doctrine, Reverend Woods, then in his seventies, remained a vibrant and impressive man, always boldly stating his position. He also never concerned himself with staying on script. So while our focus was on pre-trial publicity, Reverend Woods sparked a conversation about an aspect of the case that, to be honest, we hadn't given much thought.

Through the decades there had been a prevailing sentiment among investigators that while the Klansmen had no doubt bombed the church, the

explosives they set probably went off at the wrong time. There was even testimony in the Chambliss trial along those lines. Several witnesses in our
investigation indicated the alleged bombers had stated as much. Reverend
Woods, to my surprise, asked me if I thought the bomb had been designed
to kill people. I responded that it was generally believed the plan was for it
to go off in the early hours of the morning, when no one was around, but a
malfunction somehow caused a fatal delay.

"Well, I am very disappointed in hearing you say that, Doug," he
said.

The old warhorse put me in my place: "If you remember, two weeks after
the church bombing, there were other bombs, allegedly by the same corps
of Klansmen." He was referring to two bombs on Center Street. One was a
decoy. "The other went off, and that bomb had nails in it, and that bomb
was most definitely designed to kill people," he said. "We believe that by
the time September 15 rolled around, and the schools were being integrated, the Klan felt like it was time to hurt somebody, it was time to kill
somebody to try to stop the movement."

It was, to say the least, a eureka moment for me. We had been pointlessly searching for a motive other than the Klansmen wanting to continue
their scattergun "Bombingham" campaign, but now the specific rationale
and intent were crystal clear. The civil rights movement in 1963 was building an unstoppable momentum through the Children's Crusade, the "I Have
a Dream" speech, and the integration of Birmingham schools the week before the bombing. The only conspicuous resistance the segregationists had
offered was Wallace's farcical stand in the schoolhouse door. The Klan, feeling impotent, was angry and desperate, murderously so. They were seeing
their segregated way of life sliding away.

The clarity provided by that exchange shaped our case in multiple ways.
Most importantly there would be no hedging, qualifying, or underplaying
the Klan's actions. From that point forward, we never suggested that the
bomb did not go off when it was supposed to or wasn't meant to kill specific targets. Instead, we embraced the concept that it was indeed detonated
to inflict maximum carnage.

Occasionally I still hear suggestions that as evil as they were, the Klan
did not intentionally target children at that Sunday morning service. My
only reply is to suggest that if there are people with intimate knowledge of
the sequence of events who want to correct or clarify what we know, they
can always step up to set us straight. No one, including Blanton or Cherry,
has ever come forward.

Open Discovery Policy

Getting it right in a courtroom is only part of the battle; minimizing what can go wrong is just as vital.

There was plenty of room for mistakes due to the age of the investigation and the variety of tools used to construct the case, including reams of handwritten notes and seemingly countless FBI evidence sheets, photos, and tape recordings.

Understanding the context in which the original inquiry unfolded was key. Knowing there were clandestine alliances between various groups and understanding the involvement of various levels of government and their agencies helped explain the prioritization of some issues over others. It was also important to realize that secrecy was a major concern. Make no mistake, informants and potential witnesses put their lives on the line to provide evidence. Unless you understood who was who, it was easy to misinterpret or misread material.

With so many elements at play in this cold case, I made a decision early on to have an open file policy. That is, I intended to make available to the defense all of the evidence gathered in the course of the investigation. Such a commitment was a major challenge for an investigation stretching back almost four decades, during which time much had changed in the way the FBI compiled and kept its records. The sheer volume was staggering. In fact, I found three separate sets of records: the case file itself, informant files containing information obtained from the FBI's confidential sources, and files kept on various individuals, including most of the active Klansmen in the area.

My primary motivation for making them all available to the defense was pretty straightforward. There could be things in the files that were potentially exculpatory—helpful to the defense—even if based on hearsay. Prosecutors are required to hand over exculpatory evidence before a plea is entered and routinely do so with material that obviously falls into that category. In this old, complicated case, there was much evidence that could be misread or difficult to assess. I wanted to ensure everyone was on the same page before a jury was engaged. I certainly didn't want to get into a situation where a promising prosecution effort came to nothing halfway through a trial because evidence deemed exculpatory suddenly popped up. Additionally, should we get a conviction, I wanted to protect the record on appeal.

In short, an open file policy ensured accurate interpretation of evidence, and challenges about the relevance and viability of material would be assessed before each side put their cards on the table. It would provide an element of insurance that the case we presented would be the case the jury would consider. And if we got a conviction, it would stick.

Such a policy didn't thrill the FBI; after all, the Bureau had a strict policy of protecting the identities of their informants, even those deceased. However, the Feds were committed to the case, and the directive of a presidentially appointed U.S. Attorney trumped Bureau policy.

While internal grumbling, fretting, and negotiating were necessary in pushing the case forward, at least the public noises of discontent and anger about the defendants' bail situation had died down a little.

Understandably, the clergymen didn't cease talking about the case. However, they seemed to avoid direct public condemnation of Blanton and Cherry. This reduced the chance the judge would feel the need to move the trial to another city, less tainted by a presumption of the defendants' guilt. Not having to worry about a change of venue allowed us to focus more fully on piecing together a formula for perhaps the most important pillar of the process—jury selection.

A gut feeling isn't a bad way to make key decisions when assembling panels. However, in a case so racially charged and drenched in history, a methodical approach that included a good bit of research seemed in our best interest.

Not long after the indictment was handed down, I took a trip to Los Angeles to meet with jury experts at the firm Vinson & Demitri, including Stephen Paterson. He had worked for the federal government in the Oklahoma City bombing case as well as the prosecution of Louisiana Governor Edwin Edwards. The Goldman family had also hired him in the civil case that ultimately found O. J. Simpson liable for the wrongful death of Ronald Goldman and battery of Nicole Brown.

I had not used jury consultants on a regular basis, but we needed all the help we could assemble, as prosecuting white men for crimes against blacks had been traditionally among the toughest of legal tasks. It had been all but impossible to convict Klansmen of racially motivated crimes back in the day, although a few recent cases proved that age-old prejudices and preconceptions did not always dictate outcomes—specifically, the cold case convictions of Byron De La Beckwith and Sam Bowers.

De La Beckwith had been tried twice for the murder of NAACP leader Medgar Evers. Both attempts resulted in mistrials. He was finally held accountable in a breakthrough cold case conviction in 1994. Bowers was behind the murder of another great civil rights activist, Vernon Dahmer, in Hattiesburg, Mississippi, in 1966. The former Klan boss had avoided jail for decades and was able to inflict wave upon wave of violence on others because of four mistrials. Finally, in 1998, he was convicted for his role in the brutal killing of Vernon Dahmer and sent to prison for life.

Those verdicts were at the back of my mind when I got a phone call from Andy Sheldon. I had no idea who Sheldon was. But it turned out my cold caller was the man chiefly responsible for putting together those Mississippi juries. Sheldon had seen the news about the indictments, and as civil rights cases were his passion, he thought he'd see if he could be of service.

Growing up white in Miami, Florida, in the 1950s, Andy Sheldon lived in a community as segregated as most places in the South. He gained a law degree from the University of Florida before submerging himself in the study of juries and the psychology of trials while earning a master's and doctorate in psychology from Georgia State University.

It was a relatively new area of expertise, and Sheldon quickly established a reputation as one of the best in the country, having assisted a lawyer friend in Lafayette, Louisiana, by analyzing the jury pool for the De La Beckwith trial.

De La Beckwith, a white supremacist of the first order, had walked the streets of Mississippi a free man for decades until prosecutor Bobby DeLaughter successfully proved to a jury of eight blacks and four whites that De La Beckwith had fired the bullet that ended Evers's life on the front porch of his home. Sheldon's pro bono work proved critical and solidified his intense interest and commitment to civil rights cold cases.

He recalled recently that during the De La Beckwith trial he picked up an Atlanta newspaper and noted the front page featured an article on Evers's murderer alongside a story about a Middle Eastern terrorist, Osama Bin Laden, who would make terrible headlines years later. It struck Sheldon at the time that the international problem of terrorism seemed to be attracting growing outrage, while in our backyard we had long tolerated domestic terrorists. Many were free and expected to remain so for the rest of their days.

Sam Bowers was a prime example. Thirty-four years after he had started a spree of murders he was still on the outside enjoying a business career and indulging his hobbies, including collecting weapons and swastikas. A native of New Orleans, Bowers lived in Brookhaven, Mississippi, in the early sixties. Not unlike the thugs of Eastview Klavern, the Navy veteran believed violence should have been used more frequently and fiercely by the Klan.

He pulled together a group of wannabe "storm troopers" for the misguided white supremacist cause. He called himself a Grand Wizard, and his band of thugs, the White Knights of the Ku Klux Klan.

Their first victims were gunned down in the summer of 1964 in a triple murder near Philadelphia, Mississippi. He eventually served a six-year prison term for those homicides but not before he took the life of another black man.

In 1966, Bowers ordered the assassination of Vernon Dahmer in Hattiesburg for his perceived sin of urging African Americans to vote. Dahmer, at the time, had four sons serving in the United States military. He kept a voter registration book in his grocery store and was an active voice in the community. Constantly aware of the KKK threat, Dahmer kept a shotgun near his bed, knowing a violent confrontation was a real possibility.

The cowardly Bowers opted to use the cover of darkness to firebomb the Dahmer home. As the family slept, incendiary devices were hurled through windows and the house was quickly engulfed by flame. Dahmer used his shotgun to blast back at the attackers, distracting them long enough for his wife, Ellie, to escape with her youngest children, despite burns to her arms. The arsonists fired a barrage of bullets, trapping Dahmer in the building long enough for him to sustain what would prove to be fatal injuries. It was an outrage of the highest order, and the involvement of Bowers was common knowledge, but he had repeatedly beat the system to avoid conviction until 1998.

Sheldon's work, a blend of psychology, instinct, and common sense, was key to putting Bowers where he belonged—in a Mississippi prison.

Since the De La Beckwith trial in 1994, Sheldon has been involved in eight civil rights cases, with seven generating guilty verdicts and the other ending in a mistrial. He says he often encountered a "let sleeping dogs lie" mentality in the South when it came to cold civil rights cases.

Not only do these "old men" escape punishment, but many completely lack remorse and would carry out the same sort of evil acts again in an instant, given the opportunity. "They operated in an environment with impunity," Sheldon said. "They didn't fear the law, and in most cases intimidated anyone who dared to speak out against them. Creating fear was their constant theme. They truly were remorseless people who considered themselves outside the jurisdiction of American society."

Sheldon became a vital member of our prosecuting team and in combination with Paterson constructed what, I have come to understand, was a groundbreaking jury selection process.

We had negotiated multiple hurdles and managed to build a formidable prosecution process, but even a fair-minded jury needed a piece of evidence to put the matter beyond a reasonable doubt. I knew we didn't have that golden nugget. We needed something fresh. And we needed it fast.

The Kitchen Tape

I had dogged my investigators with repeated requests to re-examine evidence—annoying, I realized, given that the faded handwritten notes, garbled recordings, and other pieces of evidence were thirty-seven years old in some cases and had been picked over on numerous occasions over the decades.

We went off on tangents to ensure we didn't miss anything, examining all alternative theories, as thin as they were, about who could have possibly carried out the bombing. These inquiries sometimes took days and weeks, not hours, and were draining on the team. Nothing turned our heads. There were no other plausible explanations.

The defense, hoping to come up with something to point to anyone but the defendants, tapped their network of informants and sympathetic "supporters," both in local law enforcement and the wider community, for clues. On one occasion, the defense passed on information that vital documents about the bombing—rumored to implicate someone other than Blanton and Cherry—were stashed in old files in the basement of the Birmingham City Jail. We showed up with our colleagues from the defense and proceeded to pore through reams and reams of notes and other documents, mostly the work of local law enforcement officers around the time of the bombing. Even though we found nothing of use for either the prosecution or the defense, the level of detail in the notes, reviewing mass meetings and other gatherings, made them compelling records.

Among other things, they hinted at the level of distrust between authorities and the African American community. Law enforcement, reflecting the views of many whites and politicians, was also deeply suspicious of "outsiders." It's hard not to think that if there had simply been more civilized discussion between various groups some of the pain and misunderstandings that plagued the period could have been avoided.

But that was never going to happen with Bull Connor ruling the roost in Birmingham. Law enforcement in those days was rife with segregationists and Klan sympathizers. The inflexible "us versus them" mentality of those anxious to hold on to their bit of power helped make activists out of the most forgiving, patient folks in the African-American community. The notes delivered a graphic picture of the poisoned environment in which the bombing took place. Mistrust, suspicion, underhanded dealings, and community division were achingly obvious on those pages, although there was nothing of evidentiary importance for the case.

Alternative theories, other suspects, even just finding something "new"— it was all a distraction. The case had been investigated to within an inch of its life more than once. Anything that was going to help us further was already in the assembled evidence: somewhere in that dusty, eroding pile of pages, tapes, and photographs in the 2121 Building.

I was especially hopeful we could turn up something on Blanton. He had been the intense focus of a lot of the FBI's early investigation. Cherry had managed to drag the spotlight toward himself in recent times, and his motormouth was proving to be our ally. Whatever Blanton had to say about what he did would have been expressed in those early days—around the period of the Burns tapes—before he apparently took a monk-like vow of silence.

Besides the scores of old interview transcripts and piles of notes, there were also hours and hours of tape recordings made surreptitiously with telephone taps and bugs planted in strategic locations. Just about all of these tapes had been ignored during our investigation because retired agents we talked to said they contained nothing of use.

Providing the defense with discovery was an onerous task. Not only did I open all files for inspection, we made copies of thousands of pages and provided them to each defense attorney in three-ring binders. By November 2000, because of the workload, we had yet to listen to the tapes. Much to Fleming's and Herren's dismay I told them that someone had to listen to every tape, even if previous investigations had deemed them not useful. I simply was not going to take the chance that something had been missed, be it inculpatory or exculpatory.

One written entry of particular interest had summarized the recordings made at the Chambliss home featuring the sounds of men playing checkers and mechanical owl hoots—the microphone apparently had been placed inside or too close to a cuckoo clock. There were notes about other recordings, too, from June 1964, but those tapes never resurfaced. They were of high priority to us because parts of transcripts and FBI notes we found confirmed they featured Blanton's voice. We wanted to listen to every second of those ourselves to ensure we weren't overlooking anything.

The cluttered evidence room in the FBI's 2121 Building was semi-organized chaos. Over the years, every available nook and cranny had been filled. It was like walking into a musty casino where you could easily lose track of time and, despite high hopes, knew deep down you almost certainly wouldn't hit the jackpot.

Fleming again submerged himself in the clutter of notes, boxes, and potential exhibits that had been jealously guarded over time but stored in a way that suggested no one expected ever to look at this stuff again. He gave himself a target—tapes that we knew featured Blanton's voice.

"I asked the evidence room supervisor to scavenge thoroughly through everything there for the tapes," Fleming said. "After the third time and they hadn't found anything, I asked permission to look for myself, so they let me in. I'm looking around and I'm getting ready to leave, giving up any hope of ever locating them, and I see this cardboard box sitting in the far corner under a shelf near a trash can. It had some indistinct marking on it, so I just pick up the box and start going through it. And there they were." Great big clunky seven-inch reel tapes, a bunch of them. Records indicated they were the fruits of an extensive surreptitious exercise.

In 1964, the Bureau had managed to place an undercover operative in the apartment next to Blanton and his then wife, Jean. John Colvin, an FBI technician with the electronic surveillance group, posed as neighborly James McBride. He explained his lengthy stints away from home as being a product of his job as a truck driver.

Blanton's neighbor was visited one day by a repairman who, in fact, was FBI Special Agent Ralph Butler, the man in charge of the local office's electronic surveillance units. He tore out a wall in the closet and installed a microphone wrapped in insulation next to a hole under the sink in Blanton's kitchen. The microphone was attached to an open telephone line that ran to a tape recorder back at the FBI office. The result was hours of recorded conversations between the newlyweds, Tommy and Jean Blanton, and anyone else who popped by.

In 1963 and 1964 tapes of Klan members were routinely made, as no statutory law governed the process. Attorney General Robert Kennedy approved the installation of wiretaps on telephone lines, while the FBI Director, J. Edgar Hoover, had the authority to approve the installation of bugs on the premises. Such tapes were deemed necessary to collect intelligence (usually about upcoming attacks) for "national security purposes" but were not used as pieces of courtroom evidence.

It would have been most efficient to have listened to those 1964 recordings straightaway, but that wasn't possible because the tapes were old technology and we didn't have equipment on which to play them. So we immediately sent them off to an FBI lab for conversion to audiocassette, still ubiquitous, if not state of the art, in 2000. When the converted tapes were returned to Birmingham a few weeks later, secretaries in the FBI office undertook the arduous task of transcribing them, saving us valuable time.

Herren soon got a call from a transcriber: "She told me 'you have to come up here and hear this.'" The police force veteran of scores of major crime case investigations, battle-hardened from several years of disappointment working the bombing case, didn't expect it to be anything earth-shattering.

What he heard took his breath away. He called me immediately. Normally calm and collected, Herren sounded a little as though he had won the lottery. He blurted out that they had picked up something on one of the tapes.

"Don't talk to me," I said, probably a little abruptly. "Don't tell me anything just yet. I might have to replace you on the case. We have to put up the Chinese wall to get to the bottom of this."

Herren had no idea what I was talking about but I wanted to ensure there wasn't a chance we would be tainting our case with illegally obtained evidence or material that would later be found not admissible. Until I was satisfied that the tape wasn't recorded illegally and that we hadn't breached the marital privilege, the details of what Ben had heard couldn't be shared with the team.

The defense had been aware of everything else we had to that point, prompting Blanton and Cherry to remain cocky in the knowledge that just a hint of doubt might be enough to deter a jury from a guilty verdict. A new recording of Blanton might add a few more lines to the Klansmen's haggard faces.

However, even before we knew exactly what was on the tape, I felt compelled to reiterate my open file discovery policy. "We are going to let the defense look at everything in the FBI files, the informant files, everything we've got," I told the investigators. I seem to recall Fleming's eyes bulging. But in my mind, we had no logical alternative if we were to move forward. I did not want to be accused of hiding the ball.

"What Meeting?"

The temptation to get Herren to spill the beans on what he'd heard was immense. It was the secret none of us dared talk about. But finally, in a strategy session with the investigators and Robert Posey, I asked: "So Ben, is it good?"

He grinned like a Cheshire cat: "It is really good," he said, knowing not to embellish.

"Did he use the word?" I asked.

"Oh yeah," he said, knowing I was talking about the word "bomb."

Posey and I looked at each other as if a gauntlet had been thrown down at our feet. We were going to get that tape into evidence, by God!

Posey took charge of the legal research. We had two primary concerns. First, we needed to determine whether recording a conversation between husband and wife technically breached the marital privilege. The other issue was overall admissibility.

Fleming had already checked with FBI headquarters and was told, in no uncertain terms, that because a warrant wasn't obtained for the bugging, the tape would be inadmissible. FBI files indicated that the bug placed by Butler had been authorized by the FBI Director for intelligence gathering purposes only and not for use in court.

First Assistant Bud Henry and Criminal Chief and former law professor Joe McLean helped us immensely as we searched for precedent and practice in getting such recordings before a jury. But time was tight, so I had to establish, at least, whether the conversation was between Blanton and his then wife. Herren confirmed that it was.

This pushed me to risk listening to what was on the tape. The marital privilege doesn't protect the review of conversations that constitute a crime. If we had a good-faith belief that the conversation was a cover-up or a continuation of a conspiracy, we were entitled to make a firsthand evaluation.

I hadn't been as excited to listen to a recording since Elvis shocked the world with "Blue Suede Shoes." But I found it difficult to allow myself to hope, even as I sat in my office, headphones in place, poised to listen to the tape, labeled by the Feds as "Q9."

Initially, I couldn't make out anything significant amid the sounds of domesticity on the tape. The noise was overwhelming at times and suggested listening would be a pointless exercise, just as the FBI investigators' notes had indicated decades before. There was repeated clanging (presumably from kitchen pans), shuffling, and crashing; it was hard to make out anything distinct.

Then a voice, and another. It was Jean's unruly screech and Blanton's flat, humorless drawl.

The quality was mediocre at best, but you could make out the small talk.

It was not a fight, nor were they whispering secrets. They were pressing each other for answers. Tommy wanted to know what Jean had told the FBI about where he had been the weekend of the bombing. Jean wanted to know if Tommy had been carousing with her romantic rival, Waylene Vaughn, that weekend.

It took a second or two to absorb what I was hearing. It was all so casual, so matter-of-fact. What struck me was how different it sounded from other recordings from this period. Blanton and his cronies had always been so careful in conversation, knowing they were regularly taped. But on Q9, he was answering to a higher power—Jean, his suspicious wife—and was saying a few things he could never take back.

She inquired about the weekend the bomb exploded, asking what he was doing at "the bridge," a clear reference to the Cahaba River hangout. There was also a reference to the Modern Sign Shop, another known meeting place of the violent Eastview Klavern #13.

Then Blanton, on three different occasions, anxious to know what Jean had told investigators and clearly scrambling to divert any conversation about his womanizing, refers directly to planning or making the bomb.

These three unmistakable statements were pure prosecutorial gold:

"The meeting where we planned the bomb."
"We had that meeting to make the bomb."
"Oh, we were making the bomb."

There was other important dialogue, in which Jean discussed not wanting to tell the FBI about seeing Mary Lou Holt—Don Luna's aunt and a Klan wife who we believed had knowledge of the bombing—on the eve of the attack. But we all had to lift our jaws off the floor when it came to Blanton's bomb references. Everyone had been concerned that the evidence against him was thin. But now we had statements from the horse's mouth that could very well cement his guilt in the eyes of a jury.

The ghastly, dark, and almost comical fact was that Blanton found it easier to concede he was involved in a terrorist plot that killed four little girls than admit he had been out with Waylene. He didn't discuss the bombing plan in detail, it seemed, because it didn't warrant much of his attention. But he had said enough.

SEVEN

SUCKER PUNCHED

Blanton admitting in his own words to a role in the bombing was a welcome validation of what nearly everybody associated with the case had known for decades. Yet, in a way, the kitchen tape added to our main problem—time, or, more accurately, the lack of it. Not only did we have to continue piecing together our case for presentation, but we were being pounded by defense efforts to move, stop, or suspend the trial. What's more, Blanton's team was insisting the Mitch Burns recordings not be allowed into evidence, so they would surely pull out every stop to prevent the kitchen tape's admission.

It had been more than thirty-seven years since the fatal bombing, but as an unusually chilly Birmingham winter started to release its grip early in 2001, we didn't have a minute to lose.

Looming large in the back of my mind was the fact my time as U.S. Attorney was winding down. Like every other Clinton appointment, I was fully aware that the new Republican President, George W. Bush, inaugurated January 20, 2001, would be sweeping a broom through the Justice Department. With my tenure scheduled to conclude in early spring, I was expecting a tap on the shoulder at any time. Adding to the pressure, President Bush had selected John Ashcroft as his Attorney General. The former Governor and Senator from Missouri was as conservative as they come, and his record on civil rights had not endeared him to the

African-American community. At times he had been accused of racial insensitivity.

The media focus on the case was also intensifying. The longer the buildup, the more chatter was generated in the community, which potentially added credibility to claims that a pool of jurors in Birmingham could not give the defendants a fair trial.

Opinions about the tape's admissibility were mixed and seemed to change on a daily basis. Veteran investigator Fleming was particularly concerned, which was understandable as he was a Bureau man through and through and had headquarters in his ear saying the tape didn't have a snowball's chance of making it to trial. If the tape was obtained without benefit of a court order, the Feds believed, it was a violation of the Fourth Amendment.

The trial had been scheduled for early April, so in keeping with my policy I needed to provide the recording to the defense as quickly as possible. However, I first wanted to try and improve the audio quality. The FBI lab had converted the old reel-to-reel recordings to cassettes and in the process had enhanced the copy by using filters to eliminate static and other extraneous sounds. Still, the quality left a lot to be desired, so we sent them to NASA, thinking the agency's extraterrestrial filters would help. Unfortunately, it made little difference, so as a last resort, I contacted Anthony Pellicano, the owner of Forensic Audio in Los Angeles.

I had seen Pellicano's advertisements in my old copies of *The Champion*, the magazine of the National Association of Criminal Defense Lawyers. At the time he had a great reputation as the "Detective to the Stars," which I'd checked out with a call to the U.S. Attorney's Office in Tampa, where he had been engaged in a highly publicized case. I had Fleming send him the original tapes, along with the transcripts the FBI had made.

When he completed his work, Pellicano called to say he believed he had managed to enhance the quality of the recording. He'd copied it to CD and made a few amendments to the transcript, as previously garbled moments were now clear. Most significantly, he also said that he and his staff had detected the presence of a third person on the Q9 tape.

That discovery alone was worth the extra time and cost, as we would no longer have to worry about the marital privilege. The mumbled contributions of the unidentified third party weren't significant; it was the fact that he was present, as the presumption of confidential communication between spouses is destroyed when the exchange is carried out in front of another person. Of course, we still had to overcome the fact that no court order had been issued back in 1964 to permit making the recordings.

Even though we now had an enhanced-quality recording, it remained tough to make out some of the discussion. Each member of the team—lawyers, investigators, secretaries—provided their input when it came to adding to or changing the Q9 transcript. But we craved greater clarity, and I knew there was one more person we needed to consult.

In the days before sophisticated audio technology was the norm and many undercover recordings were often difficult to hear, Belle Mills became somewhat of a legend. Blind and with particularly sensitive hearing, she was the stenographer for the Internal Revenue Service and the FBI. After listening to the kitchen tape, she made a few tweaks to the transcript.

It was now about as good as it was ever going to get, so it was time to make arrangements to provide the recording to the defense, much to the chagrin of a few good men. However, I first made the strategic decision to play the tape for Blanton's ex-wife Jean. She was the one person in our sights, other than Cherry, who could directly link him to the bombing.

Twice Blanton's betrothed, twice divorced from the Klansman, Jean had been Mrs. Barnes for decades by the time the investigation reeled her in again. Now in her sixties, Barnes possessed a grandmotherly facade and a sharp tongue. She was pleasant enough through gritted teeth yet could swiftly become belligerent and indignant for no apparent reason. The years had not been kind to her physically. We hoped she might have developed some sense of remorse, though we knew she had been willing to lie and contort her story on numerous occasions to protect Blanton.

In Blanton's first interview, in October 1963, just two weeks after the bombing, he recalled that he had gone out with his then girlfriend, seventeen-year-old Jean Casey, on Saturday night, September 14. But he couldn't remember where. The only thing he recalled was that he had her home by midnight, after which he went home and to bed. Blanton quit talking in that interview when Special Agent Frank Spencer told him his car had been spotted behind the church at 2:00 a.m. His story left plenty of time for him to pick up his buddies and plant the bomb.

Blanton and Jean later admitted they had consulted after he had walked out of that FBI interview. Amazingly, during the next interrogation, Blanton remembered exactly what happened that entire weekend, and Jean's story was essentially identical. They told FBI agents that Blanton had broken a date with Jean on Friday night to make signs, presumably anti-integration banners, at the Modern Sign Shop in downtown Birmingham. She let Blanton know in no uncertain terms that if he did not take her out on Saturday there would be trouble. That portion of the story was confirmed on the kitchen tape when Jean, rightly suspecting she was not the only object of Blanton's affections, quizzed him about what he was doing that night "when you stood me up" (leading Blanton to admit "we were making the bomb"). In the second interview, the couple also miraculously remembered the time he picked her up and where they went that Saturday night. They also changed the details of Blanton's departure after taking Jean home. They said Blanton had fallen asleep on Jean's sofa and didn't leave her house until after 2:30 Sunday morning, after the alleged 2:00 a.m. sighting of Blanton's car.

With the changes to their story, the eyewitness Agent Spencer had referred to was debunked, and the couple's alibi solidified. They had a tight strategic partnership that had endured interrogation and divorce, though their respective stories had never been fully explored in court.

Tommy and Jean's first wedding occurred in the spring of 1964, when Blanton knew he was one of the FBI's top suspects, putting any potential testimony from her out of reach for law enforcement due to the marital privilege. (They had no idea, however, that they would soon be recorded.) Not long after the FBI (with J. Edgar Hoover's explicit approval) dropped the case in 1968, Blanton apparently celebrated by divorcing Jean. This lasted until the old Klansman got wind that Baxley had reopened the case. The happy couple then swiftly got hitched again. In 1978, a year after Baxley won a conviction over Chambliss, but couldn't pull together enough evidence to indict either Cherry or Blanton, it was splitsville for Blanton and Jean.

Decades later, Jean, who had married another man, was not shy and was predictably cantankerous when a legal aide arrived on her doorstep to deliver a subpoena to appear in my office.

She was agitated: "What's this all about?"

"I don't know, ma'am, but Bill Fleming sent me here to serve you with this subpoena," responded the messenger, knowing that Fleming had interviewed her earlier.

"That old butt rash!" screeched Barnes.

My team had tried to work with her around grand jury time, but she stood firm in her story, demonstrating a loyalty and stubbornness and hinting at an underlying malevolence that was hard to comprehend.

"For hours upon hours, we would sit in a conference room, trying to persuade Jean to tell us what she knew," Robert Posey recalled. "One day she told us exactly what she was wearing on the first date she ever had with Blanton. Then we would ask about what they were doing the night before the bombing and her memory suddenly lapsed, and she couldn't recall anything."

Every time we met with Jean, the men in the room couldn't understand what was going on with her. It took young Robin Beardsley, whose vocabulary had been expanded by listening over and over to old Klansmen exchanging insults, racial slurs, and sexual references on the Mitch Burns tapes, to set us straight.

"Guys, here's a simple fact," she said, somehow without rolling her eyes. "She is still in love with him and will never turn against him."

"Aw, come on," I said. "Surely to God after all this time and a new husband she would have a change of heart."

"I'm just telling you," Beardsley said, shaking her head.

Jean had stuck to their story like glue, but maybe the kitchen tape would loosen the bind. Perhaps Blanton's sole alibi would crack, as there was an admission on the tape that she had lied to the FBI about having seen Mary Lou Holt.

Jean came to my office with her current husband, Richard Barnes. We had planned a command performance—Herren set up the tape player so we could listen through both headphones and a speaker. Copies of the transcript had been made for the investigators, the lawyers, and the Barneses to follow along. Everyone was primed for the "Perry Mason" moment when a key witness breaks down and finally blurts out the truth.

Even though she was hostile from the beginning, we all remained cordial, repeatedly thanking her for coming. I told her that we had something I thought she should hear before we turned it over to Blanton and launched into an explanation that in the summer of 1964 the FBI had bugged the apartment she shared with Blanton. Jean was furious.

"You need to hear this," I said, motioning for Herren to hit the play button.

JEAN: Well, you never bothered to tell me what you went to the river for Tommy.

TOMMY: What did you tell them I did?

JEAN: You didn't even . . .

TOMMY: What did you tell them I did at the river? What did they ask you I did at the river?

JEAN: They asked me what you went for, and I told them I didn't know.

TOMMY: They were interested in that meeting I went to. They knew I went to the meeting.

JEAN: What meeting?

TOMMY: To the big one.

JEAN: What big one?

TOMMY: The meeting where we planned the bomb.

JEAN: Tommy, what meeting are you talking about now?

TOMMY: We had that meeting to make the bomb.

JEAN: I know that.

TOMMY: I think I'll wear this sh . . . I'm going to wear this shirt.

JEAN: It's what you were doing that Friday night when you stood me up.

TOMMY: Oh, we were making the bomb.

JEAN: Really. Modern Sign Company.

TOMMY: Yeah.

JEAN: I think what got me is when they told me that Modern . . . some people at the Modern Sign Company said you weren't there.

TOMMY: Who said I wasn't there?

JEAN: Um-hum.

TOMMY: Oh, well that's . . .

UNKNOWN MALE: Jean, why don't you learn anything with the FBI. Every breath they utter is a lie.

JEAN: I know, but I didn't know that then, and I didn't know whether to think you stood me up to go out with somebody else . . . that's the first thing that hit me.

UNKNOWN MALE: Well, that's . . .

JEAN: You stood me up to out with Waylene.

UNKNOWN MALE: That's what they want to do to make you mad.

TOMMY: They want to make you mad girl . . .

JEAN: Uh . . .

TOMMY: That's when they take your mind away from you, Jean. Any, any words they utter is a lie. They sprinkle in a couple of truths in them . . . then they . . .

JEAN: Even that business about Mary Lou Holt, I didn't want to tell 'em about it . . . I didn't know what to say, and I knew who it was, but I didn't want to tell them that's who it was.

As she listened to each sentence on the recording, Jean's fury grew. I think she clearly understood that pieces of the foundation of Blanton's alibi were crumbling under the weight of his words—and hers.

She went on the attack.

"They put something together," she said, in an agitated voice that bordered on a shriek. She was indignantly implying the tape had been doctored. "That's shameful. I can't believe it!"

I explained that what was on the recording from her was consistent with other statements she had made and that we would have experts testify to the authenticity of the tape.

"They can testify any way they want. I don't believe for a short minute that I ever had that conversation. My memory is faulty, but I didn't have that conversation."

Her husband asked that the tape be played again. Her only response was "that's so sad," referring to her belief that the tape had been altered.

Posey and I tried to reason with her, pointing out how it appeared that Blanton had just used her as his alibi and only married her to prevent her testifying against him. Jean's husband, as sympathetic as he was to her, tried to get her to remember the details of their conversations. At moments she broke down in tears, but despite the many repeat airings of the recording that day, she stood by her man.

Robin Beardsley sure was right about her. After what seemed like an eternity in that small conference room, Jean and Richard Barnes said that they had heard enough and were ready to leave.

Although we failed to get the "Perry Mason" admission, the meeting was a positive for us: Jean confirmed the voices on the recording were her own, Blanton's, and an unknown third person. With that, we knew for sure that the marital privilege would not be an issue.

Not long after she left the office, I had a phone call from Blanton's lawyer, David Luker.

"So, Doug," Luker said. "You got something for me?"

Apparently, Mrs. Barnes had called her ex's legal team once she was done stonewalling me to let them know what she had just heard. We arranged for him to visit my office the following Monday.

I was anxious to see how Luker would react to the tape. Blanton had been leaning on his alibi and insisting that the perpetrator was someone else, most likely Gary Thomas Rowe. He had convinced many of those around him of his innocence. But faced with his client's admission, not once but three times, would Luker protest loudly, pledge to stop the tape's admission into evidence, or deny its obvious value?

A former cop and one of the state's best and most experienced criminal defense lawyers, Luker listened intently and followed the transcript as I played him the recording. He paused a moment, looking lost for words.

"Well," he finally said with a sigh, "I guess I better go have a conversation with my client."

Four days later I got an unexpected call from Judge Garrett. He had allowed Luker to withdraw as Blanton's lawyer and had appointed my friend and former law partner John Robbins to the defense.

My gut started to churn. We had made it over some serious legal hurdles, though the admissibility of the tape was still in question. And now we had another potential issue—with a new lawyer in the case less than two months away from trial, there was the real prospect the trial would be delayed again.

Until the Bitter End

The new defense team wasted no time filing a motion seeking to prevent us from using the tape in court. This was going to be more than a skirmish. The importance of the recording was clear to everyone.

The good news from my perspective was much of the noise about Blanton and Cherry being free on bail had simmered down. I knew, however, that I couldn't expect that to last forever. Also, my old partner and new adversary Robbins was filing repeated requests for a continuance to give him more time to catch up and prepare Blanton's defense.

I knew that Judge Garrett was not inclined to delay the trial. In fact, he told us that when he called Robbins to see if he would take the appointment, he told him, "Before you answer you need to know that the case is set for trial on April 15, and I am not going to move it." Robbins said he understood, but that didn't stop him from trying, as any good defense lawyer would.

As soon as I got word of Robbins's appointment, I gave him a call. It had only been two weeks since Louise and I had visited my former partner and his wife Lisa for dinner.

"Who would have thought it?" I said with a laugh. We were going to lock horns, but there was a degree of trust between us that ensured honorable behavior.

"Whatever you need, we will make it available," I assured him.

I met with the team and asserted my desire to ensure we did whatever was necessary to make the April deadline as well as provide evidence to the defense. "Keep in mind, if Blanton is convicted, the denial of the motion to continue will be a serious issue on appeal," I said. "The best way to protect the conviction will be to assist the defense in their preparation."

We kept news of potential complications and roadblocks to ourselves, fearing any hint of further delay after thirty-seven years would be lighting a fire of frustration in the community that would be hard to douse. Even so, the weight of community expectation fueled by increasing media coverage was hard to ignore.

I was visited one day by Reverend Chris Hamlin, pastor of 16th Street Baptist Church, who had helped set up the meeting with community leaders when Cherry and Blanton were released on bail. Hamlin reminded me of what was at stake. A sincere and learned man of faith who had inherited a church legacy unlike any other, he said, in no uncertain terms, that a failure to successfully prosecute Cherry and Blanton could have dire consequences both for the city and for race relations in the South.

"You have to understand the initial pain, the severe impact on the families of the victims. They did not want to talk about it; no one wanted to talk about it for a very long time. The coping mechanism was to do what you have to do and move away from it quickly," he explained recently. "It was too close. You deal with it privately, and that was the case even when Baxley prosecuted Chambliss." This coping mechanism was the preferred method for many right into the late 1990s.

However, the efforts of Rob Langford, my predecessor Caryl Privett, and my staff, combined with the interest generated by Spike Lee's film *4 Little Girls,* had opened a door for people to talk about how the bombing, the desecration, the vile Klan, and the multiple murders of children had impacted them. "It was incredible, the extent of the emotional outpouring," Hamlin said. "So to suddenly have that momentum stop, for that hope to be lost, would be a very powerful blow."

I reassured him during his visit that we had not made the decision to go forward without a great deal of thought and soul-searching. We both understood what was at stake. Neither of us expected, however, that in the months ahead, some of our worst fears would be realized.

Motion to Suppress

It was impossible to avoid feeling pressured by the sense of responsibility, and friends continued to express concern that failing to get a conviction would be a "stain" on my record. But I could not allow myself to dwell on the possible ramifications of failure. We were too busy ensuring the case got to trial.

Some of us in the prosecution had been lugging around a heavy burden for much of our lives about this case—an invisible anvil on our shoulders. This was an ongoing Alabama story, mine by inheritance. And my relationship with the families of the girls, especially Denise McNair's father, Chris, for over twenty-five years, and Carole Robertson's mother, Alpha—a generous and modest soul—elevated the professional imperative to an irresistible personal mission.

We would likely get one shot, both men facing a reckoning in a single trial, before time ran out and the details of the murders of four girls tumbled deeper into the archives. Age and ill health were threatening many witnesses, and the case remained largely circumstantial. But we had the precious kitchen tape, and our unwavering focus had to be to get the recording heard by a jury. It confirmed the story of the events around that terrible day we would reconstruct in intricate detail. We now had the glue to put all the pieces together and make the charges stick.

Meanwhile, the defense worked just as hard to keep the recording out of evidence as we did to get it in, leaning on the "exclusionary rule," which prevents the use of any evidence obtained in an illegal manner. Back in 1964, the recording device had been placed in Blanton's apartment by the FBI undercover man without any judicial approval because in those days there were no provisions for court-approved electronic surveillance as we have now. At the time, the FBI Director had the authority to authorize the use of electronic bugs, but only for intelligence gathering in the interest of national security, not for use in court. Klansmen, and for that matter civil rights leaders, were routinely bugged in those days. The law was changed in 1968 to require a court order for electronic surveillance. Material compiled with such judicial approval could potentially be used as evidence.

When the modern-day wiretap law was passed (in 1968) requiring court approval for any telephone wiretapping or electronic surveillance, it also provided for the exclusion of evidence if the required judicial go-ahead wasn't secured or if laws were broken during the taping process. In other words, for evidence obtained without court approval after 1968, the exclusionary rule regarding electronic surveillance was statutory law.

Over the decades, however, that rule was reshaped here and there by Supreme Court decisions. Crucially from our standpoint, the rule was tweaked to include exceptions for material seized in "good faith" or "inevitable discovery," circumstances allowing prosecutors to use evidence even if had been seized illegally. In crafting these exceptions, the Supreme Court reasoned that the purpose of the exclusionary rule was to deter law enforcement from illegally obtaining evidence in the future, rather than penalizing what had occurred in years past. In each case, the deterrence factor had to be weighed against the potential evidence's value in the "truth-seeking process."

In our case, we knew that the law that existed at the time the tape was made allowed the FBI to obtain electronic evidence regardless of its admissibility in court. That meant it was gathered in good faith. Basically, we were going to argue that the kitchen tape spoke the truth. We'd submit that it was too important to leave out of the trial and that it was recorded lawfully in 1964. Excluding the tape would provide no deterrent on law enforcement agents because their conduct was now judged by the 1968 law.

The judge planned to hold a hearing on the suppression motion just before jury selection. We scrambled to hone our submission while at the same time striving to make last-minute adjustments and improvements to our case against the old Klansmen. Our other focus was to construct a plan to secure a suitably open-minded jury.

The trial date, scheduled for the week beginning April 15, was closing in. Our preparation had been first-class, but I still wanted to satisfy myself that we had not missed something. Around the first of the year, I'd started taking home one of the many three-ring binders that contained the entire case file—material that was old, new, and everything in between. I would be up with a cup of coffee by 5:00 a.m. poring through FBI summaries of witness interviews. I knew I could not go back through every scrap of evidence, but at least I could review all of the witness interviews one more time. As I completed one binder, I'd pull another from the shelf.

It's Politics, Doug

One afternoon, while buried in planning our "down the final stretch" strategy, I got a call from Mark Calloway in North Carolina. I knew what it was about before he said a word.

The U.S. Attorney for the Western District of North Carolina, Calloway was pulling double duty as the Bush administration's grim reaper. Well, more accurately, as Director of the Executive Office of U.S. Attorneys, he was helping transition Clinton appointees out of office.

Calloway and I had worked closely together on the Eric Rudolph case in the wake of the fatal bombing at the Birmingham women's health clinic. The fugitive had lived in a mobile home in Calloway's district, and intense search efforts focused on the area. We had become good friends over the previous three years, but this exchange was all business.

John Ashcroft had been sworn in as AG on February 2, so the cleanout was on in earnest when I got the call several weeks later. Calloway tried to tread delicately—he was aware I was in the middle of fevered preparations for the trial. But his duty was to set up a rough timetable for my exit—or, at least, to get me considering it.

"We're thinking late March, maybe early April," he said.

I took a deep breath and reminded him the trial was scheduled to start the week of April 15. Calloway assured me there were no plans to take me off the case, suggesting that after I stepped down I could be appointed as a Special Assistant U.S. Attorney to see my duties through until the end of the prosecution process.

I'm pretty sure I didn't insult Calloway, but I was screamingly furious. "Let me get this straight," I said, trying my best not to shoot my friend the messenger. "These guys want to remove a presidentially appointed U.S. Attorney and relegate him to a Special Assistant U.S. Attorney just to make a political point?"

He hesitated. "That's about the size of it, Doug," he said.

The last thing I needed was any disruption to our preparation—stripping me of the title of U.S. Attorney before walking into court to prosecute one of the most significant trials in recent history didn't seem too damn supportive and would certainly impact our work. After all, the title carried weight, I pointed out. In a case so vital, it should be *the* U.S. Attorney talking to the defense, the witnesses, and the jury, not a specially appointed assistant or the like.

I understood the new Republican administration was anxious to put new appointments in place, but what they were doing seemed petty and deliberately intrusive. I had a larger than normal target on my back. I had already been approached about taking on a political role once the church bombing case was done. News travels fast, and in political circles, the talk was I might make a run for the Senate as a Democrat. Even though I had not seriously looked at political options, it made my exit from the U.S. Attorney's office a priority for some in the new Republican administration.

Whatever the administration's motivation, I simply did not need outside pressure at that time. While Calloway went off to talk to the powers in the Justice Department, I decided to cut to the chase and call the office of Alabama Senator Jeff Sessions to take the matter up with his Chief of Staff, Armand DeKeyser, a good guy and an accomplished behind-the-scenes operator.

"It's politics, Doug," he said. "And there is talk of you running."

I didn't have time to be delicate. While I knew it was likely that an arrangement would be made to ensure I stayed on the case even if I left the U.S. Attorney's office, the suggested timing of a change in my status couldn't have been worse, especially with Blanton's attorney Robbins still pushing for a continuance. There was also a very real possibility we'd have to seek to delay the start of the trial if we failed in our initial attempt to get the kitchen tape into evidence. We would file motion after motion if necessary to get that recording into court.

"Listen, Armand," I said. "I'm a big boy. I understand politics and I fully intend to resign. This is not about me, and it is not about politics. Jeff, of all people, should understand the significance of having the United States Attorney and not some assistant lead this prosecution. I'm giving you my word that within thirty days of this case concluding I'll leave office. But I'm telling you, if you force me out, I will not go quietly. I'll raise such a stink. I'll raise hell about this Attorney General, whose record on civil rights has already been questioned, trying to move this U.S. Attorney out for political reasons right in the middle of prosecuting one of the biggest civil rights cases the Department of Justice has ever had. I'm not going to go down quietly, and Armand, if I may say so, you need to help save the Republicans from themselves."

From that point on, I tried to waste as little time as possible on the matter. Fortunately, in the weeks that followed, I didn't get anything but well-wishes from the Senator's office and the Justice Department. Not a word about leaving office.

(I later learned that it was a GOP stalwart, Alabama Attorney General Bill Pryor, who came to my defense. He told Ashcroft, in front of a gathering of state AGs, that I had to stay on the Blanton and Cherry case, regardless of politics.)

I was relieved I could concentrate all my energy on the case in the mad scramble of the last weeks before trial. However, just as we were making our final preparations, we were blindsided by an issue that had the potential to be ruinous to our cause and impact the public perception of judicial probity in the South.

The Cherry Bombshell

We hadn't been privy to an ex parte motion filed by Cherry's defense some months earlier. It passed under our radar, as such proceedings—brought by one side without the involvement of the other—are often routinely initiated by court-appointed legal teams. It wasn't until another motion from Cherry's lawyers—this one seeking to dismiss the charges—that we came to understand what had been playing out without our knowledge.

The ex parte proceeding had prompted Judge Garrett to grant a request for funds to have Cherry's competency evaluated. The defense lawyers did not have to share this fact with us.

They organized medical evaluations, and when their experts came back with a finding that Cherry was not competent to stand trial, they duly filed the motion asking for the charges to be dismissed.

We were stunned. At no time in the presence of any prosecutor or investigator did Cherry appear to have any mental deficiencies, including when he was interviewed by Bob Eddy and Ben Herren for four hours in the summer of 1997 or when I met with him at his lawyer's office immediately before the indictment. Similarly, when intrepid reporter Jerry Mitchell interviewed Cherry, the Klansman seemed completely lucid and had stellar recall of events from decades before, including his attack on Reverend Shuttlesworth. However, two reputable experts had concluded Cherry was suffering from dementia and could not assist in his own defense.

Incompetence is not the same as an insanity defense, where a jury is asked to conclude whether the defendant knew right from wrong at the time of the crime. Cherry's defense was not alleging he was insane in 1963 and could not be held liable for the crime. Instead, his lawyers contended that in the intervening thirty-seven years, the now seventy-one-year-old had developed dementia to the point that he could not understand the proceedings or assist the defense.

In Alabama, once a defendant has raised the issue of incompetency and provided evidence (such as the assessment of experts) to back it up, the burden shifts to the prosecution to prove that he is indeed competent to stand trial. So when, at what was effectively the eleventh hour, the defense asked for a dismissal because of the onset of vascular dementia, the onus was on us to provide a counter in an attempt to get Cherry before a jury.

All the complaining in the world would not impact the situation. It was by no means checkmate, but there was little doubt we were cornered and had to change our tactics. Building a case to prove Cherry's competence and having him thoroughly evaluated by our experts would take time and pull our focus away from the trial. We therefore had no choice—convicting Cherry would have to wait. Blanton would be the sole defendant at the upcoming trial.

We dared not think about the likely public outcry when the news got out, but there was nothing to be done. With remarkable stealth, the prosecution team put aside the strong case we had against Cherry and focused all our attention on Blanton. The thought of delaying the Blanton case to try the pair together never crossed our minds.

On April 10, less than a week before the trial's scheduled start, we filed a motion to separate the cases so we could obtain our evaluation of Cherry. Judge Garrett accepted our petition and announced he was indefinitely delaying the old Klansman's trial.

The kind of raucous public reaction to the two men being granted bail after the indictments was not immediately repeated. Instead, with the trial so close, it was as if the city breathed a collective, despondent sigh. The snake had slithered away one more time. He was still in sight, but we had to concede we no longer had him where we wanted him.

Getting the kitchen tape into evidence had been the leading priority. But now, with self-incriminating Cherry on the sidelines and the largely zippered-mouth Blanton our sole focus, the recording was even more vital to our case.

Judge Garrett would make the decision on admissibility before trial, while the other vital issue for us, his ruling on whether publicity would prevent Blanton from getting a fair trial in Birmingham, wouldn't be made until after the jury pool assembly.

In submitting to Judge Garrett on the question of whether the tape should be allowed into evidence, both sides talked themselves to a standstill. The judge even heard from Blanton's ex-wife Jean, who was as unhelpful as usual for the most part, although she conceded it was her voice along with Blanton and a third person on the tape, thus nullifying any marriage privilege.

At one point after I had emphasized the national security angle to explain the good-faith presence of the agents when they planted the bug, Robbins mocked the notion that a bunch of Klansmen had been a threat to the nation. He opened the door for me to launch into a God and country speech before the judge: "What Mr. Robbins forgets is that in 1963 we were in the midst of the Cold War. The communist threat was thought to be everywhere. Many believed the Klan was being inspired by communists. Others believed it was the leaders of the civil rights movement who were the communists. And remember, just two months following this bombing the President of the United States was assassinated."

Neither side gave an inch on the tape admissibility. I suspect we all knew it would likely come down to what the judge thought when he listened to the recording himself.

Rather than playing the tape in open court and risking the type of prejudicial publicity that we had been straining to avoid, we asked the judge if we could play it to him in his chambers. He agreed, and both sides gathered for the pivotal moment when the judge, having heard us debate the tiniest details of the law and precedent, would witness Blanton's flagrant bomb references for himself.

Knowing the tape's contents, I focused on Judge Garrett as he donned headphones, listening intently as he took in the 1964 conversation between Blanton and Jean. Most of the attending attorneys listened along, flinching as Jean screeched and straining to decipher Blanton's drawl. None of it seemed to move the judge until Blanton said: "We were making the bomb." With that statement, Judge Garrett's demeanor changed ever so slightly. Having been sitting back taking in the other parts of the recording, wearing a good poker face, he immediately leaned forward, clasped his hands together, and bowed his head.

"It's in," I thought to myself. "No doubt, he is going to let it in."

In the Spotlight

The resilience and patience shown by Birmingham's African-American community were beyond remarkable. Despite having every reason to bubble over with anger at the plodding, stop-start nature of the justice process drawn out over more than thirty-seven years, they were biting their tongues, even now, as one of the men they firmly believed killed the girls looked to have evaded answering for his sins once again.

I could not have asked for more, but as the weather warmed in the weeks before the trial was to start, the potential problem of publicity about the case infecting the jury pool popped up again as media attention heated up. Historical features, television exposés, and, I'll admit, the occasional piece on the prosecution team—including a *Newsweek* story complete with a rather expansive photo of me standing between sculptures of growling police dogs—were all mentioned. We made a concerted effort to limit that sort of exposure as the trial drew near, but there was little we could do about the release of one of the best books ever about Birmingham, the South, and the civil rights movement.

Somewhat inconveniently, Diane McWhorter's superlative tome *Carry Me Home* was released in March 2001. Momentarily, at least, I thought all that pleading to the local African-American community not to "convict" the old Klansmen before their day in court was for nothing. A native of Birmingham, McWhorter, like anyone vaguely associated with the case, knew who did the bombing and didn't hesitate to lay it out in *Carry Me Home*. She had conducted extensive research for eighteen years and had interviewed everyone alive associated with the case.

When I heard in the media about the release of the book, I panicked. The timing was impeccable for her, not so much for us. I somehow got hold of her telephone number in New York and called, pleading with her to ask her publishers to hold the release for fear the undoubted publicity surrounding it just before the trial could add starch to the defense's contention that the accused couldn't get a fair trial in Birmingham.

Diane was certainly sympathetic. The story had been at the top of her mind for decades, and she told me that she broke down in tears when she heard news of the indictments. But as sympathetic as she was, there was no stopping the publication date.

Carry Me Home certainly made a splash on release, although it quickly became clear that as great as the book was (it would go on to win a Pulitzer Prize), its six-hundred-plus pages of exceptional, detailed historical material weren't likely to be consumed by a large portion of the potential jury pool before trial. More unnerving was the bright spotlight being shone on the case by local, national, and even international media. It was to be expected that such a key event in the civil rights era would be news, and we always tried to accommodate requests for interviews and information. After all, some of our best breakthroughs, especially with Cherry, had been obtained through the media or were the work of dedicated individuals such as Jerry Mitchell at the *Clarion-Ledger* in Jackson, Mississippi. But in the rundown to trial the less said by us, or anyone associated with the bombing case, the better.

Unfortunately, our silence only served to ratchet up the media's desire for the story, and we were besieged with requests for interviews. For the most part, we politely declined. But shaking the attention of a few outlets was difficult, especially when they were playing to my ego. *People* magazine, in particular, was indignant about my decision not to agree to a profile that would hit the newsstands just days before the trial. The editors there gave me a "don't you know who we are" lecture when I turned them down.

The CBS current affairs program *60 Minutes* shadowed me for a full day before explaining that they wanted to do a segment about me to run on the Sunday night before jury selection.

"You got to be kidding!" I said, both exasperated and disappointed. "We have a jury coming in the next day, and this kind of show could jeopardize everything we have worked for in keeping this case in Birmingham. I just can't take that chance. Besides, Judge Garrett would kick my ass if I let that happen."

The *Birmingham News* didn't have the reach or broad influence of other outlets, but it was on top of the case, and its stories had been informed and insightful. It was hard to turn down two of its finest reporters when it came to a pre-trial feature on the prosecution's case. Yet I had no choice. If any media outlet was going to be picked up by potential local jurors, it was the *News*.

Reporters Val Walton and Chanda Temple had covered the story from the beginning and had done their homework leading up to trial. They had tracked down some of the witnesses, who had obliged them with extensive interviews. Now they wanted my comments on what was to be a major feature piece to run on the Sunday before jury selection that would detail our case and expected testimony. I had gotten to know the reporters well. I liked them personally and respected them as professionals. Most importantly, I trusted them.

"Guys, this is really not something I need right now," I said, reminding them that change of venue motions would not be ruled on until the jury assembly got underway. Like Diane McWhorter, they were sympathetic but insisted that their editors wanted the story now. I understood they had a duty to their organization and like me were under pressure to do their job. But a major piece in the local paper appearing as the judge was contemplating whether media and community attention could influence the jury pool certainly wasn't going to get my cooperation and, if possible, had to be nipped in the bud.

"OK, go back and tell your editors this: We have had a great relationship and one that I would like to continue, but if this story runs you will be on your own during this trial. By that, I mean that I simply will not give any statements whatsoever, on the record or off, to the *News*. I'll talk to everyone else, but not you guys. On the other hand, if you hold off, I'll make sure we talk at the end of every day, and because the jury will be sequestered, I'll be able to lay out what is coming the next day. That way you still get your story, but it is better because you have a series of articles with exclusive information."

The Sunday article, or at least the planned detailed story, did not appear. I would later hold up my end of the bargain, feeding them exclusives each day.

While First Amendment purists might be outraged, the *News* made a decision that probably benefited the paper and the city over the longer term. Indeed, with the benefit of hindsight, I believe the publication probably held back so that jury selection would not be jeopardized. It was part of a community-wide effort for the greater good. Plus, the paper ensured it would have exclusive daily content.

The Jury

The jury system is not perfect, and there have been occasions when the decisions of trial juries have seemed completely out of touch with the facts of the case. Sadly, in the South, many of those sorts of miscarriages of justice were the work of all-white male juries standing in judgment of people of color. While that kind of blatant discrimination had greatly diminished by 2001, ensuring a jury made up of thoughtful people open to the truth wasn't as simple as selecting people of a particular racial makeup.

Preparing for the Blanton trial, my jury consultants Andy Sheldon and Steve Paterson launched an extraordinary effort to maximize our chances of minimizing jury mistakes.

Given that Birmingham was one of the most deeply religious cities in America, their recommendation was to impanel men and women who were regular church attendants—something the preacher's son, Jeff Wallace, had also suggested early in our preparations.

"You cannot pick a jury [in Jefferson County] without understanding the decisions they make about right and wrong come straight out of their religious teaching," Sheldon said, prompting an "amen" from Wallace. That tenet crosses racial and gender lines and indicates how uniquely challenging jury selection was in a city like Birmingham.

As a starting point, we put together two focus groups to get a snapshot of how the community felt about the case. We wanted to know people's concerns and prejudices, and generally what they expected or wanted in this racially tinged case from long ago. Assembling at the facilities of a marketing company in Hoover, just outside of Birmingham, the two groups were assigned separate conference rooms. Their discussions were moderated by Sheldon and Norma Silverstein, one of Steve Paterson's colleagues, while we monitored the process via one-way mirror.

In my zeal to keep leaks and information out of the media, we had each participant sign a confidentiality agreement. But I didn't want to take any chances, so I opted to disguise our intentions by also asking the participants about the Oklahoma City bombing and Eric Rudolph cases.

It's often startling, sometimes shocking, and occasionally humbling to listen to the views of diverse groups of people from our communities. In equal measure, you end up gaining insight into why our democracy works and wondering how it survives.

Viewpoints are often delivered with conviction, even when they sometimes have little relation to facts. That's when it's especially important to have a wise voice in the room—a whispered truth usually trumps a screaming lie. Moreover, relying on preconceived notions of what a person of a particular race or religion might say or believe is a mistake of the first order.

In one of the groups, a young black woman said she was surprised that white men had been charged with the 16th Street Church killings, as she had always heard that the bomb had to have been planted by blacks "because a white man couldn't get near that church at night." In another case, an elderly African-American lady verbally launched into a young black woman who was querying whether it was "all that bad" under segregation. The older woman unleashed on the youngster with a history lecture and reality check that wasn't lost on anyone in earshot. A major lesson for the team was that race might be a very misleading indicator of jury suitability.

We also did a comprehensive community attitude survey, which was Sheldon's fancy term for a telephone poll. But this poll did have teeth. In an extensive effort to try and match the demographics for our expected jury pool, we quizzed participants about their views on race relations, the Klan, and racial progress in the city of Birmingham.

One somewhat startling result leaped out and completely floored some members of our team. The vast majority, nearly eighty-five percent, of Caucasian Jefferson County citizens supported an integrated society, including integrated schools, and agreed the Jim Crow South had been intended to segregate society forever. I still remind myself of that finding when evaluating the potential in Alabama to realize the dreams of leaders such as Martin Luther King.

The data collected was critical in preparing a hundred-question survey for the eventual jury pool, which ultimately numbered one hundred men and women. Sheldon asked directly about sensitive issues, from attitudes about the Martin Luther King holiday to interracial dating and church attendance. The selection process took place in the basement courtroom of the Criminal Justice Center and lasted six days. It was an anonymous jury. No one's name was ever called out.

Moreover, unlike other public trials, the voir dire, or jury questioning process, was not done in open court in front of the jury pool. Instead, each person was questioned individually behind closed doors with only the judge, the lawyers, their research teams, and the defendant present. We did so to prevent the possibility that someone might say something in open court that would taint the entire panel, potentially delaying the trial.

It was a relatively straightforward process. We came in on Monday morning. Judge Garrett asked a few general, qualifying questions and then handed out the questionnaire sanctioned by both the prosecution and the defense. The participants would be allowed to leave after completing the form and were instructed to return Wednesday morning. We scrambled to get all the completed questionnaires copied for us, the defense, and the court.

We did our analysis over that day and a half—assigning each potential juror a score based on their answers. On Wednesday morning, we began questioning each of them, exploring their backgrounds and discussing their answers. By Friday, we had enough suitable candidates to make our selection. Judge Garrett let us think about it over the weekend.

It's called jury selection, but the term is misleading because neither party gets to select the jurors they want. Instead, it is a process of elimination, with each side striking people they do not want. On Sunday, the night before the final selection process got underway, I decided to engage in an exercise to better evaluate our choices.

Judge Garrett had said that each side would get sixteen strikes, meaning we would be striking from a pool of about forty-four. I made strikes based on what I perceived to be the priorities of both sides and ended up with seven selections—all women. Ultimately six of my final seven would be seated as jurors. I would have batted seven for seven, but John Robbins was to discover something about one of the women that made her ineligible.

When the real business of jury selection got underway, it followed the pattern I predicted. Before announcing our strikes, Judge Garrett granted Robbins's request to call back one black female for additional questioning. She had answered all questions truthfully, including whether she had participated in the civil rights movement or the children's marches.

She had not, but with a little prodding, Robbins established she was the daughter of Autherine Lucy, the first black to integrate a university in the state of Alabama, in 1956. After just a few days the University's Board of Trustees expelled her, saying it was for her own safety, but Lucy's milestone would lead to the Wallace fiasco of standing on the doorsteps of Foster

Auditorium seven years later. It was an easy decision for Judge Garrett to remove the young woman from the preliminary panel.

Due to our research, my team was fairly unified in both our approach and assessment of the jury pool. The easiest to rule out were those whose answers indicated a possible lack of racial tolerance, although that didn't necessarily equate with whether they were black or white, male or female, young or old. Nevertheless, when final choices were made, it did appear that jurors were struck or preserved along racial lines. We eliminated ten white men and six white women. The defense used twelve of their sixteen strikes to eliminate blacks.

Based on our research, we wanted jurors, black or white, who were churchgoers and parents, individuals who could relate to the desecration of a church and the death of a child. However, citing Supreme Court decisions from 1986 and 1994 that prohibited the elimination of jurors based on race or sex, Robbins filed an objection alleging that those we had struck were all white men. He asked that the court overrule some strikes and put them back on the jury.

Judge Garrett listened to our arguments. I told him that we had struck jurors because we didn't think they could make a fair decision. Several we marked out because of our fear of their racial biases, including one white man whose grandfather had been a police officer for Bull Connor at the time the bombing occurred, when many on the force were known Klan sympathizers. Another I did not believe had truthfully explained the symbolism of his tattoos. We addressed our reasons for striking each juror, outlining how each decision had nothing to do with race or sex. Fortunately, the judge ruled we had provided race-neutral reasons for our selections. The jury was set: eleven women, eight white and three black, and one black man would decide Tommy Blanton's fate. Assessing the jury pool to be relatively free of undue influence from publicity and the history surrounding the case, the judge had waved off the motions to move or abandon the trial.

We had a jury that met our criteria. There would be no getting ahead of ourselves, however, as Sheldon, a man with as much experience as anyone with old civil rights cases, reminded us that winning would be "a miracle."

In my mind, it was a relief simply to get to the point where we could finally get underway. Sure, scores of potential witnesses were on their last legs, and the Cherry competency curveball had been a doozy, but that issue was out of our hands for the moment. We could only take on what was in front of us.

My old friend John Robbins had one more pre-trial surprise in store for me. As we left the judge's chambers for the day after the jury had been settled and final administrative details agreed upon, he asked me to hang back for a moment. Everyone departed, including the judge. Robbins closed the door, and there was just the two of us.

"Listen," he said quietly, "you know I am going to try the hell out of this case, but we both have a pretty good idea of how it will turn out."

He paused for a moment. I was about to tell him that no one on the prosecution team was taking anything for granted, but before I could get anything out, he said: "I just want you to know that we are all proud of you."

We both knew we were about to engage in a pretty fierce battle, but the bonds of friendship and respect could not be trumped by adversarial lines of litigation. It was a moment I will always treasure.

The prosecution's task was to help the jury somehow experience the incident as well as stand in judgment of a story about it decades later. We had no direct evidence of the weapon used and few surviving witnesses. Our case would be won or lost by the way we pieced the story together for the jury, making it inclusive and relatable.

We had one final meeting of the prosecution team before the trial. Andy Sheldon remembers it vividly. "Jeff Wallace is a devoutly religious man," Sheldon said. "And he felt strongly that there were indeed five victims, the four little girls and a house of the Lord that had been desecrated."

The son of a Methodist minister, Wallace knew the jurors would feel an obligation to not only establish who killed the children but identify those responsible for attacking the other victim, the church. Later we would learn that every morning before the trial began, the jury would pray for discernment. Indeed, we all whispered prayers before the Blanton trial finally got underway on April 24, 2001, in the old courtroom.

The Blanton Opening

Just before jury selection had got underway, I'd taken a room at the Tutwiler Hotel, right across the street from the courthouse, to ensure I could structure my days effectively. I had always tried to separate the job and my personal life, but that line didn't exist as clearly in this case. Despite juggling a six-year-old, a three-year-old, and a teenager at home largely on her own, Louise completely understood my need for detachment during the trial.

On occasion, in the past, I had a tendency to get too consumed by work.

When working into the night, it was hard to shut down. Then, when I did get to sleep, my mind would kick-start again at 4:00 a.m., and that would be the beginning of the day. The workload was so immense with the bombing case I would have never slept if I'd adopted that kind of routine, so I drew up a few rules to follow.

The first was not to read or watch any of the media coverage about the trial. We were constructing a story, piece by piece. The media would be looking for fireworks. I did not want to lose sleep about how it was being perceived or painted by others. Certainly, I didn't want it influencing our approach to trying the case.

Second, I had to adhere to a daily routine. We would wrap up each day, discuss the plans for the next day, have a decent meal and maybe a couple of glasses of wine, and retire early.

In the solitude of my room, I'd review my part of the next day's proceedings. The key was to have the discipline to get it all done at a reasonable hour so that I could get my mind in a completely different place and, with the help of a little sleep aid, drift off for a full seven hours.

The opening day of proceedings is a bit of a blur now, but I remember wanting to be by myself that morning before delivering the opening statement, running through the things I planned to say and the way I wanted to say them.

Before we got underway, I peeked in more than once at the old courtroom. Even on the brightest spring day, it's dark and serene in there. The Jefferson County Courthouse housing the civil courts and county officers is a grand art deco building built in 1931, designed by the same firm that conceived Chicago's imposing Soldier Field. It is a bold granite and limestone building decorated with murals depicting the old South's link with agriculture, including a white woman overseeing black workers in a field, and the new South's marriage to heavy industry.

The presiding judge's courtroom is the handsome heart of the complex. There is nothing trivial about the space; it's all business, with heavy wood walls, polished timber, and leather fittings. Rarely used for major trials these days, it was deemed appropriate for the Blanton trial because it could accommodate a larger-than-normal number of spectators.

In 2001 it had changed little since the days twenty-four years before when Bill Baxley made the space his. The jury box was at that time on the opposite side of its present location to the left of the judge, but otherwise it was possible to recall effortlessly where all the players in the Chambliss trial had been located.

This, like no other trial I'd been involved in, required making a connection to the jury, taking them on a historical journey, so they understood the importance and context of what had been going on in our city decades ago. It was necessary, however, to transcend the history lesson, to imbue the proceedings with spirit, humanity, and an unmistakable awareness that we were talking about more than just events from the past. It was about real people: children.

If someone like that young woman who doubted it was so bad under Jim Crow and segregation was watching somewhere, I wanted her to gain a visceral understanding of what it was like on September 15, 1963—how that insufferable pain was still with the victims' families and, in a broader sense, the entire community.

This was a time for confidence, pride, and conviction, to piece together the story for the jury without missing a detail or leaving room for misinterpretation or uncertainty. Our case was largely circumstantial, but there was no doubt all the pieces fit. There was no doubt who murdered those girls, and there was no doubt he was among us.

The first thing I did when I walked into the courtroom—and I think it was involuntary—was to look up at the balcony. It was where I had watched nearly every day of the Baxley trial and saw brilliant lawyering, recognized the grand possibilities of the law, and witnessed the moral arc of the universe bending toward justice.

This time, it was crowded with media for Blanton. My colleagues from the U.S. Attorney's office were there, and many of the judges who presided in the building had taken time out to watch. Old and current investigators flanked religious leaders and businesspeople.

In the pew behind me, in the very first row, I glimpsed the families: Mrs. Robertson; Carole's sister Dianne Braddock; the McNairs; two of the Collins sisters, Junie and Janie; and Dr. Shirley King, the girl who "replaced" Cynthia as a foster child in the Wesley household and went on to a brilliant career—perhaps the kind of life of professional achievement Cynthia Morris Wesley might have enjoyed if the Klansmen hadn't taken her life.

I felt briefly overwhelmed: Oh my God, I am here, at this time, and these people are relying on me.

I looked around the court again and up to the balcony.

I thought of the girls. I would never know them but felt such a kinship.

I thought of Baxley and his personal commitment to ensuring that justice was done regardless of the political consequences.

We were all in place, finally. Any trepidation disappeared, and a weighty burden seemed to leave me. It was my time. Judge Garrett gave me my cue.

. . . Ladies and Gentlemen,

I said, addressing the jury,

It's been a long time. Thirty-seven, almost thirty-eight years. What we are here today about is a crime that was committed a long time ago—an explosion here in Birmingham in September of 1963.

My goal was to ensure the jury members didn't immediately drift into looking at the case as a piece of history. I wanted them to be arrested by the enduring discomfort it caused. The jury had been sequestered, meaning they'd miss their families, so I decided to use that inconvenience to help them tap into the sense of the ongoing pain for the victims' families.

I want to tell you I know you have gone through an interesting four or five days sitting on hard benches outside while lawyers are huddled with the judge. We know that was a sacrifice. The state and the defense appreciate that. We also appreciate the fact that for the next couple of weeks you're going to be sequestered from your families. Another major sacrifice. But in a sense, ladies and gentlemen, this whole case is about sequestration because for thirty-seven years the families of four little girls have been sequestered from their loved ones.

To personalize the bombing, I used before and after images of the church and photos of the girls, each with an innocent face, displayed on monitors around the courtroom. I wanted to ensure the jury was aware that the girls were doing nothing other than what people still do today on Sunday mornings in Birmingham—attending church, which itself was a victim of the horror.

The church as you see there stands today as a monument, I think, to those young girls. It's reconstructed. Built back, brick by brick . . .

And who were they? Denise McNair was the youngest of the four girls. The daughter of Chris and Maxine McNair, who will testify in this case. Denise was eleven years old at the time. She had gone to church that morning, again, preparing for the youth service. Denise was eleven. Then there was Addie Mae Collins. Her sister Junie will also testify. And another sister, Sarah, was also with them. And we'll talk about Sarah in a moment because Sarah was really a sole survivor of this terrible, terrible tragedy. Addie Mae was fourteen at the time. She was born on April the eighteenth. Last Thursday she would have been fifty-one years old.

Cynthia Wesley. Cynthia Wesley was also fourteen at the time. Her stepsister, adopted sister, Dr. Shirley Wesley King, is here from Texas and will testify. She was in the basement that morning also. Cynthia Wesley was born on April 30, 1949. Next Monday she will be fifty-one. Would have been fifty-one years old. And finally Carole Robertson. Carole Robertson's mom, Mrs. Alpha Robertson, is here and prepared to testify. Her sister Diane Braddock from Maryland is here. Carole Robertson would have been fifty-one years old . . . today.

But we're not here to celebrate birthdays, unfortunately. And no children or grandchildren. We are here because . . . Thomas Edwin Blanton, Junior, was one of those responsible for planting a bomb or placing a bomb outside the church that destroyed that church.

Breathing life into a historical recount was the aim. Once it became "real" for the jury, I gave them the context—the intensity of the segregation dispute and how the Klan reacted as it does to most things, with violence—noting, however, that this time was different, more extreme.

. . . What is important about 1963 was not just the political and social changes. Because in a bitter sense 1963 in Birmingham was about killing . . .

I needed to assert, with complete conviction, that there was nothing accidental about the process. In my mind, I thought back to my exchange with Reverend Woods when Blanton was released on bond. I wanted to be emphatic.

Whoever, I submit, planted that bomb knew that this was going to be a youth service. That is a reasonable inference that . . . you'll be able to draw from the evidence. The church was a target. The youth were a target. The people that perpetrated this terrible tragedy knew exactly where they were going and who they wanted to kill. An explosion of this magnitude is inescapable.

Before the days that the word "terrorism" came into our vocabulary, this was an act of terrorism.

I illustrated my point with a photo montage.

Cars that were parked on the street were damaged. From inside you can see the force of that explosion. The steps leading down. The rubble.

That's where the four little girls were. They were in that room. Sarah Collins is standing at that sink. She had turned her back as her sister Addie was turning to Denise McNair's side. The sanctuary was damaged. The big stained-glass window of Jesus in a somewhat ironic twist has the face blown off.

Now, how is Thomas Blanton connected in this case? We believe the evidence will show you—will demonstrate—he didn't like what was happening in Birmingham. He didn't like to see what was going on in the city and around this country.

And there was a group of men that decided to meet. And they met not out in the bright sunshine where everybody can see them. They got underneath a bridge out on Highway 280. In 1963 that was the main bridge spanning the Cahaba River. And these men would meet underneath that bridge in the darkness to talk about what had to be done in Birmingham.

I went on to list the litany of witnesses who would connect Blanton to the crime and stated again, in no uncertain terms, that 1963 was "about killing" and making the children and the church specific targets.

It went by in a blur. I hoped I'd achieved a major goal of any opening, to lay out very precisely and forcefully what we *knew* to be true, but in a sense, that would look after itself as the trial went on. I knew we could piece it all together for the jury—my job, in detailing this cold case, was to compel them to want to be part of that process.

The Klan, the trolls under the bridge, segregation, the killing of children—it was shocking, maybe too horrendous to contemplate, but there was a moment I believe I felt a connection was made. When I mentioned it was Carole Robertson's birthday on that very day, you could hear and somehow feel the jury react. Birthdays are the link between past and present for all families. I knew the good people who had been sequestered to the task all immediately thought of their children and grandchildren when I referred to Carole.

I believed I had them, by God. And I would not, under any circumstances, lose them.

EIGHT

BLANTON

A lthough I had opted against rehearsing my opening, preferring to leave room for improvisation, I had a clear idea of the points I wanted to hit before I broke the nervous silence in the old courtroom that first morning.

Andy Sheldon had helped me "choreograph" the speech, matching key points with visual aids, including photographs of the scene before and after the devastation and snaps of the girls radiating innocence.

Our case was largely circumstantial, so it was necessary from the start to relate the most complete, compelling story about the bombing rather than immediately zeroing in on the specifics of Blanton's involvement. In this uniquely challenging presentation, we had to draw on a series of facts rather than lean on one large overriding truth—it was a puzzle that needed artful reconstruction.

I didn't want the glue that held the pieces together to show. The use of visual evidence assisted in making the story more seamless, complete, and helped transport the jury back in time to a city that was a far cry from the present.

It is also easier to follow stories where you understand something about the people and places involved and can track the development of the tale chronologically. So it was important to set the scene—to ensure that the sense of the civil rights push of the time, and the Klan's related desperation, was at the center of the story.

Witnesses we called not only brought evidence of a murderous act; most, in some way, represented a piece of that larger story: that the KKK, and specifically Blanton, a willful, violent man, acted out a plan against the church and the black community that was designed to terrorize by taking innocent lives.

Sheldon and I had sequenced the photographs to give a virtual tour of the bombing scene, a kind of before and after montage, starting outside before moving into the church sanctuary.

Next came the scenes of devastation in the streets around the church—mangled cars, damaged nearby buildings—and then back to the area from where the blast emanated, including the shell of the ladies' lounge.

In a pattern we'd replicate throughout the trial, we followed those scenes and explanations of the damage inflicted by connecting with the broad emotional impact—the loss of the girls and their families' grief—before turning our attention to the intricacies of the evidence against Blanton.

Believing I had successfully engaged the jury's attention at the moment I talked about Carole's birthday, I hoped the defense would be starting on the back foot. I understood my former colleague and the defense lead, John Robbins, would recognize the prosecution's challenge was to create a coherent and believable chain for the jury that connected Blanton to the bombing. His task—the only sensible ploy—would be to chip away at the chain to create a weak link in order to introduce doubt in the juror's mind. After all, to gain an acquittal, it is not necessary to prove that a defendant is innocent. Reasonable doubt in the juror's mind is enough.

It was no surprise that Robbins attempted to malign the depth of our circumstantial case in his opening while painting Blanton as a victim of community anger over the bombing.

"You're not going to like Tom Blanton," he told the jury, laying his cards on the table. "He was annoying as hell." But, Robbins said, the fact that Blanton was an unappealing bigot did not make him a murderer.

"It's not about closure," he said, suggesting his client was taking the fall for the bombing because the prosecution was milking community sentiment.

Indeed, we studiously avoided any reference to closure throughout the trial, talking instead about finally obtaining justice for the victims and their families.

The openings had reinforced my confidence that we had compiled a case that was good enough to win the desired verdict. As is usual for prosecutors, I was more worried about the possibility of the defense producing something unexpected or a hung jury.

I knew Blanton had sympathizers out there, not the least being a significant number of former law enforcement officers. We had witnessed that when we spent time and effort investigating and dismissing "evidence" in an old jail that someone had told the defense would exonerate the old Klansman. I had no way of knowing whether the defense had tapped into that network.

The age of many of the witnesses was another worrying issue. Our grand jury witness room had been like a geriatric ward, and a few old and ill folks would testify at trial. Well intentioned or otherwise, some elderly people on the stand could potentially make inconsistent statements or get confused.

Additionally, in the absence of several key individuals, such as Baxley witnesses Kirthus Glenn and Elizabeth Cobbs, who had passed away, we were relying significantly on the various FBI tape recordings to provide some of the starch for our case.

While Judge Garrett had allowed the tapes into evidence, I remained concerned the recordings might be suppressed at the last minute. We fully intended to play a number of excerpts from the Mitch Burns tapes and the recording of the Blantons in their kitchen more than once (if possible) for the jury, so the structure of our presentation would be significantly altered if they were omitted by a late ruling.

Overall, though, I knew we could reconstruct the truth of the bombing in a meaningful way for the court. When it came down to it, my biggest fear was that a wild-card juror could be a holdout. I thought we had done more than enough to get the jury we wanted, but in the end, you just don't know.

First Witnesses

The prosecution team would share the duty of questioning witnesses. Posey, Wallace, and I spread ourselves across a table close to the jury box, while our technical guy, Bill Smith, and my clerk, Robin Beardsley, were right behind. Our media and communications assistant, Amy Gallimore, and jury expert Andy Sheldon were always in the vicinity, while witness coordinators Geri O'Byrne and Susan Banks held fort back in the war room.

The first witness was Reverend Cross, who had not only made the ghastly discovery of the girls' bodies in the ladies' lounge, "stacked . . . as if they were clung together after the bombing," but as the former pastor of 16th Street, he would detail for the jury how central the church was to civil rights movement activity in 1963.

It was difficult to watch Reverend Cross. He was not in great health and struggled to deal with what he perceived to be his responsibility for making 16th Street a "target." But his personal grief graphically illustrated the kind of issues that were unique to the time.

As Jeff Wallace had insisted, the church itself, depicted in before and after photographs that we introduced into evidence as Government Exhibits one and two, was also a victim of the attack. Reverend Cross articulated the church's role in Birmingham life, before the bombing and in its wake, emphasizing its status as an enduring symbol of hope for African Americans.

Next up, Alpha Robertson. Using a cane, Carole's mother made her way to a seat on the witness stand, only feet away from the jury.

It was April 24: Carole's birthday.

Mrs. Robertson was warm, caring, and hurt beyond words by the loss of the child she sent off to the safety of church in a dazzlingly white dress and polished black shoes. Her pain was not a memory, but still raw; her loss, a calamity.

Alpha's husband, Alvin, had driven Carole to the church early to prepare for her participation in the Youth Worship Service. Mrs. Robertson was at home not far away putting the finishing touches on her Sunday wardrobe when she heard the explosion. "It sounded like the whole world was shaking," she said softly. Robertson's personal loss was conspicuous, even after nearly thirty-eight years. At one stage I incorrectly stated how old her daughter would have been that day, and she immediately set me straight. She helped dispel the mythical quality that sometimes attaches itself to cases of such vintage, reminding everyone that the case was about the victims, not history.

Maxine McNair was beyond despairing. Denise's mother was literally in pain as she recalled the bomb scene. She had separated from her daughter once inside the church, Denise heading downstairs and Mrs. McNair to her Sunday School class meeting in the choir loft, located almost directly over the ladies' lounge. Her recollection of what she said after the bomb exploded: "My baby! My baby!" was more informative than a thousand words to a jury.

As Diane McWhorter noted in a later edition of her book, proceedings unfurled in an atmosphere of "camaraderie" between attorneys from both sides and the accommodating Judge Garrett. While my familiarity with Robbins might have helped in that regard, it was also out of mutual respect for the families who had endured so much for so long and sat only a few feet from where we discussed the gritty details of their children's murders.

Blanton just looked irritable. A veneer of incredulity would occasionally wash across him when accusations were made about his behavior, but he seemed emotionally detached for the most part. Unlike the boisterous cockiness he displayed in his youth, he was quiet and unassuming in old age. He would have blended into any crowd.

We rounded out what I called the "family phase" of the trial by calling Junie Collins-Peavey, the sister of Addie Mae Collins. Junie was counting the Sunday School offering on the other side of the basement when the bomb exploded. She later had to identify Addie Mae's body at the hospital morgue.

We also called Dr. Shirley Wesley King, the Texas psychologist who had been adopted by the Wesley family following Cynthia's death. Shirley King never met Cynthia Wesley, but without objection in court she was allowed to talk briefly about the Wesley family. Introducing the families ensured the jury could connect contemporary faces with the pain caused by this depraved act from so many decades ago.

We were primed now to visit the scene of the horror, to inspect the scenes of devastation at the church created by a powerful and deadly force.

The Bomb

A potential loose end in our case was dispelling any doubt that a bomb caused the explosion. There was no physical evidence to prove absolutely that this was the case, so we had to be meticulous in presenting a scientific explanation to the jury.

To help the jury visualize the moment we brought in two eyewitnesses, Willie Byrd and Earline Tankersley, to detail the scene: shattered windows, mangled cars, structural devastation to the church and other buildings, and dust and debris everywhere.

To explain the cause of such mayhem, we called multiple experts, including local fire and utility authorities, who emphatically dismissed the possibility of a gas leak or any other source of detonation.

It was believed that dynamite, or TNT, was the explosive material used, even though in 1963 FBI lab tests of the debris could not affirmatively make that determination. However, with several manufacturing plants in the Birmingham area, dynamite was easy to obtain and was documented to be the explosive of choice for the Klan.

An ignition device was not found, despite statements in investigative documents about the existence of fishing line and a bobber that many speculated was used to fashion a drip detonator. With the absence of physical evidence, we needed to demonstrate that nothing other than a dynamite explosion could have caused the carnage. Assistant U.S. Attorney Posey prepared and coordinated that presentation.

"We talked about how to prove it, so I went to Quantico at the FBI lab with the crime scene photographs," he said. "It was explained to us that a gas leak acts like a fireball and not like a shock wave like the detonation of dynamite.

"The debris that landed on the automobiles outside the church looked like crumpled paper, exactly what you would have with a bomb. Also, the windows that imploded in the buildings adjacent to the church also clearly, in the experts' opinion, demonstrated that it was some type of dynamite explosion."

FBI Special Agent Charles Killion, an explosives expert, testified that he was dispatched to Birmingham immediately upon receiving word of the blast. He coordinated the gathering of debris for testing and assessed the crater measuring five and a half feet across and two and a quarter feet deep created at the spot where the bomb exploded.

"There was extensive damage to the ladies' lounge," he told the court, describing the incident as "a high order explosion" consistent with a bomb.

To further demonstrate the point, FBI techs carried out an experiment, detonating ten pounds of TNT in an area littered with old cars. After the explosion, the damage to the vehicles looked very similar to the impact of the church bombing.

The FBI videoed the explosion, and we fought to get it into evidence. The defense objected vigorously, but Judge Garrett gave us the go-ahead as long as the vision was shown in real time (no slow-motion) and the audio muted. FBI tech Mark Whitworth explained the experiment to the jury.

Posey's meticulous presentation of evidence and questioning of witnesses, together with the video, helped put what could have been a tricky issue for the prosecution to bed.

The stage was set to home in on Blanton.

In his opening Robbins had skillfully prepped the jury, conceding the old Klansman was not going to win their favor as a personality. Our task was to take it a step further and go beyond evidence of his loathsome character as a Klansman, to reveal a person more than willing to commit this terrible crime. As I explained to a very nervous Waylene Vaughn during our meeting in south Alabama, we needed her to recount her firsthand dealings with Blanton to paint a picture of how easily inclined he was to extreme violence, especially against African Americans.

We felt very protective of Ms. Vaughn. From the moment I met her, I could tell she was a fundamentally good person. I doubt she'd had much luck in life, but she was an honest individual, a military veteran who didn't want to run from the mistakes of her past anymore.

We had not given her any notice that we were coming when Bill Fleming and I approached her small mobile home in rural south Alabama. She was standing on her porch when I introduced myself.

"Hello Ms. Vaughn, I'm Doug Jones. I'm the United States Attorney in Birmingham."

"Hello Mr. Jones," she said with a hint of a smile. "I have been expecting you."

In her heart, I believe she knew her association with Blanton was a mistake that would never really fade away.

She was ashamed and afraid, and had been reluctant to cooperate for fear of reviving memories of things she'd been desperately trying to forget.

However, she fought through it, bravely agreeing to appear at trial. We tried our best to support her, but nothing could alleviate the terror she felt about what the KKK and Blanton might still be capable of doing to her.

We were more worried about what the defense would definitely do to her—attack her character to try to undermine her testimony.

Jeff Wallace handled the questioning. For her day in the hot seat, Vaughn had donned a suit coat and wore her best stoic look. She could not, however, conceal her anxiety. Only a few feet away, the glum and puffy Blanton, once a well-muscled young man who sported a shock of black hair, sat glaring at the woman he courted at the same time he maintained a relationship with Jean Casey.

Vaughn recounted Blanton's penchant for attacking African Americans, trying to run one man down while declaring a desire to kill "black bastards" and using an acid-like substance on Klan targets, once prompting a group of them to give chase in a car. When they caught up with Blanton and Vaughn, the Klansman waved a gun out his car window, scattering his pursuers.

Vaughn, being a woman with a military background, presented her evidence in a forthright manner. She had an air of trustworthiness as she passed on her observations without embellishment about Blanton's occasional references to dynamite and comments about blacks, including "they should kill more of them" in response to newspaper reports about bombings.

She detailed having been with Blanton on the night of Friday,

September 13, on a date at a drive-in theater. He dropped her at her home after midnight.

We had prepped her about the likelihood the defense would vigorously question why she had been in a relationship with Blanton, but as soon as Robbins started the cross-examination, I wished I'd been more explicit. He didn't hold back, focusing on the salaciousness of their relationship and inferring she shared the Klan's racist views.

"You didn't find the Klan sexy?" he asked.

She dismissed the accusation, but Robbins went after her, getting her to confirm she would "shack up" with Blanton in hotel rooms.

"You dislike what he stands for, but you didn't dislike him enough not to go to some hotel room during this time and perform oral sex on him, did you?"

I fidgeted in my chair, feeling Ms. Vaughn's pain but also recognizing that my former partner was doing what he had to do, and doing a good job of it at that.

Vaughn held firm: "That's correct."

The prospect of Blanton's retribution worried her, even almost a lifetime later, but her resolve to be truthful, no matter the cost, was unmistakable in that answer. I suspect, in fact, Robbins's approach may have backfired. Having been humiliated, she came across as sympathetic, as she refused to cower in the face of the ugly facts and a dastardly defendant.

I was inwardly elated with her testimony. It was a job well done, and, just as importantly, Waylene Vaughn seemed to be on her way to exorcising a beast.

We had reason to feel good about our progress and were yet to unveil the tape evidence I hoped would propel us toward a conviction. However, the perplexing Mr. James Lay was again the focus of our angst, this time through no fault of his own.

A massive stroke had taken him to the brink of death just weeks before trial.

Ill and Elderly

Lay, the former postal worker who had seen suspicious activity around the church two weeks before the bombing, was confined to a nursing home in nearby Bessemer after his stroke. Bill Fleming and I visited, expecting the worst. And got it.

Making our way through the ward to Lay was unsettling. There were no luxuries and few comforts for these patients, many spending their last days in bare-bones surroundings where the misery was palpable. At the former postal officer's bedside, we established he knew what was going on around him and had the desire to communicate, although his speech was significantly slurred and he was partially paralyzed.

Lay's testimony to the grand jury had been so impactful, I was prepared to push the envelope to see if we could somehow arrange to get him into the witness box again. I wanted the jury to see him, even if they could not hear him.

During our visit, Lay, for the most part, squeezed my hand to answer yes or no to questions. When I asked him, as Baxley had a quarter century before, whether he was willing to testify, the sick old man with little time left on earth nodded his head. His doctor and nurses confirmed that they thought he could handle it.

Our plan was to transport Lay to the courtroom via ambulance. Once he was there I would read him both the questions and answers, which he had given under oath, from his grand jury testimony. Following each answer, I would ask if the testimony was true and he would nod affirmatively. Cross-examination would be difficult.

As I was preparing to bring one very debilitated witness to court, the tyranny of time asserted itself again with news that retired FBI sleuth Frank Spencer, one of the original agents on the case, was in intensive care.

Spencer's daughter was driving him from his home in Tampa to Birmingham for his court day when he fell ill. He ended up in the ICU in Montgomery, ninety miles from Birmingham, with a cardiac problem.

Agent Spencer had interrogated Blanton just two weeks after the bombing. In the initial interview, the Klansman claimed he had been out with girlfriend Jean Casey on Saturday night, September 14, but could not recall where they had gone or what they had done. But he vividly recalled that he had her home by midnight, the seventeen-year-old's curfew, and then had gone directly home to bed.

Spencer, though, told Blanton they had a witness (Kirthus Glenn) who put his car at the church around 2:00 a.m., which provided plenty of time for him to round up his buddies and plant the bomb. The cocky Klansman immediately ended the interview, left the FBI office, and called Jean. Together they "remembered" exactly where they had been that night.

The happy couple now recalled going to Ed Salem's Drive-In, one of the area's most popular hangouts, which could have come straight out of the

TV show *Happy Days*, and then went parking near Birmingham's iconic statue of Vulcan, perched high above the town.

Once he got Jean home, Blanton said, rather than heading to his house and bed, he had fallen asleep on his teen girlfriend's sofa. He and Jean now agreed he didn't leave until after 2:30 in the morning, clear of the time his car was sighted at the church.

Through thick and thin, marriage and divorce, they had stuck to that revised story. Blanton's purported faulty memory in his interview with Agent Spencer just two weeks after the bombing, and his miraculous recollection of all of Saturday night's details after conferring with his sweetie, was an important piece of our puzzle, as guilt could be inferred.

It also served to help dismantle Jean's credibility as his alibi, since on the kitchen tape she admits to lying to the FBI. Agent Spencer himself was critical because all other agents who had participated in that interview were deceased. He was the only witness able to deliver the evidence to the jury.

As we scrambled to rearrange our witness schedule and investigate whether we would have to abandon calling Spencer, it became apparent that bringing Lay into court could be a fatal move for him.

I was buoyed by his commitment to testifying, but it just wouldn't be in his best interests. I also realized that in his current condition it would be impossible to reproduce the impactful testimony he gave to the grand jury.

I went to Blanton's attorney Robbins with a proposal to allow the testimony to be read by a "surrogate" for Lay in exchange for a cross-examination about the Lay evidence that Robbins wouldn't otherwise be able to do with Bill Fleming.

The surrogate would read Lay's answers from the transcript of his time before the grand jury.

It was pretty much a no-brainer for the Robbins team as legally we would have the upper hand in any challenge to get the evidence in, by whatever method. What's more, vigorously attacking the credibility of a stroke-stricken prosecution witness would likely have backfired more than the cross of Waylene Vaughn.

Also, with Fleming in the hot seat, Robbins could go further in his questioning than he could have if Lay had been on the stand.

Given the all-clear to proceed by the defense and the court, we needed to find a surrogate. We wanted a strong presence. I hoped to enlist Reverend John Porter, a friend of both Lay and Dr. Martin Luther King.

Reverend Porter was a local legend. He is one of the "kneeling ministers" in the Kelly Ingram Park sculpture depicting the Palm Sunday prayer at the end of the 1963 march protesting the jailing of civil rights leaders.

However, the retired Sixth Avenue Baptist Church pastor was not in great health, so he respectfully declined, forcing us to continue our search. Digging through old files, and asking around, we established former Birmingham radio personality Shelley Stewart had been a sergeant in the civil defense unit around the same time as Lay.

Stewart had been one of the public voices in the call to action for kids during the children's marches, directing the youngsters over the airwaves to 16th Street in those tumultuous spring months of 1963.

A man who had risen from modest roots to be a notable presence in Birmingham over several decades, Stewart had endured an intensely traumatic upbringing—his dirt-poor father allegedly murdered his mother with an ax—to become a powerful media fixture.

Known as Shelley "The Playboy" Stewart in the sixties, he was an African-American man whose on-air presence appealed to both black and white kids.

His smooth, authoritative voice was still drifting across Birmingham radio waves in 2001, so I knew he could "perform" on cue. We had no time to prep him, other than to ask that he answer the court's questions and read the Lay grand jury testimony.

We ushered Stewart into the hushed, cavernous courtroom.

In some ways, he was the polar opposite of Lay. Stewart's rich voice resonated around the old courtroom as he read the transcript of testimony the former postal worker had whispered to the grand jury.

It put an interesting gloss on Lay's evidence of seeing three, possibly four men around the church on September 2, at least two weeks before the bombing. One man was carrying a "ditty bag" near the church, according to Lay, who recognized Robert Chambliss. He also got a good look at another man he later picked out from police photos. It was Tom Blanton.

Lay had reported the incident at the time, but the police told him he "hadn't seen a so-and-so thing," Stewart said, reading the grand jury testimony to the court.

Lay also recalled his rushing to the scene of the bombing on September 15, thinking it was a plane crash. Along with Reverend Cross he dug through the rubble in what had been the ladies' lounge and pulled up the head of one of the victims: "You couldn't tell if it was a human being or not," he'd told the grand jury.

Lay repeated to police that terrible day his story of having seen the men in a car outside the church two weeks earlier.

Per my agreement with John Robbins, as soon as Stewart finished, the defense called Fleming to the stand for further examination about the Lay testimony. It was a very unusual move to allow a defendant to call a witness in the middle of the prosecution's case, but this was no ordinary matter.

The defense implied Lay mistakenly identified the Klansmen and high-lighted one statement he'd made in the sixties when he'd suggested the car may have been black, not blue on white as he'd previously reported.

The defense suggested a black car meant it was probably someone else—possibly J. B. Stoner, the arch-segregationist who owned a dark-colored vehicle.

Fleming responded that Stoner's pictures featured in the photo lineup back in 1963 but Lay had not identified him as one of the men he saw. At the time, Lay knew Chambliss was one of the perpetrators and picked out Blanton several times from police photos.

"I'll say this about serving as a so-called surrogate witness—it was not hard in answering the questions for James Lay," Fleming said with a laugh. "But what was hard was following Shelley Stewart. He sounded just like James Earl Jones."

I breathed a sigh of relief when Robbins finished his examination of Fleming. Getting Lay's testimony before the jury was of vital importance. Unfortunately, I may have let my guard down a little at that point and made perhaps the biggest potential mistake of the trial: calling the "Klan Barber," Bill Jackson.

I had serious doubts about having him take the stand. However, Jackson had been at the Modern Sign Shop on the nights of September 13 and 14, where Blanton and company met and likely completed making the bomb. He had also attended meetings under the Cahaba River Bridge.

The day of his testimony, wearing his bifocals upside-down, a pair of jeans, a sweatshirt, and no socks, Jackson had closed his shop and hung a sign on the door announcing that he was gone to testify at the bombing trial. He lacked credibility before he uttered a word in court.

Prosecutor Posey, a picture of understatement and composure, handled the questioning, eliciting an observation from Jackson that he'd seen Blanton taking something out of the trunk of a car and moving it into the sign shop on the Saturday night. However, it was quite clear Jackson's presence on the stand was shaping up to be as much a hindrance to our cause as a help.

Knowing that Robbins would likely have a field day with Jackson on cross-examination, Posey tried to get out in front, prompting the barber to admit he had lied to the FBI on previous occasions.

"I would tell you a lie in a minute," Jackson said, in one of the very few unquestionably honest statements he'd probably made in his miserable life.

Robbins may have been rubbing his hands together in glee, anticipating getting at Jackson, but I didn't notice—I was too busy cringing. Predictably, the defense highlighted his dishonesty in the past and his history, going back to the Baxley investigation, of asking to be paid to give testimony. Jackson didn't have to say much; it was enough that he stood there looking like a clown.

In the end, Robbins on cross-examination blurted: "You're just a big fat liar, aren't you?" I think everyone in the courtroom, including the prosecution, likely nodded in agreement. We couldn't get him off the stand quick enough.

We'd shuffled witnesses while continuing to assess Agent Spencer's condition. His daughter drove up to Birmingham and visited us in the war room. She was obviously concerned and had doubts he'd be able to testify in person, although she admitted that the old agent had his ailing heart set on finally giving evidence.

I explained to her how important her dad was to our case, as he was the only agent still alive who could provide that testimony. I, of course, understood her concerns. Sure enough, Spencer committed to appearing.

On learning who the old agent was and what he was to testify to in the Blanton trial, the cardiologist in Montgomery who had cared for him canceled all his appointments and insisted on coming with the former FBI man to Birmingham. Additionally, the doctor's wife, a registered nurse, took the day off to accompany them to court. Down the hall, Judge Joe Boohaker allowed us to set up a staging area in his courtroom complete with paramedics and a crash cart.

When Agent Spencer took the witness stand that day, he was eighty-two years old, making him the oldest former FBI agent ever to testify in a trial. He was followed on the stand by another former agent, Richard Hayes, who had conducted the second interview, after Blanton had conferred with Jean.

Together their testimony of Blanton's change in alibi was vital, especially as we planned to explore what the defendant and his partner Jean discussed on the kitchen tape.

(Fortunately, the trauma of the trial didn't add to Agent Spencer's woes. He was back on his feet soon after.)

The Q9

We felt the kitchen recording of Blanton and Jean and an unidentified third person from 1964, known as the Q9 tape in the FBI's files, was the next best thing to a smoking gun.

Time and again during the trial, outside the presence of the jury, the defense would raise new grounds to suppress the tape and keep it out of evidence. Each time Judge Garrett overruled.

Getting the tape into evidence was one thing, but ensuring the jury understood the context in which the recorded conversation took place was another.

Our witnesses had alerted them to the fact that Blanton had spent parts of that weekend at the Modern Sign Shop, from where we believe the bomb was likely transported to the church. They also knew he had seen Waylene Vaughn that Friday night, September 13, and had changed his alibi for the night of September 14.

One major concern was that the jury might conclude Blanton was lying about the bomb on the tape, for whatever reason, just as he had lied about many other things. Given the defendant's hatred for blacks, it was not unreasonable to think that he might admit to killing folks rather than face the wrath of Jean for his premarital infidelity.

Sound bounces around the vast old courtroom. Even though the recording had been repaired and transferred to newer technology, allowing the sound to be enhanced, it would be hard to follow in parts. We undertook to provide written transcripts of the recorded conversation to ensure the jury could understand what was said. Robbins battled to prevent the transcripts from being used. In the end, Judge Garrett said the written documents would not be allowed into evidence. However, he permitted using them in court as an aid to understanding the contents of the tape.

From the Horse's Mouth

Robbins's desperation to keep the tape out of evidence was understandable. Even though we had enjoyed a mostly positive, at times exceptional, three full days of testimony, the defense was hanging in there, chipping away at our circumstantial case.

Once all parties knew the tape was to be played, however, you could sense a slight momentum shift, benefiting the prosecution.

We had a night to dwell on it. On Thursday evening my team drifted over to the Tutwiler for a light meal and a libation or two. It was an interesting atmosphere. We all felt good about where we were, but it was like being in the dugout of a baseball team whose pitcher is on his way to pitching a no-hitter.

Better not say anything or we'll jinx it, especially as it was time to really bring the heat on Blanton with the kitchen tape.

We had carefully shielded the contents of the recording from the media and the public, though the existence of a tape of significance was previewed by some outlets, fueling anticipation that the most important day of the trial loomed.

We were taking nothing for granted. I knew Robbins would have at least one more shot at preventing the jury from hearing the tape, even after it had been moved into evidence. I racked my brain trying to anticipate what tactic the defense could use at the last moment.

Friday morning couldn't come fast enough.

Herren, plus an FBI audio team, along with my tech guy, Bill Smith, arrived at the courtroom early to set up the tape equipment. They placed a transmitter on the counsel table that would wirelessly stream the audio to headsets worn by the jurors, the witness, the judge, the defendant, and all of the lawyers.

A wireless speaker would deliver Jean's shrills and Blanton's admissions to the spectators in the courtroom. However, neither the media nor the public would receive transcripts of the recording.

When I made my way into the courtroom, it was filling up quickly with people from all walks of life, from Alabama's first African-American federal judge, U. W. Clemon, to business folks and lawyers and schoolkids. The place was buzzing. I unloaded the briefcase of three-ring binders on the counsel table in front of me. After a few minutes, Judge Garrett entered and summoned the jury to their seats in the box.

"Call your next witness," he instructed after exchanging pleasantries with the jury.

Posey had done our research on the admission of the tape, so he was to handle the witnesses who would authenticate the recording.

John Colvin, the FBI technician, testified about posing as Jim McBride, the truck driver, and renting a duplex apartment on Princeton Avenue, next door to Jean and Tommy Blanton.

Ralph Butler, the Special Agent in Charge of the electronic surveillance group, told the court that he and Colvin tore out the wall between the apartments and placed a microphone next to a hole under the Blanton's kitchen sink.

Robbins cross-examined both men to try and find any new reason to keep the tape out of evidence. Despite his relentless efforts, it was clear we had made it over the final hurdle.

There was a distinct sense of barely contained excitement as Bill Fleming instructed the jury to don the headphones and explained briefly how the audio equipment was set up. I'd heard the tape a hundred times and knew every word of the transcript, so while pretending to follow along as it played, I instead watched the jury.

Some shifted in their seats as they listened to the bizarre exchange, and, just as Judge Garrett had inadvertently changed his expression at the mention of "we were making the bomb" in his chambers, there was a discernible reaction among jurors: heads lifted, eyes widened.

They got it, and I knew they would be playing it again in the jury room.

The reaction elsewhere in the courtroom, however, was oddly muted.

Initially I was baffled. Did they not appreciate what they had just heard from Blanton's own mouth?

Turned out, they had heard very little. It seems that when I stood my binders on the prosecution table, I had placed them between the wireless transmitter and the receiver for the courtroom speaker, negatively influencing the audio quality. About all that the gallery heard was the indistinct sound of Jean's Southern drawl and Blanton's attitude.

Spectators left for lunch shaking their heads while reporters covering the trial caucused on the balcony comparing notes to piece together what they had heard.

After lunch Robbins resumed his efforts to exclude the recordings from evidence, but this time his focus was on preventing the jury from hearing the Mitch Burns tapes. During a hearing in the judge's chambers, he contested every tape, and every potentially prejudicial word uttered on each recording, as you would expect a great defense lawyer to do.

Everyone had anticipated testimony would resume fairly rapidly, but we remained behind locked doors for hours, listening to the Burns tapes and picking through transcripts. Robbins managed to prevent a couple of prejudicial extracts from being included in evidence, though the jury would hear the vast majority of the material, the judge ruled. When we finally emerged at 4:30 p.m., at our request the court was adjourned.

(At the end of a momentous day, in an unprecedented move that acknowledged the historical significance of events, the judge let groups of spectators and reporters take turns donning the headsets to listen to the five-minute kitchen tape segment. Among them was my almost seventeen-year-old daughter, Courtney, who got an acute understanding of why I had been a little preoccupied with the case for a few years.)

While Judge Garrett granted the adjournment, having sequestered the jury, he pushed us along, ordering a rare Saturday morning court sitting when we would call our next witness, Mitch Burns, the unapologetic Klansman who'd risked his life to tape his discussions with Blanton.

I'd taken Jeff Wallace's advice and backed off Burns. There were murmurs about him being reluctant to have some of the most unattractive exchanges of the recordings divulged in public, though in the end, he was completely on board with the prosecution.

Wallace had developed a good relationship with Burns and would handle the questioning.

I suspected Burns would be a good witness, not just because of the content of the tapes, but due to his manner. He hid nothing, including the Klansmen on horseback statue on his mantelpiece in his Warrior home and the gun on display even when lawmen visited. That openness was oddly refreshing.

His continued commitment to the Klan, while peculiar, elevated his credibility. He was calling out a wrong, regardless of the fact that he shared some of the same beliefs as the defendant.

Wallace readily admitted that he admired Burns as a "man of courage," and it showed in their courtroom exchanges. Burns was relaxed and affable. He had clearly risked everything to obtain the information that exposed Blanton and Cherry but was humble in talking about his bravery, further enhancing his credibility as a witness.

The jury members again received headphones, this time to listen to twenty-six excerpts from the recordings made in 1964. There was an ugliness about the conversations that couldn't be disguised. In some ways, exposing the jurors to the tone of the discussions was as important as them hearing what the Klansmen were saying.

They were cocky and cruel, and sometimes their grossly unattractive exchanges belittled authority, women, Jews, and blacks. The jocular nature of the banter served to emphasize how terrorist acts were part of everyday parlance for Blanton, as well as for Cherry, who also could be heard flinging insults and inanity on a few of the recordings.

Blanton was the dominant character in the conversations, happily joking, for example, about "bombing" a Jewish synagogue: "They make the things dynamite proof, we'll have to go out of business. Or find something worse, you know, steal an atom bomb or a plane."

On one occasion, in a lewd discussion about chasing women, he concludes: "I'm going to stick to bombing churches."

His hatred for the FBI was conspicuous, which was not unusual for a Klansman. He stopped short a few times of incriminating himself, though occasionally he would reveal a little too much, like when he declared, "They ain't going to catch me when I bomb my next church."

It was intensely interesting for the jury, but tedious after a while for the seventy-four-year-old Burns, who nodded off to sleep during one long listening session. The old Marine, however, was always fully engaged when giving evidence. Burns described how a friend who worked at a café where he often lunched asked him to help Blanton, who was being hounded by the FBI after the church bombing.

He explained how around the same time, the FBI had repeatedly approached him to help with the investigation into Blanton. He turned them down until Agent Blake showed him the morgue photographs of the girls.

As he recalled the moment of seeing the images, the old Klansman's eyes moistened, and he choked up ever so slightly: "It was the most horrible sight I had ever seen," he said. Looking directly at the jury, he added assertively, "I told them I would do all I could to help."

Discrediting Burns was a difficult task for the defense. Robbins attacked him for his Klan affiliation but in doing so had to walk a fine line, as he would also be condemning Blanton for sharing some of the same racist views.

He also implied there was something untoward in Burns's "little thing on the side" with waitress Marie Aldridge, who had introduced him to Blanton. Robbins suggested the romantic relationship was extramarital. The negative inference was to backfire on Blanton's team.

As Robbins tried to drive home the point that there had been some hanky-panky between Burns and Aldridge in front of a courtroom gallery that included a restless bunch of young school kids, he asked: "So you were having sexual relations with Marie Aldridge?"

Burns paused, leaned into the microphone, and, with a tip of the hat to the public statements of President Bill Clinton in the wake of the Monica Lewinsky scandal, said: "I did not have sexual relationships with Marie Aldridge."

The courtroom erupted into laughter. It was so boisterous that TV crews stationed in the hall scrambled to access what sounded like a controversial uproar before realizing a moment of mirth was the source of the disturbance. I'm not sure who laughed loudest, as everyone was cackling, but it induced a pronounced and prolonged guffaw from Judge Garrett.

While Burns was on the stand, we also got the chance to clarify, via a redirect, the fact that his interest in Aldridge came years after his wife had passed. We never established whether Burns even got to first base with the waitress, but he certainly hit a home run that day in court.

The Heart of the Case

There was high expectation before and after the playing of the kitchen tape that we would call Jean Casey, now Jean Barnes. I had, in fact, said as much in my opening statement. She had been caught in a lie on the recording and quite clearly had conspired with Blanton to cover for his movements in the early hours of September 15, when the bomb was planted under the church steps, amid small weeds and thistle.

I was itching for the opportunity to expose her in court. In my view, she had been calculating and relentlessly dishonest for thirty-eight years. I'll concede she got to me as much as the Klansmen. If she didn't have a conscience, I wanted at least to humiliate her, strip her of the strange pride she seemed to take in her role in one of the most awful events in recent history.

Fortunately, cooler heads, specifically those belonging to Posey, Wallace, Beardsley, and Sheldon (essentially, my entire team), prevailed. In the end, she added nothing to our case. She would have been combative and presented Robbins with his only friendly witness.

Instead, I allowed my friends on the defense team to agonize over whether to call her or not. Chomping at the bit for a chance at cross-examination, I was disappointed, though not surprised, when Robbins told me later he would not be calling her. Released from a subpoena, Barnes continued asserting her support for the defendant by taking a seat in the front row, clearly on Blanton's side of the aisle and uncomfortably close, in my opinion, to the victims' families.

We would end our four and a half days of prosecution witness testimony with unmistakable reminders for the jury about the difficult-to-fathom horror of that September day in 1963. As I have said in many public addresses in the years since the trial, we wanted to start our case strong and end it strong, and the source of the greatest strength had always been the families.

At the start of that unusual Saturday hearing, I had carefully placed a piece of mortar and a pair of shiny black children's dress shoes on the prosecution bench. After the intrigue and occasional jocularity of Mitch Burns's spell on the stand, Chris McNair's presence in the witness box immediately focused the court back on the grim fate that befell his daughter Denise and the other three girls.

McNair was seventy-five years old but still boasted an impish grin and a booming, radio-quality voice. On this day, however, the grin gave way to a fixed, somber expression, and the usually mellifluous voice carried an uncommonly sharp edge, as if to signal his disgust at being in the same room as Blanton.

From the moment he repeated his daughter's full name—"Carole Denise McNair"—everyone present knew that his testimony would pack a wallop. McNair detailed how he'd rushed from St. Paul's Lutheran to the scene of the bombing and then on to Hillman Hospital. On entering a makeshift morgue, he knew the worst, he said, but nothing could have prepared him for the sight of his ravaged, lifeless daughter.

"There was a piece of mortar mashed in her head," he told the court. There were gasps in the gallery.

I picked up the sharp-edged mortar fragment, similar in size to the kinds of stones kids in the South skip across water. I passed it to the jury for inspection.

Amid courtroom silence punctuated by sobbing from the gallery, McNair confirmed it was the piece extracted from Denise's skull. I knew what agony it was for the old man to testify. I was, like the gallery, deeply moved by his testimony.

We were all aware that the case, win or lose, was of importance to the city, state, and country. However, our approach was to ensure, ultimately, the jury knew this was about providing justice for the victims, not making a mark in history books.

Our final witness was a victim that history had often overlooked. The four girls who died were remembered, but the "fifth little girl" who survived was often just a footnote. I wanted to change that.

Sarah Collins Rudolph emerged alive from that devastated church lounge but had endured many challenges in the years since, not the least her recovery from horrific injuries, including complete blindness in one eye and impacted sight in the other.

The photograph of Sarah in the hospital in September 1963 that we displayed to the jury is an image that will never leave me: large, starkly white bandages over each eye of this little black girl. She looked helpless as well as hurt, completely at the mercy of those around her.

In the decades since she had tragically received little or no support from the city or the state. She struggled through adulthood, haunted by the events of that day.

The only eyewitness to the last moments of her sister and friends' lives, Collins Rudolph plunged the court into a firsthand account of what, I'm sure, many on hand had tried not to contemplate in too much detail.

We all knew how her account would end—it was excruciating listening to how excited the girls had been, how bursting with energy and beauty they were that day in the church basement. We were all there, in our minds and our hearts, with little Sarah as she washed her hands in the ladies' lounge, turned, and saw her sister tying the sash of Denise's new dress.

Then, a sound. Debris came crashing down.

Darkness as the fallout from the explosion blinded Collins.

She told a hushed court that she remembered calling for her sister: "Addie, Addie, Addie." Her voice rising with each word, much like it had thirty-eight years earlier.

"Did she answer you?" I asked.

"No, she didn't."

"Did you ever see your sister alive again?"

"No, I didn't see her again."

And with that, holding back my galloping emotions, I looked to Judge Garrett: "Your Honor," I said, "the state rests its case."

There was no cross-examination from the defense.

We adjourned the Saturday session around noon.

We could breathe a little easier until the defense put its case before the court on Monday. At least I could devote the rest of the day to my family and maybe carve out a bit of Doug time that evening.

It was a picture-perfect afternoon, warm and sunny without the inevitable oppressive Birmingham humidity, which was still a month or so away. I think I hugged my family just a little bit more than usual that day. The emotional impact of the closing witnesses was raw.

The Defense

John Robbins would only call two witnesses when court reconvened Monday morning.

His first witness was a recall—Bill Fleming. He again tried to cast doubt on Lay's observations two weeks before the bombing and produced an FBI book containing numerous photos of suspects.

Robbins suggested that Lay's description of the man outside the church that night fitted both J. B. Stoner and Dr. Edward Fields, the racist leaders of the National States' Rights Party. Their photos were in the FBI book, and Lay had been asked to look through it during early investigations.

When I got my opportunity to question Fleming, he noted that there were some men in the photo book who had the same general physical description as Blanton. We also pointed out to the jury that Lay had looked through the photos but did not identify either Stoner or Fields. In fact, he picked out Chambliss and Blanton as those he'd seen two weeks before the bombing.

The second witness was a church member who had seen a car displaying Confederate flags speed away just before the bomb exploded. It was the defense's effort to suggest the bomb had not been planted but thrown from a vehicle.

Eddie Mauldin, seventeen at the time of the bombing, testified seeing a Rambler station wagon cruising near the church. One of the two white men aged in their twenties in the car appeared to have a walkie-talkie. (Robbins had already established that neither Blanton nor Chambliss owned a Rambler.)

Mauldin thought they might have been police, even though the car prominently displayed the Confederate insignia. "That wasn't unusual at the time," he said. According to Mauldin, the car sped off abruptly moments before the bomb detonated.

We all place special significance on anything we see, or think we see, before a notable incident, yet Mauldin had not witnessed anything thrown from the car. Additionally, the inference that a bomb of enormous magnitude was tossed from a car and rolled to a stop underneath the bottom step at the side of the church was a very big stretch, but it was about all the defense had.

Blanton declined the opportunity to tell his side of the story, which was not a surprise. It seems that all of these old racist defendants were quick to deny their involvement to whoever would ask, except when they had to take an oath to tell the truth.

A sad parade of Birmingham's white supremacists had denied all knowledge of the incident in interviews and grand jury testimony, and any remaining scraps of humanity aligned with Blanton would have likely hindered, not helped, his cause, so Robbins opted against calling anyone else.

The defense team clearly felt their best chance to instill doubt in the mind of the jurors was to attack the quality and credibility of our witnesses. It seemed to me that rather than shooting for an acquittal, Robbins now was working for a hung jury. All they had to do was find one juror to stand firm in the belief reasonable doubt existed.

We knew Robbins would make that pitch and do his best to malign Burns, Vaughn, and Lay in his closing. To counter that approach, our final remarks to the jury would have two primary goals: first, to present an assured, comprehensive narrative linking all the circumstantial evidence while providing historical context, and second, to dispel any doubts the defense cast on our case and our witnesses.

In criminal trials, the prosecution has the burden of proving the defendant's guilt beyond a reasonable doubt. The burden never shifts to the defense, but there is one clear procedural advantage for the prosecution. The state goes *first and last* in closing arguments, with a lone defense argument sandwiched in the middle.

This was especially advantageous in the Blanton case, as we could present the big picture of a very old case first, then counter the defense's potshots at us when we had the last word to the court.

We opted for the buttoned-down and thorough Robert Posey to present our initial argument, while I would hopefully tie the facts and the emotion of the case in "responding" to the defense. I had pushed everyone so hard. Now I relished the thought of having a last word.

Posey took a different approach than me. I framed my argument in my head, over and over, making notes to prompt me but also ensuring my address was a free-flowing stream of consciousness. My colleague, always the stellar student, prepared by writing down every word and learning his address by rote.

"I memorized it, knowing that based on the emotions of the jury that I might have to adapt as I delivered it," he said. "I admit, I choked up at times even as I was memorizing it."

He wasn't alone—just saying the girls' names was enough to induce a conspicuous emotional reaction for many of us.

Andy Sheldon had encouraged Posey to "go as far as you feel comfortable, and then take it a step further."

"I went over my closing time and again," Posey said. "I practiced and practiced just trying to get through it."

We got to court early on May 1, 2001. On that day, thirty-eight years before, Dr. King, Andrew Young, James Bevel, and others had been finalizing plans to launch the children's marches from 16th Street the next morning.

My team had gathered for a final briefing before we headed into a packed courthouse. The gallery was bursting at the seams, full of familiar faces: business leaders, judges, lawyers, staff from the office, and many of Posey's peers, including church associates and friends. He saw his wife Jan and two daughters, Grace and Lily, ages eleven and eight.

Nearby, my wife Louise looked nervous. She'd been able to break away from mom duties, having deposited first grader Carson at school and Christopher in preschool. Courtney got to skip school and was in the gallery, in her Sunday best after a quick change of outfit. ("I was into grunge at the time," she recalled.)

Mom and Dad sat not far behind the McNairs and Alpha Robertson. Toward the back of the courtroom, the prosecution's number one cheerleader, Bob Eddy, came to watch the culmination of decades of work.

I don't know how Posey felt, but it was striking how supportive the atmosphere seemed, and there was an energy in the room that told me he was about to do something special.

He didn't disappoint.

I knew Posey would have a challenge in the initial moments, getting over the hump of saying the girls' names without losing his composure.

"There are four indictments for the murder of four little girls," he told the jury, eyeing each member of the panel.

"One for Cynthia Wesley, one for Carole Robertson, one for Denise McNair, and one for Addie Mae Collins.

"Four little girls in church on a Sunday morning."

Soft-spoken, mild-mannered Posey was on his way, delivering a closing for the ages. It was mesmerizing. He followed our loose pattern of developing the theme, addressing the facts, then turning directly to Blanton, before closing with the emotional turmoil of the girls' deaths and the issues of responsibility and accountability.

We again used multiple photos to link the story, and Posey interweaved technical evidence with emotive language and images. For example, in discussing expert testimony that indicated the shockwave from the explosion was indicative of a bomb, he said:

"Jack Crews, the fireman . . . felt the shock wave at the fire station and when he got to the church he saw the damage, and he saw the children's bodies were burned and mutilated . . .

"But the shock wave felt by Mr. Crews at the fire station was not the only shock wave created by this bomb."

Showing a slide of the severely injured Sarah Collins, Posey continued: "There was a shock wave of excruciating pain that swept over Sarah Collins as she lay in the rubble of the ladies' lounge, blinded in both eyes, crying out for her dead sister, Addie.

"There was a shock wave of grief that swept over the McNairs and the Wesleys and the Robertsons as they learned that their children had been senselessly murdered.

"There was a shock wave that swept all across the Earth, as the world learned of a horrible crime committed in Birmingham, Alabama."

Posey had us in the palm of his hand by the time he faced Blanton.

"This defendant didn't care who he killed, as long as he killed somebody, and as long as they were black.

"Who would do such a thing?"

His explanation drew on the depiction of a despicable man we had built courtesy of the evidence, mostly from Waylene Vaughn and Mitch Burns. He reminded the jury of Vaughn witnessing Blanton's attempt to hit a black man with his car, his affection for violence, and we replayed an extract of the Burns tapes, bringing home Blanton's obsession with 16th Street, his disrespect of the church and the children who died.

The jury heard again: "I'm going to stick to bombing churches."

Posey broke down the lie of Blanton's alibi, drawing on the evidence of Frank Spencer, Jackson the Klan barber, and the kitchen tape.

"This is a tape of Blanton's confession of guilt in this crime."

We showed a slide of the transcript of the tape as it rolled.

TOMMY BLANTON: They were interested in that meeting I went to. They knew I went to the meeting.

JEAN BLANTON: What meeting?

TOMMY BLANTON: To the big one.

JEAN BLANTON: What big one?

TOMMY BLANTON: The meeting where we planned the bomb.

JEAN BLANTON: Tommy, what meeting are you talking about now?

TOMMY BLANTON: We had that meeting to make the bomb.

JEAN BLANTON: I know that.

JEAN BLANTON: It's what you were doing that Friday night when you stood me up.

TOMMY BLANTON: Oh, we were making the bomb.

Playing the tape aloud, without the use of headphones, and scrolling through the transcript on the large screen and televisions throughout the courtroom was a calculated move.

It was the first time that the spectators and the media had been able to read the transcript. (I made sure that nothing blocked the area between the transmitter and speaker.)

Turning off the recorder, Posey drank in the silence for a few moments. He then sought to reinforce the idea that Blanton not only made the bomb but was engaged in delivering it to the church by referring to Lay's evidence. The Klansman was one of the men who may have tried to place an explosive device at the church two weeks earlier.

Showing a slide of Blanton, Posey went in for the kill.

[This is the] same man who rode around Birmingham committing random acts of violence against black people. The same man who we hear on tape saying "They're not gonna catch me when I bomb my next church."

The same man who, even a year after the horror of Sept. 15, 1963, can be heard on tape cursing the name of the church where these children died.

The same man who lied to the FBI about the Klan, and about what he was doing that Friday and Saturday night before the bombing.

The same man who, when his wife asks: "What did you go to the river for?" says three times on tape that he was at a meeting where they made a bomb.

That same man is seen at the church with Chambliss, in the middle of the night, with a satchel in his hand, at the very spot where the bomb exploded that killed these children.

Ladies and gentlemen, this is the man who committed this crime.

Just as the courtroom tried to catch its collective breath, we put up slides of the victims, one by one.

This is Cynthia Wesley. This is Carole Robertson. This is Denise McNair. This is Addie Mae Collins.

His voice began to crack as he continued.

This defendant killed this beautiful child, because of the color of her skin. He murdered these four worshippers in God's house on a Sunday morning because he was a man of hate.

The hatred, the intolerance, the injustice, perpetrated by this defendant must not stand unchallenged.

The deaths of these four little girls must not be in vain. Don't let that happen. Don't let the deafening blast of his bomb be what is left ringing in our ears. Don't let it drown out the voices of these children.

On behalf of the state of Alabama, and on behalf of these four little girls, I ask you to find this defendant guilty as charged.

To this day—at this moment as I write late at night—Posey's closing brings a lump to my throat.

Angling for a Hung Jury

Robbins's final plea for his client, as expected, relied heavily on attacking the credibility of the witnesses who helped us paint a picture of Blanton as a vicious bigot.

He went after (the absent) James Lay, alluding to an episode of depression the former postal worker endured when he was an aspiring paratrooper in the fifties. Robbins also suggested that back in 1963, Lay had not positively identified Blanton.

It wasn't difficult for him to impugn the integrity of the barber Jackson, but Vaughn and Burns were greater challenges.

Vaughn, Robbins told the court, had harsh things to say about Blanton, who, the defense suggested, was "not that good-looking." However, Robbins noted, that didn't prevent her from continuing to date Blanton, and never once reporting him for alleged crimes against black folks in the sixties.

I knew how much fear Vaughn lived in, both as a young woman and later in life. Unfortunately, that fear would only intensify if I didn't get a conviction against Blanton.

In attacking Burns, Robbins challenged the assertion that the Klansman became an informant out of civic responsibility, arguing instead that he was just out for the money that the government was paying him—$200 a month plus the costs for weekend forays with Blanton. He dismissed the recordings as the irrelevant ramblings of "drunk rednecks."

My former legal partner returned to his opening statement salvo, the idea that Blanton was an awful Klansman, but that didn't make him a murderer. He urged the jury not to find Blanton guilty just because he was a hater, or because they felt the need to convict someone in a case that had been troubling the community for so long.

While my team had studiously avoided talking extensively about the historical resonance of the crime, Robbins opened the door to that issue when he urged the jury only to look at the evidence presented, rather than be swayed by the horror and significance of the event. Emotion, he suggested, should not play a role in their deliberations.

As we expected, he angled for that hung jury, focusing on the idea that there were holes in our account. Referring to the prosecution's statements that our case was like a puzzle, he argued that "missing pieces were reasonable doubt."

He asked the jury to consider the idea that if the evidence compiled by the FBI in the mid-sixties was essentially the same as we had used in Blanton's trial, why hadn't the Klansman been prosecuted decades earlier?

"If evidence in this case is so great and if it's there . . . why not in '65?" he asked. "What has changed?"

He was implying that if there were doubts then, there should be doubts now.

"Return a verdict that you know is right, and you can all look yourself in the eye with a verdict of not guilty," he implored the jury in his conclusion.

It's Never Too Late

When my turn came, I felt an odd sense of calm. Perhaps Posey's performance had inspired me. I embraced the opportunity to have a last say.

I would counter a few points the defense had made, defend our witnesses, and remind the jury members of some of the key facts we'd presented. But Posey had done a masterful job of laying out the details in his address; I wouldn't labor the retelling, just provide the bullet point version to help them put the puzzle together one more time.

We had stuck to the evidence throughout the trial, deliberately avoiding melodrama or repetitiously referencing the historical significance of the case to the point that the jury, I sensed, had perhaps heard enough of the "hard" facts.

It was now time to wrap those details into the bigger picture, to acknowledge the length of time it had taken to get Blanton before the court and to talk about what it meant to the community.

Robbins had implied the state was seeking closure on an emotional, historical case by fingering Blanton, despite "missing" pieces of the puzzle. There was no great value debating that by revisiting the evidence again, piece by piece; instead, I saw it as an opportunity to inject the proceedings with the passion we had barely contained.

Posey had been meticulous and stuck to his brilliant script, so when he injected emotion it was remarkably impactful. I was going to ad-lib for the most part—have a conversation, refute the defense, and demonstrate the fire in the belly we all had about this case.

I had reread Bobby DeLaughter's book about the De La Beckwith conviction, *Never Too Late*, in preparation for my closing. I planned to borrow a few themes he touched on. My contention would be that time had been an ally to Blanton, but that his time was up. This wasn't about closure; it was about justice.

Again, we would use visual aids in the telling, photographs of the girls, the bombing scene, and the church among them. I turned to the sequestered jury, made eye contact best I could with each member, took a deep breath, and gave it my best shot.

It has been a long time. It has been eight days. That's a long time. It's been a long time for Birmingham. It's been a long time for the families that you see on the front row here. It has been a long time.

. . . Mr. Robbins, both in his opening and in his closing, he talked about the fact that he wanted you to judge this case with the passage of time . . . he's asked you, what's different?

Well, ladies and gentlemen, the passage of time is exactly what this man [Blanton] wanted.

. . . He wanted the passage of time to be on his side to fade the memories of those little girls and what happened on September 15 . . . Tom Blanton wanted the passage of time to fade the memories of the witnesses . . . He wanted the passage of time to eliminate witnesses.

But there's something that Tom Blanton didn't understand, folks. It's never too late. It is never too late for the truth to be told . . . It is never too late for a man to be held accountable for his crimes. It is never too late for justice.

I didn't dispute that much of the key evidence had been gathered decades before, though I pointed out that the tape recordings probably would not have been included in a trial in the sixties. The material hadn't "changed" over the years, I said, conceding Robbins's point, but the way the criminal justice system operated in 2001 was different from the days of all-white, all-male juries.

What has changed? Mr. Robbins asked . . . The evidence, he says, is the same as it was.

But what has changed? . . . Look around. Look in the jury box. Look at the people you have spent the last eight days with.

Look around the courtroom. Upstairs and downstairs. We have changed. Look around you everywhere. Black men and white men. Jews and gentiles. Protestants and Catholics.

Now, I've got to admit that's not my line. Okay? And maybe we haven't completely fulfilled "The Dream," but we have sure come to focus more on it than we were in the early years when Tom Blanton roamed the streets of Birmingham.

We have come to focus more on our lives and our understandings. And we have come to focus on evidence.

. . . It took a long time for this country to focus on the fact that black citizens were treated as second class or no class. It took a long time for Birmingham and America to come to grips with the fact that liberty and justice for all was really an empty saying for a lot of people in this country.

The big changes were in the way we viewed, understood, and valued the evidence, and the treatment that black issues now received in the criminal justice system.

Without getting bogged down in history, I referenced how those necessary reforms gained momentum because of the work of activists such as the Freedom Riders and those involved in the children's marches.

Blanton, who had been able to exercise his propensity for violence without accountability under Jim Crow, had felt exposed and threatened. He hit out.

And Tom Blanton saw change and he didn't like it.

Tom Blanton and his buddies saw change. They saw it again in the fall. Reverend Cross talked about the schools being integrated for the first time in 1963.

> On September 15, 1963, these little girls were going to worship.
>
> They were in the one place that everyone should feel safe. They were in the one place where they could go, and they could get away from the marches, and they could get away from the Klan, and they could do what you do in a church. You worship and have a youth service. But not on this day. Not on this day.
>
> Because at 10:25 or 10:22, whatever time the clock said, time stood still for Birmingham. Time stood still . . . as that explosion ripped through the ladies' lounge.

As Jeff Wallace had emphasized, the pious city of Birmingham was also outraged that a storied and intensely important church had been attacked—"people who would destroy a house of God" were nothing less than terrorists, I told the jury.

We went to great lengths to provide photos of the destruction of the church itself, with a special focus on the stained-glass window that remained intact except for the face of Jesus.

> A bomb . . . that blew out that face right there. Just as it destroyed those four girls, who were piled together in the ladies' lounge.

As we revisited photos of the church and the girls, I sensed unease among the jurors. Robbins had pushed his "reasonable doubt" agenda by inferring we were relying on the emotion of the case to cover "missing" pieces of the story. I wanted to diffuse that—to let the jury know it wasn't a ploy of some sort—that it was OK to feel that way in response to the evidence.

> Now, Mr. Robbins has spent a lot of time talking to you about emotion. But remember, ladies and gentlemen, the state of Alabama didn't put the emotion in this case.
>
> The state of Alabama presented evidence. The state of Alabama didn't put the emotion in Ms. Alpha Robertson's voice, Maxine McNair's voice, in Mitch Burns's voice. That emotion the state of Alabama contends was placed there by Tom Blanton.
>
> And the emotion is as much a part of this case as anything.

It is that which he placed there. He killed. He placed the emotion. And to this day it remains.

You saw through the witnesses, Ms. McNair, Ms. Robertson . . . because a mother's heart never stops crying . . . it's tough to think about. But the state of Alabama didn't place that bomb.

I also wanted to undercut the defense's assertion that if we didn't know every single detail of the story of the bombing, it amounted to reasonable doubt about Blanton's guilt.

Mr. Robbins talked to you about the state's case and the fact that cases are like puzzles. That's absolutely true. I told you at the beginning of this case that the evidence doesn't always match the horror of the crime. We're not on *Perry Mason*. We're not on *Law and Order*. We're not at a movie. But cases are like puzzles.

Now what Mr. Robbins was wrong about, Mr. Robbins gave you the impression that in order for you to convict Tom Blanton that every piece of that puzzle has to come together to form a complete picture, and that is not the case.

Perhaps Mr. Robbins kept all of his puzzles together when he was a small child.

I didn't.

But when I put my puzzles together and there were a couple of pieces missing anyone could walk by and see what the picture was. Anybody could walk by and tell it was the picture of a clown, a scene, a children's story. And in this case, ladies and gentlemen, anybody can walk by and see that the puzzle forms the picture of Tom Blanton.

I also needed to address succinctly Robbins's attempt to undercut the character of our witnesses. There was not much that could be done about Jackson, so I merely reiterated his role as a witness to Blanton's attendance at meetings at the Modern Sign Shop and under the bridge.

I was fairly confident Vaughn and Burns had been convincing witnesses and, despite their flaws, their honesty on the stand was conspicuous. I opted to remind the jury members that we didn't attempt to sugarcoat anything for them.

We have never put anyone up there and tried to tell you anything other than what they were. Whether it was Ms. Vaughn, or
Mitch Burns, or Bill Jackson.

Lay was another matter. His absence from court deprived the trial jury
of the chance to see the quiet, sincere individual who had addressed the
grand jury. Robbins had taken a shot at his mental health, so I pointed out
that he'd endured a "rough time" as a black man in the fifties in the services.
But, I noted, that had not prevented him from serving his community as a
volunteer civil defense officer on top of his full-time occupation.

I sought to portray him, accurately, as a man who acted honestly and
responsibly in the face of racial hostility and had assuredly identified Blanton at the time of the bombing.

I didn't want to get bogged down in reciting the evidence again, but I
wanted to ensure the jurors had their heads wrapped around a few damning snippets and could see the pieces of the puzzle laid out in front of them.

I went over how Blanton's alibi for that night had changed after he consulted with Jean to cover his tracks, and, of course, I played the kitchen tape
one more time. I paused the tape after each sentence, repeating the words
from the transcript displayed on a monitor in the courtroom.

That, ladies and gentlemen, is not circumstantial evidence. That
is direct evidence. That is a confession out of this man's mouth.

I also reiterated a few damning statements from the recordings with
Mitch Burns.

You heard the testimony of Mitch Burns, and you have seen the
transcripts . . . there are things that are very instructive on
those tapes.
"What are they going to do when I bomb my next church?"

In wrapping up, I wanted to ensure with my final words the jury could
easily assemble the parts of the story.

. . . Planning the bomb. The Cahaba River. The meetings . . . the
Modern Sign Shop. Robert Chambliss. September 2, James Lay.
They all come together. Are there pieces missing? Yes. But we

can see clearly the picture. We can see clearly the pictures from Tom Blanton's own mouth.

We come here in this time and place . . . to do justice. And it's not cheapened. It's not been thrown around. It's real. And we come here because there were four children who died and the world changed, and we changed.

. . . We come here because a mother's heart never stops crying . . . we come here because we do remember, and [with] every day that passes . . . Tom Blanton gets older, and that is a mockery of the deaths of those little children.

Ladies and gentlemen, there are a lot of people looking.

But there's only four that matter. Denise, Cynthia, Carole, and Addie.

Carole would have been fifty-one as we opened this trial and Addie would have been fifty-one as we closed the evidence today.

Those four are the people that look down for hope and inspiration. Those are the people that look down for justice. Those are the four who are waiting.

. . . Sarah called out "Addie, Addie, Addie" in cries of pain.

Today, let us call out to Addie. Let us call out in joy and happiness to Addie and her friends Carole and Denise and Cynthia. That today, in this time and place, we did justice.

And, at long last . . . they can rest in peace because it's never too late for that, and Tom Blanton can finally be held accountable for the crime he committed in 1963.

The Wait

As I waited for Judge Garrett to dismiss court for lunch, I realized why Baxley had seemed so limp when I shook his hand following his closing argument. I was drained—mentally and physically. The next few minutes passed in a blur, though I recall leaning down to Mrs. Robertson to receive a gentle embrace.

Some folks who had taken the time to sit through the arguments made their way to where we were packing up to have a word with Posey and me. My old friend Eli Capilouto, the Provost at the University of Alabama at Birmingham and now the President of the University of Kentucky, was so emotional when he grasped my hand he could barely get out the words "thank you."

I had no real idea what impact my closing argument might have had on the jury. I did know, though, that if you have enough people telling you that you did a great job, you start to believe it.

We were buoyed by positive feedback, and I was feeling pretty good as we headed across Linn Park to lunch at the Birmingham Museum of Art. However, Jeff Wallace made sure I stayed grounded.

"That was a really good argument, Doug," he said.

I could sense there was a "but" coming.

"But I thought you might have hit a home run with that stuff about the puzzle."

Of course, I bit. "What do you mean?"

"Well, talking about the missing pieces to your puzzles was good, but I thought for sure you would throw up the picture of the stained-glass window and say 'Tommy Blanton blew out the face of Jesus on this stained glass, but everyone in the courtroom knows who that is.'"

I wanted to drop to my knees.

How could I have missed producing what would have been one of the great closing argument analogies? I tried to reconcile my oversight with the notion that only the son of a preacher like Wallace would have thought of it.

In the afternoon, the judge charged the jury on the law, and we retired to the war room on the other side of the courthouse, silently resigned to a long, excruciating wait for the verdicts. It was about 2:30 p.m. I felt like I was in a fog, unable to properly function until it cleared. The thought of a wild-card juror unsettled me, but we'd done our job, including producing a few moments of great impact, which made up for a few slipups.

Optimism for a guilty verdict was apparently pretty low among most spectators and the media. The media coverage of the last few days of the trial, I realized after the event, had been a little strange. It was clear, in retrospect, the detail and importance of the kitchen tape had been lost on some, likely because of the poor audio quality of the tape and my transmitter snafu.

Few dared to think with any great conviction that a guilty verdict was likely, and there was concern that a not guilty decision would spark civil unrest.

Reverend Abraham Woods, Caryl Privett, and civil rights attorney Rodney Max had sat together in the courtroom balcony through the closing arguments. They shared an intense concern about how to keep the peace should Blanton receive a "get out of jail pass."

Indeed, anticipating the worst, Woods and Max were instrumental in scheduling a candlelight vigil at the church that night to pray for justice and peace.

However, Bob Eddy wasn't in any doubt. The old investigator placed a call to Bill Baxley to tell him that he believed the closing arguments sealed the deal, and a guilty verdict was likely. Whether it would be a celebration or a protest was in the hands of the jury. Either way, I was quite sure we wouldn't hear their decision that day.

Robin Beardsley was due to begin her final exams the next day, so I told her to go on home and study.

A little after five o'clock we got word the judge was going to release the jury for the night, necessitating our return to the courtroom. Wallace headed over before me.

As I approached the metal detectors outside the courtroom, I was still kicking myself for missing the opportunity to bring the damaged stained-glass window into my closing.

My cell phone rang. I barked a greeting.

"Where are you?" Wallace asked with a hint of urgency—maybe Judge Garrett wanted to get home quickly.

"Right outside."

"Well, you need to get on in here."

I hustled into the courtroom. Wallace was standing stoically in front of the judge's bench.

"What's up?" I asked.

"We have a verdict."

"No, no," I said, shaking my head. "He's just letting them go for the night."

"Doug," Wallace said emphatically, as he looked me dead in the eye, "we have a verdict."

Wallace swears he watched all the blood drain from my face.

The jury had been out for only about two and a half hours. I was rendered speechless for one of the few times in my life. I never expected such a quick decision and did not know what to make of it.

Amy Gallimore, our media coordinator and assistant, wandered into the room. Later she told me I was standing alone, "ashen, almost white." She tried to reassure me—she believed the evidence was too strong for an acquittal to be possible and the verdict, in her mind, had to be guilty.

It seemed to take forever for everyone to assemble. Some regulars like Diane McWhorter were caught off guard and looked like they might miss the moment. I sat in the seat that I had occupied for the last eight days and waited restlessly, my hands clasped tightly on the table and my right foot shaking almost uncontrollably below it.

Court reporter Julie Carter got my attention.

"It's OK Doug," she said quietly.

I cocked my head a little and asked, "What do you mean?"

She smiled ever so slightly: "It's going to be OK."

My panic subsided slightly. Court reporters and bailiffs know things.

And then the jury filed back in.

Just moments before, it seemed, I'd been contemplating having a bourbon. No, two or three. Now we were all back in place.

This was it.

Blanton looked angry; everybody else looked scared.

The jurors seemed jittery. I couldn't read them. A few made eye contact, but their expressions told me nothing. We had worked so hard to select these folks but at the end of the day, there was no way to know for sure how they would perceive the evidence.

At 5:50 p.m. on May 1, 2001, the forewoman, a black woman, was asked if a verdict had been reached.

She seemed to be shaking as she stood.

"Yes, your honor."

She's more nervous than me, I thought.

Blanton had been charged in separate counts of the indictment for the death of each girl. Four verdicts would be read, and because it was tried under 1963 law, it was also up to the jury to impose any sentence.

She was trembling now. Definitely.

Blanton looked anxious. Good.

"In case number . . ."—her voice cracked, she was struggling—"we the jury find the defendant, Thomas Edwin Blanton Jr., guilty of murder in the first degree and set punishment of life in prison."

I heard people exhale. I stared at the table before turning to look at the faces of those girls' families. Oh my God, they'd suffered so. Chris McNair smiled. A tired smile.

The forewoman's voice cracked with emotion again as she announced each decision. By the time she reached the fourth and final verdict, she was so overcome she could barely get the words out. "Thomas Edwin Blanton Jr. . . . guilty . . . murder in the first . . . life" was all she could muster.

Judge Garrett polled the jury, and each member affirmed the verdicts. He then turned to Blanton: "Do you have anything to say before sentencing?"

The murderer feigned indignity. He looked pompous, but I knew he was terrified.

Give me the finger now, Tommy.

Blanton said the most intelligent thing I'd ever heard him utter: "No, I guess the Lord will settle it on Judgment Day." With that, Judge Garrett swiftly sentenced him to life in prison and gaveled the trial to a close.

Hands cuffed, head down, Blanton was led out for the final time. There was no side or back entrance to escort prisoners in and out, as the courtroom wasn't regularly used for criminal trials, so Blanton had to be taken down the main third-floor hallway to the public elevator. He passed through a sea of spectators and media on his way to an Alabama prison. Inside the courtroom, the atmosphere was subdued; in fact, an eerie silence descended like a shroud over the space. The collective relief was overwhelming. We all stood there, numb for just a moment before the spell was broken.

I went straight to the families; tears rolled down their cheeks. We hugged.

Only three parents were still alive to see justice rendered: Chris and Maxine McNair, who had remained in the courtroom throughout, and Alpha Robertson, who had retired to her home following the closing arguments.

Immediately after the trial, the McNairs, who had rarely spoken to anyone about the crime over the last thirty-eight years, including their two daughters, declined to comment to the media, while Mrs. Robertson offered a brief word to the few reporters who reached her by phone.

"I'm very happy that justice came down today, and you know, that's enough, isn't it?" she said. "I didn't think it would come in my lifetime."

I knew we'd be besieged by media as soon as we walked out of the courtroom, so I had asked Gallimore to shepherd everyone to the steps outside where we could accommodate all inquiries. Before heading out, I made my way to the defense counsel to embrace my old law partner, Robbins.

He and his team had tried a great case under difficult circumstances. It was my time to tell him how proud I was of him.

I had one task I wanted to complete before leaving. It's not my usual practice to talk to the jury immediately after a verdict, but at Andy Sheldon's suggestion, I was to pay the panel members a visit. I felt such an exceptional judicial experience would only be complete if I saluted the folks who had been sequestered and given the daunting challenge of assessing such a cold and controversial case.

The forewoman's battle to hold back tears as she read the verdicts was evidence of the intense emotional toll on all the jurors. When I walked into the jury room, there was a magic moment of serendipity. Emotions were high, tears flowed, some heads were bowed in contemplation. There were no high fives or any celebration. Instead, there seemed to be a wordless acknowledgment that something necessary and righteous had at long last been achieved.

As I thanked them for their service, weary faces with bloodshot, puffy eyes focused on me in a way so vastly different from the intensely inquisitive looks I'd become familiar with in the courtroom. There was no longer the need to be detached.

"What you've done for your community is something very special," I said. "I know this was hard, but this is history. I don't need to tell you, but I want to assure you that you got this right."

If there ever was a time that the words of Dr. King were proven true, that "the arc of the moral universe is long, but it bends toward justice," it was on that day, at that time, in that jury room.

Outside, it was bedlam.

Robin Beardsley had been working out at the gym when the breaking news on television revealed the verdict. She scrambled back to the courthouse and on arrival was stunned to see hundreds of people on the granite and marble stairs leading to the entrance. In the streets around the building, hundreds more, men, women, and children milled and celebrated.

Many people had been planning to attend the vigil, so the news of the conviction came as a joyous surprise. It was a carnival-like atmosphere, and from an attorney's point of view, like winning the Super Bowl.

My path through the courthouse toward the media pack outside had been clogged with friends and spectators wishing me well and thanking the team. I was immensely gratified. Before heading outside, I took a moment to call Louise, who had been watching the live coverage on television. She had lived every moment of the trial with me. We had a brief, emotional exchange, and I was ready to go.

On exiting the building, it was like a scene from a movie. The crowd erupted in cheers and what seemed like one hundred microphones were thrust toward my face. I could see people, young and old, high-fiving, even dancing.

That was my first major jolt of understanding about what the case had meant to the community. To that point, I'd been completely consumed with the process—with the task of trying to ensure we made the case in the most comprehensive and accurate way. The noise around the trial had all been peripheral.

"They say that justice delayed is justice denied," I said. "Folks, I don't believe that for a minute. Justice delayed is still justice, and we've got it here in Birmingham, Alabama."

A whirlwind of news interviews followed, all the while with my cell phone blowing up from people calling. I couldn't take most of the calls, but when Bill Baxley's number popped up, I found a quiet spot to talk for a few minutes.

"I am so happy for those families," he said, barely containing his genuine excitement.

We discussed a few details—shared experiences of getting a deserved verdict—before I had to go.

"Doug," he said in closing, "I am so proud of you and what you did for those families and for all of us.

"You are my hero!"

"Bill," I said, a little stunned, "thank you. I think I did pretty good."

Blanton, as was expected, appealed. But with Alabama Attorney General Pryor personally arguing for the state, the old Klansman's conviction was later confirmed by the Alabama Court of Criminal Appeals.

It Really Happened

The legal team, sans Beardsley, whom I sent home with an order to study, gathered at the Tutwiler later for a celebratory session that was a combination of relief and joy. We were joined by some of the regular media folks, including Diane McWhorter, and other local luminaries.

Amy Gallimore was fielding media calls left and right, and my cell phone continued to buzz every few minutes. I took a call from the Governor and in between drinks skipped across the street for live media interviews with Geraldo Rivera and others. I turned down the offer to fly to New York for *Good Morning America*, opting instead to stay with the locals, with whom I had developed such a great relationship, but I committed to a satellite interview with *GMA*'s Charlie Gibson bright and early the next day.

As the evening started to wind down, I got another reminder of just how much the case meant to many folks. Kevin Sack, the Atlanta journalist who had covered the trial for the *New York Times*, walked into the bar with his computer.

"Want to see the front page of tomorrow's *New York Times*?" he asked.

His story "Ex-Klansman Is Found Guilty in '63 Bombing" was passed around. As soon as she saw it, Birmingham native McWhorter burst into tears.

"It really did happen," she said.

On my quiet drive home, a couple of things from the day replayed in my mind: the verdict being read and the look of relief on the faces of the McNairs when I turned to them. It had been a great day. But one thought was spoiling the party and wouldn't leave me: "Cherry. He's still out there."

NINE

POLITICS AND DEMENTIA

I couldn't sleep.

I'd been lying in bed watching the clock move toward midnight, ending a day a lot of us had feared would never come.

When 12:01 came up, it occurred to me I hadn't planned for anything much else for about three years other than working toward getting a bomber convicted of murder. Now it was tomorrow, and everything seemed a little daunting. Family, work, politics: there was a lot to do.

There also was an overwhelming "what just happened?" sensation. High on a cocktail of pride, elation, and exhaustion, I was trying to digest the last twelve hours or so.

It was a bit of a struggle to revel in the "victory." Blanton was where he belonged, so I could finally indulge in a celebration, but it ate away at me that Cherry was still out there, feigning dementia.

The Baxley Tirade

We had consulted experts and compiled a comprehensive evaluation for presentation to Judge Garrett that argued the former Klansman was fit to stand trial, but since he'd been diagnosed as medically incapable, it wasn't really a debate—we had to provide absolute proof that the accepted evaluation was wrong.

Candidly, we held slim hopes of success, and that pessimism was fed by our collective exhaustion. We were all working to expose Cherry and have him follow Blanton to court and eventually jail, but legally, the burden of proving his competency meant we'd have a very steep hill to climb.

The elation of the Blanton verdict quickly gave way to rumblings of discontent in the community about Cherry's status. It played into a largely unfounded but persistent suspicion that authorities had concertedly blocked the African-American community's access to justice in the bombing case.

That undercurrent of unease flowed a little quicker when my friend and hero Bill Baxley had a piece, stridently critical of the FBI, published in the *New York Times* after the Blanton verdict was handed down.

Baxley wrote bitterly that in addition to obtaining a conviction against Chambliss he would have been in a position to go after the other two bombers, Blanton and Cherry, if the FBI had handed over to his investigators the crucial tape recordings used in my team's prosecution of Blanton.

"This was evidence we desperately needed in 1977—evidence whose existence FBI officials had denied. Had it been provided in 1977, we could have convicted all three of these Klansmen," he wrote.

Baxley went on to insist, "Most of the tape recordings admissible against Mr. Blanton in 2001 were admissible in 1977. . . .

"What excuse can the FBI have for allowing Mr. Blanton to go free for 24 years with this smoking gun evidence hidden in its files? . . . I do know that rank-and-file FBI agents working with us were conscientious and championed our cause. The disgust I feel is for those in higher places who did nothing."

Baxley called it as it was, and much of his disgust was shared by many of the investigators who had worked the bombing case over nearly four decades.

There is little doubt deliberate efforts were made at various stages, mostly back in the sixties and seventies, to block or limit access to sensitive files relating to FBI informants or agency undercover efforts.

While Baxley may have had a struggle getting some of the sensitive material into evidence in 1977, I'm sure the knowledge that the recordings existed alone would have propelled him to push feverishly to take Blanton and Cherry through the system.

Baxley's piece touched on issues that needed to be out in the open, though the timing made things a little uncomfortable for people still engaged in hauling Cherry to justice. Disgruntled elements in the community linked the FBI's past behavior to the Cherry situation, and despite Baxley's praise of the rank-and-file agents, Fleming and Herren felt tainted by inference.

It prompted a response in 2001 from the very image-conscious FBI Director, Louis Freeh, who was battling attacks on the agency's credibility on a number of different fronts at the time. He agreed the investigation had taken far too long. He apparently vented his anger on his blameless regional offices. The local guys who had done such a fabulous job were being diminished by the Bureau's top brass. It wasn't a good way to endear yourself to the rank and file.

An FBI spokesman was forced to acknowledge the agency had failed to give tapes and other evidence to investigators but denied they were "purposely withheld," which was the kind of public contradiction the Feds had often used when it came to the bombing case.

As he was prone to do, Baxley had said what many had thought for decades. I would have preferred, though, if he'd given us a heads-up about when he planned to do it.

The Cherry Ruling

My stint as U.S. Attorney officially ended on May 31, 2001. However, my responsibilities to the bombing case continued, as it was under state jurisdiction. My special appointment before the Blanton trial as an Alabama Assistant AG was designed to take in the Cherry prosecution too.

A July date had been set for Judge Garrett to assess recent medical evaluations of the old Klansman, and that looked likely to be when my association with the bombing case would end. Preparing for the hearing wasn't a full-time job, as there was only so much Robert Posey, Jeff Wallace, and I could do as we waited for our medical experts to form opinions about Cherry's mental health status.

We struggled to admit it to each other, but realistically there was very little chance Cherry's case would go to trial. We knew it would be difficult to meet our burden in a battle of experts.

Even before the Blanton trial, I had started weighing options for the future, approaching a local litigation firm, Whatley Drake, about the possibility of coming on board.

The partners, Joe Whatley and Jack Drake, were old friends and willing to be flexible with my other commitments, including the Cherry case and the possibility, raised by several friends and local Democratic Party leaders, that I might dip my toe into politics. The firm handled plaintiff cases all over the country and had made a mark. I had a positive reputation that could benefit the business and perhaps help further extend its reach.

Politics, a career focusing on litigation—it was all ahead of me, but my primary focus was Cherry as I wrapped preparations for the July hearing into his competence.

Before Blanton's trial, both former Eastview Klavern trolls dismissed my entreaties for them to come clean, or at least point the finger at each other. Now, with Blanton put away, Cherry should have been exceptionally anxious about his chances of staying out of jail. His dementia ploy was his last, best chance of avoiding a deserved fate.

Most who knew Cherry understood that while he wasn't the sharpest tool in the shed, he wasn't burdened by a mental condition that should have prevented him from standing trial. However, his legal team had done a good job in compiling medical evidence to back that claim.

What we expected to be the final decision on the matter was to be delivered by Judge Garrett after the July hearing. He was taking evidence from two experts brought in by the defense who submitted Cherry was suffering from vascular dementia, perhaps reflected by dark areas in his brain, visible in tests. We, on the other hand, had two authorities advising that Cherry, while possibly suffering from some form of mild dementia, was in no uncertain terms a great big fake—although that wasn't the medical terminology they used.

Here was a man suddenly devoid of memory and apparently unable to process the simplest of intellectual tasks. But the idea that he was telling his evaluators that two plus three equaled six was to us a bigger indicator of his cunning than his craziness.

Unfortunately, the heavy burden was squarely on our shoulders to prove that Cherry was competent. The fact that there was a credible diagnosis of dementia meant it wasn't enough to provide testimonies about the limited extent of his ailment.

The judge ruled against us.

On July 16, 2001, the court announced that "the State had not presented sufficient evidence to overcome the burden of proving competency by clear, convincing and unequivocal evidence."

It was disheartening, though not entirely a surprise. There had been no compromise in our commitment to bring him to trial, but it felt as though the chance was lost on this occasion, and though it was not the final decision, realistically it was likely to be the end of the road.

"The window of opportunity" to prosecute Cherry was closing, I conceded to the media while referencing Alabama's heavy burden of proof when it came to overturning a mental illness ruling. I was drained, disappointed, and a little angry but fully understood the judgment.

I had no intention of pretending to the community that there was much hope of holding him accountable. I had been open and honest throughout the investigation and trial process and didn't feel it appropriate to start fudging the truth now.

That, it turned out, may have been a mistake.

Kevin Sack's story datelined July 16, 2001, in the *New York Times* led with: "An Alabama judge all but ended the prosecution of the 1963 Birmingham church bombing case today by ruling that the sole remaining defendant, Bobby Frank Cherry, was mentally incompetent to stand trial."

Members of the African-American community bristled over the decision and soon exploded in anger, having suppressed their feelings for decades.

Through the initial FBI investigation in the sixties, amid Baxley's inquiries, the diversion of resources to the Rudolph case, and the bail decisions, they had done well to hold their tongues, but no longer.

Matters swiftly threatened to get out of hand. The release of all that pent-up anger sent people into the streets. It felt as if a lot of the behind-the-scenes work to patch race relations over the years and to try and make up for past injustice, plus the euphoria over the Blanton verdict, had evaporated overnight.

There was a feeling of "enough is enough." People were emboldened, and red-hot-poker angry. A considerable proportion of their fury was directed at my team. For me, it looked like one of my final duties in relation to the bombing case would result in bitter disappointment and a bunch of people I loved screaming abuse at me.

It was obvious the odds that Cherry would never face trial had dramatically shortened. Indeed, it looked like a fait accompli.

In a portion of a court order that was barely noticed at the time, Judge Garrett did not rule out completely the possibility Cherry could be found competent in the future, but for the moment, it was over. A further hearing was scheduled for August. We assumed that would likely be a formality in the process of locking down the dementia judgment going forward.

Community sentiment was aggressively negative. Personal friendships were tested, including my long-standing relationships with some black religious leaders and, most disappointingly, Chris McNair.

Public protests about the decision culminated in a mass rally one steamy summer afternoon with about one thousand people gathering at Linn Park howling their disappointment, frustration, and anger. Reverend Abraham Woods was, of course, a leading voice, insisting Cherry should be hauled into court on a stretcher if necessary to face murder charges.

He was morally right. Unfortunately, the law stood in the way.

I wanted to explain the situation—stress that we were in what felt like a legal checkmate—but no one was listening. When I wasn't being ignored, I was being yelled down. I'd gone from hero to zero in a matter of months.

Little did I know that Judge Garrett had a little surprise in store.

On August 10, with protesters picketing the courthouse, the judge ordered Cherry to be committed to the custody of the Alabama Department of Mental Health and Mental Retardation for evaluation and to determine if he could be restored to mental competency. Put simply, he was saying Cherry may have been unable to stand trial at the time of testing, but the judge wanted to see if the seventy-two-year-old's mental state would remain an issue in the future.

It was a brilliant move that respected the opinions of the experts and the letter of the law while ensuring common sense wasn't ignored.

Cherry entered the maximum security Taylor Hardin Secure Medical Facility in Tuscaloosa four days later and would stay there for the next seventy-one days. He was released October 24.

The public animosity about Cherry and the state's inability to try him did not wane.

It was a brutal time, in many respects. It felt as if much we'd worked for had been undermined.

I was at a loss to adequately convey the legal bind we were in and, frustratingly, not at liberty to speculate that his time in the mental facility held at least a possibility of reigniting the case.

September 11, 2001

I had taken up an opportunity at Whatley Drake on June 1, immediately after my tenure as U.S. Attorney concluded.

With Cherry sent away for testing, it was time to refocus. I could at least put in a bit of extra time with the firm, and I got to entertain the idea of taking a meaningful step toward building a political presence. At the urging of friends and political colleagues, I announced in August I was planning to seek the Democratic nomination to challenge Republican Senator Jeff Sessions in June 2002. Law and politics made for a long day, but at least I didn't have to talk to Klansmen.

As I slowly built a political campaign, I pulled back somewhat from the Cherry case at the insistence of Attorney General Bill Pryor, although I remained on board in a consulting capacity.

Meanwhile, Don Cochran, a Missouri-born former Green Beret and razor-sharp attorney, had slotted into the Cherry prosecution team and was working diligently with Posey to compile a comprehensive case on the dementia issue to present to Judge Garrett.

Word from Tuscaloosa was that Cherry was turning his memory loss and incapacitation on and off. When surrounded by staff members he diligently lapsed into deep dementia, but during the day, he would slipup, gladly entertaining conversations complete with favorite memories of his preferred sports teams. It apparently didn't occur to him that he was under observation, with cameras, and was being scrutinized by experts around the clock.

Cherry would be flooded by his professed affliction when formal testing was conducted, but seconds before and after he was his chatty self. On one occasion he turned red with fury as he repeatedly cussed about me—a sure sign of mental adroitness.

Experts said he recorded such low scores in the testing process, they believed it took an extraordinary awareness of what he was doing to be able to manufacture such a result. Just as my experts had opined, Cherry was malingering—faking it. It's possible to do that for an hour or two at a time, but not over seventy days.

When we received word that the examination was complete, Judge Garrett summoned the legal teams to review the outcome of the defendant's time in Tuscaloosa. We gathered December 3, the Tenth Judicial Circuit Court in Jefferson County's Criminal Division hosting all parties. Dr. Kathy A. Ronan from the Taylor Hardin Secure Medical Facility testified that in her opinion Cherry was indeed mentally competent and should stand trial for the murder of the four girls. Cherry presented no evidence to rebut Dr. Ronan's findings.

In their brief to Judge Garrett, Cochran and Posey thoroughly detailed an argument for Cherry to be ruled competent and refuted the defense contention that the court had already issued an inflexible ruling on the issue.

In his initial order, Judge Garrett had ruled that Cherry was not competent to stand trial "at this time" and had ordered the defendant to undergo further testing.

Our brief to Judge Garrett emphasized that the mental health experts who had declared Cherry incompetent had met with him for only a few hours, while medical staff at Taylor Hardin had conducted an extensive evaluation from August 12 through October 24, including times when Cherry was unaware that he was being tested or observed.

According to Dr. Ronan's report, the assessment of the staff was unanimous: Cherry was faking his lack of memory to appear incompetent when in fact he was "fully capable of understanding the case against him and assisting in his defense."

Garrett ruled that Cherry was mentally competent and capable of standing trial for the murder of the four girls.

Effectively, the decision rang the bell to start the third and final round of the thirty-eight-year pursuit of the three principal suspects in the bombing of 16th Street Baptist. The prosecution had hauled itself from the canvas and was ready to go toe-to-toe again, though I would likely be a ringside spectator when the trial got underway in May.

When I put myself out there as a potential Democratic Party candidate for the Senate, a Cherry trial had looked unlikely.

It was a decision I'd taken having made a calculated guess that my immediate future would probably be spent working as a litigator, rather than being swamped by the intense pressure of a major criminal trial. But even before Cherry was ruled competent, the ground had shifted.

On September 11, 2001, the attacks in New York and Washington ensured Birmingham, a town that had endured too much in the way of terrorist-induced tragedy, was a weary, sad place. Grief-stricken by the unthinkable losses and anxious about what the future would bring, a memorial service at 16th Street Baptist for the victims focused the attention of the city.

As I walked up the steps to enter the church, I encountered Reverend Woods. With the terrible images from the Northeast at the forefront of our minds, and the dreadful fate that had befallen four girls that same week thirty-eight years before, as always, lodged in our hearts, the pertinacious pastor looked at me and, not for the first time, said something profoundly impactful.

"Doug, that's what this Cherry business is about. It's about terrorism; it's about stopping the idea that this can happen without consequence and ensuring it doesn't revisit this city or this country again."

Getting Cherry to trial wasn't something I could do much about, despite what the community may have been led to believe. It was in the hands of the medical experts and Judge Garrett. However, I needed to hear what Reverend Woods told me to be reminded of the singular importance of doing whatever I could to bring Cherry to justice. I could do nothing about the World Trade Center, but I vowed not to meekly surrender the fight in Birmingham. Once again, the old civil rights foot soldier had shown me the way. Over the ensuing months, the terrorist attacks dramatically impacted the political climate around the country. The prospect of an Alabama Democrat displacing GOP Senator Sessions had always been a long shot, but the chances dwindled to almost nonexistent. The country was rightly rallying around the Republican President.

It wasn't appropriate to dwell on differences. I didn't agree with everything the Republican leadership was saying, but it was no time to score political points. A unified approach, one that unequivocally backed the resolve of the American people to hold those accountable for acts of terrorism, was required. The political reality was that GOP tough talk was what the country needed to hear. Democrats joined in. Presenting an alternative approach wasn't a realistic option.

When Judge Garrett made his ruling on Cherry in December, I already knew in my heart that I would not make it to Washington this time—whether I stayed in the race or not. I did not withdraw immediately, despite knowing my candidacy was doomed.

I shifted my attention to making a meaningful contribution at Whatley Drake and pondering how I could fully re-engage with the Cherry case in a way that ensured the old Klansman would meet the same fate as Blanton.

In January 2002, before I officially dropped out of the Senate race, I traveled to Montgomery to meet with Attorney General Pryor about the case, which was, after all, a state prosecution he controlled. I laid my cards on the table, letting him know I believed I could make a positive contribution to the prosecution if there were a way I could be reappointed to the team on a full-time basis.

Unfortunately, he was too sensible to be moved by my enthusiasm and succinctly told me my campaign for the Senate wasn't something that could coexist with a prosecution role of such extreme importance.

"Doug, it is just too important for the state. We can't take a chance on it getting sidetracked," he said.

Deep down I knew Pryor was right, and I would have certainly made the same decision had I been in his position. The prosecution team was in great hands with Cochran, Posey, and Wallace, who would now have to knuckle down and construct a trial strategy. I didn't feel I could poke my nose too far into their business unless asked.

More out of a sense of duty to the people who backed me than anything else, I continued to campaign for the Senate nomination for a while, but my heart wasn't in it. As a Democrat, raising money for the campaign was almost impossible at that time, and I felt in some ways the kind of politician I wanted to be wasn't the candidate my party was looking for, rightly or wrongly.

By February it was time to pull the plug. I didn't call a press conference but issued a media release. About three o'clock that afternoon I answered my phone to a pleasant surprise. Bill Pryor was calling from Washington, D.C.

I expected him to sympathize with me.

"I want you to come back and try the Cherry case," he said without preamble.

I hadn't seen that coming.

Pryor explained he'd heard about my pulling out of the political race, and that had been the only issue he needed to be resolved before offering me an opportunity to return to the fold.

"But what about the team that is in place?" I spluttered.

"I will take care of that," Pryor said. "This has been your case, and you have the trust and confidence of the families. . . . You need to see it through."

I felt for my colleague. "But there is a new U.S. Attorney who I am sure would like to see this through."

"I will figure this out. It's just a matter of you wanting to do it."

I probably thought about it for two seconds before accepting his offer. It would be back to burning the candle at both ends, hours of endless frustration, encounters with obnoxious people, and a paltry salary.

I couldn't wait.

PART
THREE

PART

THREE

TEN

CHERRY

There was tension.

I understood my return to the prosecution team would ruffle a few feathers.

Cochran, Wallace, and Posey had done great work while I had been trying to initiate a political career. They were buried in the process of formulating a plan of attack for the Cherry trial, which was scheduled for May 2002, just two months away.

When I returned and took over the lead role again, I was sensitive to the possibility that it could disrupt their routine, and I knew there would be questions about whether part of my motivation was glory seeking.

That couldn't have been further from the truth. At the age of forty-seven, I was putting my stop-start career on hold once again and asking the indulgence of my employers and family. The fact is, I felt an intense personal desire to bring it home one more time, as we say in the South, especially after Reverend Woods and the SCLC reminded me of the importance of holding everyone accountable. Cherry was the last Klansman standing.

My colleagues had worked with dedication in my absence. I wanted to ensure they knew I did not take that for granted. Cochran and Wallace were especially close, having worked in the DA's office together for several years, and I did not want to disrupt the team's chemistry. Subsequently, I initially tried to tread lightly, perhaps too lightly.

I too readily agreed to a few things I might normally have challenged. The guys, for example, had decided Posey should deliver the opening statement. I had no doubt my friend who had excelled so brilliantly during the Blanton trial would do the job again, though I was personally disappointed I wouldn't be setting the tone for the Cherry hearing as I had in the Blanton trial. Nevertheless, compromise was an important part of reestablishing myself on the team and any unease quickly dissipated. In fact, we were quickly united by a shared fear that the Cherry trial could be derailed again.

A budget crisis in Alabama resulted in the state refusing to fund criminal trials, and some were postponed. Our prosecution had been bankrolled by the Feds but was to be tried as a state matter. For several weeks, about a month before Cherry was to enter court, we feared Alabama would refuse to cover the costs, likely bumping the old Klansman's judgment day back again.

Such a development would have produced a very ugly reaction from the community. Fortunately, the funding issue was resolved before we began the process of selecting a jury.

Surrounded by Lies

The Cherry prosecution was markedly different from Blanton's. We did not have eyewitnesses conclusively connecting Cherry to the scene or a clear admission on tape that he made the bomb. However, the old Klansman with the motormouth had been caught out on numerous occasions changing his story to the authorities, saying the kinds of things only a man who believed he had beaten the system would say. We would be able to offer a parade of witnesses testifying that Cherry had boasted about his nefarious deeds, including the church bombing.

Mitch Burns would again be a significant courtroom presence, assuming we could get the tapes of his discussions with Blanton and occasionally Cherry into evidence.

The defense, led by Mickey Johnson and Rodger Bass, would challenge the recordings' admissibility at every opportunity.

We planned to assemble an appropriately ugly portrait of Cherry. It would be immediately clear how despicable he was, especially from family testimony, but we had to tie his capacity for violence to his hatred of blacks and school integration.

Years before, when we had interviewed Cherry in Texas, he had been unable to refrain from regaling the investigators with tales from his past. Without prompting he had blurted: "Hey, did you know that one time I busted old Shuttlesworth right in the nose and busted his head open with my brass knuckles?" He was talking about the incident outside of Phillips High School.

Later, with the help of journalist Jerry Mitchell of the Jackson *Clarion-Ledger*, we would find video from a news station that captured on film the assault on Reverend Shuttlesworth and his wife outside Phillips in 1957. Sure enough, Cherry was right in the middle of it.

That piece of history would be the first piece of the puzzle connecting Cherry's bigotry and capacity for intense violence to the issue of school integration and ultimately the church bombing.

Mitchell also confirmed what our investigation had established about Cherry's alibi for the night of Saturday, September 14. It was completely bogus.

In the interview with Eddy and Herren, Cherry admitted that he had been at the Modern Sign Shop earlier in the evening. However, he had insisted he was home by ten o'clock Saturday night to watch his favorite television show, live studio wrestling, and to care for his cancer-stricken wife, Virginia. He repeated that story to Mitchell in an interview for a newspaper piece. Our B.S. radar went off at the same time as Mitchell's, and, after a little digging through old TV logs and medical records, it was easy to prove Cherry a liar. There was no wrestling on television on Saturday nights during September 1963—broadcasts didn't start until 1964. And while the Klansman's wife died of cancer several years later, she did not have the disease at the time.

Another key piece of our puzzle came courtesy of some first-class work by Don Cochran. Buried in the mountains of evidence, notes, and miscellaneous material assembled over nearly four decades was a five-page handwritten account, signed by Cherry on October 9, 1963, detailing his whereabouts on Friday night, September 13.

The FBI had swiftly come to suspect the then thirty-three-year-old Cherry had played a major role in the bombing. On October 9, 1963, two agents, Joseph Ayers and Carl Welton, conducted the first official interview with him.

The normal custom of the FBI, established by J. Edgar Hoover decades earlier, was to take notes during interviews, then, back at the office, use the notes to write up an official witness statement. But on this occasion, the two agents sensed the importance of what Cherry was saying and decided to handwrite a statement then and there and get him to sign it.

In the document, he describes his whereabouts in the lead-up to the bombing. Cochran was especially riveted by Cherry's admission that he had been at Merle Snow's Modern Sign Shop the Friday night before the attack. The statement read:

On Friday evening, September 13, 1963, I went to the Modern Sign Co. on 3rd Avenue North between 16th and 17th Sts., run by Mr. Snow. I arrived there about 5:30.

I went there to visit and lend a hand in making signs for a motorcade which was to be in protest of Birmingham school integration. During the evening, people I recall coming there are Bob Chambliss, Tommy Blanton Jr., John Frank Jones, and Stevens whose first name I do not know.

Chambliss came about six or six-thirty in the evening, went out for a sandwich and then came back and stayed there till about midnight. Tommy Blanton Jr. came there about six or seven o'clock, went out for a sandwich with Stevens.

A short time after he returned from the sandwich, he and Stevens went to get some mineral spirits for the sign painting job. Tommy Blanton made a few calls which I think were to his girlfriend. Tommy left the place about nine-thirty or ten o'clock at the latest.

I recall that there was a young man there, who is a barber, working at the Paradise Barber Shop. This man could be Bill Jackson. He came about the same time as Blanton. He worked on the signs and then went to eat and brought his girlfriend back with him.

The girl was very pretty and looked to be about fifteen-years-old. He and his girlfriend stayed till about 12 o'clock midnight. The girl had dyed her hair gray. Mr. Snow and I closed the shop a little after midnight.

I have read the above statement of this and from other pages and it is true and correct to the best of my knowledge.—Signed Bobby F Cherry.

Here was Cherry's specific admission that he was at the Modern Sign Shop with Chambliss and Blanton on the Friday night before the bombing. Cochran saw the slam dunk. Coupled with the "oh, we were making the bomb" conversation between Blanton and Jean on the kitchen tape, it corroborated Cherry's involvement. It placed him with the convicted bombers on the night they "made" the device.

While it was likely Cherry's statement—his own words—would be admissible, we knew it would be a fight to get the kitchen tape before the jury. That recording was made June 28, 1964, more than nine months after the bombing, and Cherry was not a part of the conversation.

Under the co-conspiracy law, statements made after a crime is committed are generally not admissible, but Cochran found an exception.

"Under Alabama law," he wrote in his article "Ghosts of Alabama," "if, after the commission of the crime, some of the conspirators participate in concealing the crime by suppressing or fabricating evidence, then there is a 'continuing conspiracy to conceal' and any statements made during the course of and in furtherance of this conspiracy to conceal will be admissible against those involved in the conspiracy."

There was a very long list of evidence linking Cherry and Blanton after the bombing, conspiring to cover their tracks—not the least being Mitch Burns's testimony.

The Last Appeal

The goal was to hold Cherry accountable by whatever means necessary. But I longed for the whole story to come out.

Cherry remained obstinate. Despite Blanton's conviction and his own failed attempt to be ruled legally incompetent to stand trial, Cherry clearly believed, at age seventy-one, having survived a heart attack (in 1988), stints in jail, and accusations of child molestation and spouse beating, he could beat the bombing rap. He'd lived a violent, pathetically selfish, and confused life but somehow had managed to stay out of prison for most of his rotten existence.

Even though he talked way too much to anybody who would listen, he was still protected by the Klan's "kiss of death" threat and an extended family that was reluctant to commit to bringing him down. He had put his seven children into foster care after his wife Virginia died but had stayed in touch often enough to bring pressure to bear on them over the years. Despite his abhorrent treatment of those around him, only Teresa Stacy, his granddaughter, was prepared to condemn him unconditionally. Even her father, Bobby Frank's son Tommy, hedged—not that it got him off the hook with the wicked old man, who shunned him for even talking with authorities.

Cherry had already turned down the opportunity to cut himself a break before the Blanton trial by giving up information on his former Klan colleague. Now, with nothing to barter, he had nothing to lose by putting us to our burden.

So in searching for the full story the community needed, I had nowhere to turn but to Blanton again. I didn't expect he would readily admit guilt, but I thought maybe, just maybe, after almost a year in an Alabama prison where he'd allegedly been beaten up by a prison guard the first week in, he might have a change of heart (if he had one).

If I offered to have him moved to a less oppressive federal facility, perhaps he'd be willing to pass on a bit of detail. Moving him out of the state system seemed like it was probably more than he deserved, but it might prove to be worth it for the community's sake.

About a month before the Cherry trial was scheduled to get underway, Jeff Wallace and I took the plunge, visiting Blanton and his lawyer John Robbins. We quietly had the bomber transported to the Jefferson County Jail from his new home at the St. Clair Correctional Facility outside Birmingham. At the time, he was probably clinging to the faint hope that his (eventually unsuccessful) appeal of the murder convictions would succeed, but the reality of a harsh life behind bars was sure to have kicked in during his first months in a tough state facility.

We wanted to avoid news of the meeting being leaked to the media, so we arranged to meet in the jury room of the courtroom in the basement of the Mel Bailey Criminal Justice Center. It is the same space where Blanton had watched intently as lawyers for the prosecution and defense questioned prospective jurors in his case. And it was the same location where jurors would soon be deciding the fate of Bobby Frank Cherry. Sheriff's deputies remained outside to ensure our conversation was completely private.

Blanton didn't completely ignore me this time. He clearly assumed we were there to horse trade. I began by reminding him of our earlier meeting and that I didn't lie to him—I told him what I was going to do, and I did it.

"I'm not going to lie to you now either. The fact of the matter is I don't have as much to offer as I did then."

I went on to tell him that even if he were to help me and admit he was guilty, we would let his appeal go its normal course. "I won't do anything to get you out of jail, but I believe that I could get you moved to a safer and more comfortable federal facility."

Just as he had done in our meeting two years earlier, Blanton listened with his best poker face intact. I knew I was not offering much, so I decided I would hold out one more carrot.

"You know, Chambliss died in prison and you probably will too. But if you cooperate with us and accept responsibility for what you did there's at least a chance that might not happen."

I went on to tell him again that the community needed someone to tell the story and apologize for what had happened. If he could just find it in his heart to do that, I would commit to speaking to the families and leaders of the community about not necessarily opposing parole down the track. "I can't promise you anything," I said, "but my commitment is to try."

It was then that he interrupted to say, "Well, you're really not offering me anything. I don't like the Feds anyway."

There it was. To that point he hadn't at any stage said "I didn't do it. I can't help you." Instead, he just grew impatient with my refusal to put a better price on getting the truth. In my mind, it was just as strong an admission as he had made on the kitchen tape.

Robbins weighed in, pointing out to Blanton that the chance to move to a federal facility was a pretty big deal, even if he hated the Feds.

Finally, Blanton had enough and let loose. "I'm not going to do anything," he said emphatically. "This whole deal is political. You guys had your say, but I never got to tell my story. I can't help you."

With that, I didn't have to play the nice guy anymore. He'd given me the figurative middle finger once again, and now it was my turn.

"Don't you give me that crap you son of a bitch," I said, almost instinctively. "You had every chance to tell your story. You could have taken the witness stand and told your story. Hell, even Connie Chung tried to interview you, but you wouldn't talk!"

At this point, he was no longer making eye contact.

"Besides, you knew that if you took the stand, I would slice you to ribbons on cross-examination."

There was a moment of silence laced with tension before he finally looked up. "You're probably right," he said.

"Hell, I know I'm right."

And with that, Wallace and I left the room, disappointed but not surprised.

It would be more than twelve years before I would see Blanton again.

Sheldon's Jury Magic

The media interest in the Cherry case was extraordinary, much more intense than Blanton's. Cherry always seemed to be portrayed as more of a villain, even before the dementia ruling. Maybe it was something to do with his name—Bobby Frank seems to have a familiar good ole boy quality to it.

As expected, the defense filed motions to move the trial out of Birmingham, but we were confident Judge Garrett would keep it in the city. This time, though, he wanted the trial held in the smaller Mel Bailey Criminal Justice Center basement courtroom. A modern, fairly soulless complex, all parties and, indeed, the gallery would be in close proximity. It would be like being locked in a box under fluorescent lighting.

While the local community was anxious to see Cherry in court, and Birmingham newspapers published scores of stories about the case, there was a tense anticipatory silence about the trial itself. Discussions in churches and at community gatherings had replaced the near riotous public outcry demanding the old Klansman be brought to the bar of justice, which initially threatened our ability to keep proceedings in the city.

The defense objected strongly, but the judge ordered the hearing be held in Birmingham as scheduled.

My team had conducted a mock trial in preparation for the real thing, which helped solidify a few plans for presentation of the evidence. I purposely did not participate, watching instead from behind a one-way mirror. I had become the face of the prosecution, and it was important not to let the "jurors" know who was conducting the exercise.

In my view, the most crucial pre-trial work in the weeks leading up to trial would be strategizing and planning for jury selection. Thankfully, Andy Sheldon had secured a modest contract with Bill Pryor and was on board again. In my mind his involvement in the Blanton trial was not just an unqualified success—he was part of the team.

On May 6, a full year after the Blanton conviction, Sheldon handed out a questionnaire that contained input from both the defense and the prosecution to a jury pool of 114 citizens. We pored over the information about each juror, using both the answers to the questionnaire and the notes we had made during the voir dire, the preliminary examination process. On a Sunday afternoon, a day before we would convene in the courtroom for the trial to get underway, the prosecution team gathered in the Whatley Drake conference room to decide who were our preferred panelists and, more importantly, who were not. Sheldon guided us. Our model juror preferences were much the same as in the Blanton case: family people, churchgoers, those with an affinity for their community.

Several selections were quick and easy, but the process wasn't as swift as last time. It became difficult establishing who each prosecution team member favored. We needed to map it on a whiteboard, but nothing big enough was available.

Then I remembered.

I went to the back of the office and pulled out a four-by-eight-foot corrugated "Doug Jones for U.S. Senate" sign that was slick and white on the back.

"At least this will be good for something," I said.

Wallace propped it up on a chair and proceeded to map our choices as if he were plotting the D-Day invasion.

With Judge Garrett presiding, it would take a full week for the defense and the prosecution to settle on the dozen individuals who would determine the guilt or innocence of Cherry. To preserve the integrity of the selection process, and ensure potential jurors were not exposed by the media, the judge followed the same procedure as with Blanton. Selection was carried out in closed court, with potential jurors questioned one at a time, never in the company of others.

We ended up with six white women, three white men, and three black men.

Judge Garrett had once again decided to sequester jury members for the duration of the trial. He called in extra support from the Sheriff's Department to assist the panelists in getting home to pack some belongings before heading to the downtown hotel where they would live during the trial.

Meantime, back in the basement courtroom, Mickey Johnson and Rodger Bass were giving us all we could handle with motions to exclude three of the most important pieces of the Cherry puzzle. The first was the defense effort to keep out the video of the Shuttlesworth beating. Johnson argued that the film from 1957 had been made too long ago to be relevant and had no probative value to the church bombing case.

Cochran had the case law to back up our contention that the bombing was tied to efforts to integrate the Birmingham schools, while Posey and I chimed in on Cherry's propensity for violence to stop black and white kids from going to school together. What he did in 1957 was a reaction to the same issue that came to a head in September 1963.

It was not lost on us, or I think on Judge Garrett, that the defense lead, Johnson, did not attempt to argue that the man in the white shirt on film reaching in his pocket during the beating was someone other than his client.

The defense also argued to exclude the kitchen tape, Johnson submitting that Cherry's name was not even mentioned. But Cochran laid out the other evidence that bound Blanton's statements with other co-conspirator utterances, thus ensuring their admissibility, we believed.

Finally, Johnson and Bass took aim at the Mitch Burns tapes. Like Robbins a year earlier, they suggested the recordings amounted to little more than unreliable chatter among a couple of drunks. It was all pure hearsay, and irrelevant hearsay at that, they argued.

We had anticipated their argument and added a few excerpts featuring not only Blanton and Burns but Cherry as well, who bragged about lying to the FBI.

As is often the case with motions to exclude evidence, Judge Garrett withheld final rulings until we got into the trial and he could consider them in light of other evidence. The defense would hammer the issues at every break in the proceedings, imploring the judge to exclude the recordings and the Cherry note.

Coming back to the case after an absence, I always felt I was playing catch-up in some way. There were even fewer hours in the day than during the Blanton trial.

In those tense weeks before the Cherry trial, my fear of failure was acute. We weren't just taking a shot at a cold case, as we had with Blanton; there was an expectation of success.

The trial preparations were unsettlingly demanding, and lingering unrest over the case in the black community made me anxious. Additionally, the constant media attention surrounding Cherry was intense and occasionally intrusive. Every moment in the build-up to the commencement of the hearings was covered by national and international outlets, many of them camping out with their equipment in the streets of Birmingham. I couldn't shake the thought that a failure to get a guilty verdict in the case might generate a riotous response. Still, I knew we were well prepared overall.

Having had the benefit of going through the process with Blanton and a mock trial for Cherry, we strode into the courtroom before Judge Garrett on May 14 with a degree of confidence.

I was personally dismayed at the absence of a key team member. Jeff Wallace, a critical voice in the Blanton trial and throughout the investigation, had opted to bow out of the trial team during prep. I was disappointed, though I understood my esteemed colleague's reasoning that four trial lawyers in a courtroom was simply too many.

The room seemed too small for such a big affair. My team huddled together to the left of the judge. Posey, Cochran, and I were closest to the jury box, while the investigators, Herren and Fleming, our media coordinator and assistant, Amy Gallimore, and the IT team were on a bench behind us.

All eyes were on Cherry, resplendent in a blue suit. A tall man with distinctive features, he had a swagger about him. Even though Cherry occasionally looked to be at war with himself as well as the world around him, he tried to project an air of confidence.

He was an arrogant man who had conned his way through nearly everything and had obviously walked into court convinced he would do it again. The suit gave him a façade of respectability, but you got the feeling he might explode at any moment.

Posey would give the State's opening statement, hopefully picking up from his incredible closing in the Blanton trial without missing a beat.

In what would be an emotional case, we wanted to start coolly, with a detailed overview of our case. We would follow a plan of attack similar to our approach in the Blanton trial, initially providing historical context and focusing on the church and the heartless targeting of innocent children because of the Klan's outrage at school integration.

Unlike the old courtroom, our more intimate surroundings meant noise from the gallery and around the court was more noticeable. Reactions from spectators would feed the drama of testimony and legal conflict. We would again use photographic references, visible to the jury on monitors. The room fell into an almost deafening silence as Posey addressed the court.

He immediately harkened back to 1963, when John F. Kennedy was President and George Wallace had become Governor of Alabama for the first time on a platform of "segregation now, segregation tomorrow, segregation forever."

The history lesson sizzled, with Posey explaining that oppression and discrimination had resulted in school kids taking to the streets in protest, only to be assaulted by authorities wielding fire hoses and dogs.

He segued into a close examination of Cherry's character—his decades-long objection to desegregation and his propensity for extreme violence.

The last time that desegregation had been attempted in Birmingham was a few years earlier when a black preacher named Fred Shuttlesworth tried to enroll his children in Phillips High School.

They were met by a mob of Klansmen, who beat Shuttlesworth to the ground. One of the men in the Klan mob was the defendant, Bobby Frank Cherry, and Cherry would later brag about how he hit Shuttlesworth in the face with a set of brass knuckles. A news cameraman caught the beating on videotape, and we expect to play that tape for this jury.

Posey indicated we'd then turn to the evidence linking Cherry to the church bombing, including the multiple admissions he'd made over the years to friends, family, and acquaintances:

His children knew the story. His granddaughter heard him brag about it. His son-in-law heard it. His brother-in-law, Wayne Brogdon, listened on many occasions to this defendant tell about what he had done to the church in Birmingham in 1963, and about the children who were killed.

It was a puzzle the prosecution would help jurors assemble, Posey said. My colleague had put the first pieces in place.

The Defense Surprises

Mickey Johnson, the defense lead, was an excellent attorney, and a scrapper. He wasn't one to back away from confrontation but had a low-key, folksy way about him that jurors could relate to.

Johnson, admirably, would get straight to the point, a quality that enhanced his believability. As expected, he immediately went after the credibility of the witnesses who would testify about Cherry's admissions, suggesting whatever they said could not be believed. That didn't overly concern me. We had a diverse group poised to reveal what Cherry had said to them over the years. It would be difficult to dismiss every witness as lacking credibility.

Johnson, however, certainly got our attention when he revealed his overriding strategy: a wholesale dismissal of the credibility of the investigation. The defense contended it was flawed from the beginning, as the prosecution would not have focused on Cherry as a primary suspect but for "lies" told a year after the bombing.

He did not mention her by name, but clearly he was talking about Mary Frances Cunningham's statement to investigators in 1964 when she alleged she had been an eyewitness to the Klansmen placing the bomb under the church stairs.

It seemed not to matter to the defense that Cunningham had subsequently recanted that statement on numerous occasions. Certainly, we had no plans to try and fashion evidence to comply with her original story. (As noted previously, Kirthus Glenn's story was remarkably similar, but she had long passed, and we wouldn't be able to introduce her Chambliss trial testimony.)

Johnson's ploy would obviously bring Cunningham to the stand, which we anticipated would be entertaining, if nothing else, especially if the defense made the mistake of implying she had an affair with Deputy Hancock.

Our first witness would be the indomitable Alpha Robertson.

The small courtroom meant the visual tools were even more prominent for the jury. Due to the room dimensions, we employed a single large screen positioned in front of the panel instead of a series of monitors.

Mrs. Robertson had been confined to a wheelchair and was in failing health. She hadn't wanted to go through the trauma of appearing again but bravely compelled herself to do so. Her raw, emotional testimony was as effective as in the Blanton trial, perhaps more so, with the screen projecting a six-foot-high photo of a serene Carole.

Sitting in her chair next to the screen she swelled with pride describing her daughter's dress that day: "They were wearing white dresses. She also had her first pair of little heels, black pumps."

She explained that she was dressing at her home a few blocks away when the explosion shattered the serenity of that Sunday morning.

"It was just an awful sound, like something shaking the world all over," she said.

The jury, along with the rest of the courtroom, could not conceal the emotional impact of this amazing lady's heartfelt testimony.

Afterward, Mrs. Robertson grasped Amy Gallimore's hand and thanked her for all we were doing. We were not only grateful for Carole's mother's presence but also relieved her time on the stand was done. Every sentence she uttered, every memory she invoked, was painful. What an exceptional woman.

Having made the court aware of the emotional weight of the case, we wanted quickly to lock in Cherry's long history of violence and opposition to school integration.

James Armstrong, one of the great civil rights foot soldiers, who famously enrolled his sons Dwight and Floyd in formerly all-white Graymont Elementary School, enraging the Klan in 1963, took the stand.

We displayed a photo of that day. It showed Armstrong escorting his two sons to the school alongside Reverend Shuttlesworth and attorney

Oscar Adams. "Five days later," he said, reflecting, "the explosion was at the 16th Street Church."

A witness or participant in many of the pivotal events of the civil rights era, Armstrong painted a vivid picture of Birmingham in the late fifties and sixties, reflecting on Wallace's "segregation forever" speech, the dramatic impact of the children's marches, and the presence of Dr. King in the troubled city.

He also recalled being at Phillips High School when Reverend Shuttlesworth planned to enroll his children in 1957 to test the *Brown v. Board of Education* decision on school integration. Armstrong said he heard a commotion while waiting for Shuttlesworth to arrive. On investigation, he saw numerous white men beating the pastor and his wife.

There was a "crowd around them, covering him," he said.

Armstrong, a self-employed barber, later was involved in a lawsuit along with seven other families to integrate the schools. As others dropped out of the action when their jobs were threatened, Armstrong became the lone plaintiff. It culminated with him enrolling his boys at Graymont in 1963.

We had footage of that Shuttlesworth assault in 1957 we wanted to show the jury to point out Cherry's involvement and his propensity for violence. The young man who filmed the incident, Jimmy Parker, by then in his sixties, was next to testify. He had graduated from Phillips High School in 1957 and had gone back in September to get his transcripts to enroll in college. When he came out of Phillips that day, there was a "ruckus" going on outside.

An aspiring television cameraman working for our local PBS station, he grabbed a sixteen-millimeter camera and shot about fifteen white men beating a black man, Shuttlesworth, and four other people, while up to forty other white men looked on.

He remembered "a couple of people swinging real hard . . . and one of the guys you could see reach in his pocket and pull out something." He didn't know what was in the man's hand but thought it might be a roll of quarters as he took a swing at Shuttlesworth.

Cochran had Parker identify a DVD made from the film he shot, but by agreement with the court we held off playing it for the jury until we could prove that it was Cherry in the film assaulting the former Bethel Baptist Church pastor.

Our next witness would provide that opportunity.

Bobby Birdwell was the first witness we produced who would say he heard Cherry talking about the bombing. He was just twelve years old in 1963 and lived around the corner from the Klansman's family in Ensley, a community to the west of downtown Birmingham right near my hometown of Fairfield.

He and Tommy Frank, Bobby's oldest child, were friends. On visits, he'd heard various emphatic declarations from Cherry, including "my kids will never go to school with niggers," on numerous occasions. A few days before the bombing, Birdwell was in the Cherry house when he saw a white robe with "cutouts in the eyes."

"That's my daddy's," young Cherry told him.

Birdwell testified that he and Tommy went into the kitchen, where Cherry and three other men were sitting "talking and everything, you know."

"And I heard them mention [the] bomb and 16th Street."

He told the jury that he heard about the bombing just a few days later, but he didn't tell anyone what he had heard. "I was scared, you know . . . there was a lot of hatred."

Cochran played the DVD of the Phillips High School incident for Birdwell and the jury. At the point when a sandy-haired man reaches into his pocket, Cochran paused the video and used a red-dot laser to point to the attacker apparently foraging for a weapon.

Birdwell indicated to the court he knew the man.

"And who is that?" Cochran asked.

"Bobby Cherry."

"Any doubt in your mind?"

"No, sir."

Cherry's brass-knuckle attack on the leader of the Birmingham civil rights push in 1957 was evidence of his propensity to violently protest school integration years before he played a crucial role in the church bombing.

It was time to focus squarely on the bombing.

Reverend Cross, the former 16th Street pastor, had suffered three strokes but summoned all his strength to testify one more time. During his stoic appearance, I asked him to verify the contents and context of photos that included the scene and the girls' bodies in the morgue. His horror was visceral as he described the bodies as "mutilated and scarred up." He identified the bodies of the girls taken in the morgue (though the jury would not see the images until later).

Maxine McNair told the Cherry jury the same story she had related to the Blanton jury a year earlier and the Chambliss jury almost twenty-five years ago. Her despairing cry of "my baby, my baby," was no less heartfelt, no less impactful.

During the lunch break on that first day, I was reflecting on how well our opening gambit had played for the court when Gallimore tracked me down. She'd been sitting with the families all day, and I expected a report of how they were responding to proceedings.

"There is a lady out there sitting with the families who says she is Cynthia's sister," she said.

Bill Fleming joined us as I took it in.

The Wesleys were both deceased, but I hadn't thought to reach out to Cynthia Wesley's blood relatives from the Morris family, who, I believed, did not attend the Blanton trial.

"Are you sure?" I asked.

"She sounds legitimate."

Fleming knew what I was thinking. Siblings were walking, talking connections to history—they help juries understand the full, shattering impact the loss of life delivers. But Reverend Hamlin had told us over the years that some animosity had built up between the Morris family and the Wesleys.

"Remember," Fleming said, "we have heard that there might be some bad blood between these folks."

The Morrises reportedly had felt aggrieved for decades, believing they were snubbed at Cynthia's funeral, forced to sit in the back while the Wesleys were coffin-side.

I had been looking at photos of Cynthia Wesley off and on for about four years. Her large eyes and wide smile hinted at a personality mature beyond her fourteen years. When Gallimore introduced me to Eunice Davis, I knew at first glance she was Cynthia's sister. They shared kind and caring eyes. I immediately felt an attachment.

I apologized to her for not reaching out to her family. She was gracious in the extreme and willing to provide me with a rundown of what had been going on in her life during that turbulent year of 1963. One of eight children—five girls and three boys—and the daughter of a single mother, times were "kind of rough back then."

A social worker convinced her mother to let Cynthia live with the Wesley family to ease the caregiving burden. Eunice, at the same time, took on a caregiver role with all her siblings, learning to make the most of the very little the family had. She seemed to be the glue that kept them together and would reach out regularly to Cynthia.

Their bond was strong, which made the way she learned of her sister's death even more painful. Eunice heard about the church bombing on the radio. She was the family member charged with the duty of traveling to the Wesley family home to confirm the death.

Her story riveted me. It was as if Cynthia herself was giving a firsthand account of her family's struggles. Acting on trial instincts, I told Ms. Davis that I would like to call her as a witness. She agreed, saying she wanted to do something for her sister. It was a bit of a risk, as we'd not done any preparation.

"I understand that there was some friction between your family and the Wesleys after Cynthia died," I said. "But I don't want to get into any of that. This is for Cynthia, OK?"

She understood and agreed.

That afternoon I called her to the stand, where she repeated the story of how she'd learned about her sister's death while Cynthia's photograph gazed across the courtroom from the screen. Davis captivated the jury just as she had engaged me. Stepping down from the stand, she flashed a smile that was uncannily similar to Cynthia's gentle grin, evident in the photo still dominating the room. The Morris family had finally been included in the story of seeking justice for their child.

We ended the day with another sister, Junie Peavey, Addie Mae's sibling, who had been counting the Sunday School offering when the bomb exploded. Sixteen-year-old Junie had taken on the grisly task of identifying the body of her sister, and the image was as stark in the courtroom as it was in 1963. It was an emotional conclusion.

The defense had made the strategic decision not to cross-examine most of the witnesses. There was not a lot to be gained from querying their extreme emotional response to the bombing.

Before heading home and trying to gather my thoughts for the next day's proceedings, I raced to catch the ill and aged Reverend Cross before he traveled back to his Atlanta home with his daughter Barbara. I had long had great respect and affection for the old minister. The psychological toll the bombing had taken on him was terrible, but he remained a compassionate and thoughtful man, summoning great resolve to be a terrific witness.

He was certainly one of the unsung heroes on that terrible day, braving entry into the destroyed ladies' lounge to find the bodies, then grabbing a bullhorn to keep peace in the streets by reciting part of his Sunday School lesson: "A Love That Forgives."

Before they left the court, I told Reverend Cross how much I appreciated him and how much it meant to everyone that he had appeared again for the girls. He said nothing for a moment, taking my hand in both of his.

"I am so happy I got to meet you," he said.

I was overwhelmed. I managed a "thank you," as I choked back the tears. "You can't imagine what that means to me."

On my way home to my family that night, I marveled at what a journey it had been. Often we are caught up in the demands of the moment, and during trials, I am always battling anxiety. It's hard to focus on anything but the case itself. But, for that moment at least, I was able to take a step back and recognize what a privilege it was for me to know people such as Reverend Cross, Mrs. Robertson, the McNairs, Junie Peavey, Eunice Davis, and Sarah Rudolph. Despite their overwhelming, never-ending grief, they had not tumbled into bitterness and cynicism. I invested just a little bit more of my heart and soul in the case that day.

Burns Tapes

The challenge to prove a bomb caused the devastation on September 15, 1963, was the same imperative it had been in the Blanton trial. With no physical evidence to draw on, we again would rely on the testimony of explosives experts.

Additionally, Cochran had sought the opinion of a leading pathologist of what he could glean about the nature of the girls' injuries from the various reports and photographs. This, we believed, would add substance to the evidence that a bomb, not a gas explosion or the like, had killed and injured.

In calling Dr. Robert Brissie, a professor of pathology at the University of Alabama in Birmingham and Chief Coroner and Medical Examiner of Jefferson County, we had a witness of unquestioned qualifications, with extensive experience in the lab and the courtroom. I knew firsthand the caliber of witness he was, having cross-examined him on several occasions during my time in private practice. But I admit I felt uneasy about the fact that during Dr. Brissie's testimony, we would seek to admit into evidence and show the jury staggeringly graphic photographs of the girls' bodies in the morgue.

We had attempted to introduce the photos into the Blanton case, but the defense had successfully objected, insisting they were prejudicial. We opted not to push the point for a variety of reasons, including the fact that using that sort of overwhelmingly impactful material can often backfire.

Our aim wasn't to shock the jury into a conviction but rather guide them to a logical conclusion of guilt.

I had mixed feelings about the use of such material in the Cherry trial. I think it was the defense lawyer side of me coming out.

I believed that such photos were potentially more prejudicial than probative, not to mention downright morbid. But my fine colleague Cochran had focused intently on getting Brissie to testify so he could introduce the photos to demonstrate his point that the injuries were consistent with a high-order explosion. His position made sense, even if it unsettled me.

The doctor, as expected, was a splendid witness, and the jury seemed intrigued as they followed his explanations as to how the girls died. He detailed that high-order explosive-type detonations cause two types of injuries: primary injuries from the sheer shock wave from the explosion itself and secondary injuries from flying projectiles.

Cochran carefully guided Dr. Brissie through all the photographs and documents from the period that Brissie had examined to formulate his opinions decades later—autopsy drawings and photos of the scene, including the devastation inside and outside of the church.

When it came to displaying the photos of the girls' bodies, Judge Garrett ordered us to angle the large screen so they would only be visible to the jury.

It made me very uncomfortable. The horrified looks on the faces of those jurors said it all. Just the day before they had seen the large photographs of each of those children, dressed in their Sunday best, or in the case of Denise McNair, in her pajamas holding her doll.

The families sitting behind me knew exactly what the jury was seeing, as they had seen the carnage firsthand. There was an awful lot of emotion in both trials, but this was a moment of great pain.

Dr. Brissie, without emotion, offered commentary and concluded: "It would be my opinion that the decedents died as a result of extensive blast injuries that resulted from both apparent secondary blast injuries and most probably primary blast injuries also."

I don't know about the jury, but I had a hard time refocusing. I kept imagining how difficult that testimony must have been on the families.

I was glad that Posey then plunged us into a careful scientific evaluation of the bombing scene with experts. He questioned former Alabama Gas Corporation employee Richard Harris, who declared a natural gas leak could not have caused the explosion, before calling one of the explosives investigators who had done the lab work in 1963.

Charles Killion had been employed with the FBI from 1948 to 1973. When he retired, he established the Virginia state forensic laboratory. As the Feds swept into Birmingham in the wake of the church killings, Killion said his initial impression of the scene was it had not been "a low-order-type explosion, such as gas. It was a high-order explosion."

He testified that authorities found nothing that could be identified as a remnant or piece of a bomb device despite extensive searching. He noted, however, that this was not necessarily unusual and that pieces are often just simply "consumed in the blast."

The FBI had taken samples from the area, including residue that they had hoped would produce some evidence of the material used to detonate the bomb. However, nothing conclusive was found. The agent agreed those results might have been different if scientists back in the day had had access to today's technology.

Posey and the team did a thorough job reinforcing the theory that a bomb, and only a bomb, could have caused the explosion.

There had been no major slipups, and our case was coming together just as planned. But I was anxious to get back to putting Cherry front and center.

We had been the targets of so much criticism over the competency issue that I was more than ready to get into the meat of our case by rolling out those who implicated Cherry in the bombing. The nasty old Klansman's declarations over the years to friends and family were damning. It was time to stifle our critics by playing all our best cards.

Cochran called Ralph Butler for his last, historic testimony. The old agent began his career with the FBI in 1955 and was working in New York when he was transferred to Birmingham in November 1963 to work the church bombing.

His area of expertise was electronic surveillance, which is why he came in contact with informant Mitch Burns, who was being handled by Special Agent John Downey.

Butler explained to the jury how he would meet with Downey and Burns regularly to install the bulky reel-to-reel recorder in the trunk of the Klansman's car. After each outing that Burns would take with Blanton and others, Butler would remove the tape and the recorder and give the recording to Agent Downey.

Ben Herren took the stand to identify the Burns tapes. He also explained to the jury how we had prepared the transcripts for the jury's use—a painstaking process that began with the FBI steno pool and group efforts among the lawyers, investigators, and Burns himself.

However, as we prepared for Burns to take the stand, the defense, not unexpectedly, once again objected to the tapes' admission. Judge Garrett took us into his chamber to hear arguments. Cochran again spelled out his belief that a conspiracy existed between Blanton and Cherry, ensuring the legality of the tape evidence. Johnson insisted there was no evidence of a conspiracy and, in fact, the pair hardly knew each other.

In the end, the judge allowed us to introduce all but one of the tape excerpts we wanted to use. It was a very important victory.

On the stand, Burns detailed his affection for Marie Aldridge, the waitress, and how he came to hook up with Blanton after being approached by Agent Brook Blake. He noted that the horrendous photos of the deceased girls compelled him to act.

"Now, were these pictures of the little girls alive?" Cochran asked.

"They were mangled," Burns responded, "and it was sickening to look at. I almost vomited. It made me sick."

It was at that point, he told the court, that he agreed to become an FBI informant and his car was rigged up with a microphone in the radio and the recorder in the trunk. Conversations in the car were captured on tape. Once the Klansmen left the vehicle, they were out of range. Several significant conversations occurred away from the car. Burns recounted them for the jury.

The first took place at the National States' Rights headquarters. Blanton had urged Burns to go there so Dr. Ed Fields could publish a story about how Burns, like so many other Klan members, was harassed by the FBI.

When Burns arrived, Cherry was there. Talk almost immediately turned to the church bombing, which had occurred well over a year earlier.

In his typical braggadocious way, Cherry told Burns he'd been interviewed by the FBI and had taken a lie detector test, but he had "lied all through it. I didn't tell them shit."

Another conversation Burns recalled took place at Cherry's house one night. When the church bombing case came up, Cherry said: "They [the FBI] think the bomb was made somewhere else."

We also had a great anecdote from Burns about a discussion in the car on a day when the recording device was not installed. Unfortunately, we were prevented from entering it into evidence, courtesy of an upheld defense objection. Burns was poised to tell the tale of the day they were cruising to

Cherry's house. As they turned down a street running behind the Klansman's home, Blanton allegedly said: "This is the alley I almost missed the night we bombed the church."

Johnson succeeded in keeping that one out of evidence and fought like hell to keep the other admissions away from the jury, but he could do nothing about the tapes.

As we prepared to play the recordings, a hush fell over the court.

The recorded sound of a distant siren filled the room, then Blanton—perhaps mocking the police—jovially asks: "Where were you guys when the church blew up?"

Cherry: "Yeah, we're just trying to make a bomb . . . we ain't got ours made yet."

On another excerpt, Cherry talks about being a demolition expert in the Marines, and ponders unexploded bombs found in Birmingham: "Probably had the wrong kind of caps in them."

Blanton: "What kind of batteries do they use?"

"Hell, I don't know what kind they used," replies Cherry. "Hell, a flashlight battery would have set it off. Hell, they have had it in there when a clock, the alarm, or something . . . the mother-fucker makes contact, you see."

The jury also heard Blanton admonishing Cherry, telling him to stop talking: "Careful what you say around this boy," Blanton said, referencing Burns. "He doesn't know too much. Let's keep it that way."

Johnson's cross-examination was not as combative as John Robbins's in the Blanton trial. The defense, this time, opted to question Burns's memory and the context of the discussions.

After thirty-eight years, on the third day of his Cherry testimony, Mitchell Burns's role as an FBI informant was complete. Burns again had emerged as a pivotal witness: assertive and trustworthy. The irony was obvious—a Klansman playing a major role in efforts to bring justice for black families, and I knew he would have done it all again if he had to.

Our case was picking up momentum, and we planned to introduce the kitchen tape the next day. Although it didn't feature Cherry, it was still a critical piece of evidence, helping to connect the activities of the convicted bombers with the defendant.

As they had in the Blanton trial, Agents John Colvin and Ralph Butler set the scene, explaining the process of planting the microphone under the Blanton kitchen sink.

Johnson wasn't going to let the recording into evidence without a fight.

Another round of arguments outside the presence of the jury took place be-fore Judge Garrett issued his final ruling to let the tape into evidence.

Bill Fleming testified about finding the tape during the most recent in-vestigation.

"Agent Fleming," Johnson asked on cross-examination, "have you heard Bobby Cherry's voice on that tape anywhere?"

"Not on this tape, no, sir."

This allowed Johnson to return to his opening statement theme: that the investigation had relied on witnesses who were not credible, meaning that leads pointing in a different direction were ignored.

"You're a trained investigator. Can you tell the ladies and gentlemen if you have a procedure which you follow to make a determination . . . if it's truthful?" he asked.

"Well, we don't go around with a crystal ball," Fleming said with a soft counter-punch.

Judge Garrett gave the defense considerable leeway on cross-examination.

Over my many objections, Johnson was able to focus on Mary Frances Cunningham's 1964 statement implicating Cherry, Blanton, and Chambliss. He accused the investigators of not letting go of her accusations even though she had recanted them years later.

He queried why the reopened investigation didn't focus more on Bob Chambliss and the "fourth" man, Herman Cash.

"We were not going to focus our resources on people who were dead," Fleming said.

It was a real test for the veteran agent, but he was more than up for it. He carefully detailed how the investigation came together and why certain lines of inquiry were followed.

To ensure we milked the drama of the kitchen tape and provided the jury with context, Cochran convinced us to call Blanton's on-again, off-again crush, and bride, Jean Casey Barnes. Unlike at the Blanton trial, Barnes wasn't a potential asset for the defendant. All we needed was for her to identify the voices on the tape (hers, Blanton's, and the unknown third person's) and place Blanton at the Modern Sign Shop on Friday night.

With her ex-husband finally behind bars, my long-held desire to attack her credibility in court had been largely extinguished. Her testimony was brief but significant.

Cochran asked: "Ms. Barnes, at one point on the tape and in the tran-script, there's a mention of a Friday night. I think the specific quote is: 'that

Friday night when you stood me up?' Do you know . . . what Friday night you were referring to?"

"That would be the Friday night before the bombing on Sunday morning," she responded coolly.

She testified that Blanton called her from the Modern Sign Shop. She called him back there, and he broke off their date (and, as we established in the Blanton trial, went out with Waylene Vaughn).

When we played the tape, it was not the borderline smoking gun it proved to be in the Blanton trial, but it was a stunning courtroom drama nonetheless. The jury ate up every word, the recording clearly audible to the entire room.

As it was played, Cherry squirmed and smoldered in his seat. I'm sure that Johnson and Bass had instructed their pompous client to keep his facial expressions and body language in check, as jurors always watch for signs from the defendant. But Cherry was not the type of guy who could rein himself in.

Having established Blanton's whereabouts that Friday night, we now set about placing Cherry with him.

Retired FBI agent Carl Welton, a soft-spoken man who reminded me of my step-grandfather, Auburn Grey, was one of four former G-men who would testify about the conflicting statements given by Cherry in his interviews.

Bill Fleming and I had visited with him in his Macon, Georgia, home before seeking the indictments so that we could talk to him firsthand about his importance to the case.

Welton and his now deceased FBI partner Joe Ayers had interviewed Cherry about his whereabouts that Friday night and had the foresight to get him to sign the handwritten statement. Before I introduced that into evidence, I walked Welton through the inconsistencies in Cherry's statements during that period.

Welton was stationed in Macon when he got the call on September 15, 1963, to head to Birmingham to assist with the church bombing investigation.

During seven meetings with the Feds over eight weeks, Cherry tried to massage his alibi slightly on each occasion and ended up contradicting himself. He had initially said that he didn't know Blanton well, but then would talk about him carrying around a "big ol' knife" that he "kept flipping around like a nigger."

He also said he had not seen Blanton the week of the bombing, but later revealed that Blanton came by his house the night of the bombing, and the pair talked about it.

For a couple of hours, the jury listened as I walked Agent Welton through each of the interviews he had conducted with Cherry, often skipping back and forth between interviews to highlight inconsistencies. It was painstaking but effective. The truth from an innocent man does not contain inconsistencies like those Cherry produced, all within months of the bombing.

The signed statement was icing on the cake.

On cross-examination, Johnson noted that Cherry did not make admissions in interviews and sought to highlight the fact that he volunteered information when asked even though he did not have to.

As I listened to Johnson all but say that his client was a good citizen doing his part to assist the FBI, it occurred to me that it wasn't only the inconsistencies that were important.

What Cherry had failed to say was just as telling. On redirect, I questioned Welton about some of the defendant's alibi, which we would break down later for the court. The agent duly stated that at no time during the interviews did the Klansman say anything about leaving the Modern Sign Shop on Saturday night before the bombing to go home to watch live studio wrestling. Nor did he mention his wife was bedridden with cancer, as he was to allege later.

To drive the point home, I asked the agent if he had seen Mrs. Cherry when he was at the family home for his October 9 interview.

"I think I did," he said.

"Was she bedridden?"

"No."

By the time Welton stepped down I felt we had positioned Cherry exactly where we wanted him—with Chambliss and Blanton when they were making "the big one."

Willadean on the Stand

It is wise to weigh carefully the positives and negatives of introducing a witness with an obvious personal agenda into the reconstruction of an event you're soberly relating to a jury.

If we'd opted to bring out Cherry's ex-wife, Willadean Brogdon, too early in the case, it would have amounted to a step in the direction of committing prosecutorial suicide. But by the time we were ready to unleash her on the court, the jury had a solid outline of the events of 1963 and a sense of the defendant's bizarre history.

In a case that featured more unusual characters than a P. T. Barnum sideshow, Ms. Brogdon was a headline act whose body language revealed a repulsion for Cherry that knew no bounds.

As Rick Bragg wrote for the *New York Times*: "Willadean Brogdon, who once left her then husband in a cloud of dust on the side of the road in Mt. Olive, Alabama . . . could never be called an impartial witness."

Posey had the honor of guiding Willadean through her story, detailing how in the late sixties she drove an eighteen-wheel tractor-trailer as one of only a handful of women truck drivers in the country. In 1969 she was hauling explosives for Baggett Trucking when she met Cherry, also a truck driver, at a stop in Indiana where they had coffee. They collided again at a truck stop in Birmingham, and by May 1970 she had moved in with him in the Magic City.

She recounted seeing his Klan robe, "white with red stripes on the arms and gold on the shoulders," and talked about how he was proud of being a Klansman, dancing around in the KKK uniform for her and her children.

Posey asked Brogdon if Cherry ever said anything to her about the 16th Street church.

"His car broke down . . . on Fifth Avenue, and I went to get him. And he pointed out the church and said that was the church that he put the bomb under the steps. He said he lit the fuse to it. And he said that he regretted that it was children that were killed, but at least they couldn't grow up to have more niggers."

Brogdon said Cherry would regularly talk about the bombing in his sleep, so much so she was moved to record him muttering about the church and the children. The tape, she said, was lost in a house fire.

The former flame-headed trucker, now gray and retired but with a persona that suggested she was still as tough as a four-dollar steak, also detailed a family trip to Atlanta.

There they stayed with friends of Cherry's and visited the city's zoo. There was another man visiting at the time who she would later learn was Robert Chambliss, "the best bomb maker in this part of the country," her then husband told her.

Posey asked: "Did Bobby Cherry say anything about Chambliss with respect to the church bombing?"

"Yes . . . that he was the one who built the bomb. He said they were all together the night the bomb was built."

Brogdon's relationship with Cherry was, to say the least, tumultuous. We knew that we had to avoid the prejudice that comes from testimony about domestic and child abuse. She described leaving Cherry and moving to Chicago without getting into the reasons.

She explained that Cherry found her in the Windy City and moved in with her. Brogdon's nephew, Charles Ferris, lived with the family for a time, and her brother, Wayne Brogdon, was often around.

When she and Cherry moved back to Birmingham from Chicago in 1972, Brogdon decided she'd had enough, opting to make her move to change her life on the trip to see Cherry's sister at Mt. Olive, just outside the city. With her kids in the backseat, she pulled up so Cherry could stretch his legs. "Bobby stepped out of the car, and I put my foot on the gas."

She never looked back. The next time she "laid eyes on him" was when she walked into the trial courtroom.

Johnson's cross-examination was like a sparring match. He would jab about inconsistencies in the dates and times, and Willadean would rope-a-dope until she could counter with a hook. At one stage Johnson kept asking her to repeat her answers, prompting Brogdon to offer: "Maybe you ought to write some of this down."

Johnson suggested she had described the front steps, not the side stairs, of 16th Street Baptist when testifying that Cherry had told her he planted the bomb, and the defense homed in on the volatility of their relationship.

The implication was she had the motivation to bring Cherry down. Johnson also raised issues that potentially reflected negatively on her, including losing a custody battle for her children and being charged with kidnapping at one stage for bringing them to Alabama.

At that time, Cherry had taken her to see Art Hanes, the same lawyer who represented Chambliss years later, who the Klansman claimed could get her out of anything. Although she spent a few days in jail, the case was ultimately dismissed. She got her children back and remained in Birmingham.

Johnson, harping on the idea she wanted to get back at Cherry, asked about the fire in Chicago that took the life of one of her children. It had occurred not long after she left the Klansman in the dust, and she had always suspected it was an act of revenge.

She indicated she had always lived in fear of Cherry, who kept weapons under his pillow and beat her. The defense was seeking to portray her as a woman out for revenge, but relating some of their domestic horror stories also helped build Cherry's image as a violent man who was prepared to do anything.

She told the court that after several years of separation, she was relieved when her sister told her "Robert" had gone to jail for the bombing. She said she had assumed that it was Cherry, when, in fact, it was a reference to Chambliss's 1977 conviction. She only became aware Cherry wasn't in jail when she read the newspaper story in Glendive, Montana, in 1997.

When Johnson finished his cross-examination, he had successfully provided proof that Brogdon harbored a deep dislike of Cherry, but both the defense and Brogdon had landed a few blows worthy of a heavyweight fighter. By the time she finished, it was a performance that included enough material about lovin', hatin', tragedy, and trucks to fill an entire country western album collection.

Posey couldn't say "no further questions" quick enough.

Even after Brogdon was excused as a witness, she couldn't conceal her contempt for Cherry, whom she stared down more than once. As she left the stand she asked the judge, "Can I sit in the courtroom?" which she did for the remainder of the afternoon. She listened as her brother Wayne testified that Cherry had talked about making the bomb, but it wasn't supposed to hurt anyone. She also heard her nephew, Charles Ferris, tell the court that on another occasion Cherry said that the church "was supposed to be full of niggers" when the bomb exploded.

During testimony by "the Brogdon clan," as Johnson described them, Cherry tried to look fierce, alternating between furious and indignant.

"Throughout the trial, I sat behind Cherry," said Amy Gallimore. "He was beyond narcissistic. He had an intimidating persona, and I can easily understand why he had bullied his way through his life, beating up women and slapping around his children. You could just sense evil in this man."

The inescapable circle of guilt was closing around Cherry. Our last witness of the day, Michael Gowins, was involved in a life-and-death battle with his health at the time, but I had let him know how important his testimony could be, and he duly appeared.

Gowins had called the FBI after seeing Cherry on TV in 1997, recognizing him as the man he knew in Dallas back in 1982.

When Herren and Fleming first interviewed him, he was already gravely ill. With Cherry's case delayed for a year, I feared Gowins probably wouldn't be around when we finally got the Klansman to court. But he had held on— barely. Now confined to a wheelchair, he wore a breathing apparatus and needed an oxygen tank in the courtroom to counter his severe emphysema and chronic obstructive pulmonary disease.

Gowins detailed his encounter with then carpet-cleaner Cherry at the Munger Apartments in Dallas in 1982. The former Klansman, in conversation with Gowins and his mother, had compared "Mexicans" in Texas with "blacks" in Birmingham. He allegedly said, "I had to get out of Birmingham because the niggers were taking over."

Struggling to breathe during his testimony, Gowins added: "And they [Cherry and Gowins's mother] was talking about the Klan and all about that and all about the 16th Street Church. And then he said, 'you know, I bombed that church.' And that's when it got real quiet. Nobody said anything else."

On cross-examination, Johnson tested Gowins about the consistency of his statements over the years. While the defense questioned the quality of the witness's exact recall, Gowins's responses offered the opportunity to repeat many of the most damning Cherry statements.

I don't think we could have ended the day's testimony any better.

The defense was obviously feeling the pressure of Cherry's words, particularly his repeated use of the word "nigger." Johnson asked the court to order witnesses, recounting Cherry's conversations, not to use the word again. "They've made their point . . . enough is enough."

Frankly, we were all sick of hearing it, but it was woven into the fabric of the case, and it would have been disingenuous to have witnesses paraphrase. Judge Garrett said that any witness could repeat direct quotes that contained the word.

The next day of trial would be the last full day of what Herren described as a family reunion of former FBI agents. When the indictments were announced in May 2000, the phone lines at the Birmingham FBI office lit up like a Christmas tree with retired agents from around the country who had worked the case. They all wanted to know how they could help.

Each day they would come over to the courthouse to be part of the action even though as witnesses they couldn't sit in on the trial. Judge Garrett had allowed us to use his courtroom upstairs as the waiting room for most witnesses, but the old agents liked being closer to the action and would hang out just outside the judge's office.

It was an area directly behind the judge's bench and the witness stand, from where they could more easily interact with the trial team, especially Amy Gallimore, to whom they had taken a special shine. Each day, it seemed like the old boys got a little rowdier. They were having a ball. Judge Garrett couldn't help but notice.

During one of the morning breaks, he talked to Ben Herren: "Ben, we are hearing all of that talk in the courtroom. You're going to have to keep them quiet."

Herren undertook to pass the message along, explaining: "Judge, look, every one of them has a hearing aid, and that's probably the reason they're so loud."

Gallimore had the task of trying to keep the old agents occupied, a job she relished, but it likely contributed to the problem, as a few of them were prone to showing off for her. She laughed when she recalled their reaction to Judge Garrett's decree for silence: "They kind of acted like little children who had been reprimanded by their teacher."

The happy reunion continued, though at a lower decibel level. Just had to turn up those hearing aids.

Of their tribe, we had already called former G-men Colvin, Butler, Killion, and Welton. Now it was time for Downey, Murphy, and Shanahan to dig Cherry's hole a little deeper. Agent John Downey joined the FBI in 1957 and was assigned to the Birmingham office in August 1963, shortly before the church bombing. Over the next couple of years, he interviewed Cherry six times and handled Burns as an informant.

We focused on summarizing how flexible Cherry had been with what he'd told authorities over the years. With Downey on the stand, we gave the jury a list of key points, displaying them on the monitors to reinforce the frequent variations in the defendant's story.

We got the chance to highlight several key statements, including Cherry's assertion in September 1964 that "the only reason I didn't do the church bombing was maybe someone beat me to it."

Johnson seemed to feel that statement's sting and tried his best to minimize its impact, arguing with the agent over its significance. The defense claimed it was the statement of a man acknowledging his bias but maintaining his innocence. To Downey, however, it revealed Cherry's frame of mind. Significantly for us, it gave the witness the opportunity to repeat the phrase over and over.

Even more damning, Cherry went into stunning detail during one interview about his experience in demolitions, and how to make a fuse for a bomb. It was not what you would expect from your typical eighteen-wheel truck driver.

Downey said that during an interview, Cherry said he in no way participated in the bombing of the 16th Street Baptist Church but added that he had training in the use of explosives while in military service.

When asked how he would detonate an explosive, Cherry stated that he would use either a fuse that he would light by hand or an electric blasting cap detonated by an alarm clock mechanism. He added that another type of detonator featured chemicals in conjunction with a fuse and blasting cap.

Cherry went on, stating that either nitric or sulphuric acid would be placed in a plastic container similar to the type used to hold pills. Powdered sugar and another chemical with explosive properties would then be mixed and inserted into a large size gelatin capsule of the type used by farmers to administer medication to livestock.

He advised that the gelatin capsule would then be dropped into the acid container, dissolve, and cause a chemical fire of intense heat, capable of igniting a dynamite fuse.

In his very thorough analysis, Cherry cautioned that when dropping the capsule into the acid, care should be taken to clean off the outside of the capsule, since any of the material contained in the capsule on contact with acid will ignite and can burn the skin.

Despite the level of detail he provided, Cherry reiterated that he had not seen this process used or tested and could not recall where he had learned of the need to be cautious in its execution.

After Agent Downey left the stand, Posey called our FBI bomb expert, Mark Whitworth. He used a video produced by the FBI lab to demonstrate the explosive effect of potassium chlorate and sugar after releasing it into sulfuric acid—as described in stunning detail by Cherry.

Former Agent Robert Murphy, at the time an administrative law judge in New York, testified that he too had interviewed Cherry on several occasions; one time Cherry talked about how he would go about pulling off the bombing if he had done it.

He said: "One man would be the lookout . . . while the other would drive to the area, park his car and plant the bomb."

Cherry also repeated a familiar Klan theme to Murphy: that "the church bombing was committed" by black folks.

"How could anybody have sneaked up on that church by their nigger guard without being seen?" he had asked.

It was an especially interesting comment given what we had heard from James Lay in the Blanton trial. It is certainly not much of a stretch to think that Blanton or Chambliss would have told Cherry about Lay after they cruised near the church just two weeks before the bombing.

On cross-examination Johnson somewhat sarcastically stated, "for the fifteenth or sixteenth time," that Cherry had denied any involvement in the bombing of the church. But the defense, no doubt, cringed each time his speculation about explosives—or, worse, his boasts to others about his role in the attack—came up.

We closed our parade of former agents with Fleming's old friend from his first office in Philadelphia, Neil Shanahan.

Having had the opportunity to spend some time with these guys in the days leading up to their testimony, I would have loved for the jury to have heard their many stories about Birmingham in the sixties.

Shanahan, in particular, had been involved in so many things, and he could spin a tale as well as anyone. But for our purposes, Shanahan stuck to detailing Cherry interviews that painted a picture of a man filled with hate who couldn't keep his stories straight.

While Cherry never admitted to investigators that he was involved in the church bombing, it was clear he wanted very much to brag to the agents about his knowledge and "expertise."

As Shanahan stepped down, it occurred to me how astonishing the much-maligned FBI's contribution had been to the case. In total, during the Blanton and Cherry trials, we called up half a dozen or so former agents. All were in their seventies or eighties, and none had testified in decades. But to a man, they were as competent as in the days when they were professionally active. Not only did they take the time to review the old reports to refresh their memories about this part of the investigation, but they were also sharp on cross-examination.

If not for the tenacity of Agents Welton, Downey, Murphy, Shanahan, Spencer, and the scores of others who hit the streets of Birmingham after the church bombing, we would never have been able eventually to haul Blanton or Cherry to court, much less succeed in convicting them.

To borrow a phrase from Reverend Cross—I'm really glad I got to meet them.

Teresa Stacy

We had worried during the Blanton trial about what the defense would attempt to do to the Klansman's former girlfriend Waylene Vaughn on the stand. If you've made conspicuous mistakes in the past, a courtroom can be a brutal place to be confronted with those truths.

Cherry's granddaughter Teresa Stacy had been a runaway at sixteen, an exotic dancer, and a drug addict. It was a great testament to her strength of character that she had turned away from that destructive lifestyle and built an admirable, even enviable, life as a responsible adult and parent.

However, just as Vaughn was maligned in the Blanton case, the Cherry defense team would focus on nothing but Stacy's early life struggles and use them to try and undermine her testimony about her grandfather.

It gave us pause before asking her to testify.

"I had been impressed with her," Fleming said, "but you always worry about a witness with such a tarnished past."

I was convinced she would be strong on the stand. She carried herself with great poise and had a calm demeanor that was a testament to the thoughtful woman she had become. She was also a vastly different physical presence than just about every other witness, many of whom were elderly or in bad health. Stacy was young and attractive. When she arrived to testify, she was a picture of self-assurance, elegantly attired in an off-white suit; she looked anything but the confused teen the defense would focus on.

Cochran wasted no time getting to the substance of her testimony, asking right out of the chute if she ever heard her grandfather make any statement about being involved in the bombing of the 16th Street Baptist Church.

"He said that he helped blow up a bunch of niggers back in Birmingham," she replied.

She recalled Cherry had been on the front porch of his trailer in Texas at the time and seemed "braggish." She acknowledged that she, in turn, bragged to a couple of friends about her grandfather's claim.

She conceded she never thought it anything but "bragging" until she saw his press conference denying his involvement. It was then that she "put two and two together" and called the FBI.

Her direct testimony before the Cherry jury lasted only a few minutes, but it was powerful. Here was a family member painting the final strokes of a picture that was incredibly consistent through all witness testimony.

Johnson pounced on Stacy's checkered past, having her admit to a drug and alcohol addiction as a teen to the court. Crucially, in the course of saying her drug of choice was cocaine and opening up about her mistakes, she was unflappable, listening carefully to questions before answering, and responding politely. A "yes, sir" or "no, sir" on the stand goes a long way.

Johnson implied she had told the FBI the bombing was a "constant source of boasting by your grandfather" but she shot back: "No, I didn't say that. I said it was common knowledge in the family," and that she had "heard it for years in the family."

The defense cast aspersions on her motivation for testifying. She acknowledged that she had hoped that her cooperation might get her brother out of jail, but it had not. Johnson suggested her new notoriety had yielded a "spread" in *Glamour* magazine, an interview with *Texas Monthly,* and an appearance on *Good Morning America*, resulting in a change in her life.

She responded calmly: "Why should I let this change my life?"

As she walked from the witness stand, you could sense the tension in the courtroom. Cherry sneered, while a substantial number of his family members bristled in the gallery, apparently incensed she would speak the truth about her appalling grandfather.

Stacy was a clear winner for the prosecution.

"She had cleaned up her life from the days when she was a chronic drug user," Posey said recently. "Even more important, she didn't hesitate to admit her lifestyle issues from her teenage years. She was unflappable. Afterward, Judge Garrett would tell me that she was the best witness he had ever seen in all his years in the legal profession."

Gallimore shared the widespread admiration: "She was a beautiful young lady. She had morphed into this mature person who carried herself with dignity, and there was no doubt she was telling the truth. She personally impacted me deeply."

Cherry's Words

I felt we had scored big with the retired agents pointing out the remarkable inconsistencies in Cherry's interviews. But the 1997 interview Bob Eddy and Ben Herren staged with Cherry in Texas was the most complete ever conducted, and in many respects provided the pieces to construct the definitive tale of the defendant's life in Birmingham.

On the stand, Herren reminded the jury of Cherry's Klan and white supremacist associations, from Robert Shelton, the Grand Dragon of the KKK, to Robert Sidney Thomas, the Exalted Cyclops of Eastview #13, to Tommy Blanton, Robert Chambliss, Troy Ingram, Hubert Page, and Dr. Edward Fields, among others. Cherry even said that he had been Shelton's security guard before the bombing. (That was probably a lie, but what the hell.)

The former Birmingham cop Herren also laid out Cherry's boasts in the interview, including his unprompted declaration that he had "whipped Shuttlesworth in 1957 in a high school demonstration," bopping the minister "between the eyes with a pair of brass knuckles."

There was also an incident at the Krystal Kitchen Restaurant, a Birmingham establishment where Cherry said he "split a nigger's head open" with a pistol after the man called him a son of a bitch. Herren passed on that the defendant at the time of the interview had declared "the statute of limitations has run out on that one."

Herren detailed how Cherry explained that on the night of September 14 he was at the Modern Sign Shop running a silk-screen press, even though he had earlier said he had broken his back and probably couldn't even carry a lunch box.

Cherry saw Chambliss and Blanton there together with a couple of others. "He said they did not come to work, and he did not know what they were talking about."

To slam the door shut on any doubt Cherry had rolled out lie after lie to create a flimsy alibi, we finally had the chance with Herren on the stand to expose the defendant's nonsense about watching wrestling on TV and caring for his sick wife on Saturday, September 14.

Herren explained Cherry had insisted he was home by ten o'clock that night.

We brought down the sledgehammer, noting TV logs proved there was no wrestling broadcast that night—in fact, the sport wasn't televised until 1964. What's more, we produced documentation to prove that Mrs. Cherry was still years away from being stricken with cancer.

Not only had Cherry lied, repeatedly and insistently, regarding his whereabouts in the hours leading up to the bomb being planted, but Herren also painted a picture, using the Klansman's own words, of a man who boasted about his history of violence and racism.

He noted the 1997 interview ended with Cherry volunteering: "Birmingham is a little fucking Africa, more niggers than whites."

If the jury members were not fully aware of Cherry's capacity for dishonesty, treachery, racism, and violence before Herren took the stand, they were fully briefed by the time the investigator stood down.

We had started our testimony by making an emotional connection with the jury, and we would conclude in a similar fashion.

Seventy-six-year-old Chris McNair once again told the story of September 15, 1963. How at St. Paul's Lutheran he heard a noise that sounded like thunder. How he rushed to be with his wife and daughter at 16th Street, but he was too late; Denise had been killed.

At the Hillman Hospital, he saw a cousin who had "found the room that they were using for a morgue.

"And in there we went, and there were the four girls lying on the table." He identified Denise's body: she had "a piece of mortar that was smashed into her head."

There was a heaviness in the air as McNair left the stand and took the seat in the front row of the courtroom where he and Maxine had been all week.

Sarah Collins Rudolph, the sister of Addie Mae and the lone survivor among the girls in the ladies' lounge, was once again our last witness. She testified with a large photograph of Addie on the screen in front of the jury.

No one in court dared make a sound as she related the last seconds of the lives of her sister and her three friends, Addie, Carole, Cynthia, and Denise, who had been standing together by a sofa, Addie tying the sash on Denise's new dress, before a monstrous sound and darkness.

We brought up the photo on the screen of little Sarah, eyes patched over with gauze. Thirty-nine years later, the lone survivor re-enacted calling out for her sister: "Addie, Addie, Addie!"

There was no response, she told the court.

I had heard Sarah's final words to her sister on the stand before, but I was overwhelmed. I'm not sure how I retained my composure. After a few moments, I shattered the stillness in the room, turning to Judge Garrett, offering: "The state rests."

Even though Sarah's call to her sister wasn't answered that fateful morning in 1963, I got the feeling it was heard that day in 2002, and not just by every sobbing observer in court.

The Cherry Defense

I felt good about our case. It had been a relatively seamless presentation, featuring twenty-two witnesses. It was highly emotional every day, and we had constructed a detailed, telling portrait of Cherry, a man moved to extreme violence by his opposition to school integration.

We'd worked to use his words against him and reconstructed his role in the bombing in detail, placing him with the convicted killers using the wildly different statements he'd given to the FBI and focusing on his familiarity with explosives, his involvement in the Klan, and his bitter hatred for black people.

Still, our case was largely circumstantial, and the defense knew it only needed to induce doubt in one juror's mind. We knew what was coming from Mickey Johnson and his team: a focus on trying to fault the investigation itself.

On Saturday, May 18, 2002, after a series of legal arguments outside the presence of the jury, Johnson and Bass began the defense of Bobby Frank Cherry with none other than the enigma, Mary Frances Cunningham.

Cunningham, seventy-seven, looked put out. She didn't want to be there, and I must say we would have preferred she'd stayed at home. It was somewhat of a desperate measure by Johnson's team, but there was the potential for something unexpected to happen.

The irony was that Chambliss's sister-in-law would have been the best possible witness for the prosecution if she hadn't initially embellished the information she had by telling authorities she had followed the Klansmen to the church.

Nearly four decades later she didn't hesitate to admit to the court that in 1963 she had been giving information about a possible bombing plot involving her brother-in-law, Robert Chambliss, to Jefferson County Sheriff Deputy James Hancock. (Johnson had the good sense not to delve into the much-rumored intimate, if not illicit, relationship with Hancock.)

The information about the bombing, she said, came from her sister, Tee Chambliss, Dynamite Bob's wife.

Hancock, she explained, did not act on the information, either before or after the explosion.

More than a year later, on December 7, 1964, according to an FBI recorded statement, she told the FBI "that I was a witness to somebody putting down the bomb," that "somebody" being Bobby Frank Cherry.

However, in court, she said emphatically: "I did not make that statement."

While we knew she had recanted her tale numerous times since, we did not expect her actually to deny making specific statements in the first place.

Johnson handed over a copy of the FBI document, a regulation FBI-issue 302 form, to Cunningham and asked her to read it. Initially, she declined, as she told the court she hadn't brought her reading glasses. After a pair of glasses had been borrowed, she went through the document, saying she was "very well aware of the contents."

She said that she first saw the statement when Bob Eddy showed it to her during the Baxley investigation in the seventies and that she had "absolutely" told him at the time that it was not true. She added she had related the same thing to Bill Fleming and Ben Herren when they came knocking in the late nineties.

Johnson also had her admit that of the four names mentioned in the report—Chambliss, Cherry, Blanton, and Herman Cash—the only one she knew was Chambliss.

The defense got some value out of Cunningham's presence, as they were able to discredit her to a degree; however, we were clear (and would make the point in closing) that our case was not leaning on her story or her value as a witness.

We opted to forgo cross-examination, as it could have been perceived as adding weight to the idea that we put some credence in the recanted Cunningham account.

Eddy was called to the stand and testified that Cunningham had told him that the story contained in the December 7, 1964, memo was not true. However, the old investigator explained that rather than denying that she ever gave the statement, Cunningham had told him that she had repeated things she had heard from the FBI.

Working hard to tarnish the foundations of our investigation, the defense recalled Fleming to the stand with the intent to impeach him on a statement he'd made to the grand jury—that "informants tell us that Mr. Cherry exited the vehicle and placed the bomb under the staircase."

Johnson submitted that the assertion Fleming had made was based purely on the recanted statement from Cunningham.

Time and again, before the statement was read to the court, I strenuously objected to Johnson's efforts somehow to condemn the legal worth of the entire investigation on the basis of the one comment from Fleming in grand jury proceedings.

In retrospect, we probably should have specifically mentioned in the grand jury that Cunningham's statement had been recanted, although, at that stage, we had yet to explore fully whether she would be of use as a witness.

Fleming survived a tough examination from Johnson. He stuck to his guns and referenced the fact that our case was built on an array of evidence. He diligently avoided referencing Cunningham's 1964 statement to the FBI, despite the defense's attempts to get him to bite.

Johnson also quizzed Fleming about our witnesses, implying they had credibility issues. Again, the veteran agent stayed strong, defending the witnesses and taking the opportunity to repeat some of their most impactful testimony.

The defense made a valiant attempt to undercut our case. While I thought that much of Johnson's argument was just a smokescreen, he had wisely not tried to attack much of our evidence head-on.

I hoped the Cunningham appearance amounted to little more than a distraction, but with juries you just never know.

Judge Garrett adjourned early Saturday, wanting to give the sequestered panel members some time with their families. The defense had only a few more witnesses. Closing arguments were just around the corner.

It was a restless weekend for me.

Don Cochran would do our first closing, and I knew he would provide a thorough overview of the case. I also knew that my rebuttal to Johnson's position that the investigation was flawed from the start would be hugely important.

Monday's testimony for the defense was largely uneventful. They called Bill Jackson, the Klan barber, who offered little except for the opportunity for me to regret having called him in the Blanton case.

Two of Cherry's grandsons testified, ostensibly to counter Teresa Stacy's evidence that their grandfather's involvement in the church bombing was common knowledge among family members. They seemed like nice young men, but I didn't believe their denials that Cherry had boasted about the church bombing countered Stacy's firm contentions and stunning presence.

Johnson's team threw a Hail Mary pass by calling Robert High, a minister of a Mabank, Texas, nondenominational church, to talk about Cherry's participation at his house of worship, where the congregation was a mixture of blacks, whites, and Mexicans.

It only took a little push during my cross-examination to establish that Cherry didn't start attending this admirably diverse church until 1997, following the reopening of the case and our interview with him. I have often joked that I had saved more souls as a prosecutor than Billy Graham. Everyone seems to find Jesus when they are headed to or have been in prison.

My friend Carolyn McKinstry was somewhat of a reluctant witness for the defense. She had called Johnson the night before and said she had a doctor's appointment that would prevent her from taking the stand. Judge Garrett, however, ordered her to appear.

McKinstry repeated the story she had told, which had garnered considerable public attention in the past, that as a fourteen-year-old member of the 16th Street community in 1963, she happened to hear the telephone ringing in the church office on the morning of September 15, 1963.

On answering, she said the caller, a man, said, "The bomb will go off in three minutes." Before she could tell anyone, the explosion tore through the building.

In a documented interview with the FBI in the immediate wake of the bombing, there was no record of McKinstry saying she received the threatening phone call, although in court she insisted she had told agents about it.

The defense suggested that the agents failed to document her statement about the call because it somehow did not fit the FBI narrative of what had happened.

It was another defense attempt to discredit the investigation. However, I didn't feel Johnson's claim had much weight. Whether the FBI did not record it or whether a young black girl recently traumatized by a bombing that took the lives of her friends failed to tell them, there was absolutely no evidence of an FBI cover-up or of any conspiracy.

As we expected, the defense rested without calling Cherry as a witness. I think they realized he'd said more than enough over the years.

It was down to the business of considering closing arguments. Perhaps it was because we were in sync that Cochran and I didn't feel the need to consult each other about what our last statements would contain. We had divided up the witnesses and followed a coordinated pattern in the prosecution, so we were all on the same page about the strengths and weaknesses of the case.

I was pleased my closing in the Blanton trial had garnered praise, but frankly, I'd been a little disappointed. I am my biggest critic, and I felt it could have been more comprehensive.

I wasn't going to change my style—I would work with notes rather than a fully prepared text. But I felt the need to draw on multiple sources. In preparation, I reread Bobby DeLaughter's closing in the Byron De La Beckwith trial and took special note of points made by Andy Sheldon.

Conceptually, I knew what I wanted to say but had difficulty piecing it together. Crumbled paper began to pile up in my little study at home on that Monday night as I hit a wall trying to arrange my thoughts.

I decided I needed a break and headed for the screened-in back porch.

Passing through the den, I noticed that my daughter Courtney was watching one of my favorite movies, *The Shawshank Redemption*, the tale of a banker in prison for a double murder who earns the respect of fellow prisoners for his upstanding moral code and quietly indomitable spirit. Rather than proceed to the porch I plopped down with Courtney to catch the end of the show.

Fresh from victory in high school student council elections, Doug Jones poses with his ride for the homecoming parade in the fall of 1971.

A Clinton administration nominee, Jones's appointment was approved by Attorney General Janet Reno. Following Senate confirmation, he was officially sworn in as a U.S. Attorney in November 1997.

More than thirty-six years after the bombing and twenty-two years after Chambliss was convicted, Jones and Jefferson County District Attorney David Barber announced indictments against Blanton and Cherry. They also outlined the case's shift from federal to state jurisdiction.

Tom Blanton was the first suspect to be tried by Jones. His trial began on April 24, 2001. Here, Robert Posey and Jones are in discussion with Blanton's counsel, John Robbins, at a pre-trial hearing.

Tom Blanton's car. Ms. Glenn recognized the vehicle as the one she saw behind the church in the early hours of September 15, 1963.

Blanton was convicted on May 1, 2001. Jones took questions from a large media pack outside the courtroom.

Bobby Frank Cherry's decision to hold a press conference to announce his innocence sparked calls from numerous valuable witnesses. His distinctive look reminded many of incidents that they had tried to put behind them.

Jones and investigator Bill Fleming head into court for the first day of Bobby Frank Cherry's trial before Judge Jim Garrett, May 14, 2002.

Cherry's granddaughter Teresa Stacy was an impressive witness for the prosecution.

Willadean Brogdon, shown here being cross-examined by Cherry defense counsel Mickey Johnson, gave valuable testimony in her former husband's murder trial. After leaving the stand, she remained in court to observe proceedings. Cherry was ultimately convicted on May 22, 2002.

Doug Jones, before Judge Garrett, points to the defendant Bobby Frank Cherry during closing arguments.

The Blanton prosecution team. *From left to right*: Bob Eddy, Bill Fleming, Robert Posey, Doug Jones, Robin Beardsley, Ben Herren, and Jeff Wallace.

Doug Jones announced his candidacy for the Senate in May 2017. He won the Democratic primary in August and beat Republican Roy Moore in the U.S. Senate special election December 12, 2017. Here, he poses with the original election team. From left to right: Nancy Ellisor, Kent Haney, Giles Perkins, Joe Trippi, Doug Turner, and Louise Jones.

Doug and Louise Jones join Congressman John Lewis on the Edmund Pettus Bridge in Selma, Alabama, the site of bloody clashes between civil rights protesters and law enforcement in 1965.

Joe Biden stumps with Jones in Birmingham. The former vice president was one of the few national figures to feature in a campaign that focused tightly on local issues.

Jones's daughter Courtney and her children, Ever and Ollie, on Senate Election Day, 2017.

Doug Jones with wife Louise and sons Christopher (*left*) and Carson, celebrating the election victory.

On their twenty-fifth wedding anniversary, Jones and wife Louise celebrate his Senate victory in front of supporters in Birmingham.

Having seen the film a few times, I recognized that the story had progressed to when Andy, the main character, has escaped from prison. His recently released friend, Red, is following clues in search of him.

We hear Red, played by Morgan Freeman, reading a letter left by Andy: "Remember Red, hope is a good thing, maybe the best of things, and no good thing ever dies."

In an instant, a jumble of images popped into my head: the photo of Denise and her Chatty Cathy doll, pictures of the children's marches from 1963, the sight of the girls' mothers battling to give testimony about the bombing in the long search for justice.

Hope. A good thing. Never dies.

I dashed back to my study and wrote furiously.

I had a frame for my closing, a tone and a theme I could tailor to the facts of the case and use in a rebuttal to the defense.

The Closings

I'd been operating with blinders on for the week of testimony. While the media coverage was everywhere, I'd deliberately avoided seeking out opinions about how we were proceeding from anyone except those in my tight circle.

I knew there were scores of media representatives in town, but I'd kept my head down and my focus on the next day's testimony. But with the finishing line not far away, I took a look around at what was going on outside the court for the first time in a week.

When I arrived Tuesday morning, it was as if a fog had lifted to reveal batteries of media vans and personnel. There was a crowd outside the courtroom and a buzz throughout the Mel Bailey complex. Spectators, including Louise, had arrived early. Many were unable to fit in the courtroom and had to listen from outside.

The bombing case would never cease to define Birmingham, but the curtain was closing on the biggest drama the city had seen. I didn't allow myself to dwell on the thought, but if we could get Cherry, perhaps it would help usher in a new era for the Magic City.

I take little pleasure in others' discomfort, but I have to admit that I was pleased to see Cherry was irritable. He appeared as if he were looking for someone to blame for something as he entered the courtroom.

There had been various Cherry family members in the gallery for much of the trial, and he anxiously looked around for support. The packed house made locating any one particular person difficult, and he looked distressed.

When Judge Garrett gaveled us into session, all eyes went to Don Cochran.

"You may proceed," said the judge, who had presided over both bombing cases with welcome authority and, on occasion, extraordinary patience. He fully understood the history and the importance of the moment.

Cochran efficiently packaged our comprehensive circumstantial case, getting out in front of the defense by dismissing their suggestion that we were leaning on Mary Frances Cunningham's recanted statement. He emphatically told the jurors the only material we wanted them to consider was the evidence presented to the court over the previous six days.

The former Marine showed the video of the Shuttlesworth beating again and, methodically, in a PowerPoint presentation, took the jury through all of Cherry's statements to law enforcement, highlighting the inconsistencies. The court had heard it before, courtesy of agents Welton, Downey, Murphy, Shanahan, and Herren, but to see the lies side by side on a large screen was damning.

Harkening back to a rock song of his youth, Cochran told the jury: "Rod Stewart had a song out a few years ago about you've got to look for a 'Reason to Believe.' Well, sometimes that's what you have to do . . ."

Among those reasons was the evidence of the Blanton kitchen tape, which placed Cherry with Blanton and Chambliss when "they planned and made the bomb."

More reasons to believe: the multiple admissions Cherry made to his family and acquaintances—the bragging—on the back porch of the trailer: to Willadean, to Charles and Wayne, to Michael Gowins, and as overheard by young Bobby Birdwell.

Individually or together, the jury, he said, had a reason to believe that Cherry committed the crime of murder.

Johnson and Bass had done a great job for their client. They were always prepared and knew the case file just about as well as anyone. With that knowledge, I'm sure Johnson knew he had a steep climb to overcome the mountain of self-incrimination Cherry had amassed over the years.

In his closing, Johnson attempted to play down the impact of Cherry's penchant for talking about himself: "There is only one statement I know that was consistent in all of the many interviews and 302s that you read of Bobby Cherry's. And that is, he said: 'Look, I did not do—I did not have anything to do with bombing that church.'"

The defense, however, also had to address the fact that several witnesses had said Cherry had made admissions of involvement.

Johnson understandably opted to attack the character and credibility of the witnesses, especially Willadean Brogdon, Wayne Brogdon, and Charles Ferris—"the Brogdon bunch."

Willadean had an ax to grind, he insisted. The trial was her chance for revenge against a man who had treated her poorly. The defense also noted flaws in her record—the kidnapping charge and various misdemeanors—and Johnson wondered aloud why the Brogdons had remained silent about Cherry for so long.

He recalled Stacy's lurid past, too, and noted her desire to see her grandfather pay for what he had done. He also questioned the accuracy of Birdwell's recall of visiting the Cherry family home as a child. He struggled, however, to poke holes in Gowins's testimony about Cherry's very direct statements about his involvement in the bombing.

Ultimately, the defense fell back on the idea that the entire investigation was based on a lie—Cunningham's 1964 statement. He referred to the case as a "multiple choice prosecution" that focused only on the four men named in that (recanted) statement: Cherry, Blanton, Chambliss, and Cash.

He suggested the jury reject the evidence presented by the prosecution on the basis that it evolved from a flawed foundation.

It was, in my opinion, drawing a long bow in search of an acquittal, though he did not have much else with which to work. There were elements of our case the defense simply couldn't counter by any method other than suggesting everything was tainted. Interestingly, there was virtually no mention of Mitch Burns in Johnson's close.

Johnson made a plea for the jurors to set aside personal feelings that they might have about his client. They should focus instead on what he called dismissively the "feel good prosecution" cynically constructed by the state to make up for Alabama creating "an atmosphere of hatred among people" in the sixties and failing "so miserably to protect the lives of these children":

"Nothing we can do here can add anything to the importance of their memories.

"But if you convict someone, unless you have in your heart of hearts the belief that this person beyond a reasonable doubt is guilty, then I suggest to you that you detract from the value of the memory of those children."

I had a lunch break to consider the rebuttal. I don't remember eating much. The rest of the prosecution team left me to my thoughts.

Even though we had not compared notes on our respective approaches to the final arguments, Cochran's remarks in closing had set the perfect tone. It allowed me to pick up where he left off to complete one long narrative while occasionally diverting to quash any defense claims.

I finished my preparations early enough to make sure Louise got a good seat. I was thrilled she was able to witness the end of the process, whatever the result. It had been a long and demanding campaign for her, too.

This was it.

A fork in the road of nearly thirty-nine years of agony for the families and endless frustration for the community. Decades of a man, an evil, weak man, walking around causing havoc, ruining the lives of people who could not run away from him fast enough.

And there he was. Cherry, sitting there in court like an indignant, overgrown schoolboy. Apparently angry he was in any way being held accountable for this trail of destruction he'd left in his selfish wake.

This was different from the Blanton experience. It was the last time this tragedy would be reviewed in a judicial system that had let the victims down for so many years. I'd spent some time, too much time, thinking we wouldn't get this chance to hold Cherry accountable. That amounted to a sense of guilt after Blanton's conviction, then, almost shamefully, resignation. But now the chance had come.

One chance.

The families looked apprehensive. Louise smiled encouragement. I moved around the counsel table and directly faced the jury.

May it please the Court, counsel, and ladies and gentlemen.

I reiterated the context of the bombing—the Klan's hatred of school integration—and set about breaking down the defense's push to distract from the evidence by raging about the notion of a faulty investigation.

It is about the state of Alabama versus Bobby Frank Cherry and no one else today.

. . . I bet forty percent of Mr. Johnson's argument was about something that the state of Alabama never brought before you.

Would you expect the state of Alabama to put someone up there who has recanted a statement?

The defense, I argued, had inserted a straw man in the case (Mary Frances Cunningham), only to attack her and cast aspersions on the entire investigation.

It was important to outline that it wasn't necessary to know every specific detail of the crime to make a decision on Cherry's guilt. The Klan's silence for thirty-nine years had ensured bits and pieces of the puzzle would remain hidden, but that had not interfered with the big picture.

> These cowards that hid . . . underneath their hoods.
>
> We're not talking about men—ladies and gentlemen—who walk down the streets of Birmingham in broad daylight carrying a bomb, or talked in open forums like this and said . . . "we're going to bomb a church, would anybody like to join us?"
>
> Bobby Frank Cherry and his Klan brothers, if you could call them brothers, were the forefathers of terrorism. They met in secret. They met in their homes. They met after hours.
>
> And after this murder, they decided that they've got to keep their mouths shut. And you have not heard a single one of them, no one that was associated with the Klan, that has come forward and talked about this case.
>
> Ladies and gentlemen, that is the shroud of secrecy that the state and the FBI for thirty-nine years has had to try to punch— to lift the shroud and the veils of those robes away from the likes of this defendant and his friends. It has been a painstaking process.

But, I reminded the jury, others had revealed the key details the Klan had tried to hide—from the kitchen tape to the evidence of those who overheard or spoke to Cherry about the bombing.

The defense had tried to discredit the witnesses, but, I reminded the court, even Mickey Johnson could find no reason for Gowins, a sick man with much to lose by coming to court, to lie.

I added:

> You know, the one person that Mr. Johnson barely mentioned was Mitchell Burns.

While Cochran had meticulously laid out the case in his close, it was my job to ensure the jurors were not of two minds about Cherry's character. I wanted to make it clear he had the ability to make the bomb and spotlight his obvious efforts to try and cover his tracks once he realized he was under the spotlight of law enforcement again.

We don't know how this bomb exploded, ladies and gentlemen, but we do know this: From this man's own mouth, he was pretty good at it. He had a number of ways that he could explode a bomb.

. . . Mr. Johnson talks also about the defendant's metamorphosis as if he too has changed. I submit, ladies and gentlemen, what Mr. Johnson referred to you is a sham. It is a mockery of everything that is right and decent in this society because Reverend High told you that that church didn't even come into existence until 1997.

Agent Herren and Bob Eddy go to Texas, and for the first time in years, Bobby Frank Cherry is questioned. And then, lo and behold . . . Bobby Frank Cherry starts going to church with black folks and enjoying their company.

Ladies and gentlemen that is such a mockery. That is such a mockery of everything that is decent in this world. And using, as he used in 1963—somehow using religion and God's house for his own purposes is such a distortion and should be totally rejected.

I wanted to pick up on Cochran's mantra "reason to believe" by mentioning the key evidence, but also to remind jurors of the link between Cherry's violent disposition, his hatred of blacks, and his desperation when it came to preserving segregation.

The importance of the tapes and Blanton's admission, ladies and gentlemen; the importance of [Cherry's] written statements, and all of the statements to the FBI—where they were, what they were doing, how he knew Chambliss, how he knew Blanton. Not merely their associations but their kinship, their bond—they give you, ladies and gentlemen, as has been said to you, a reason to believe.

They give you the reason to believe Bobby Birdwell. They give you the reason to believe Willadean Brogdon. They give you the reason to believe Wayne Brogdon, Teresa Stacy, and Mr. Ferris. Probably above all else, Mr. Gowins.

I added that the jury also had "reason to believe" that Cherry wasn't just a Klan hanger-on, he was "a man of action."

How do you know that?

At that moment I motioned for Bill Smith, our tech guy, to hit the play button on the video of the Reverend Shuttlesworth beating outside of Phillips High School in 1957.

I remained silent as the tape rolled and the jury saw again how Cherry jumped into the middle of the fracas and reached into his pocket to pull out brass knuckles so that he could cause serious damage. When the video stopped, I looked at the jury and said:

That's how we know that.

As I approached the conclusion, I suggested to the jury that Blanton told Cherry not to say too much around Mitch Burns because, indeed, they knew way too much.

I hoped I had degraded the defense's intimation that we just wanted to bring Cherry down to close the door on the case. I reiterated how we had let the evidence lead us, and it had sent us directly to the defendant, time and again.

That was the sober, "just the facts" setup. I wanted an emotional finish. The jurors had seen the incredible ugliness of the crime during testimony. To close, I wanted them not only to recognize Cherry's role in violently taking lives but to understand that it was his attempt to derail an entire community.

Ladies and gentlemen, I know you're getting a little tired. Trust me, we all are, but I want to close up here by coming back to one of the images that I know you have seen several times. And it's an image that stands out among all of the others in this case, an image that I believe captures everything about this case and about our world, then and now.

At that moment Smith put a photograph on the screen directly in front of the jury and to my right.

It's a picture of Denise taken by her father holding her best friend, a white Chatty Cathy doll.

And this picture, ladies and gentlemen, says it all from start to finish. It is an image of innocence but also a snapshot of the reason she died.

It is an image of children who marched the streets of Birmingham because they simply wanted the same opportunities as others.

It evokes the images of this great tragedy . . . Sarah Collins lay blinded calling out for her sister—"Addie, Addie, Addie"—not knowing that Addie's lifeless body lay only a few feet from her.

It is an image of death—of a mother, Maxine McNair, crying out, "my baby, my baby," after the explosion ripped through the sanctuary where she was and as the body of her daughter, this beautiful child, and her three friends lay directly beneath them in the rubble.

But, ladies and gentlemen, it is also an image of hope, the dream, if you will, that all God's children can live together. In 1963, it was the hope of a race of people. Today it is the hope of all of us.

Bobby Frank Cherry tried his best to destroy that hope, but because he was blinded by hate, he could simply not understand that hope is a good thing, and good things never die.

I could see tears in the eyes of the jury. The image of Denise holding that doll does that. I battled to contain my emotions to finish. My voice cracked occasionally.

In a cemetery not far from this courthouse, there is a well-kept grave with a headstone that simply says this: "Carol Denise McNair. November 17, 1951. September 15, 1963. She loved all—but a mad bomber hated her kind."

What a timeless statement.

It is as if Denise and her friends are calling to us today with a message that is as important as it ever has been—that in the state of Alabama and in the United States of America, we value our children, and we value human life regardless of race, creed, or color. And we will bring to justice and hold accountable those who would take those lives from us.

I fought back tears.

I know that you are ready to analyze this evidence, to follow your oaths, to follow the law, to examine your hearts and consciences, and to base your verdict accordingly. And I submit to you, ladies and gentlemen, that after you have done so, there can be but one verdict in each case for each child. One verdict. Final justice.

I ask that you hold this defendant accountable, that you find him guilty of the murder of Addie Mae Collins, guilty of the murder of Cynthia Wesley, guilty of the murder of Carole Robertson, and guilty of the murder of Denise McNair.

And when you do, ladies and gentlemen, as the saying goes, justice will truly roll down like a mighty river, because you, ladies and gentlemen, are the channel through which that mighty river of justice flows. And when it flows, as I believe the evidence proves beyond a reasonable doubt, the world can stop shaking, and the souls of these four children can finally be free.

Bobby Frank Cherry hated their kind. He is a murderer who has lived among us, and it is time that we have held him accountable for his crime against humanity.

The courtroom was extraordinarily quiet. I was a physical and emotional wreck.

Judge Garrett recessed for an afternoon break. As soon as the jury retired to the jury room, I headed straight out of the courtroom in search of seclusion in the area behind the bench. It was the same spot where all of the retired agents had gotten a little too gregarious. The witnesses were gone now, and it was a place of solitude.

I was totally drained and needed a few minutes just to pull myself together. I didn't second-guess what I'd just expressed to the jury. It was beyond me at that stage, and I suspect I knew deep down I'd done what I needed to do. It was up to the jury.

When I walked back into the courtroom, the first person I saw was Louise, standing by the rail that separated the lawyers from the spectators.

"You did great," she said as I got a much-needed hug. I could barely talk.

After lunch the judge instructed the jury and sent the panel to deliberate. There was nothing to do but wait.

A massive media pack had descended on the court complex, perhaps anticipating a relatively swift verdict, as had been the case in the Blanton trial. There was little doubt that members of the media were also impacted by the trial. For some, such as the representatives of the British Broadcasting Corporation, who were there most every day, it was a strange story from

America's mysterious South, which required much backgrounding for their viewers.

For others, such as Rick Bragg from the *New York Times*, it was deeply personal, despite the journalistic desire to be objective. Bragg had become a best-selling author and Pulitzer Prize winner. He'd come a long way from his rural Alabama roots growing up in nearby Calhoun County. Like me, he had been insulated from the civil rights movement as a kid.

Bragg, however, got an early taste of segregation's dysfunction when he was taken to a George Wallace rally in Sylacauga in the early 1960s, where he was told whites were superior to blacks. This concept didn't sit well with a little country boy whose black neighbors helped feed his family after his father had abandoned his mom and him and his two brothers.

"My job is to write about the trial," Bragg said. "My job is to capture it. My job is to do the best that I can with it. I think that a lot of writers and editors want to pretend that they go in with this pure and perfect objectivity. It was very difficult to go into that trial with any real objectivity, very difficult to go into that trial not caring one way or another how it came out."

Far from being an opportunity to avenge or in some way revel in Cherry finally facing court, this "old crime and this still fresh agony" was a physical and mental test for most everyone on hand, he noted.

"There were times in the trial when I guess maybe I had forgotten what that dark corner of the South was like, and at the end of the day when you would walk outside, and you would see that it's 2002, you would be very happy that the calendar kept flipping," Bragg said.

The Verdict

The jury deliberated for only a short time before retiring for the evening. I was a little numb from it all that night though appropriately worried that the verdict thirty-nine years in the making should be the right one.

The next day, May 22, 2002, Bobby Frank Cherry showed up in court wearing a gray suit. At least he would look relatively distinguished in cuffs when they took him away—I hoped.

After only a few more hours, we were informed a verdict had been reached. I heard the media scramble. The court staff assembled.

My team looked as nervous as I felt.

Judgment.

The jury forewoman, a tennis pro at one of the local country clubs, tried to announce the verdict with confidence but was quickly engulfed by emotion.

We strained to hear every word and collectively held our breath until she was able to work through her emotions to announce "guilty" on four counts of first-degree murder.

I was vaguely aware of Cherry reacting angrily. There was noise from the gallery—I locked eyes with Chris McNair. His smile was neither wide nor conspicuous, but it was there. It was a combination of "about time" and "you done good, my old friend. Thank you."

Judge Garrett asked the seventy-one-year-old Klansman if he had anything to say. Still defiant, an angry Cherry said, "Yes, your honor. This whole bunch lied all the way through this thing."

He turned to my team. Pointing his finger in our direction, he continued: "They all lied. That Doug Jones, that bird there [Herren].

"They all lied about me. I told the truth. I don't know [why] I'm going to jail for nothing."

In the small courtroom, Gallimore was too close to Cherry for comfort. "I could literally have reached out and grabbed his finger while he was pointing. He was in a rage."

Judge Garrett sentenced Cherry to life in prison on each count. The bailiffs handcuffed him and led him through the side door to an elevator. He and his gray suit were off to Jefferson County Jail.

Relief and exhaustion tempered elation.

Bill Fleming was near tears before the media descended on him as he left the courtroom. "It was a case without fingerprints, eyewitnesses, and evidence," Fleming said. "You could only hope the jury would know the hate in this man's being."

I had been concerned about the Cherry verdict. I never doubted his guilt, but I was worried the lack of evidence that had the kind of impact the kitchen tape provided in the Blanton trial would result in the jury failing to convict him of what we all knew he did.

I'm not exactly sure what level of community backlash a not guilty verdict would have incited, but I know it could have been ugly and, likely, damaging to race relations and the city.

A few minutes before I fronted the media outside the courtroom, I wanted to be alone with my thoughts. It was hard to focus. It was a victory, but beyond that, there was a profound righteousness about the fate that had finally caught up with Bobby Frank Cherry.

The truth had finally shone through. The darkness that accompanies the maintenance of deceit, a sense of denial and shame that was born with the bombing many decades ago, receded.

Hope had successfully intervened and Birmingham, Alabama, was a different place than the one it had been the day before.

The country, in the wake of the September 11 attacks, had talked of little else but terrorism for six months, and now a hideous terrorism event instigated and engineered on our shores was finally resolved, in a sense.

I was besieged on leaving the court.

Several microphones were thrust in my face: "Why is it important to prosecute these civil rights cases?"

I reiterated some of the thoughts I had after the Blanton trial: "You've heard the saying justice delayed is justice denied. That's just not the case. Justice delayed just does not have to be justice denied. It's still justice no matter when you get it.

"I think it's very important for victims, and I think it's very important for the community. We are a nation of laws. Sometimes those laws are Jim Crow segregationist laws that need to be overturned, but we're still a nation of laws and people need to be held accountable.

"What happened to the black community in the civil rights era was abominable . . . to be able to go back and to try to reach back in time to right those wrongs, to seek that justice, that's what this country is about."

As I was talking, Reverend Abraham Woods, Reverend Fred Shuttlesworth, and several other black leaders, along with Junie Collins Peavey, Addie Mae's sister, strode toward the media pack, arms interlocked, singing triumphantly.

When the cameras closed in, Reverend Woods, as only he could do, launched into a laundry list of issues the African-American community had in Alabama and the South. How he managed to focus on anything other than the elation of getting Cherry behind bars at that moment was beyond me. But the old bull had been waiting for this sweet victory for so long; I guess now seemed as good a time as any to let fly about ongoing injustices.

It gave me a chance to escape the media for a few moments. As I scurried away with the intention of making a few calls, one to Alpha Robertson, another to Andy Sheldon, who was overseas, I got a reminder that sometimes there is nothing you can do to make some people happy.

One of the irrationally angry voices during the controversy of the Cherry competency hearings was activist Frank Matthews. I understood his passion. I recognized he and others in the black community had felt betrayed by the justice system. But Lord, he seemed a hostile man.

But now, as he closed in on me outside the court, at least we had finally put Cherry where he belonged. I hoped we could let bygones be bygones.

"You wouldn't even shake Reverend Woods's hand," he said, without any preamble.

What was he saying? And he was getting in my face.

"Not even shake his hand."

In my haste to get clear of the media, basically to give Reverend Woods the stage, I realized I may have overlooked an attempt by the pastor to say congratulations.

I tried to explain to Matthews that there was nothing in it, but, not surprisingly, he was having nothing of that. Sheesh.

At least he stomped off promptly, allowing Fleming and Herren, who had assumed the role of bodyguards, to relax.

I finally called Mrs. Robertson.

She answered the phone at her Smithfield house in west Birmingham. As dignified as ever, she not only discussed the verdict but passed on how happy she was that I had given up the Senate race. It was touching to hear her reflect on how she never thought she'd live long enough to see three convictions for the murder of her daughter. "Justice has prevailed," she later told the press.

I resumed doing media interviews for what felt like an eternity. At one stage, out of the corner of my eye, I saw reporter Jerry Mitchell: "How does that feel?" he asked. "Better than some Senate campaign, I bet."

Indeed, it was.

We celebrated the victory that night, and I privately toasted Bill Baxley. I thought of Howell Heflin, my mom and dad, my wife and kids, even my childhood. The promising world I had reveled in as a kid was not just a mirage after all.

Next day, we all stumbled into the war room to clean it out. Herren said he had been to his office, where he'd found a plastic and wooden feathered bird perched on his desk. He'd helped convict two terrible murderers in a couple of the most significant cases in history, and all he got was a new nickname.

ELEVEN

EPIPHANIES

It is a great, largely unknown irony that Reverend Fred Shuttlesworth, that giant of the civil rights movement, may have been a little less strident in his denunciation of segregationist forces if authorities had just been slightly more courteous to him early in his career.

He would have been no less a force of nature: relentless, necessarily obstinate, and, no doubt, if he hadn't found activism, activism would have found him. Indeed, his commitment was extreme, reaching a point in the 1960s when Shuttlesworth, the survivor of multiple Klan bombings and assaults, believed he would have to die for any meaningful change to occur in Birmingham, according to the current pastor of Bethel Baptist Church, Reverend Thomas Wilder.

Yet when the man who would go on to be a founding member of the Southern Christian Leadership Conference first took over at Bethel in suburban Collegeville in 1953, his vision wasn't necessarily to become the scourge of Southern segregationists. His ambitions were more modest, largely limited to servicing the Bethel brethren, his flock.

Issues in Collegeville at the time revolved around the welfare of workers in local heavy industry—the mills, factories, and rail yards that still dominate the hardscrabble neighborhood a few miles north of downtown Birmingham.

Wilder said Shuttlesworth told him that he took up the cause of residents and a local nightclub near the church, one of the few establishments servicing the many thousands of laborers in that community. Gunshots sometimes rang out at the bar, so the pastor thought it prudent to seek a discussion with Birmingham police to put into place measures to ensure keeping the peace and allowing hardworking people to enjoy the club safely.

"But they completely ignored him," said Wilder, who served as Shuttlesworth's driver before his death in 2011. "In fact, they were downright rude and just told him to go away."

This, of course, was like waving a red flag at a bull.

"Basically, that's what got Reverend Shuttlesworth started," Wilder explained. "He came to understand clearly just how [blacks] were being treated by the police and others, and he became that loud and powerful voice in the movement. If they'd only bothered to respond to his very reasonable request for a discussion, who knows?"

I'm sure some people have a grand vision from the get-go, but the Shuttlesworth experience likely mirrors how many of us come to be better informed and more concerned about our communities. We can be intellectually aware of an issue, pay genuine heed, and express a heartfelt opinion, but there is nothing quite like experiencing something firsthand.

I found myself in a professional situation as a federal prosecutor where my colleagues and I had to draw on all our expertise to address a lingering wrong. I had understood before I became U.S. Attorney that the bombing was a horrific crime committed at a time when the city and country were going through tumultuous changes. But in doing that job, my eyes were opened wider than they had ever been, stirring something in me with which I am still coming to terms.

The experience of being forced to look very closely at how the actions of one group not only ended lives in a most gruesome way but also stripped so much from so many more in my beloved, sometimes befuddled town has been enduringly visceral.

Maybe it was a bear hug from an impressively large stranger in Home Depot in the wake of the Cherry conviction that sealed the deal for me. Certainly, the flood of thank-yous that greeted me every day at nearly every turn was a startling insight into what the trials meant to a wide cross-section of the community. Even as I welcomed the chance to return to a "normal" career, I suspected I wouldn't be filing the bombing trials away in the archives and resuming my old life.

I don't believe I turned into an activist by getting to know those girls, their families, and a community's struggle. There is no doubt, however, that the experience was transformative. Along the way, hopefully, I became a better person. Perhaps that's the biggest difference we can strive to make.

Moving On

It was my plan after the media attention had died down never to have to consider an image of Bobby Frank Cherry and his bulbous nose again. I could finally stop replaying Jean Casey's fingernails-on-a-blackboard voice in my head and respectfully file away those terrible photos of the girls' charred bodies.

The only big case I wanted to look into was one full of aged bottles of bourbon. If I had to see the inside of a courtroom, I didn't want to do it until I'd had a chance to catch a few baseball games and hit the water to fish unsuccessfully for several days.

I owed a huge debt to my colleagues at Whatley Drake, who had stood by me during my aborted Senate run and throughout the Cherry trial. I needed to spend time sharpening my class action legal expertise and get a bit of office grunt work under my belt. I also was desperate to check back in on a real family life. The unconventional demands of the previous few years robbed me of time with my loved ones, plus there was the small matter of trying to make a little money after four years of a steady, if less than extravagant, full-time federal prosecutor's paycheck.

It also was time to rebuild a few important relationships. The reaction of some members of the community to the Cherry situation before he was ordered to stand trial had left a mark. My team had been attacked and maligned, and the strength of several friendships had been tested.

There was a sense, too, that Birmingham was a little tender after the emotion of the trials. Predictably there were a few in the community who still questioned whether two "old men" should have been pursued for something that happened long ago. I could barely muster the energy to argue. Surely the culpability for murdering four girls doesn't diminish when you qualify for AARP?

Additionally, there were a couple of suggestions in the media and academic circles that we were lucky to get the convictions given the large volume of circumstantial evidence. In my mind, and as I far as I can tell, anyone who spent actual time involved with the case knew such an assertion missed the mark by about 180 degrees.

It was clear that the overwhelming collection of small truths had locked in the undeniable proof of guilt. Men and women had been convicted on far less, in far less meticulously assembled cases. Back in the day when bias and racial imbalance were recurring features of Southern justice—or injustice, as was often the case—the old Klansmen would have likely scurried away again. This time, however, they had nowhere to hide, and no one to lean on.

Predominately, though, the reaction to the convictions was positive, uplifting, and, in the case of the lady in Home Depot, all-enveloping. Throughout Alabama, you could all but hear the collective sigh of relief. Birmingham could get on with being all it should be, rather than struggling in the hole that Bull Connor and others before him had been digging for a hundred years.

Significantly, this new chapter in the nearly forty-year saga was the cue for many who had seemed to be barely clinging to life to finally let go.

James Lay died shortly after the Blanton verdict, and about a month after they locked up Cherry, John Colvin, the FBI technician who placed the bug in Blanton's apartment, succumbed to cancer.

On August 11, 2002, Alpha Robertson, aged eighty-three, passed away after battling cancer and a series of strokes. Mrs. Robertson to this day remains an inspiration. Her quiet, resolute faith, her ability to focus on the positive, and her unswerving devotion to her family made her a beacon of hope.

Exposure day after day to wanton individuals such as Blanton and Cherry generates a toxicity that threatens to infect others. Mrs. Robertson was the cure for that ill, a relentlessly good individual—the "moral center of the universe," according to Andy Sheldon. I suspect she willed herself to hang on to life until justice had been rendered in behalf of her precious daughter.

She had lost her husband in 1974, another cruel blow in a quality life devoted to education in her role as a librarian. She took some solace from the naming of two schools after her daughter in Chicago. The Carole Robertson Center for Learning was a source of great pride. Bill Fleming called her "the strongest person I've ever known," and he's known a few.

Mrs. Robertson died on a beautiful Sunday afternoon at her home. I had hoped to see her that day in New York City at the Harmony Awards Dinner, given by the Congress of Racial Equality, but before we were scheduled to depart, she called to tell me that tests had come back that were not good and that she could not go. I went by to see her in the hospital before I left and gave her a rose I'd picked from Louise's garden. It was our last time to be together. At her funeral later that week in Birmingham, her son Al took my hand in both of his. "Thank you for coming," he said quietly, "and thank you for what you did. It was because of you she died with a smile on her face."

A few months after Mrs. Robertson passed, I attended Mitch Burns's funeral. He had died of a heart attack a couple of days before Thanksgiving. Burns lived and died a Klansman and a segregationist, yet he had risked everything to try and secure justice for those girls and their families, not only at the trials decades after the fact but while the atmosphere in Birmingham was beyond oppressive and the murderers were at the height of their perverted powers.

Another key witness, Michael Gowins, died a year after the Cherry verdict from complications of his COPD and emphysema. Over the ensuing years, Ben, Bill, and I, or a combination of us, would attend funerals for Reverend Cross, Agent Frank Spencer, and Agent Ralph Butler.

One night in the fall of 2004 I was moderating a civil rights panel at the 16th Street Baptist Church when Reverend Shuttlesworth, one of the participants, took a phone call. He motioned me over to the corner of the sanctuary: "I just got a call from the *Birmingham News*. Bobby Frank Cherry has died in prison."

After the guilty verdict, Cherry had been sent to Kilby Correctional Center, outside Montgomery, Alabama. He was transferred out at one point but ended up back at the Kilby medical unit after being diagnosed with cancer. In the twilight of his life, an appeal he'd lodged against his conviction was heard by the Alabama Court of Criminal Appeals, which upheld the original decision shortly before Cherry died on November 18, leaving Tom Blanton the lone surviving bomber.

Spreading the Word

I have been involved with many civil rights programs and panels over the years, sharing the stage with legends such as Reverend Shuttlesworth, a forthright and intensely entertaining man who epitomized the vigor and righteous spirit of the movement. I was honored and humbled to be a speaker at his funeral in 2011.

In those months after the Cherry conviction, however, I had no real desire to talk about what had dominated my life for the previous five years. Even though the outpouring of support following the convictions was at times overwhelming, I really didn't expect anyone else would find the story to have little more than passing historical interest. But in the fall of 2002, my friend and fellow lawyer Scott Powell asked me to join my hero, Bill Baxley, in an off-the-cuff talk about the bombing convictions to the Inns of Court chapter in Birmingham, an association of legal professionals.

Baxley and I had never really compared notes about our respective bombing trial experiences, but I knew firsthand what he did, and he had tracked our progress carefully. He was still bristling (is still bristling) over the FBI's refusal to hand over investigative materials, such as the tape recordings, that proved so invaluable in the Blanton and Cherry cases. However, his review of the Chambliss conviction focused on the brilliance of Bob Eddy and his investigative team and the key moments of the trial, including Dynamite Bob's refusal to take the stand.

Our presentation went down well. I was surprised at the audience's receptiveness; they had a thirst for knowledge about the legal ins and outs of the process but also craved information about the history and context of the case. Many shed tears.

I felt like we were onto something special and suggested to Baxley that we should do it again. Perhaps next time I'd be a bit more organized and bring a few photos and supporting materials to add to the presentation. Sixteen years later, we're still at it, talking about the 16th Street bombing case to lawyers, civic organizations, and educational groups around the country.

Even if I had wanted to try and put the bombing cases aside for a while, it swiftly became clear it wasn't an option. Our modest presentations became something more than a lesson about history and notable courtroom experiences. In some cases, they were clearly cathartic experiences for many of the attendees and, undoubtedly, a form of self-prescribed therapy for me.

Reconstructing what happened in Birmingham in the sixties by necessity includes an analysis of why it happened. That requires talking about the city and the South, then and now, comparing and contrasting, explaining differences and sometimes noting similarities between eras.

We turned down more invitations to do talks than we accepted; however, over the years we tried to ensure we spoke to diverse audiences.

Sometimes they'd look familiar: caring husbands, fathers, uncles, and grandfathers, like me, proud sons of the South. A couple of generations of hardworking, mostly well-intentioned white men and women, some carrying a heavy, maybe even unspeakable, burden having grown up in families that supported segregation. Or perhaps they were academics, teachers, students, or even kids; the faces of the peers of my daughter and two growing boys staring back at me, wondering how people like me and my parents' generation could have possibly allowed this to happen.

"It's not like that anymore," the kids would say, more out of hope than experience.

Of course, there is plenty of evidence to back that up. To be sure, the transformation in the South and beyond has been head-spinning at times. As Alabama's pre-eminent historian Wayne Flynt points out, one in four representatives in the state's legislature now is black, and in some counties all representatives are African-American when only fifty years ago there were no black legislators at all.

A couple of generations of African Americans have capitalized on government and business initiatives that reflect Dr. King's dream, reaching great heights in the corporate world, and across the country, many conspicuous signs of racism have been forced underground or eradicated.

While racial insensitivity and vilification still blurt from the mouths of newsmakers, even successful presidential candidates, it's largely frowned upon with great intensity by our civil society. And when it comes down to it, that's what we want for our children. Certainly, it's what I wanted for Courtney, Carson, and Christopher—to grow up in an environment where all people are afforded the same dignity and respect.

I'll admit, when I started talking to people about the bombing, discussing the context in which it was allowed to occur and comparing it to contemporary attitudes and conditions, I felt like we were talking about two very distinct times. It was more like a history lesson on how bad things were back then, and I took pride—I still take pride—in asserting that the successful prosecution of the old Klansmen helped end something terrible in our history.

Through the 2000s, however, the "it's not like that anymore" contention became less credible.

My family had flourished in an environment blessedly free of much of that obviously hateful dialogue in a happy home and more tolerant city. My daughter married and had two children; my eldest son, having inherited my love of the Birmingham Zoo, developed an intense interest in the animal world; and my younger boy became my best fishing and hunting buddy, as we shared his fierce love of the outdoors.

However, by the time my eldest boy, Carson, was dealing with junior high school, the notion that tolerance and social progress would continue to transform the South wasn't the assured assertion it had been decades earlier. Certainly, suggestions that we were living in a "post-racial" world were abject nonsense. We had no more ended racism and segregation in society than we had eliminated terrorism.

Déjà Vu

Rather than having shed the legacy of Wallace and other Southern demagogues, by the mid-2000s the Republican Party had effectively picked up the tactics of division to strengthen GOP domination of politics and ideology in the South. To a large extent, this move was changing the fabric of the Grand Old Party nationally.

Democrats failed to respond as they began to lose power in Alabama and other Southern states. They surrendered meekly, as the GOP had done in the face of the Southern bloc from the Jim Crow era. The best effort the Democratic Party could muster was to preserve pockets of influence—black influence.

With great political cynicism, both major parties indulged in gerrymandering, the act of deliberately fashioning a political advantage by changing electoral boundaries.

The redistricting process is often manipulated by the party in power to protect the incumbent. Politics had become more about getting into power and holding on rather than doing anything that might represent leadership or a true representation of the diverse interests of a wide range of people. This was blatantly the case in the South, and it permeates Washington today.

The emergence of Barack Obama as a national political force perhaps helped camouflage this slide back toward the bad old days of manufactured splits in society. Some pundits suggested the rise of an African American as a contender for the country's highest office was proof positive that society was now color-blind. No need to worry about discrimination and the manipulation of the broad political system, they'd say; everyone is now on equal footing.

It was, of course, a convenient and sinfully misleading assertion that had dramatic consequences. Repeated chants that hundreds of years of racial oppression were no longer a major consideration in American life gave fresh force to those wanting to peel back civil rights protections for minorities.

Rather than engaging in constructive critiques of the homegrown flaws in our democracy, our collective focus was again directed toward the terrible influence of "outsiders." This time, they were challenging America's borders—Latinos to the South and Middle Eastern terrorists charging in from everywhere.

Politicians have long relied on convincing us there was a bogeyman out there, and only they could protect us from him. But this reached new levels in the decade after the September 11 terrorist attacks.

A "tough hand" was the only way to deal with the threats—strident law-and-order restrictions had "cleaned up" cities like New York, and harsh prison sentencing was lauded as having put a dent in the "war on drugs." In fact, the main result of those programs for the community was the dent they put in taxpayers' pockets, as the prison system burst at the seams, and we jailed more people than any other country in the world.

At least forty percent of people incarcerated in the massive law-and-order "cleanup" through the nineties and noughts were African-American, and most of them were from below the poverty line. Once again, a great swath of black people had lost their hard-fought right to vote, earn a living, and share the spoils of enterprise and hard work—this time because of felony convictions and incarceration.

If it wasn't obvious a few years before we elected our first black President, it was undeniably clear that the America Obama was to inherit as Commander in Chief in 2008 was being weighed down by some attitudes not far removed from those peddled a half-century before.

Far from being on equal footing and united by common causes, we were a country divided once more. The appearance of a black leader had merely allowed bigots to camouflage their hate as policy criticism or political debate.

Make no mistake: especially in the South, where the level of antagonism toward immigrants reached frightening levels in the late 2000s, racism and other discriminatory behavior remained dangerously pervasive; they had just become more covert.

As Professor Flynt explained: "What we have are new proxies. This is all about race, make no mistake. The Republicans over the course of the last decade knew that."

Obama's comprehensive victory nationally couldn't divert attention from the fact that he got little support from the white community in the Deep South. In Alabama, just ten percent of the white vote went his way—the lowest in the nation.

Carson, though, headed to his nearly all-white junior high school the day after the vote wearing a celebratory T-shirt featuring the new president's image. He didn't expect all his school friends to celebrate with him, but he could hardly believe being repeatedly abused as a "nigger lover."

On occasion, especially around the time of Obama's election in 2008, I would sometimes hear emphatic declarations at my talks from the audience that what happened in the past has nothing to do with present-day challenges. After all, now we had a black leader. But an honest evaluation of then and now did not allow such a comfortable summation; on the contrary, I was increasingly startled by the similarities.

Despite the welcome election of a black President, the seeds of terrorism, political demagoguery, and intransigence were disturbingly alive and well. Our political representatives were poles apart in Washington and state legislatures. Religion was being wielded as a weapon, and the level of xenophobia, especially in the South, was staggering. The "new era" felt uncomfortably familiar.

I vaguely recalled rhetoric in the 1960s about the end of government-sanctioned segregation meaning we were all suddenly on a level playing field. In the wake of that basic civil rights reform, moderates turned their backs on the creep of extremism and the rise of a demagogue, leaving the door open to violence and turmoil.

Many of the good people of the South in the fifties and sixties ignored or were deceived by the resilience of their bigotry. Sixty years later, the welcome presence of an African American in the White House was apparently evidence that the bad old days of division were behind us.

But I, for one, vowed not to be fooled again.

TWELVE

HONORING THE CHILDREN

The fifty-year commemorations of several key civil rights–era events were opportunities to recognize how far we have come in the South.

While the grief of the girls' deaths is a constant, there was official acknowledgment in 2013 of the positive impact of their unwitting sacrifice. In May, the families of the 1963 bombing victims were summoned to the White House. Carole, Denise, Addie, and Cynthia were to be posthumously awarded the Congressional Gold Medal, the country's highest civil honor. Alabama's sole Democrat in Congress, Terri Sewell, and Republican Congressman Spencer Bachus sponsored the bill to make that possible, and President Obama was to sign it into law in the presence of family members and a few dignitaries in the Oval Office.

The girls' relatives and the politicians joined the President at the Resolute desk for the signing ceremony on May 24. I was honored to have been invited by my old friend Congressman Bachus to attend in his stead.

Carole Robertson's sister Dianne Braddock, Lisa McNair and her mother Maxine, Attorney General Holder and his wife Dr. Sharon Malone Holder, Surgeon General Regina Benjamin, Congresswoman Sewell, Birmingham Mayor William Bell, and 16th Street Baptist Pastor Arthur Price were on hand to witness the signing.

As the President addressed us before bringing in the throng of media, I could not help but notice that mine was the only white face in the room.

If nothing else, it was an indication of the progress we have made regarding the opportunities embraced by African Americans seeking high office over the last fifty years.

The media were waiting outside to be allowed in to record the signing. Before they crowded into what I consider one of the most sacred of spaces of our democracy, President Obama took a moment to pass on a few thoughts. There was an unpolluted thirty-second silence before he spoke with great sincerity about how the horror of what happened on September 15, 1963, changed the country. He acknowledged that most of us in the room that day wouldn't be in such exalted positions (himself included) were it not for the girls' unwitting sacrifice and the righteous response it inspired. With a nod to me, he also noted that it took a "proud son of the South" to bring justice after so many years.

The media entered, and the bill was signed. Four months later, we gathered again amid the marble and sandstone beauty of Statuary Hall in the U.S. Capitol. The sculpture of Rosa Parks peered over the shoulder of dignitaries as the official Congressional Gold Medal ceremony was conducted.

The medal inscription carries the girls' names and reads: "Pivotal in the Struggle for Equality, September 15, 1963."

One of the few things Washington seemed to agree on, for that day, at least, was that the tragedy of the girls' deaths was the catalyst for unprecedented, significant advances in the civil rights struggle. It was a grand bipartisan gathering at a time when Washington was mired in disagreement, conflict, and standoffs.

It was not the time to dwell on partisan politics, nor was the commemorative service five days later at 16th Street Baptist in Birmingham reflecting on the half-century since the girls' deaths. Overall, the fifty-year commemoration of the bombing was a positive occasion, overflowing with inspirational speeches and spiced by occasional scuttlebutt, such as why the city's own Condoleezza Rice, in town for a number of commemoration events, failed to join other community and national leaders in church for the actual memorial ceremony.

Yet, there was an underlying anxiety flavoring many conversations. The commemoration was a rare opportunity for leading civil rights activists, academics, old foot soldiers, and community leaders from across generations and the country to get together. It was striking how they all expressed acute concern that the advances from decades of reform were quite suddenly and ferociously under attack.

Divisiveness in Washington and state legislatures across the country had given rise to an atmosphere in which no-compromise politicians were rallying around legislation and initiatives that resembled throwbacks to the Jim Crow era.

This had spilled over into the judiciary, with the Supreme Court embracing concepts that quashed the fruits of years of civil rights struggle. In a June 2013 ruling the Court effectively gutted the Voting Rights Act—the monumental 1965 legislation preventing electoral disempowerment of minority and many other would-be voters.

The Act was introduced to ensure those who wanted to vote could register to do so. It was a federal action to safeguard against states introducing measures to keep the poor and traditionally marginalized from qualifying to be on the voting rolls.

However, the Supreme Court ruling *Shelby County v. Holder* effectively nullified the core of the Act. The judges' decision by a five-to-four vote included an explanation that said the precautions and safeguards for potential voters offered by the legislation were no longer relevant—in a sense, suggesting there were no longer potential racial imbalances in the registration process. With that, one of the greatest pieces of reform legislation in American history, the method by which a generation or more of African Americans came to embrace and make use of their right to vote, became impotent.

Confronting the attendees at the 16th Street Baptist Church commemoration was the fact that the highest court in the land had decimated the very legacy of the girls' sacrifice.

While the Selma-to-Montgomery marches had forced Washington to approve the Voting Rights Act, it was the horror of September 15, 1963, that spurred Diane Nash, James Bevel, and others to push the nonviolent protest movement in Alabama toward the goal of making the vote more obtainable for blacks.

The term "slap in the face" is inadequate. The Supreme Court decision and Congress's subsequent dismissals of moves to reinvigorate the Voting Rights Act were full-blown assaults on basic rights. Salting the wound, the changes seemed to be handed down with an imperious detachment.

Standing in the 16th Street Baptist Church, I watched politicians and other leaders join hands to sing "We Shall Overcome" to commemorate the girls' deaths. The faces of some of the foot soldiers were contorted by emotion—although from what I'd learned from the trials and in the years since, I knew not every tear they were shedding was about the past.

I had to quell my own growing anger about the fact that we were dismantling the positive changes made possible by the efforts of thousands during the civil rights era. I sang, smiled, and celebrated, but I also was furious.

While acknowledging we'd come a long way, I could not hide the feeling that we'd taken a wrong turn in recent years and, in a sense, ended up where we'd started, more than a half-century before.

Eighteen months later, on March 7, 2015, at the fiftieth anniversary of Bloody Sunday in Selma, Alabama, that feeling was even more pronounced.

The Tea Party–infused GOP had taken control of the U.S. Senate in the midterms and promised to continue to block President Obama's every legislative move. The sky was blue over Selma, but a dark cloud loomed in the minds of most participants.

Louise and I had the honor of attending the event. We were in the esteemed company of some of the old foot soldiers in Selma, who could only shake their heads at some of the politicians on hand. Some of the same people obstructing the reintroduction of voting rights protections were getting political mileage out of being present at the commemoration of the bloody incident that forced Congress to introduce reform and protection for marginalized voters in the first place in August 1965.

In fact, some of those giving lip service to civil rights were champions of a rash of contemporary legislation that looked like it was straight out of the Jim Crow playbook, from voter ID laws to immigration policies such as Arizona's SB 1070—the "show me your papers law" that focused heavily on targeting those with the "wrong" skin color, accent, or dress. Not to be outdone by Arizona, Alabama had its own draconian anti–illegal immigration bill, HB 56, that supporters tried to justify by saying aliens were taking jobs from locals.

Bobby Frank Cherry's suggestion to Michael Gowins in Dallas in 1982 that Hispanics should be subjected to the same fate as blacks in Birmingham was an ugly reference to invoking racial violence. Decades later, while the tactics weren't quite as crude, there was no doubt some lawmakers were making it their mission to treat immigrants, legal or not, with the kind of legislative disdain long endured by African Americans.

It wasn't just immigrants who were feeling the wrath of the courts and legislatures around the country. Gay Americans were constantly being made to feel like second-class citizens. Plus women's rights, including equal pay for equal work and the right to make health decisions regarding their bodies, were under attack, increasingly for purely political purposes.

The belligerence of all parties in Washington and the narrow interests being served in state legislatures around the country were eerily reminiscent of standoffs in the pre–civil rights era. These echoes of the past were evident to many who had fought against direct discrimination and marginalization a half-century ago, risking their lives in some cases in a bid to end segregation.

Standing on the Edmund Pettus Bridge in March 2015, I was unsettled by how easy it was to picture a time in the near future when we could again be contemplating the "how could we have let this happen?" question that had haunted me as I investigated the church bombing.

Disturbingly, the answer would be similar: extremists fighting to set the agenda in an environment poisoned by political polarization where the middle ground and the pursuit of compromise have been abandoned. We were divided and segregated again, if not by law, then by economics.

That feeling of unease I had about the possibility of a backlash in the wake of Obama's election in 2008 had sadly proven incontrovertibly accurate. Not only did we hear echoes of an ugly period of our country's history, but we were to some extent repeating it.

The eruption of protest in the wake of the deaths of African-American men, including Eric Garner in New York and Michael Brown in Ferguson, in recent years at the hands of police galvanized elements of the contemporary civil rights movement, creating its new public face, Black Lives Matter.

The parallels to the early sixties were uncanny, and when you see (Bull Connor–like) armored vehicles in the suburban streets of Ferguson, Missouri, as part of a heightened militarized response to protest, experience tells us matters may get far worse before they improve.

I was in the midst of writing this book, contemplating, in part, how to avoid sounding like a scaremonger, when Freddie Gray, a twenty-five-year-old African American, died after being taken into police custody in Baltimore. His death on April 19, 2015, sparked protests and was used as a symbol in riots that resulted in looting and lawlessness. Amid fires, property destruction, and street battles, a terrified American city had to be shut down.

At both the September 2013 bombing commemoration and the Bloody Sunday anniversary in Selma eighteen months later, I had reluctantly raised the possibility with colleagues that it might take something as horrendous as the murder of those four girls to bring the message home that divisiveness was facilitating dangerous dysfunction, and reform was again overdue.

And then it happened.

I was heartsick when twenty-one-year-old white supremacist Dylann

Roof violated the sacred space of the Emanuel African Methodist Episco-pal Church in Charleston, South Carolina, one of the most famous black places of worship in the country, on June 17, 2015, by fatally shooting nine churchgoers.

I was enraged all over again by our complicity through collective si-lence. Once again political and social dysfunction had coalesced as mur-derous toxicity. I couldn't blame my parents' generation for this one.

Then and Now

For the most part, my talks around the country, often with Bill Baxley at my side, have remained focused primarily on the process of prosecuting the bombers. We take turns recounting what happened, how it happened, and how the old Klansmen finally faced justice. The presentations are in-credibly well received, and attendees are anxious to participate in discus-sions about the bombing, the girls' legacy, civil rights, and the terrible old Klansmen.

Of course, we occasionally run into a few people who just don't want to know: the "why dwell in the past" crowd. I understand it is difficult to face ugly facts about people and places from years gone by, especially if you have a direct connection to them, so I used to ignore those who chose to look away.

But I won't do that anymore. You can't un-see what we've witnessed in the last few years, and it's quite clear there are fundamental wrongs that need to be addressed swiftly before the divisions in this country perhaps become irrevocable.

I have learned valuable lessons through my involvement in the bomb-ing case and especially in the years since. Many of them have been per-sonal, but unquestionably the most impactful is that the worst parts of our history repeat themselves unless people of goodwill speak up and take de-cisive action. Uncomfortably for some, we do have to look back at the bad old days to recognize that the same factors that used to poison society are responsible for the current wave of divisiveness and extremist behavior.

After the Charleston shootings, inspirational author and lawyer Bryan Stevenson lamented our country's inability to deal honestly with our his-tory of racial injustice. He talked extensively about the legacy of slavery and how it echoed through the South and beyond over decades through lynch-ings, terrorism, segregation, Jim Crow, and, indeed, Dylann Roof, who wanted to start a "race war."

When you talk about slavery in this country, especially in the South, you get many white folks, and a few black folks as well, staring blankly, or out the window, waiting for you to stop retracing a path back hundreds of years. However, the Charleston shootings follow a very direct, uncomplicated route to the 16th Street Baptist Church bombing of 1963. It's a short journey, though certainly not painless, and is another chapter in our failure to adequately address the underlying causes of inequality.

To ignore positive changes in race relations, especially in the last fifty years, would be disingenuous. But we will continue to repeat atrocities unless we accept, across the political spectrum, that segregation, acute bias, and domestic terrorism are as threatening today as they were a half-century ago, if not more so.

The trolls under the Cahaba River Bridge in 1963 were desperate. With the dismantling of segregation, they decided they'd take matters into their own hands. If only they'd waited a few decades, they would have seen not all hope was lost for their dismal kingdom.

Even before Donald Trump blustered onto the national stage with a cynical, self-serving political agenda comically reminiscent of George Wallace's, the contemporary political landscape bore striking similarities to those dark days when one party dominated vast tracts of the country.

In the South, the GOP has ruled the roost regardless of the comings and goings in the White House for much of the last twenty years. At the same time, Democrats in the South have lurched from being ineffectual to occasionally shambolic outside the comfort of core blue areas.

Where there is a large black population, the Democratic Party often has been content to accept and cling to a pocket of power, but elsewhere, progressives are so marginalized and dominated that many Democratic candidates have felt the need to out-Republican the Republicans in order to try and win elections. At the same time, the national Democratic Party machine has backed away from the South as if it was an irredeemable basket case: home only to rednecks, racists, and those who rant about religion.

There was a brief moment around 2006 when former Vermont Governor Howard Dean, in his capacity as Chairman of the Democratic National Committee, advocated a "fifty-state strategy" to strengthen the party's roots everywhere. But he was swiftly howled down by national strategists.

The GOP, by contrast, was politically astute, fighting every electoral battle, at every level of government, in most corners of the country, like it was a presidential poll. By 2010, Republican dominance in the South was complete. The lack of an effective two-party system was catastrophic for the South during Jim Crow, and now we have a political structure, aided and abetted by gerrymandering and the unseemly influence of money in politics, that in many ways is just as perverted as the Dixiecrat reign.

The dearth of an effective moderate voice in an atmosphere of extreme partisanship leads to confrontation, politically and socially, yet we've abandoned the middle ground and handed the agenda, in many instances, to those on the extreme.

The volatile 2016 presidential race was a product of this maladjusted environment, which reeked of the rotting remnants of another age even before Donald Trump began stoking the fires of racism and division.

Mark Kennedy, the former Alabama Democratic Party Chair, is married to former Governor Wallace's daughter, the delightful and brilliant Peggy Wallace Kennedy. He believes her father, the advocate of "segregation now, segregation tomorrow, segregation forever," would be stunned that the current sociopolitical climate reflects many of the same discriminatory qualities that looked to be vestiges of the past by the 1970s.

"I have told my wife in several conversations that if your daddy were here today and looked over this landscape, he would be absolutely amazed that the power of hate and fear are in full bloom," Kennedy said.

Far from being an anachronism, Wallace, with his victory-at-any-costs approach and his creed of zealotry, was the prototypical intransigent voice of political self-interest that echoes loudly in Washington and state legislatures around the country today.

The Governor and his Southern Democrats were the architects of dog-whistle politics used by all sides of government and have been embraced by many Americans, some who stumble into perpetuating bigotry and bias without even realizing.

Just as the Birmingham church bombing ushered in a positive period of national reflection, perhaps the political chaos we're currently negotiating will lead to a necessary reset of our moral and ethical path. But in my view, only a broad coalition—a bipartisan commitment to common sense and true reform—can protect against yet another, perhaps catastrophic, backlash.

In the wake of the 2016 presidential election, Louise and I felt compelled to at least make an effort to be part of that process. And I knew, as I did before the bombing trials, that there were already tools in the system to get us back on track.

Why?

Recently I got together with Jeff Wallace and Robert Posey at the Tutwiler Hotel bar for a chat. I will be forever grateful to both men and the rest of the prosecution team not only for their contributions to our effort to hold Blanton and Cherry accountable but for the fact that they helped me understand the importance of what we were doing. It wasn't that we ever discussed it in those terms. Rather, I saw it in their actions, then and now.

"We were just doing our job," Wallace said, as we reminisced about what the case meant to each of us. But minutes later, as has always been his way, Jeff couldn't bring himself to say the four girls' names.

Posey, too, was unsettled. Sitting at the Tut bar enjoying a local craft brew, he went silent for a moment before gently reciting a small piece of his breathtaking closing argument in the Blanton case:

"This is Cynthia Wesley. This is Carole Robertson. This is Denise McNair. This is Addie Mae Collins. This defendant . . . murdered these four worshippers in God's house on a Sunday morning because he was a man of hate. The hatred, the intolerance, the injustice, perpetrated by this defendant must not stand unchallenged."

Posey had committed his closing to memory in 2001 and practiced for many hours to control his emotions. Sixteen years later the only way he could bring himself to say the girls' names without being overcome was by drawing on that discipline.

The trials were part of our job, and thankfully, we did it pretty well, convincing the juries to see the bombing as something other than a piece of regrettable history. It was an evil act against children that still rightfully induced outrage, unfathomable grief, and horror. Professional detachment in this case was not an option, especially with the thought in the back of our minds that many of us had a personal relationship with the time and place of this atrocity.

Not having the luxury of looking away, I found I was not only horrified by the bombing but wounded by the sense that good people—my people—remained silent for so long, allowing that toxic environment to evolve.

When you talk to white folks today about those times, it is striking how little they say they knew about the race issue. Some of that is defensiveness and guilt, but it's also a predictable product of the segregated society that was the norm for so long. After all, an underlying idea of segregation is to exclude that which you don't want to deal with.

We remain segregated today not by law but by economics and the hijacking of our political process.

Of course, if you said too much about those sorts of issues in the fifties and sixties you were labeled an enemy of democracy. "Race Mixing Is Communism," the banners at segregationist rallies screamed. Now, in 2019, you're a bleeding-heart liberal extremist, a member of the Washington elite, and perhaps, ludicrously, branded a racist for talking about race.

I am none of these things. I am like my dear mother and father, who loved their children, respected people, went to church, and worked hard. The only difference is they didn't get to see in detail some of the ugliest consequences of segregation. I did, and it would be remiss of me not to speak about it.

What do two murderous Klansmen who committed a terrible crime more than fifty years ago have to do with the need to renovate aspects of our political system? Everything, because they represent the ugly truth of extreme political, economic, and social division.

Linking the situation in the 1960s with today isn't an empty scare tactic or an attempt to trumpet my personal political views. It is about those four girls and thousands more we should have protected. It is about ensuring those people who did speak up and walked the walk are honored. It is about ensuring that individual liberty is preserved, not abused, by the few who have the means to impact all our lives. It is about gently prodding the collective conscience that made America powerful *and* compassionate.

I want my grandchildren to be able to attend school wearing a T-shirt the day after America elects its next black President and not be called a nigger lover. I want all our kids to have a real shot at a decent piece of the pie, and I want that gentleman who is deliberately staring off into the distance to turn and face me, you, and an uncomfortable history, and discuss how we can ensure it never happens again.

THIRTEEN

ONE MORE CHANCE

For much of the Trump presidency, the administration, recognizing that fear of crime is a potential vote winner, has shamelessly propagated the myth that the country is in the grip of out-of-control rises in lawlessness.

However, once "tough on crime" Attorney General Jeff Sessions was removed from office and presidential advisor Jared Kushner got in his father-in-law's ear, there was an abrupt about-face and, unexpectedly, common sense briefly emanated from the White House. To the President's credit, in December 2018 he backed a bipartisan criminal justice reform bill that goes some of the way to addressing our sentencing laws and incarceration practices, which are a global disgrace.

We have been unquestionably misguided in pursuing an excessively punitive policy against some who break the law, but that doesn't mean there are easy answers in America's law-and-order debate.

I have much sympathy for those impacted by malfeasance, and, indeed, I am not blind to the injustice visited on some criminals. Having operated as a prosecutor and defense lawyer, I'm acutely aware that lives can be destroyed by both crime and punishment. The fate of two convicted men, especially, has been at the forefront of my mind for many years, and the unexpected intersection of their cases, on a personal level, helped compel me to try and act on the lessons of history.

Both before and not long after Blanton's incarceration, I met with the former Klansman, hoping to convince him to fill in the missing details about the bombing. The investigations put the pieces together, so we had a clear picture of key facts, but the families of the four girls, the black community, the state of Alabama—anyone with an interest in history—had the right to know every detail.

Despite Blanton's apparent absence of compassion for his fellow human beings, I'd hoped he might understand it was in his best interests to provide the whole story. He would still be held accountable for his actions, but any cooperation would be noted and possibly go some way to making his time behind bars shorter and more bearable.

He opted to swat me away and ended up in one of Alabama's harsh and overcrowded prisons, a deserved fate. However, I've always thought if somewhere along the line Blanton was to admit to a degree of personal responsibility for the bombing it would be a positive for the wider community. Perhaps, in those circumstances, a slightly less dire jail experience would be a suitable acknowledgment that there is value in truth and the desire for forgiveness.

However, the incarceration of Chris McNair, at age eighty-five in 2011 on corruption charges, introduced me to a new level of personal angst about Blanton. I was repulsed by the prospect that the father of one of the victims, a friend, might die behind bars before his daughter's killer passed.

The Sewer

McNair had decided to stay in Birmingham after Denise's death and made an enormous contribution during three decades of public service, despite having every reason to turn his back and get the hell out of the place, away from the people who took his innocent daughter in the most gruesome way. He held his ground, taking a seat in government alongside a man who supported those who murdered his child. He became an unusual conduit between black and white communities in Birmingham while always shadowed by the reality of bigotry and the memory of that unconscionable act.

When elected in 1973, McNair was one of the first blacks to take a seat in the Alabama legislature since Reconstruction. And from 1986 through 2001, he served on the Jefferson County Commission, where he was often celebrated as a progressive, evenhanded administrator.

From early in his adult life, he had been a man who was on his way to being part of Dr. King's vision for a reformed South. A talented, educated

African American no longer paralyzed by the prejudice of the Jim Crow era, he had the vision to overlook vestiges of segregation and build a professional future in the broad Birmingham community.

McNair was at ease envisioning a world where he would be, as King described it, "the white man's brother, not his brother-in-law."

"He was like that for as long as I can remember," said his daughter Lisa, who was born a year after Denise died. "We grew up around black and white people. It wasn't strained or anything; it just was what it was."

In 1996, some of those white friends, all of whom did business with Jefferson County, offered their "assistance" as McNair expanded his photography studio into a multipurpose arts center that would also feature the respective art skills and culinary expertise of his daughters, Lisa and Kim. A centerpiece of the development would be a memorial to Denise, using Chris's photos and memorabilia.

However, the *Birmingham News*, with an investigative zeal that has sadly disappeared from most newspapers today, looked into allegations that Chris's "baby" was the result of the largess of some of the businesses he was vetting to potentially work on Jefferson County infrastructure projects.

The business leaders, it was alleged, had tried to ingratiate themselves with McNair to get his crucial support for them to participate in a $3.2 billion overhaul of Birmingham's antiquated water and sewer system, and he had sought their economic favor as part of a quid pro quo agreement.

I represented McNair in what was always going to be a very tough bribery and conspiracy trial in the spring of 2006. The prosecution's evidence was pretty solid, and our only real defense—one McNair insisted on—was these were friends and there was no quid pro quo. He was found guilty by a jury in one case and pled guilty in another.

On September 19, 2007, he was sentenced to five years in prison and ordered to pay $851,927 in restitution but remained free on bail pending the outcome of appeals. We took the case to the Eleventh Circuit Court of Appeals, only for the conviction to be affirmed on May 12, 2010. We filed a petition for a writ of certiorari in the hope that the U.S. Supreme Court would take up the case, but it was denied on March 7, 2011.

McNair was required to report to the Federal Prison Camp in Marion, Illinois, on June 6, 2011. I volunteered to drive him. His brother Harold and my associate Anil Mujumdar accompanied us on the six-hour trek through northern Alabama, Tennessee, and the tip of Kentucky into eastern Illinois. On arrival, we were informed we couldn't accompany him into the facility. We said our good-byes from the parking lot, where prison personnel gathered his numerous medications and his sleep apnea machine before a guard escorted him into the stark main building.

It is one of those snapshot moments I expect will repeat on me until I leave this earth. McNair, struggling to walk, accompanied by the guard, made his way to the jail entrance, turned, and as if he was off to camp, gave us a reassuring wave, a "thanks, I'll be OK" sign-off. And with that, a tired, sick, elderly man seemed to let go of the ledge to which he'd been clinging during a long and difficult climb out of despair. The absence of mercy was conspicuous at that moment. It all seemed resoundingly cruel, although I clearly understood why it was happening.

The likelihood he would die before Blanton while incarcerated was a dark, faith-testing possibility. Throw away the key to Blanton's cell, I thought. Good riddance.

Over the next few years, I set up appeals and mobilized support for a clemency bid. There were a few encouraging signs, but nothing came of them as McNair's health swiftly deteriorated behind bars.

In August 2013, we prepared to commemorate the fiftieth anniversary of the bombing without McNair. But then, a phone call.

As I was helping my son Carson move into his college dorm at the University of Georgia, Attorney General Eric Holder called. He and I had talked about McNair earlier, and I knew he was revamping the "compassionate release" program to reduce the number of elderly, infirm, low-threat prisoners in custody. Chris McNair fit the new criteria, according to the AG, and with judicial approval would be released.

I still get chills thinking about that conversation. When I got off the phone, I was excited but also strangely exhausted. I guess I'd had Chris on my mind in some way, shape, or form nearly daily since at least 1997, when I took on the bombing case. I'd known of him nearly all my life and been friends with him for nearly thirty years. And now, on this day when I was battling a little melancholy as I prepared to say farewell to my son, I had received word that I could stop agonizing—stop being eaten away by the sadness of it all.

Something was going to go right for Chris McNair—a hero, a victim, a whipping boy; a man too black or not black enough; a leader and a felon— but most of all, at least to me, an elderly father who had lost his precious daughter when he was in his prime and she had not yet had a chance to realize her promise. Mercy. Sweet mercy.

On August 29, I was scheduled to fly to Rochester, Minnesota, to fetch McNair from a prison medical facility (without alerting the media). My plan fell through as the sun rose. The pilot was unavailable, and there was a distinct possibility McNair's only chance to get home before the fiftieth commemoration of the church bombing would be lost. I had to get him before 5:00 that afternoon, so I made a circuitous round-trip journey on a string of commercial airlines. I saw several American airports that day and managed to get Chris back to Birmingham late at night. Louise met us at the airport and we headed to a little McNair family celebration shortly after midnight.

On arrival, there was culinary carnage in the small space of the family home where Kim had worked her magic. Amid a battalion of small appliances, cooking utensils, baking trays, cake tins, and assorted pots and pans, Maxine McNair, confined to a chair at the center of the room, was holding court.

"I have missed you, old man," she said as Chris trudged in. She struggled to stand and embrace him. Bending his tired frame, he supported her and brought her in close: "I have missed you too baby."

No wasting time; it was late. Chris was ushered to the table and surrounded by family, fried chicken, okra, collard greens, beans, sweet potatoes, gravy, and pie. He was where he belonged. Only one thing—one irreplaceable treasure—was missing, although for some reason, you had the feeling there had been some unseen hand involved in making the pieces fall where they did that day.

McNair's release lifted the fog a little for me. I wasn't as blinded by rage at Blanton or inclined to despair about what I couldn't do to change things for the better. Compassion still existed, right there alongside the rule of law.

I soon found myself wondering whether, on the way to eighty years, Blanton might have mellowed. Even though he was still a belligerent and angry man around the time of his trial, the second half of his life wasn't littered with examples of the kind of violence he exercised as a bullheaded, undereducated twenty-something.

Pull up his mug shot on the Alabama Department of Corrections website these days and an image of a half-smiling old man with thick glasses appears. It could be a headshot from central casting for a Christmas elf. Looks, however, can be deceiving. I know what the elf is capable of. But maybe time and isolation had changed him, I thought. And frankly, the opportunity to milk a little remorse or maybe even an admission from him was slipping away.

Blanton's freedom over the decades following the bombing must have felt a little like a kind of purgatory. Most who remembered the case knew he was associated with it in the worst way, and his old racist networks had gradually dismantled.

As a middle-aged curmudgeon, he apparently moved from job to job in the Birmingham area as the stain of the bombing followed him. When we were preparing our case, Jeff Wallace happened to be in the Walmart in suburban Hoover and couldn't resist wandering into the gun department, where Blanton, one of the most violent men in Birmingham in the sixties, was working, helping customers purchase firearms and knives.

Blanton eventually studied law, likely in search of a way to keep himself out of court rather than as a path to a career. He fortunately never passed the bar.

I paid Blanton two visits after McNair was released. One on a warm summer's day in 2014 and another in 2016, when the media was overflowing with "Hillary Clinton this" and "Donald Trump that" in the rundown to the presidential election. At that time, Thomas E. Blanton also was contemplating his first encounter with the parole board.

Blanton's life sentence made him eligible for parole after fifteen years. He is serving his time in the St. Clair Correctional Facility near Springville, about thirty-three miles northeast of Birmingham. The prison, rated among Alabama's worst, is regularly embroiled in controversy. It has capacity for about 1,300 prisoners but houses about double that number, including 365 serving life without the chance of parole. In recent times at St. Clair, there were six killings over a thirty-month period and numerous serious assaults. Located on six hundred acres in semi-rural surroundings not far from Springville village, population 2,500, the jail is an easy half-hour drive up I-59 from downtown Birmingham.

After all these years of being a criminal defense attorney, you'd think I'd be used to jail visits, but there is never anything routine about them. The horror of walking into a place where you can feel the absence of hope is startling.

The buildings and facilities at St. Clair, like many in the Alabama system, look like throwbacks to the 1950s. During my first visit, I checked in with the warden, who explained Blanton spent most of his time in his cell, rarely taking advantage of the five hours a week he was permitted to venture out of the tiny space where he lived in isolation from the rest of the prison population. He had no visitors other than the occasional encounter with his daughter, and his health had been deteriorating. He was particularly troubled by eye problems.

An escort led me through the bowels of the jail to an outside area where there was a small shack-like structure, more cleaning supply closet than meeting room. I took a seat on one of a few chairs at an old table and suddenly Blanton appeared with chains around his ankles and his hands handcuffed behind his back, a withered version of the man I'd last seen thirteen years before.

At my request, the prison guards agreed to handcuff him in front of his body rather than behind his back, and he took a seat opposite me, looking every minute of his then seventy-seven years. At first he did not recognize me, but when he did he almost immediately inquired, "Why are you here?"

For a second or two, I didn't have an answer. Why was I talking to a murderer who had been involved in one of the worst crimes in Alabama history and duly received his just punishment?

I explained, as I had during previous meetings, that the families would benefit from knowing more about what happened all those years ago. "And this community is yearning, not so much for blood anymore, but a sense of reconciliation," I said while hearing a voice in my head scream *apologize, damn it!*"

As I had always been with him, however, I was honest about my intentions. I told him I was writing this book and I believed it provided the perfect opportunity for him to come clean and begin the reconciliation process.

"I don't know anything. I can't help you," he said.

He may not have felt like helping anyone, but he certainly knew a lot.

For the sake of the exercise, I told him, we could pretend he hadn't played an active role in the bombing itself, but he certainly knew what had occurred.

"Well, I can tell you who did it," he said, bantering.

I knew who he was going to name, the individual every Klansman blames for just about every KKK act of terror and violence in the last sixty years.

"Gary Thomas Rowe."

Since being exposed as an FBI informant in the Viola Liuzzo murder trial, Rowe, deceased since the late nineties, had become the Klan's fall guy. Most everyone who investigated the 16th Street Church case suspects Rowe may have known a little more than he let on about the bombing, but he was never part of that inner circle of Klavern members who planned and carried out the crime. They didn't trust him.

Blanton, recognizing that theory wouldn't hold up to scrutiny during our conversation, switched to blaming the "system," insisting he was the victim of several conspiracies. He wasn't passionate about this perceived injustice—it was as if he were reciting scenarios he'd concocted during those long hours alone in his cell.

One included the fact that his lawyer John Robbins had been a former partner of mine when I was a defense attorney. We had been in cahoots, Blanton alleged. The other was that the tape evidence we had sent to a specialist for enhancement had been doctored.

He had latched onto this thread years ago when Anthony Pellicano, the Los Angeles private investigator and audio specialist who had enhanced the quality of the kitchen tape at our request, was convicted of firearms, explosives, and wiretapping violations in cases that had no relation to ours.

It was something for Blanton to cling to and he had made noises about all sorts of appeals. He hadn't followed through.

Listening to Blanton scratch around for ways to avoid admitting guilt or remorse, I got the impression he had even started believing some of this nonsense. Rather than allowing himself to dwell on the horror he'd been part of in 1963, he'd focused on making himself a victim and indulging his perception of himself as someone with good enough legal chops to beat the rap.

An apology, obviously, would involve him admitting to himself what he'd done. Given that many people in the Birmingham community without anything to hide preferred to avoid looking at history, it's little wonder one of the perpetrators of the bombing couldn't abide facing the dreadful consequences of his hotheaded youth.

In August 2016 Blanton was up for parole for the first time, having served fifteen years of his multiple life sentences. There was no expectation he'd be released, and certainly no one associated with the prosecution of the bombing case was suggesting he'd changed in any way to merit any form of benevolence. However, if Blanton were going to apologize or mutter any sort of remorse, now would be the time.

I planned to attend the hearing in Montgomery on August 2 to address the parole board, along with family members of the victims. I would be advocating for his continued incarceration, but before that day I wanted to give him another chance to show remorse.

It had been with a mixture of disappointment and relief that I'd driven away from my last encounter with Blanton empty-handed. I would have preferred an admission, but his delusional behavior somehow made it less of a burden to put the whole matter aside once more.

I felt uneasy about returning to St. Clair. Another visit felt as if I were paying too much attention to his ramblings, but maybe he had changed. Perhaps he even thought he had a shot at getting out.

On the trip up I-59, I had a feeling that my growing anxiety was not solely about the prospect of walking into that sad place and looking that regrettable history in the face again. It was Donald Trump. His campaign rhetoric, every utterance covered on radio, was disturbing to say the least, and there was a discernible undercurrent of support for him in Alabama and beyond. I used to think Trump had about as much chance of being elected as Blanton had of being released. I knew that wasn't the case anymore.

I lumbered into the St. Clair facility at my allotted time. One guard standing at a lone metal detector greeted me and sent me toward the heart of the prison with a note authorizing my encounter with Blanton.

Unescorted, I headed down a long hallway painted blue and white and featuring motivational phrases such as "Make peace with your past so it won't spoil your present." A little odd, as not many prisoners would have seen the messages, but they were sound enough advice for staff and visitors to this troubled place.

I hit another security checkpoint, where I left my driver's license, before proceeding through a steel door at the guard's instruction. I was outside now but still felt closed in, under a covered walkway next to an open area surrounding the mundane red-brick, metal-roofed buildings that housed the general prison population.

I came to a halt at another barrier. Ahead of me was the segregation unit. I had enough time to contemplate the irony that Blanton had gotten what he desired—to be segregated—in at least one way before a guard ushered me on.

Through another barrier, I encountered an official who would escort me the rest of the way. About twenty yards ahead, on the other side of yet another fence, I could see Blanton at the end of a sidewalk, handcuffed, his hands behind his back. The gate to the segregation unit swung open, and silently we headed to the "closet" where we'd met previously.

Once inside, I requested they allow Blanton to have his hands at his front and the guard complied, locking the handcuffs in a more comfortable position.

"How you doing, Tom?"

He was calm and looked in better health than on my last visit. Contemporary dark-rimmed glasses had replaced the coke-bottle-lensed spectacles he wore previously.

"Been a while since I have seen you," he said, his voice strong.

I suggested it was probably about two years and to my surprise he offered: "August 25, 2014."

Blanton rarely had a visitor. I guess any contact with outsiders, welcome or otherwise, was memorable.

Our exchanges were pleasant enough—no racist rants. We got down to business quickly, as I raised the issue of his parole hearing in Montgomery, asking him if he had plans to attend.

"Why, you want to be my lawyer?" he joked.

I wanted to take the discussion in the direction of talking about the possibility that he could demonstrate some remorse.

There was no doubt the hearing was on his mind. In his odd, self-aggrandizing way, he referenced it as a big event for the community, saying he thought that there would be riots there. He was concerned someone might try and take him out with a sniper rifle.

I told him that I didn't think there would be an issue, as the only attendees, besides me, were likely to be family members of the victims and a couple of advocacy groups opposing parole.

At times during the conversation, he seemed gripped by the paranoid and conspiratorial mindset I had witnessed in earlier encounters. I tried to broaden the discussion to keep him talking.

We chatted about his ex-wife, Jean Barnes, briefly. He'd obviously been in contact with her and related that her husband had died. And we talked about lawyering. When I told him I recently had been in São Paulo, Brazil, on a case, he explained how after the Civil War, some Confederate soldiers had moved to just north of that city and founded a town called Americana.

Blanton, the KKK hitman, seemed jealous that Southerners had set up a community in the most racially diverse nation on earth.

I asked him about his decision to go to law school—whether it was a reaction to the scrutiny he was under.

"Yeah, I guess that was it," he said, shrugging, adding he'd taken the bar exam twice.

When I commented that he didn't make it through, he replied, "That's what they said." Another conspiracy.

He launched into a rant about the Feds trying to take over local police departments, suggesting the recent attacks on law enforcement and civil unrest were being orchestrated by federal officials so that they could set up some sort of dictatorship.

He also wrapped in the Clintons and the Democratic Party, saying they were part of a corrupt conspiracy. His views were bizarre and baseless, but on some level reflected the fake news peddled by the alt-right and others during the presidential campaign.

We started going around in circles. Before it got too nonsensical, I once again told him that folks were looking for a sense of remorse, noting prisons were expected to serve three purposes—punishment, deterrence, and rehabilitation.

He knew what I was asking him to do. "You wouldn't want me to lie to them, would you?" he said before returning to his stock explanation that Gary Thomas Rowe "did it."

"Put aside my firm belief in your guilt," I said. "And put aside your steadfast maintaining of your innocence. Let's forget about Gary Thomas Rowe. I know you met with Chambliss and Cherry and others and I firmly believe you know exactly what happened—the who, what, where, and when. That is a story that needs to be told, and you are the only one left to tell it."

We discussed many of those who had died, before, during, and after the trial. Blanton was strikingly quiet during this exchange. In the end, he neither conceded nor denied he knew what happened.

I could sense he was about to retreat into another conspiracy theory. It was time to sign off, but before I did, I wanted to know if any of his views had changed over the years.

"You were pretty rough back in those days," I said. "You didn't like blacks, Catholics, or Jews."

He looked uncomfortable but blurted: "We all change to some extent."

In wrapping up, I told him that it would likely be the last time I would visit but again suggested he get in touch if he ever wanted to talk. I had given him four chances to set things straight, to find it in himself to face his past in order to have a future. Each time he'd declined. He took my card—I suspect to get rid of me.

The guard escorted me out. On the way, he asked me if I was Blanton's lawyer.

I set him straight, telling him I prosecuted the old Klansman.

"Y'all should let that old man go," the guard said.

I explained that Blanton had walked free for thirty-seven years after he killed the four girls. "I know, and I'm black and all," he said, "but y'all ought to let him go. Nobody needs to die in prison."

There was no sniper, no riots, and not much fuss when the Alabama Board of Pardons and Paroles took a little over a minute to refuse Tom Blanton parole. The prisoner had not been invited to attend the hearing, which accepted eloquent addresses from several of the victims' family members, including Dianne Braddock, Lisa McNair, and Sarah Collins Rudolph.

I asked the board to deny parole to send a message about those motivated by hate to commit acts of violence. Blanton will be up for parole again in 2021, when he'll be about eighty-six.

I expect most of the details of that terrible day in 1963 will accompany Blanton to the grave. As part of the big picture, I guess it doesn't matter. History can't be reversed, and justice, eventually, was served. Yet it's hard to ignore the idea that a single sincere utterance of "sorry" would be cathartic, and I suspect not just for me.

Stranger things have happened, especially in this bombing case, which has occupied so much of my life and indirectly been part of so much of what has happened in the South and beyond over the last fifty years.

Coincidences, moments of luck, and happenstance were key features in connecting me to the case and eventually played important roles in the successful prosecutions. The universe seemed to indulge us when we needed it most. I quietly hoped it was not too much to ask for the planets to align one more time on my personal journey of redemption and discovery.

To date, there has been no apology from Blanton, but less than a year after Donald Trump was inaugurated as the forty-fifth President of the United States, I was granted another moment of kismet.

FOURTEEN

CONNECTING THE DOTS

When a child dies, scores of lives are shattered.

The killing of the four girls in the 16th Street Baptist Church bombing and the two boys who died from gunfire in Birmingham the same day created a deep crater of despair and remorse in 1963. But around that well of grief, over the decades, something life-affirming has grown.

Initially, at least, the blast shook us out of a stupor. It was an alarm to warn about the creep of a smothering darkness that could only be repelled by fundamental change, not only to laws and mores but, eventually, to hearts and minds.

I learned much from the bombing investigation and trials—about my city, state, and country; justice; our people, good and bad; the dangerous absurdity of racial prejudice; and the destructiveness of divisiveness.

Indeed, I feel like I've grown more in the last twenty years than I did in the first forty.

With that knowledge and the benefit of retrospect comes a sense of responsibility—a compulsion—to act rather than pontificate about the fact that we are obviously repeating mistakes of the past. Silence and inaction are the reasons we got into that mess in the first place.

My presentations with Bill Baxley had been opportunities to encourage conversation about our past and future in Alabama. But as the tide of extremist sentiment rose, especially in response to the election of our first black President and later with the explicit backing of Donald Trump, I battled a feeling of powerlessness.

There I was during August 2016 driving back to Birmingham from the St. Clair prison and trying to shake off the lingering ill effects of a conversation with the still-cocky, unapologetic Tom Blanton—killer of four girls. On the radio, presidential candidate Trump was recklessly insulting and berating critics and cleverly appealing to angry or marginalized chunks of the electorate open to xenophobic bluster. The delusions of a craven, racially motivated murderer and the rhetoric of a demagogue. What decade was this again?

What could be done? Probably very little. Trump was embraced by a Republican Party willing to turn a blind eye to deviance for the sake of power, while the Democratic Party in the South and many places beyond had dwindled to the point that it was a fragmented and often compromised presence.

Some of us in Alabama probably knew even before Trump that he had a real shot at the GOP nomination and even the presidency. After all, we'd grown up with George Wallace. I had been worried for some time, before the New York businessman and TV personality emerged as the frontrunner, that he was, inadvertently or otherwise, tapping into a deep well of disdain for the national Democratic Party and even Republican establishment politics. It also was disturbingly clear to me that the lid the Civil Rights Act had put on the cauldron of racial dissent in the sixties was being removed. Many long-suppressed, still-boiling emotions were released into the atmosphere.

The George Wallace–like rallies, dog whistles, and outright bigotry justified as "straight talk"; the anti-intellectual, superficial knowledge gussied up as policy proposals and reform: it was the kind of us-versus-them nonsense that Alabama, in multiple acts of self-harm, including the unqualified investment in Jim Crow, had endorsed since Reconstruction.

In my anxiety-laden discussions with civil rights leaders in recent years, it had been hard to ignore the possibility that with so many key reforms under attack, someone cynical and self-serving could emerge—as Wallace had—to tap into the zeal of the disaffected and defensive. Donald Trump seemed to be that person.

If it had only been ranting racists getting behind him, I would have expected his bid to flare then die, probably petering out last in the South. But he was aided and abetted by a Republican Party so eager to regain the White House that they would ignore his personal failings and divisive rhetoric. And crucially, there was unmitigated anger across a broad section of the electorate at the perceived cynicism and condescension of the Democratic Party toward voters in many parts of the country.

As we closed in on the election, I was disturbed, but not surprised, by Trump's political resilience. I clung to the hope, if not the belief, that Hillary Clinton and Bernie Sanders had done enough to expose the insanity of it all. Certainly, I didn't share the outlook of several friends at the Downtown Democratic Club gathering the Friday before the election who were busy planning their trips to Washington for a Clinton inauguration. I suspected a few Republicans were making similar plans.

When Trump registered a more than 28-point victory in Alabama—the largest margin since Richard Nixon defeated George McGovern in 1972—the surprise for me wasn't his local dominance but the extent of his national appeal.

My personal priorities at the time had been dominated by my law business, my family, and the deteriorating health of my aging parents. For the most part, I left the election postmortems and political plotting to friends and colleagues. But something in my gut was gnawing away.

I couldn't bring myself to watch the Trump inauguration. It was the first presidential inauguration I'd missed, either on TV or in person, since 1976. I opted, instead, to go deer hunting. I was happy to turn my back on it all for a day, but I knew I'd have to do something. I was not going to be complicit by watching divisiveness become even more entrenched in Alabama and the nation.

Governor Jones?

While the Republican Party's cynical appeal to the vulnerable and disenchanted infuriated me, I had to concede that Democrats had no one to blame but themselves for handing Republicans such a rich political opportunity.

In national politics, Democrats had all but deserted the South over the last few decades, and their outright condescension toward those outside blue strongholds has been as maddening as GOP opportunism.

As anxious as I am for the indefensible attitudes of some of my Southern brothers and sisters to change, I am acutely aware the best approach to spreading wisdom is not always confrontational.

You don't want some highfalutin, big-city liberal storming the dinner table to tell grandad he's a gun-loving, racist old fool and belittle aunty for her emphatic commitment to the evangelical church. Are Southerners defensive, sensitive to criticism, and suspicious of outsiders? Hell, yeah. And you would be too!

Investigating the bombing had provided me with daily reminders of the obvious: that long-held attitudes and ideas aren't swiftly discarded even when their merit has been undermined long ago. As much as we don't want to talk about it, clearly the seeds of white supremacy didn't disappear when the KKK became less of a Southern community fixture, and it's just as obvious that the impact of institutional oppression is ongoing for African Americans.

Meanwhile, the GOP, during thirty years of dominance in the South, has enjoyed the spoils of being less politically tone deaf than Democrats. Conservatives had people on the ground to turn LBJ's fear into a reality. On securing passage of the Civil Rights Act in 1964, the President reportedly speculated that the Democratic orchestration and support for the legislation would hand power to Republicans for decades.

Since Ronald Reagan recognized the strength of the white evangelical vote in the eighties, conservatives and ultraconservatives have become entrenched at every level of government. They did so by playing a long and patient game, delivering a disciplined and consistent, if often divisive, message.

The Democrats' answer in the South has been to bark indignantly from afar or occasionally offer a candidate hoping to tap support from African Americans. In recent years, on state and national ballots, many Democratic Party nominees have masqueraded as "Republican Lite" candidates, anxious not to be associated with progressive policies. In doing so, they have abandoned any point of difference with the GOP and played right into Republican plans.

The irony, I believe, is there is a flourishing desire to get away from the stifling and destructive politics of divisiveness in Alabama. The will of growing numbers of well-educated millennials, as well as immigrants and a more politically active black community (especially women), has only been thwarted by Republican manipulation of elections through gerrymandering and voter rights suppression. A groundswell of common sense and community-based advocacy has been evident but has received too little structural support from a unified party machine.

The GOP obliteration of Democrats in the South in the 2010 and 2014 midterms and dominance in the 2016 presidential election were predictable tribulations. But we need to remember that many of the people who voted for Obama in large numbers everywhere—even in parts of Alabama—were part of the same electorate that elevated Trump to power.

It's simple. People want real, discernibly different options. The community is increasingly willing to get to know what a person stands for, and crucially, they want a focus on issues that unite us across party lines, not divide us. The practice of making a judgment based solely on the party of representation is the default in the South. There has been little effort to change that to stimulate a true, competitive two-party system.

In writing off the South—with the occasional exception of waving from Washington during presidential election campaigns—Democrats retreated to their corner. They didn't try to speak to marginal or "lost cause" electorates, and more importantly, they did not listen to voters about their concerns on everyday issues.

Identity politics on a national level for the Democrats has been an issue that helped kill their chances to make a connection with diverse populations outside the blue states and regions. In squandering this opportunity, they lost sight of the party's core qualities, which are based on principles of equality and a chance for all. That identity requires embracing policies that nurture the working and middle classes regardless of race or religion, with a focus on issues such as healthcare, jobs, and education.

At the very least, it was apparent to me that more local moderates and progressives needed to get some skin in the game to change how Alabamians perceive politicians, even if it meant, well, losing a few more elections while closing the gap between the parties in the electorate.

That was the discussion I was having with my beloved wife as we struggled to come to terms with the notion that the soon-to-be-inaugurated President was a brazen New York real estate tycoon whose victory owed much to the success of his appeal to struggling workers in some of the poorest parts of the nation.

"And do you think one of those sacrificial Democratic Party lambs should be you?" she asked, while we enjoyed a moment of domestic serenity, having recently become empty nesters.

"Not exactly," I offered a little too meekly. "I think there could be a chance to have an impact on the Governor's race."

This wasn't untrue, even if a Democratic victory in the 2018 Alabama gubernatorial race was unlikely. Republicans start every poll as the favorites, but since GOP dominance was completed in 2010, the state had endured one embarrassment after the next. First was the draconian immigration bill HB 56. Then the Speaker of the House was indicted and convicted of violating the very ethical principles he had championed. And, of course, our Chief Justice, the so-called "Ten Commandments Judge" Roy Moore, was removed from office for a second time. By the time of the Trump inauguration, Alabama Governor Robert Bentley was entangled in a sex scandal that put him at risk of impeachment.

Nevertheless, Republicans still had a deep bench in Alabama. Democrats would start any contest for statewide office as an underdog. Part of the attraction of the Governor's race, though, is that unlike a federal election process, there wouldn't be an endless stream of funding for the GOP cause and an opponent could potentially run a high-profile campaign on a tight budget.

I fancied my chances to shake things up a bit in the Alabama capital of Montgomery, although it would be a tough slog and mean a big change in my professional life. Yet another one.

Louise has endured much over the years because of my political and professional interests. It's only been in recent times we've finally been able to regularly enjoy our city together, catching up with friends we've seen too little of due to work and family commitments. A girl from Cullman, long a conservative stronghold north of Birmingham, she had married a lawyer with good prospects. She got an attorney preoccupied with civil rights cases, sports memorabilia, Alabama football, and national politics.

After decades of watching me switch-hit between prosecution and defense duties and tolerating multiple occasions when I had to restart my career in private practice after stints in modest-paying, highly stressful government jobs, the path in recent times had finally started to look a little less complicated. Or so she thought.

Even though Louise didn't shut me down immediately, I knew the idea of the final chapter of my career being spent in Montgomery would not be an easy sell.

"Montgomery!" she said, as we sipped cocktails around the pool in the home we'd built gradually over decades in the leafy suburbs of Birmingham. "We'd have to move to Montgomery?"

"I mean, we'd be spending a lot of time there, but the Governor also gets access to a beach house on the coast," I hastened to add. "Not sure what condition it's in but, hey—a beach house!"

She remained unconvinced. "Montgomery?"

I thought I'd let it sink in. Maybe for a month or three.

To be honest, I wasn't entirely sure whether the Governor's race was where I should focus my attention. My heart had long been with national politics. But Alabama had been exclusively sending conservative senators to the Capitol for a quarter of a century, and there was every indication that wouldn't change for another twenty-five years.

I made a note to myself to ensure that when I was next in Montgomery on a legal matter, I would take a closer look at that fine city and make a list of its charms.

The Sessions Seat

I'd mentioned my gestating idea of running for office to two of my long-time buddies, Giles Perkins and Doug Turner, invaluable Democratic strategists in a state where they get too little love. They seemed about as impressed as Louise was with my gubernatorial aspirations but shared my desire to bolster the party at the grass roots and make it competitive at every level of politics.

Immediately after the 2016 election, there had been talk that Alabama's Jeff Sessions, who had been elected to the Senate in 1996 upon the retirement of my old boss Howell Heflin, would be Trump's pick for Attorney General.

My old acquaintance Sessions was the first sitting senator to endorse Trump, and his reward—a nomination to become the country's top lawmaker—sent a chill down the back of many moderates.

The seventy-year-old was in his fourth term, and during his time in Washington had been no friend to civil rights, actively advocating draconian judicial measures and hacking away at the Voting Rights Act. He was also among the loudest anti-immigration voices in the federal sphere, making him an early partner in Trump's destructive stand on preventing others from coming into this country of immigrants. And as a law-and-order guy, it was predictable Sessions would pull back on the substantial progress toward criminal justice reform made by cops, lawyers, politicians, and academics during Obama's last year.

I expected my Democratic Party friends to vent vigorously and perhaps tear out the few remaining clumps of their hair that had survived the stressful events of November 8, 2016, when Trump beat Clinton and the South took another huge step in the direction of the 1950s.

However, when we got together at a ceremony honoring Giles for his work in developing an award-winning park in downtown Birmingham, Turner, always a numbers guy, seemed strangely buoyant. "In a special election," he said, "the Sessions seat could be taken by a Democrat. That is where you should be looking."

I just shook my head. It had been twenty years since a Democrat represented Alabama in the Senate, and since then the state had been painted several more coats of Republican red.

I had been aware that Sessions's appointment as AG would necessitate his vacating his Senate seat, but an election for his spot would not be held until November 2018, concurrent with our statewide elections and the federal midterms. Alabama Governor Bentley confirmed that date when he appointed Alabama Attorney General Luther Strange as the interim replacement for Sessions.

I probably would have more of a chance of success in the Governor's race, but if I was honest with myself, I had to admit the Senate had been my goal for a long time. My brief stint working for Senator Howell Heflin had cemented that desire and helped clarify my political philosophy. I recently revisited the Senator's farewell address, in which he noted how voters felt alienated from Congress, where gridlock was a constant problem. He urged bipartisanship and advocated a cross-aisle focus on what he called "compassionate moderation" to reach agreement on difficult issues. This was in 1996.

Maybe there was a chance to be competitive, but I would be a long shot at best and was concerned that a competitive Senate race in 2018 would necessitate bringing in tons of money that would hurt our overall chances in other statewide races.

"Besides," I said, "it has gotten so ugly and partisan up in Washington that I am not sure that is where I want to be anymore."

"Well, I understand that," Turner replied but he wasn't going to let it go. "I think legally the Governor is going to have to call the Senate election much sooner than 2018." To emphasize the point, he later emailed me a copy of the Alabama statute that appeared to back his theory. He was insistent, my old political colleague, although I continued to look toward the Governor's race.

Let's Make This Happen

Everyone had election fatigue. It seemed a little premature for a son of the South to be speculating on any future political possibilities, and, frankly, when it came down to it, I was a little overwhelmed by personal matters, specifically my parents' health.

Dad was not only restricted physically, he was also deteriorating mentally and needed constant care that his dear eighty-four-year-old wife could no longer provide. Fortunately, the family was around, providing great comfort to Gloria and Gordon. My sister, Terrie Savage, came in regularly from Hartselle with her husband Scott, and my daughter Courtney was settled in Birmingham with her family. My two boys, Carson and Christopher, made a beeline for their grandparents whenever they returned home from college in Tuscaloosa and grad school in Colorado. Louise did a lot of the heavy lifting. Thank goodness she was always just a phone call away.

As the curtain slowly comes down on my father's life, I'm immensely grateful he got to witness our efforts to get justice for the girls. He's a good man, and like so many men of that time, he'd silently carried the unresolved issue of the church bombing around in his bag of personal regrets for many years.

Mother, meanwhile, remains my greatest supporter. I may not yet receive the same level of adoration as Alabama football coach Nick Saban, but I will happily settle for second place behind the football coaching legend.

Gloria's great thrill is watching her grandkids grow into responsible adults. Courtney married the love of her life—bringing another attorney into the family, Rip Andrews. They are raising two beautiful girls, my beloved granddaughters, while Courtney recently received a doctorate reflecting her interest in social justice issues. Carson earned a master's degree and is realizing his long-held goal of being a full-time zookeeper, while Christopher is finding his feet as a conservative-leaning business student at the University of Alabama.

I also was reluctant to impose the intensity of a campaign on my wife at a time when she was enjoying watching her children flourish and making the most of being free of daily mom duties. A recent trip to the Bahamas with girlfriends was something she was keen to replicate. A few times.

My reticence to discuss a possible political future with her started to dissolve on January 21, 2017, the day after the Trump inauguration.

I had an unusual Saturday meeting planned at my firm's offices with a new client. Weekends are usually blessedly subdued in downtown Birmingham, though I knew that as part of a national movement there was a plan to stage a women's march in Birmingham in the wake of Trump's official ascent to office. Louise wanted to go but couldn't find a friend to accompany her. Eventually, she decided to go alone. I believe organizers had hoped to get a few hundred folks to participate.

From my firm's offices, if you peer through the tree line, you can see both Kelly Ingram and Linn Parks, primary sites for protesters to assemble for marches and rallies over the decades. I was in the midst of my unfussed weekend work obligation when noise from the street started echoing around downtown. I peered out the window to catch a glimpse of the march—maybe I'd see Louise. But instead of a few hundred dedicated souls, there were about ten thousand women, men, and children hollering, chanting, and singing. It was thrilling to hear and see this kind of ebullience and energy in the Magic City.

I figured that Louise was down there somewhere and later learned that my son-in-law Rip was marching with my granddaughters while Courtney was out of town. Perhaps I was finally taking off my man goggles. There was such enormous energy, an unmistakable groundswell for change. The question was how to keep it going and translate it into making a difference.

Over the ensuing weeks, I continued to nibble around the edges of the idea of instigating some sort of a run for Governor. Perkins and I met a couple of times and Turner kept running the numbers. However, when impeachment of the Governor became inevitable, and Bentley resigned in April, it all came to a head. His replacement, Lieutenant Governor Kay Ivey, announced the special election for the Senate was to be brought forward, just as Turner had predicted.

The primaries would be in August, and the head-to-head between the GOP and Democratic candidates for the vacated Senate seat would be held on December 12. Even with that, though, I remained somewhat focused on the Governor's race and requested a lunch meeting with Giles and Doug to really get into the details of what a gubernatorial campaign would look like.

My friends, however, had other plans. "Jones," they said without ceremony as I walked through the door of Perkins's house, "sit down. We need to talk."

They laid out how they believed we could win the Senate election but also stressed how vital it was for a Democrat to simply be in the game— really in the game. That knee-jerk reaction among Southern voters— Republican: yes; Democrat: no—had to change.

"We're in trouble," Perkins confided. "We really do have to find our feet again. If we concede this Senate seat in a special election where there is this much energy, we can write off 2018. It may be the last chance for Alabama."

My colleagues believed I was a Democratic Party challenger who couldn't be dismissed out of hand. I had a public profile and a good relationship with the African-American community. Despite lingering racist sentiment in the South, the bombing prosecutions were largely viewed positively. And while I was known as a Democrat, I didn't have a history of shifting my position to accommodate the prevailing political winds—or, for that matter, stepping back from a particular point of view to appease certain groups.

At the least, in Alabama, getting someone with a positive public profile to stand as a Democrat represented great progress.

Turner, ever the stats guy, had broken it down and proceeded to regale us with a dazzling array of possibilities that, in summary, went something along these lines: if we got record numbers of African Americans out to vote, swayed more women our way at the polls, got most of the independents, and convinced moderate Republicans to turn their back on extremism, we'd have a chance.

"That's all it would take?" I asked.

I didn't get a laugh. Turner was convinced we had a shot, and even Perkins the pessimist thought we had a shot. Despite the devastation of the presidential election, there were distinct signs of grassroots mobilization in Alabama of Democrats, and that process was likely to accelerate.

The Trump administration was no friend to African Americans, and Sessions, one of the loudest and most disdainful voices about the Black Lives Matter movement, was barking about the need for "tough" prosecutions at all levels of the criminal justice system, which to many in the black community simply meant incarcerating more African Americans. Women, across many demographics, were up in arms at Trump's sexism and bragging about sexual assault, and many moderates in the GOP were as disgusted as Democrats with the tenor of Trumpism, even if they tried to keep it under wraps. Moreover, we were all convinced that the two leading Republicans, Luther Strange and the "Ten Commandments Judge" Roy Moore, had significant political baggage that could help provide a path to a Democratic Party victory.

It was an outside chance, but my friends were right. At the very least, a strong Democratic showing would help the party stay on the map in the South and reinforce the wilting two-party system.

"And here's the other thing," Perkins noted. "This is where your heart has always been."

Damn. They knew exactly which of my buttons to push. I began pacing the room in much the same way as I do in brainstorming with my legal team about an upcoming trial. I got it. But I wanted it known that I would not be adjusting my beliefs or backing away from difficult positions for the sake of votes.

I told them of a conversation I had during the 2012 presidential election with my old friend Joe Biden. We were discussing the need for more candidates and public servants to be authentic and true to who they were. He told me he was often asked by candidates: "What can I say to win my race?" His response was simple: "You are asking the wrong question. You should be asking, 'What am I prepared to say even if it means losing?'"

I wasn't trying to be difficult, but Biden's comments had resonated, as I had long believed that Democrats in Alabama had lost their souls in futile efforts to simply cling to a vestige of power. I couldn't abide the prospect of yet another Alabamian bowing down to pressure to appease the powerful, watering down positions, or pandering to ultraconservative voters. Perkins and Turner were of the same mind.

I headed home for a pre-dinner cocktail around the pool with Louise, who I suspect expected me to present my case to take on the Governor's race. Finally, after about fifteen minutes of chitchat but nothing political from me, she opted to go there.

"So how did the lunch go?" she asked.

I had some explaining to do: "Well . . ."

I think I made her dizzy with my sudden change in focus.

She still needed convincing, and I needed more reassurance that it was the right move. With our friends Kent Haney and Nancy Ellisor, Louise and I headed to California, where Baxley and I were to do our church bombing presentation. It would provide us with a great opportunity to talk it over with the closest of friends. The fact that we were in wine country was a bonus.

In the meantime, Perkins convinced me to have one of the great Democratic Party strategists, Joe Trippi, fly in on our return so that he could provide his valuable insight for an all-hands decision meeting.

At a dinner on the evening of my sixty-third birthday, Trippi, Perkins, and Turner laid out the case for the gathering. Kent, Nancy, Louise, and I asked questions. Many questions. At the end of the evening, the consensus was that I seemed all in, Louise maybe not so much. It took the weekend and discussions with the family to come to the decision that this was something that we both felt compelled to do.

The first target: win the Democratic primary in August before taking on the Republican candidate. Interim Senator Luther Strange was favored to be the nominee, but we believed it was more likely to be Roy Moore, the far-right-winger who had been twice removed as Chief Justice of the Alabama Supreme Court.

Kitchen Table Issues

Operating on a shoestring budget, Perkins found us a warehouse in the gentrifying Birmingham suburb of Avondale. The Doug Jones for Senate headquarters. The poster out front looked good.

"Seems like a lot of space for just a few of us," I said, my voice echoing around the cavernous room.

But Giles—whom I took to calling Yoda given his knowledge of the political universe, his ability to mentor me, and his nuanced understanding of Alabama electioneering—assured me that word of my entering the race had been well received and there was already a stream of interest.

"Before you know it, this place will be packed with volunteers," he said, probably lying.

I was anxious to throw myself into the task but also had obligations with several legal clients. The summer was a constant juggle of lawyer time and candidate campaigning. Fortunately, my law partners helped take up the slack. My still-young firm with Greg Hawley and Chris Nicholson was bubbling along and we needed help to ensure we maintained momentum. Fortunately, an old friend, Cissy Jackson, had gotten back into the legal game as she prepared to send her youngest child, one of Christopher's classmates, off to college. Along with my longtime assistant Tyler Florence, she kept all of the trains running on time in my absence.

At the same time, I was dealing with the difficult decision to place both Mom and Dad in an assisted-living facility. Falls had made my mother's ability to get around problematic, and Dad's condition had deteriorated to the point where he needed around-the-clock care. They were in the same facility but different care areas. It was a terrible blow for Mom to leave her home of more than thirty years, but she was as comfortable as she could get in a private living area where she had a big-screen TV to watch news items on the next Crimson Tide football squad. It's never off-season in Alabama.

My head popped up on the big screen regularly, too, as the campaign rapidly gained traction. There was the usual tone of dismissiveness from the media about a Democrat having a shot of winning in 'Bama, but our headquarters was filling up quickly, just as Yoda had predicted: lots of young people, many women, a strong representation of African Americans. There was definitely something in the air.

Trump was backing Luther Strange for the GOP primary—reluctantly, we suspected. The mutineer from the alt-right, Steve Bannon, was hot for Roy Moore. The former judge's disruptive influence in every role he'd held over a career that included episodes of extreme homophobia, religious zeal-otry, and blatant racism suited the mayhem the hardcore Trumpists wanted in Washington.

The late Speaker of the House Tip O'Neill famously said that "all poli-tics is local," and from day one, our policy was to keep a local focus on the race. We did not want or need to get dragged into discussions that involved Trump or even Sessions. They had plenty of detractors out there who we felt would keep our base energized without me bashing them at every turn. To be successful we would need some Trump voters to cross over. And we were going to move with caution when it came to other hot-button topics such as guns and abortion.

Kitchen table issues—employment, wages, education, access to medical care, cost and standard of living—were our focus, and not because they were "safe." They were actual issues everyone in Alabama faced every day, be they Republicans, Democrats, or people who'd given up on politics years ago.

We would not avoid answering questions about guns, race, abortion, religion, immigration, and gay rights, but we would always bring the dis-cussion back to what everyone, black and white, male and female, young and old, had in common rather than blustering on about what was perceived to be dividing us. I believed then as I do now that at the end of the day, Ala-bamians have more in common than that which divides us, and my job was to bring that message home.

We also wanted to reconnect Democrats with their core values and ideals—fundamental fairness and equality, respect for each other, no dis-crimination, and everyone getting a fair shake—good wages, jobs, health-care. The Democratic Party's historical and central calling is to fight for basic rights for people in the working and middle classes who need an advocate.

Over the last twenty years or more, the GOP and extreme right-wingers have enjoyed largely unchallenged opportunities in the South and beyond to exploit social and cultural issues that divide us rather than to offer ways to move forward. They seized the political stage and used it to depict and define Democrats as disconnected, uncaring elites. We wanted to make it understood that the Democratic Party was a pretty big tent, with shared ideals but room for diversity of opinion and debate.

For reasons of acute self-interest, Trump and Bannon had been steal-ing the rhetoric that for so long had been the language of the party of the "everyman." We wanted it back, though, and in this fight we weren't going to throw bombs—we were going to defuse them.

Contemporary politics, especially Trump politics, is about tribalism. I wanted none of that. The plan was to defy logic and make our campaign about doing what's best for regular folks—all of them.

To borrow a bit of baseball parlance, we would play small ball while our opponents tried to hit us out of the park. It was the kind of methodical approach that worked for me in the church bombing case too. Be transparent. Be honest. Hide nothing. I fully intended to give essentially the same stump speech to the Chamber of Commerce that I would to African-American ministers.

My primary chances seemed strong, although some Democratic Party kin were uneasy that a half-dozen candidates had thrown their hats in the ring, including Michael Hansen, the first openly gay candidate for statewide office in Alabama, and a mystery man with a familiar name, Robert Kennedy Jr. (no relation).

While the swell of support was encouraging, there were pockets of resistance within the party that would stay in place through primary day.

During the primary, money was only trickling into the campaign. It was difficult to convince anyone other than my closest friends to invest in our race. Fundraising "call time" was a necessary evil that I avoided like the plague. We did, however, raise enough to begin to hire a few full-time staffers, including campaign logistics king Wade Perry. We also placed radio ads and worked on a social media platform via Facebook while searching for low-budget ways to promote the cause.

Having been involved in a few traditional campaigns, I had pushed to spend a few pennies on yard signs, although Perkins pushed back, saying "yard signs don't vote."

A meager investment, however, proved fruitful. So many people started asking for the signs it became annoying. When homemade signs started popping up, my esteemed colleague relented, and we ordered a couple of thousand. They flew off the shelves and started popping up in places where no one expected, like rock-ribbed Republican areas around Birmingham and Mobile.

Social media, ironically, latched onto the story of the popularity of the old-school method of promotion. We got a big bang for small bucks, and yard signs remained an integral part of the strategy throughout the campaign.

Fortunately, we swept to a comprehensive victory, with more than sixty-six percent of the vote in the primary. Our modest budget would go further now that we didn't have to worry about funding a runoff against a Democratic opponent.

The Republicans weren't so decisive. Moore and Strange would have to compete in a runoff. That gave us a chance to get a jump start on the campaign proper, mostly under the radar, as the media and popular opinion seemed to believe it didn't matter what we did, since the GOP would be providing the winning candidate. Most had already written us off, some saying we had a ten percent chance at best to win the December 12 election. We, however, knew different, and not just from our own polling, which suggested we had a chance at grabbing better than forty percent of the vote against either opponent.

You could feel it. Our headquarters was suddenly packed with volunteers, and I couldn't walk down the streets of an Alabama town—and I was walking through a lot of them—without being besieged by well-wishers. "Doug Jones for Senate" yard signs, a leading indicator, were popping up everywhere, outside homes in wealthy suburbs and the hardscrabble streets of some of the country's poorest neighborhoods.

What I didn't expect was the core sentiment most people expressed in those brief personal encounters. I was thrilled to be wished good luck but overwhelmed by the number and sincerity of the thank-yous I received. If ever there was a sign I was doing something that people had been waiting for in Alabama for too long, it was "Thank you for running." That was a huge win right there.

The intensity and extent of the support jumped exponentially when Roy Moore won the Republican runoff, vanquishing Trump's pick, "Big Luther" Strange. It was a victory for Bannon and an opportunity for us.

We'd been feeling good about our prospects against Strange. He was staunchly conservative, very much in the mold of Sessions, and a safe pick for Republicans, but there were questions about his appointment and whether a deal had been cut with the discredited Governor he was investigating. In addition, he had wrapped himself in the D.C. establishment that at the time appeared to always be at odds with the President.

Moore was tricky because of his evangelical base, but for the love of God, we had to have a chance if we played our cards right. The man was a political disgrace who routinely condemned just about everyone outside his tiny circle of influence. He regularly invoked what could be considered hate speech against homosexuals and Muslims and was a vocal part of the "birther" movement that questioned the legitimacy of Barack Obama as

President. Notably, he also clearly violated the separation of church and state by installing a monument to the Ten Commandments at the Alabama Supreme Court building, which led to his first ousting from office (he violated a federal court order to remove the monument). Moore won back the Chief Justice role in November 2012, and while on the bench made his opposition to same-sex marriage known. In 2016, having prohibited Alabama probate judges from issuing same-sex marriage licenses in defiance of federal law, he was again suspended from office, ending his second tenure as Chief Justice.

It was tempting to go for the jugular straightaway, to clobber voters with condemnation of Moore the man. But that would have come at the cost of building our own positions. Instead, I bit my lip (until it bled more than a few times) and let Roy's record speak for itself. The plan was to come down hard on his record later in the campaign, although we didn't really get the chance when other disturbing events from his past came to light.

Moore had little going for him other than the fact he was tribal. He wanted nothing more than to draw us into a slagging match on social issues because it would divert from the total lack of substance of his campaign.

The pundits continued to dismiss our chances, but at every turn, we were being overwhelmed by community support and enthusiasm. Our fundraising efforts, after a modest start, went into high gear after Moore launched his campaign with a typically oddball stunt—pulling out a little pistol on stage at a rally while dressed in a cowboy outfit.

Money wasn't exactly pouring in, however, and the national machine was hesitant to go all in backing us, simply because outside of Yoda, Doug, and me—and maybe a few other dreamers—no one really thought we could win. Many political colleagues around the country offered moral support and expressed keen interest, but frankly, there were still elements of that long-prevalent dismissiveness of Dems in the South.

The national leadership of the party got us, but I'm not so sure their staff were of the same mind.

To be fair, we didn't go out of our way to protest their perception—preferring to focus on our own process—and some polling (much of it with voters with landline telephones rather than cell phones) gave us about as much chance as the conservative media was predicting, somewhere around next to none.

But the "radical" idea of at least reestablishing a meaningful Democratic presence by running quality candidates in the progressive ghost towns of the South and the heartland meant we weren't always being dismissed out of hand. Progress!

I also had a positive relationship with both DNC Chairman Tom Perez and Tim Kaine, the influential Virginia Senator and former vice presidential candidate, who shared my desire to reinvigorate Democrats in the South. Both men were among the first to encourage us to go for it.

A few weeks after my discussion with Turner and Perkins, Perez played a video to his colleagues that was a snapshot of my presentations on the church bombings and a pitch for the community to be alert to the creep of extremism. I understand it brought some to tears and helped elevate the argument that it may be worth backing noteworthy Democrats in even the most "unwinnable" seats. On seeing the video, Perkins became more convinced we were on the right path: "If that is really you," he said, "I will make you a U.S. Senator."

We also benefited early from the wisdom of national strategist Joe Trippi, who brought Twitter guru David Yankovich to the campaign. He had great success building on the efforts of volunteers out of Tuscaloosa to turn heads our way. He was especially good at chiding Roy Moore, and pretty soon my following on social media boomed. Increasingly, people of goodwill were comparing my record with my opponent's. The thought of Moore being a United States Senator was abhorrent to so many people.

It was gratifying and much-needed encouragement, although it was also a reminder to keep a tight focus on the table where my bread was being buttered. I made a fairly easy and early decision with the backing of my political troika (Perkins, Turner, and Trippi) to resist the temptation to drink in too much of what was going on outside Alabama. In a sense, this mirrored my approach in the bombing trials.

I didn't ignore national media, but I wasn't going to chase them. And when it came down to it, what was most relevant to my race was the involvement of locals, not the opinions of cable news talking heads.

We crisscrossed the state, while a ballooning group of volunteers from all over Alabama and other states pounded the pavements to spread the word, planting thousands of "Doug Jones for Senate" yard signs and crowding into headquarters and branch offices to make phone calls to voters—more than one million by the campaign's end.

With the help of my friend and PR guru David Davis, we kept the growing national media interest in the campaign at arm's length and prioritized local outlets. Former *Montgomery Advertiser* reporter Sebastian Kitchen was our point man for that strategy. We were welcomed enthusiastically by "black" radio, for example, and tried to be available for studio interviews. We also advertised heavily across the airwaves of traditional African-American stations, big and small.

My background of involvement with the black community helped generate interest in some regions where a politician was not always welcomed with open arms or likely to get a lot of attention. And the support of young black mayors and other African-American elected officials in places such as Birmingham, Selma, Montgomery, and Huntsville was heartfelt and invaluable.

In many areas, including some remote rural areas, there were extraordinary plans to try and overcome the barriers that folks, especially in the African-American community, face simply getting to the polls. There was a concerted effort to ensure transportation would be available on election day. These drives were sometimes orchestrated by Democratic Party operatives in the communities but just as frequently by members of African-American churches and other civic-minded groups.

Aside from one stirring campaign launch in Birmingham featuring my buddy Vice President Joe Biden, we deliberately declined the generous offers of support from several other high-profile figures. We wanted to keep it "Alabama." Outsiders from the world of politics, entertainment, and sports would just stir the defensive mindset of my opponent's supporters.

Biden, a working man's public servant, was the perfect person to show folks it was OK to be a Democrat—another pillar on which our campaign was built. We had been confident we could draw a crowd at the Birmingham Jefferson Civic Center, and we were anything but disappointed on arrival to see that the lines to get in extended several city blocks. Inside, before we started the rally, more than a thousand people were making a racket as backstage, the former Vice President got on one knee to talk in private with my mother.

It was a great gathering. The enthusiasm was over the top. I got to speak for the first time about being on the "right side of history," a refrain we'd continue to use until the campaign's end, and let the electric crowd know I'd learned much from Biden over the years—"some would say a little too much," I joked, donning a pair of Bidenesque aviator sunglasses. As he always does, Biden delivered.

Most of our community rallies and meetings, however, were planned as intimate occasions in halls, senior centers, and churches. When more people than anticipated started showing up, it was a hint we were doing something fundamentally right.

In college towns such as Tuscaloosa and Auburn, there was a great undercurrent of interest from students, especially young women presumably offended by President Trump's frequently insensitive and sexist comments.

More than once, I was told in no uncertain terms that Alabama deserves better politically than what we've endured for so long. The enthusiasm wasn't confined to the state. While I wasn't monitoring national coverage of the campaign, the number of messages from well-wishers and an influx of campaign contributions and volunteers from across the country were startling. Louise and I met a retired couple who had squeezed into an RV and driven from Colorado to Dothan to campaign for us, and there were scores of stories like that.

We traveled so much and so often that it became hard to keep track of time, though Louise, looking forward to a return to normalcy one day, if not a trip to the Bahamas, would count it down daily. It was a physical grind, but every so often you got a reminder of what it meant to folks—maybe it was an encounter with a long-suffering Alabama Democrat or a Republican horrified by the idea that old Roy was the best their party could do, or kids waving "Doug Jones for Senate" posters. More than once I witnessed elderly people trudging miles to knock on doors on my behalf.

My God, what an acutely important responsibility I had.

During a trip to Mobile, a city where the statewide Republican dominance of recent decades was strongly evident, we were trying to wrap our heads around the fact that we were getting the same enthusiasm and positivity we'd felt elsewhere. Was it a sign of something special or were we just overwhelmed by our first campaign?

Meetings with local officials and religious leaders in Mobile were to be followed by a relatively small fish fry for supporters at the home of a supporter on the Dog River.

A giant setting sun lazily reclined on the horizon as we chugged down the river toward the gathering. We got there early and marveled at the beautiful setting from a vantage point on a pier. It was so engrossing that Louise and I didn't notice the guests arriving . . . and arriving. I had hoped to shake hands with a few local supporters, but within an hour there were four hundred of them.

At some stage, Louise and I looked at each other in amazement. Oh yes, this was really happening.

Our strategy to keep it local and ignore the noise from outside Alabama was tested at times. There were even hints that some within the Democratic

Party wanted to replace my strategists with campaign organizers with a "broader" outlook.

"They think we're yahoos," Perkins said, in the midst of putting together an extraordinary campaign alongside Turner and Trippi.

There were also well-intentioned liberals from outside Alabama wanting to rush in and save us from ourselves. Some believed we were wrecking a chance to lecture conservatives by talking about being prepared to compromise. Fortunately, former Democratic Party leader Howard Dean stepped in to placate them.

"Compromise" seemed to upset a wide variety of factions, especially when we made a campaign television spot drawing on Civil War history. I spoke about the Battle of Gettysburg clash on Little Round Top between troops led by Colonel William Oates of Alabama and Colonel Joshua Chamberlain of Maine, making the point that the time for fighting was over, and the opportunity for compromise through negotiation was the best way forward for the country (especially 154 years later).

The fact was that we couldn't please everyone and we had no intention of trying to. We knew our state; we knew our own minds. If we burned a few bridges on either side of the ideological fence, so be it. We would stay focused on being firm but reasonable and keep faith with the idea that my opponent's repeated failures in public life would cost him dearly, even with Trump supporters who knew the importance of having a Republican in the Senate to maintain the GOP's numbers advantage.

We knew there would be a certain percentage, maybe thirty-five to forty, depending on turnout, who would vote GOP even if Beelzebub were the candidate, but we deliberately tried to control the level of rancor between my opponent and me to ensure there wasn't too much to hate about me and perhaps enough to like to turn folks my way.

I got as good an indication as any that the strategy was working when I was doing voter research before the Alabama-Louisiana State University game on November 4.

OK, it wasn't research.

Heading up the elevator to get to my seats in Bryant-Denny Stadium in Tuscaloosa with Louise and my childhood buddy Fred Metz and his wife Sophia, I was surrounded by about twenty potential voters. The four of us were wearing our "Doug Jones for Senate" buttons, and I was engaged in conversation with a gentleman from Huntsville, a Republican who indicated he would be voting for me.

Our conversation and my button caught the attention of a middle-aged woman who was not short of an opinion. I wasn't profiling, but I had her pinned as a Trump voter before she let me know it in no uncertain terms.

She sidled up to me and took a look at the button. "Are you Doug?" she asked as everyone in the elevator listened in.

"Yes, ma'am."

"Hmm. You Republican or Democrat?"

"I'm a Democrat."

And with that, she audibly grumbled and very deliberately turned her back on me.

The other twenty or so in the elevator snickered and awkwardly began to look at their shoes. She had made her point—one we're used to in the South.

I couldn't resist and wasn't about to let this moment pass. I leaned in and stage-whispered over her shoulder: "Ma'am, do you know who my Republican opponent is?"

"No," she gruffly replied.

"It's Roy Moore," I said with a chuckle.

"Shiiiiiiiiiiit!" she bellowed, cracking up the emptying elevator.

Fred and I high-fived. There was a bounce in my step as Louise and I walked to our seats: "Get ready, honey," I told my wife. "I think we've got this!"

I saw the woman a little later. "You know I'll have to vote for you," she said with a smile.

"I appreciate that."

"You've got to help Trump, though," she said.

"Hey, if it's in the interests of Alabama, I absolutely will do everything to help President Trump. I promise you."

And I meant it.

Sexual Assault Allegations

Believe it or not, the bombshell was a double-edged sword from a political point of view. Our internal polling numbers were looking great and we were ready to move in for the kill on our terms. But all of that changed with one newspaper story.

I was utterly disgusted with my opponent when at least nine women came out to accuse him of sexual misconduct when he was a thirty-something

Assistant District Attorney. Several of the victims were teenagers at the time of the alleged impropriety, and one was just fourteen years old.

The media went nuts and my rapidly expanding team of campaign workers, especially the sharp communications team, understandably thought Moore had handed us the election. For years prior to the November 9, 2017, *Washington Post* story that broke the news, there had been persistent rumors about Moore's behavior as a man in his thirties, including his reputation at the Gadsden Mall, where media reports would later contend he'd been banned for questionable, even predatory, behavior. But that wasn't gossip we had planned to explore. Moore had disgraced himself amply in other ways, as far as we were concerned.

The women's stories, however, were incredibly impactful, and not just because of their obvious credibility. They rammed home how messed up one of Alabama's leading figures had been for a long, long time. It was a terrible indictment of our state and politics that this man had been elected to statewide office twice.

While some of our supporters were popping champagne corks, we were more circumspect, anxious even.

Our campaign had been built around a sure and steady approach and the avoidance of personal attacks. We knew that if we went after Moore for his detestable behavior rather than his incompetence, we risked derailing our own process and basically waking the slumbering giant of Southern tribal politics.

Effectively, we would have mobilized his base for him. People who would not have bothered voting, and those of his supporters who did not even know an election was looming, would undoubtedly have come out of the woodwork. Discussions would have been dumbed down to "he said, she said" and "fake news" distractions, taking us away from our analytical assessments of his inability to propose or do anything useful for the state.

An initial pullback of GOP support for Moore from Washington meant the plug was pulled on a river of funds for his campaign. At the same time, our fundraising took off. Money poured in from everywhere, allowing us and supporter organizations to finance blocks of advertisements, especially television spots detailing Moore's record. Those campaign pieces did outline Moore's missteps, including the accusations of his sexual predation. However, I deliberately did not buy into extensive personal criticism of him on the campaign trail. There was no value in me reiterating what folks already knew.

I made it clear, however, at every opportunity that I believed the women and that their voices, like so many others in the "Me Too" movement, should be heard.

Moore completely disappeared from public view—not that he'd been ubiquitous, having refused any opportunity to debate or discuss any issue. His only statements were personal attacks on me and, later, denials of sexual misconduct and accusations against the women who came forward.

The few calls for him to step away that came from GOP establishment figures in Washington were countered by loud hollers of support from the Bannon faction and Alabama Republican figures, including our State Auditor, who compared Roy's sexual contact with a teen to Joseph's relationship with Mary. Many months after the fact, I still have no words to respond to that comment.

The most valuable Republican critique of Moore, from our point of view, was that of Alabama's long-serving GOP Senator. When Richard Shelby said publicly he would not support Moore and indicated he would write in the name of a "good Republican" instead, he gave others the green light to do the same. It was a message to the crucial demographic we were trying to attract, moderate GOP voters and independents. If we could not get those voters over to our side, having them write in or stay home was a vote in our favor.

Shelby would repeat his condemnation of Moore just a few days before the election on CNN, and we quickly used his words in one of our TV spots

Make no mistake: we certainly got a numbers boost, especially at first, from news of Moore's indiscretions, but we also sensed a jump in his support from his base. Certainly, media coverage of the election went through the roof, ensuring every tiny pocket of rural Alabama would know December 12 was polling day.

When the GOP national machine decided to reverse its decision and came back, all guns blazing, to support Cowboy Roy, the tone and regularity of the attack ads against me intensified markedly. I was being called everything under the sun, most frequently a baby killer for refusing to back away from supporting women's right to choose.

For the most part, it was water off a duck's back, but it was tough on Mom. Gloria had that big-screen TV on every waking hour and every few minutes had to endure seeing me accused of murdering children.

Moore's team, and President Trump, also tried to paint me as "weak on crime"; a lackey of the national Democrats "Schumer, Pelosi, and Hillary Clinton"; and someone who was going to snatch away Alabamians' guns. This amused all who knew me.

In a measured response, we put together a campaign advertisement that outlined my background as a hunter and gun owner. When the film crew visited my home to shoot the piece, they got a glimpse of my gun safe, which is impressively well stocked. I declined their entreaties to use an image of it as some sort of counter to Moore's firearm fixation.

When the President came out in full support of Moore about a week before the election, my opponent definitely got a substantial lift. Polling was erratic during the campaign, but there was uniformity in the bump he received every time Trump publicly backed him or denigrated me.

I'll admit, down the stretch it became very difficult to hold the line and refuse to react when President Trump or Moore was insulting me.

"Kitchen table issues, Doug. Keep it to kitchen table issues," I would remind myself.

By keeping it local, we passed up multiple opportunities to get what may have seemed like priceless exposure. Keeping it local didn't stop national exposure, however, as late-night talk show hosts, for example, laid into Roy. We just couldn't afford to reinforce in any way the GOP contention that we were in the pocket of Democrats outside of Alabama or pandering to those "liberal elites."

While Moore's team kept him from public view, I was out there every day with Sam Coleman, a veteran communications guy, engaging with folks, including increasingly large gaggles of media members. Each time we followed the same script: providing a few remarks on the kitchen table topic of the day before fielding a couple of questions from Alabama media followed by the national press, all of them hankering for a personal attack on Moore or Trump only for me to pivot back to the issues.

In the privacy of my own home, I allowed myself to be indignant and infuriated by the insults and misinformation directed at and about me. Hell, I wanted to joust with the guy and knock him off his pretend cowboy horse, but we kept our discipline on the road. If Nick Saban had been a political strategist rather than perhaps the greatest college football coach ever, he would have been proud of us. We worked on the fundamentals and knew our process. Things went right, things went wrong, but we stuck with our process and never got rattled by extremes.

I finally did let Roy have it in a major speech I gave in Birmingham to kick off the final week of the campaign. While I had stayed with the "don't make it too personal" program, I had made it clear that I wanted to do a "closing argument." I did not know how the election would turn out, but I knew that if I lost the race, I would never forgive myself if I didn't make that speech my way.

Moore was an easy target. I didn't have to spell out his sins. Instead, I wanted to note how his outlook and posturing were antiquated, an insult to Alabama, and, frankly, immoral.

I always try to keep it real in speeches. This one had been stewing a while.

Deep down, most of us know what's wrong and what's right, especially moms and dads. I prodded them: "We need to look at this as parents, not voters. Will we tell our daughters that if you are abused and if you speak out you will be believed, and Alabama will stand with you regardless of when you come forward?

"Or will we tell our young sons this behavior, this disturbing behavior, is OK? If you're powerful enough or important enough, Alabama will simply look the other way?"

Moore's few public appearances had been stage-managed theater, and he'd tried to depict himself as the tough Southerner and me as "soft"— easily manipulated by the "anti-gun, anti-Christian" national Democratic Party. Personally, that sort of idiocy didn't make a dent, but it was a great example of how Southern conservatives rely heavily on a very limited playbook that demonizes restraint and common sense.

"I am a supporter of the Second Amendment," I reminded the people of my state. "When you see me with a gun I will be climbing out of a deer stand or a turkey blind, not prancing around on a stage in a cowboy outfit."

It felt good when that segment of the speech went viral.

The last stages of the campaign went by in a blur. I was joined on the road at various times by family and close friends, including a group of great buddies and former U.S. Attorney colleagues—Greg Vega from San Diego, Walter Holton from North Carolina, and Don Stern from Boston. Also, a couple of genuine future presidential prospects: former Massachusetts Governor Deval Patrick and former Newark Mayor, now junior senator from New Jersey, Cory Booker, were energy personified, hitting the road with me and meeting up with the great Alabama Congresswoman Terri Sewell and other Alabama officials to urge folks to get the vote out. Even though Patrick and Booker were "outsiders," they helped carry the message of our commitment to the African-American community and reflected the vigor and energy of the new wave of Democratic Party identities.

While we were blanketing the state with appearances, we always maintained a heavy focus on the black community. Congresswoman Sewell campaigned tirelessly, assuring African-American voters that "help is on the way" if they supported me in the December 12 election. We also did a huge event in Pritchard, just outside of Mobile, with civil rights hero John Lewis, who revved up the crowd with soaring oratory. Terri was instrumental in ensuring that the event was a success, and over the last weekend of the campaign we had a flurry of activity by members of the Congressional Black Caucus, including Chair Cedric Richmond, Hank Johnson, and Sandy Bishop. If they weren't coming in for events, they were recording robocalls that connected us with thousands (as did President Obama's robocall contribution late in the campaign).

The almost nonstop travel around the state was exhausting but exhilarating at times. A special treat was the chance to take in numerous civil rights hubs, none more significant than Selma. When our little caravan rolled into the town where Martin Luther King Jr., John Lewis, and hundreds of others had stood bravely on that bridge on Bloody Sunday, it was moving to see my campaign posters alongside "Vote or Die" placards. These messages were displayed in the front yards of modest homes that had rarely, if ever, hosted a political message. The mobilization of the often-sleepy base was tangible in Selma.

The eloquent former Massachusetts Governor Patrick and Congresswoman Sewell joined me at the historic Brown Chapel, the staging ground for the voting rights marches and protests in the sixties. The city's young Mayor, Darrio Melton, hosted a gathering with a handful of the church's flock, including Congresswoman Sewell's mother.

I was struck by the intensity of our all-too-brief discussion. It was clear this predominantly African-American city was all in on the election. "I'll be taking four people with me to vote. We all should take four people with us," declared one of the women, likely aged in her seventies. Clearly, the spirit of the march to Montgomery that changed America never left this place.

There was a feeling we'd done all we could as I indulged with a nightcap in my kitchen during the last week of the campaign. It felt like the first time I'd stopped moving in weeks—and I was suddenly overcome with mild panic and a sense of despair. Up until that point, I'd been carried along by the enthusiasm of the campaign and, to an extent, the righteousness of the cause.

The idea of losing to Moore was horrifying—and a distinct possibility. I had always been worried about not winning, but now I was desperate not to lose, afraid I would be letting the state and the country down.

The community had so much riding on this. So many people had given their all.

Giles Perkins had major health challenges as an against-all-odds two-year survivor of pancreatic cancer. Every day when I saw him, I wondered how he had the strength to go through this unbelievably stressful process.

The previous day he had texted me: "My wife told me earlier that she used to think God was keeping me alive to see our children grown," he wrote. "But she now says she believes it is to get you into the Senate."

He added the next day that his message may have been as much a product of a fine bottle of pinot noir he'd been drinking as melancholy, but his sincerity and dedication, as well as his wife Hillery's, were beyond doubt and reflected the sort of commitment of hundreds of people.

I was terrified I would fail them. The voters too. A 111-year-old woman's family had sent a photo of her struggling to fill out her absentee ballot for me from a hospital bed. "She stayed alive for this day," they said. "Thank you."

Election Day

It was my twenty-fifth wedding anniversary. Oh, and election day.

The polls were all over the place; as usual, most favored Moore, but notably the few surveys that didn't rely solely on landline phone calls had us up, suggesting younger voters might be unusually influential.

Nevertheless, even though the vast majority of professional observers suggested it would be close, just about every prominent pundit said Moore would triumph.

President Trump had directly urged Alabamians to vote for Moore. He made the appeal in Pensacola, Florida, just across the border from Mobile. We thought it bizarre that the President would not actually come into Alabama, but then again, I'm sure that his advisers did not want him to be seen in the flesh with Moore given the allegations. In any event, his appearance definitely had a positive impact for the Republican candidate—although, as had been the case throughout the campaign, that surge in support seemed to dissipate rather quickly. We were thankful the President made the appeal several nights before the election rather than on its eve.

Accompanied by Carson and Christopher, a slew of supporters, and a media posse, Louise and I voted in our Mountain Brook neighborhood, then visited a few polling stations before bracing for the election-night watch party at the Sheraton in Birmingham. There was not much else to do other than to try and remain reasonably calm.

I tried not to dwell on a gut feeling I had that we would defy every pundit and win the thing. It was a feeling that had grown stronger since we had enjoyed a group dinner at an upscale Birmingham restaurant a few nights before.

It's the sort of place where well-heeled Alabama Republicans are probably the best customers, but on that night, the quiet hum of the eatery was interrupted by suited men and women insisting on wishing me well and guaranteeing their vote would go my way.

On the eve of the poll, my confidence was reinforced as Charles Barkley, the NBA legend, spoke with passion at a campaign rally in Birmingham. He basically said all the things I wanted to say but, due to self-censorship, couldn't. In his direct, engaging way, Sir Charles, a proud Alabamian, lectured on the need for the state to turn around its national image and reject its association with people like Moore.

As we left, a supporter shook my hand vigorously. "You got this," she said.

Yes, I believe we have, I thought.

By December 12, my team and I were revisited by the kind of shared tension that enveloped my group as we closed our case against Blanton—the sense that the pitcher was on the way to a perfect game. *Nobody say anything, just keep doing what you're doing.*

We kept it simple. The guys charged with helping me on the road with communications and security, including off-duty police officer Heath Boackle and Alabama's finest drivers, Beau Bowden and Garrett Stephens, ferried me around to perform a few domestic duties, chief among them getting Louise a card and an anniversary gift.

I spared no expense on the present, a sparkling piece of jewelry, but, crushed for time, I opted to grab an anniversary card from Walgreens.

What? They have a great selection.

In fact, it was an unexpectedly meaningful excursion to the pharmacy. There were still a few remnants of snow on the ground, as Birmingham had had a rare five-inch early December dump a few days before, but the sky was a rich blue and the sun was glinting off the cast-iron statue of Vulcan that hovers over the city.

The symbol of Birmingham's past as an iron and steel industry hub is more a familiar fixture than an inspiring attraction, but from the Walgreens parking lot, located within throwing distance of Red Mountain, where Vulcan has been located since 1936, the creation of sculptor Giuseppe Moretti was an arresting sight.

With Birmingham's symbol looming over me, I walked into the store, made my selection, and lined up at the counter. But before I could pay, the sales attendant, a middle-aged white woman, walked out from behind the counter and embraced me.

"I voted for you. I really hope you win," she said.

There was something about that moment. In some ways, it was similar to the monumental hug of thanks I received from the African-American woman in Home Depot after the Cherry conviction.

A white woman from Walgreens, in the shadow of Vulcan, just gave me an unexpected and sincere declaration of support. For some reason, that convinced me we had it. I returned the knowing glance of a colleague who had witnessed the exchange, but we said not a word. We were on the way to the perfect game.

At a late lunch, I got the feeling all over again when a friend sent a photo of a scarfed white woman with steely features and expensive clothes near a suburban polling station. The caption said: "She voted for you!" There was little doubt in my mind that it would have been the first time she ever considered backing a Democrat.

And the Winner Is . . .

Things weren't going so well. There were a few tears among family and friends.

We were in a private suite for the family at the Sheraton. Down the hall, my buddy Kent had a room, and on consecutive floors below us, other family members and friends had gathered to mingle and watch the results reported on big screens. In the ballroom below the hotel lobby, what appeared to be a couple of thousand supporters were packed in for the campaign's election watch party.

It had started OK. It was pretty much neck and neck as expected, as the first twenty-five percent or so of the vote was counted, but then Moore started to pull away. It was clear rural votes were coming in and giving him a healthy lead. At one point I calculated it was about fifty thousand votes. I was getting pretty depressed.

The experience of closely watching Alabama political contests my whole life told me that was a deficit that was hard, maybe impossible, to overcome. For most of the evening, we remained about eight to ten points behind.

With eighty percent or so of the vote counted, the thing keeping the mood buoyant in the party was my four-year-old granddaughter Ollie, who had come along with older sister Ever, her mom, Courtney, and father, Rip Andrews, expecting me to defeat "Hillary Crimson." As the adults in the room grew somber, she offered medicinal hugs and kisses.

I was also an occasional source of comic relief. Somehow, I had managed to get a bloodstain on the collar of my freshly starched white shirt when I had visited supporters in a suite. Louise and her buddy Heather Cooper were madly washing it—I had no other dress shirt—so I wandered about in a T-shirt emblazoned with the image and moniker of blues rocker George Thorogood.

I tried to remain positive, but, realistically, things weren't looking good.

It was awful witnessing Mom's despair. She had endured watching her son be insulted and belittled for months, and now the chief offender seemed set for victory.

Watching the numbers on television, I felt ill. It wasn't the fact that I was going to lose; it was the idea that a man like Roy Moore was going to win and represent Alabama to the nation, the world.

Oh, my poor home state. I've let you down. My family, friends, campaign colleagues . . . it bordered on unbearable.

I had to get it together. As my buddy Fred Metz loomed up to give me a sympathy speech, I was trying to formulate how I'd address the crowd with dignity. I would emphasize that we'd run an honorable race, one that had thrown down the gauntlet to extremists while also showing Alabama that real issues should be our priority, not political point scoring and power grabbing. It was a new dawn for Democrats despite defeat.

I was pondering how I'd get the words out when Kent and my son-in-law, Rip, diverted my attention from the television to the *New York Times'* online coverage.

"Doug, you really need to look at this," Kent said.

Kent and Rip had both been monitoring the *New York Times'* real-time "needle" estimating the candidates' chances of victory, based on an analysis of where both current votes and the still-uncounted votes were coming from. It still had me as something like a sixty-three percent chance to be the winner, and we had not dipped below sixty percent for over an hour.

"Maybe you should be preparing a victory speech," Kent said.

I knew some of the Black Belt counties were yet to be counted, and Jefferson County, where Birmingham is located, was still to report a vast majority of its vote, but already more than eighty percent of the total vote was accounted for. How could this be?

I recalled the same needle during the presidential campaign: the agony of watching it steadily and swiftly dismiss Hillary Clinton's chances of winning after she'd been estimated to be an almost certain victor for much of the night.

"I think we need to move downstairs," Kent said as the needle began to tick upward in our favor.

For a moment I didn't know whether to be devastated or elated—though I certainly knew I had to change my shirt. Win or lose, George Thorogood probably wasn't appropriate. I put on the freshly ironed (scores of times) dress shirt; we packed the family up and headed down to friends on the floors below.

In the minutes it took to get there my chances of winning had leaped again. It was that quick and that crazy.

With about eighty-seven percent of the vote counted, we drew even. Kent and a few others were saying I had it in the bag. Around that time, I noticed the numbers coming in from Dallas County, where Selma was the urban hub. We were just outside the family and friends suites when the television coverage showed we'd taken the lead. Guess those fine women at Brown Chapel each took four other people to the polls.

A muffled roar moved through the hotel. It sounded like the spectator cacophony that used to roll through Birmingham when the Crimson Tide played games at the ramshackle Legion Field.

Within minutes there was talk that the AP, CNN, and the *New York Times* were going to call it for our team.

Oh my God, is this really happening? And then it did. We had no sooner left the friends and family suites and headed to the elevators than we heard a second eruption from the ballroom. At that moment, we knew we had pulled off what no one outside of our team thought we could. Louise and I paused and held each other tightly, savoring the end of one incredible journey together and the beginning of another.

A gang of us crowded into a service elevator. Mom was in a corner with her walker while towering above us was six-foot, six-inch Charles Barkley, who was oblivious to the bruising he had inflicted on Doug Turner's legs. The former NBA superstar had pounded on my buddy's thighs in frustration when they sat together watching some of the less attractive vote calculations coming in earlier in the night.

I was lost for words. Numb. I just stared at Louise.

Sir Charles spoke up: "I've done a lot of really great things in my life," the Olympian, All-Star, and NBA MVP boomed. "Things I would have never dreamed doing. But this is the greatest night of my life."

The roar as we got to the ballroom was deafening. It was mostly celebratory, but I suspect there were hollers of relief too—a couple of decades' worth. Backstage was just as crowded and noisy. The exuberance of the friends and family around me was remarkable.

My team was pushing me toward the stage. "Shouldn't I wait for Roy to concede or make a speech or something?" I asked.

"He ain't gonna say shit," my campaign advance man, Stephen Groves, shot back. "You gotta get up there!"

And I did.

Less than thirty minutes before, I had been shaping a speech to thank supporters and urge them to take the movement forward. Now, I didn't know what the hell I was going to say, but I wanted to emphasize unity.

Louise and I walked onstage, followed by family and a throng of friends and supporters as music blared, the crowd roared, and red, white, and blue confetti swamped us. We could not get the crowd to quiet down, nor did I really want to. It was the dream of a lifetime and we savored every minute. I think the only one who enjoyed it more was my granddaughter Ollie, who, as a four-year-old, rightly took it in as if the party were for her.

"We have shown the country the way that we can be unified," I said as I felt confetti and a little bit of history rain down on me.

"This entire race has been about dignity and respect. This campaign has been about the rule of law. This campaign has been about common courtesy and decency and making sure everyone in this state, regardless of which zip code you live in, is gonna get a fair shake in life."

We won by about 22,000 votes, or 1.7 percent. Voter turnout was more than 40 percent, exceeding the predictions of 20 to 25 percent. The major cities were our strengths—Birmingham, Mobile, Montgomery, and Huntsville—while we got Obama-like numbers of African-American support, grabbing 96 percent of the black vote in the Black Belt and winning diverse Jefferson County by 84,000 votes. African-American women, especially, turned out in droves and voted for me by a whopping 98 percent to 2 percent margin.

Just as Doug Turner predicted, African Americans, a surprising number of white suburban women, and quite a few moderate Republican and swing voters came our way. Young people were our champions, voting in great numbers across the state, especially in college towns.

It was a victory for the selfless door-to-door campaigners, the scores of phone bank operators, and the person I referred to as my running mate, Louise. She worked crowds better than I could and headlined some events on her own around the state in the crucial final stretch. She was my margin of victory.

The GOP's Senate advantage would soon be down to 51–49.

Two Parties Are Better Than One

In the rundown to the 2010 midterms, immigration was, as it is now, a hot topic. It tends to bring out the worst in politicians, offering some a chance to regurgitate the bogeyman narrative: the idea that Americans need protection from hordes of aliens.

It's a deceitful simplification of a complex issue, and in 2010, some Democrats in the South saw a chance to try and muscle in on the debate. They weren't, however, planning to counteract GOP sensationalism with cold, hard facts about the positive impact immigration and foreign workers have on our state and our country. No, some of the most hateful and dishonest political advertisements maligning immigrants came from Democrats, pandering to people who were not going to vote for them anyway. They got wiped out.

Seven years after those midterms and about three weeks after my election, I was surrounded by family and friends, including Vice President Joe Biden, at my Senate swearing-in. I hadn't had much time to digest what our election victory meant, if anything, for the bigger picture, but one thing I knew for sure, it was an overdue endorsement for Democrats to be Democrats in every corner of the nation.

Pummeled into submission, some in the recent past had felt it necessary to present themselves as "Republican lite" candidates, while others sought to be more outraged than the GOP about immigration, abortion, and guns. They even tried to out-Christian the evangelicals. On the other side of the ledger, there were forces within the national party that banged the liberal identity drum so hard, centrists couldn't be heard over the noise.

At least I got to make a point, not only in Alabama but nationally, that there is some value in being authentic: true to yourself while respectful of opposing views.

Several commentators have suggested my victory would likely have been far greater if I had not stood my ground on advocating for women's rights. Others believed even mentioning responsible gun ownership, as I did during the campaign, could have cost me dearly, while elements in my own party had wanted me to be more assertively law-and-order focused. But that would have been pandering.

The bottom line is you can stick to your principles and still represent a vast and diverse group of people.

We were a pretty good test case for any push to reinvent the Democratic Party around the country outside true-blue states. A few things now seem self-evident. Certainly, a one-size-fits-all model for Democrats is a mistake. We have a big umbrella to cover a big country, so let's use it and ensure a Democratic presence in every contest—all politics is local. Adapting the core message of inclusion and fairness to the demands of a specific region isn't only politically savvy, it's a responsibility.

We are seeing change at the grass roots in the Democratic Party, and, I believe, it's only a matter of time before the Republicans come to terms with the fact that they have built a house of cards, constructed on a foundation of gerrymandering, extremism, and political opportunism.

The coming generation of voting Americans, in all its racial and religious diversity, is already beyond wringing hands about issues such as gay rights and racial discrimination. Certain rights in their eyes are non-negotiable. Sure, as old ideas are exposed as discriminatory and unjust, their defenders' voices will become louder, more desperate, and more defiant, but we are witnessing the final throes of concepts that will eventually be exposed as serving only the narrow interests of a particular group.

That was true of the Klansmen who used to meet under the Cahaba River Bridge and plotted violent responses to racial integration. It also applies to those contemporary politicians who service discrimination, hatred, and, chiefly, their own interests, by latching on to a hot-button idea held dear by a segment of the community and cynically using it to secure and solidify their power.

As these people dig trenches between us—again—parts of the country struggle with extreme poverty, third-world healthcare, and appalling educational opportunities, and have to overcome manufactured barriers to merely vote. The middle class is a pipedream for tens of millions who felt abandoned by the Democratic Party machine and are used by the GOP.

No more.

This is where we turn it around.

In the South, we talk a good game about hospitality and inclusion, but our history paints a different picture. This divisive nonsense started below the Mason-Dixon line a long time ago, but it's also where positive change—stop-start, spluttering change—began and will eventually flourish.

We are glimpsing what is possible, even under the most testing circumstances. More women, young people, and minorities are getting skin in the political game.

Some of my Democratic Party colleagues look to changing demographics and the surge in political will and envision turning many red states blue, even locking up power for generations to come, just as the astute Republicans did. But my wishes and expectations are a little more modest. Our focus, as much as I want Democratic Party success, must be on rediscovering and facilitating a system where both political parties are competitive.

Donald Trump's rise to the presidency was a symptom rather than the cause of the imbalances and sometimes manufactured weaknesses in the two-party system. Those issues remain whether he or his ilk are in the White House or not.

When one party is overwhelmingly dominant, its representatives simply retreat to their corner and strategize to solidify that base, often by redistricting. When there is a lack of diverse voices, it's the loudest, most extreme (better funded) voices within the ranks that win out. They run not to serve the community but to make sure they hold on to power. They don't end up working for the betterment of everybody. Sometimes they end up working for no one but themselves. U.S. Senators should represent not only the people who voted for them but those who voted against them and the people who didn't vote at all.

Reinvigorating the two-party system means competing for votes on issues, hearing from different places on the political and ideological spectrum, and plotting a way forward collectively.

Compromise within party ranks and across the aisle isn't a sin; it's a necessity.

I want a healthy Democratic Party, but I also hope the GOP can rediscover its soul.

The necessary reshaping of the Democratic Party will be a work in progress for some time to come. There is some speculation that the way to once again differentiate the donkey from the elephant is to move the party to the left, but I'd suggest that ignores all the lessons we've been learning since conservatives started to take a vice-like grip on power at all levels of government in so many parts of the country.

It's not a matter of moving left or right. It's a matter of moving toward the people. Repopulating and reenergizing the center. The radical middle.

It's not how the GOP cynically grabbed power, but it is how this country became an unparalleled democracy.

I wore a pair of Howell Heflin's cufflinks to my Senate swearing-in. I walked down the aisle of the Senate floor escorted by Vice President Biden. My new colleague, Tina Smith of Minnesota, who was also being sworn in that day, was escorted by another former Vice President, Walter Mondale.

I looked up into the family gallery to see the friends and family who had made the trip to share in the moment and blew Louise a kiss. It was an intensely emotional moment to be back in the space where I had served as a staffer for the great Senator Heflin nearly forty years before—and to be in his seat, to boot! A swearing-in reenactment with Vice President Pence in the Old Senate Chamber after the official ceremony gave Louise and the boys a chance to be active participants in the process.

I accepted the challenge to represent the people of Alabama in the spirit of Biden's advice—to be prepared to say things of conscience even if it meant political defeat. There are many others, I believe, in the South and across the country who share that kind of commitment, especially in light of what we've endured in recent years.

The grand notion of serving the public isn't dead and, I'm convinced, is gaining traction again as the full extent of attempts to undermine our institutions and pervert our process come into clear, unmistakable view.

Tension between competing factions will remain immense, but the divisions we have been dealing with have forced us to look back—as far back as the ultimate divisive fight, the Civil War, and to slavery and Jim Crow.

That reflection is key to constructing a future that won't be derailed by a single authoritarian figure or the will of a minority who wish to strip this country of its glory: its diversity, tolerance, and compassion. It exposes the ongoing cynical efforts to appeal to generations-old prejudices in order to maintain a culture of divisiveness that locks economies into a cycle of failure and creates a delusion that compels many of the most vulnerable to vote against their own best interests.

The enemies of this united country are desperate. They are losing as the nation becomes more diverse and its population better educated. Let's put an end to the civil war they continue to prosecute.

I have been very lucky. Being confronted with the human side of some historically important processes, I've come to understand how vital it is not to give up, even when a fair outcome looks remote.

Hope.

It's what Robert Chambliss, Tommy Blanton, and Bobby Frank Cherry couldn't kill. Hope didn't wane when Oswald shot JFK, and it didn't die when James Earl Ray murdered Dr. King, or Sirhan Sirhan gunned down

Bobby Kennedy. Hope was inherent in the actions of the families of the victims of the Charleston shooting who forgave Dylann Roof.

It was hope for equity and justice that propelled good people to finally speak up and end segregation in the sixties. And it is the reason I encountered countless Alabamians in 2017 who expressed a desire to reform the harsh image of their state, to focus on what is possible rather than resigning themselves to what they've been conditioned to believe is inevitable.

On several occasions over the years, I wanted intensely to put the church bombing case behind me. It dominated my life and, especially in quiet moments, its ugliness was sometimes overwhelming. To be sure, to this day, I'm only half-joking when I say one of my greatest fears is that when the light starts to fade on my time here on earth, the last thing I'll hear in my head will be Jean's shrill "Well Tommy . . ."

But, recognizing what those cases meant to others and how relevant they are to our present-day challenges, I am reminded of what a privilege it was to be involved.

Delayed justice didn't provide closure, but it was a form of community and personal redemption. I am a more complete person for it, and maybe the world is a slightly better place too.

ACKNOWLEDGMENTS

Writing this book has been a labor of love over several years. Along the way, I have been blessed by the advice and encouragement of scores of great people. Some are mentioned in the book, many are not. Be assured, I am thankful to you all, although I must immediately single out my wife and inspiration, Louise, who has been my constant and wise consultant.

Although I had ideas about this book relatively soon after finishing the Cherry trial, it was my friend, the Pulitzer Prize–winning author Rick Bragg, who sat me down in my law office and sketched out how best to put it together. For advice, I have also often turned to another Pulitzer winner, Diane McWhorter, who has likely forgotten more than I will ever know about civil rights history in Birmingham.

Over the years, my fellow lawyer Kirk Wood would constantly needle me with: "When you going to finish that book?" Finally, recognizing that my day job was getting in the way of my writing, he introduced me to Steve Townsend, a gifted journalist whose additional reporting was invaluable to getting this project off the ground.

Kirk also connected me with my literary agent, Lois de la Haba. From our first meeting, she let me know she saw something special and timely in the story. Lois lent her creativity to help build the manuscript and, along with her associate Marilyn Myers, offered advice for specific changes. If there is a patron saint of this book, it is Lois. It was she who introduced me to my collaborator, Greg Truman, an incredibly talented storyteller with insight into how best to weave many facets of a story into a single body of work. My gratitude and respect for him as a writer is eclipsed only by the enduring friendship that we developed.

All Points Books Editorial Director Adam Bellow and the team at St. Martin's and All Points have been models of patience, efficiency, and professionalism. Adam is rightly revered in the publishing world and I have benefited immensely from his astute guidance.

Back home in Birmingham, my longtime legal assistant Tyler Florence has been multi-tasking and laboring hard on my behalf for years. *Bending Toward Justice* might not have been completed for another ten years had it not been for Tyler.

Many of the prosecution team are still plying their trade in the South. I am privileged to have worked with them. Robert Posey, Jeff Wallace, Don Cochran, Bill Fleming, Ben Herren, Bob Eddy, Robin Beardsley, Amy Gallimore, Bill Smith, Andy Sheldon, Steve Paterson, and Norma Silverstein also helped me compile this story.

Rob Langford and Caryl Privett deserve special recognition for having the foresight and courage to re-open the bombing investigation, and I need to salute the vision of former Jefferson County District Attorney David Barber and former Alabama Attorney General, now Eleventh Circuit Court of Appeals judge, Bill Pryor. Their actions allowed me to stay on the bombing cases when they were taken from federal control and placed in state hands.

I am also lucky to have led a U.S. Attorney's office of rare talent. I am particularly indebted to my old team of Bud Henry, Joe McLean, John Ernest, and Mike Rasmussen, Jim Lewis, Will Chambers, Cindy Kelly, China Davidson, and Stephanie Braswell.

I would be remiss if I did not acknowledge the early investigative work by the many FBI agents and personnel who did so much immediately following the bombing to try and bring the perpetrators to justice. And of course, to construct our case, I had to climb onto the shoulders of Bill Baxley and his team of lawyers and investigators, headed by Bob Eddy, who prosecuted Robert Chambliss in 1977. Along with my old boss, Senator Howell Heflin, another great public servant, Bill serves as an inspiration and example for my service in the Senate.

I am a United States Senator today because of the thousands of folks in Alabama and across the country who contributed to my campaign. I am indebted to every one of them, and thankful beyond expression to my core campaign team: Giles Perkins, Doug Turner, Kent Haney, Nancy Ellisor, Joe

Trippi, Thomas Rossmeissl, Wade Perry, Beau Bowden, Jess Vaughn, Garrett Stephens, Trey Forrest, Chris Mosley, and Bennet Murray. When Giles started formulating my campaign, he was a two-year survivor of pancreatic cancer. As of this writing, he is a three-and-a-half-year survivor. He is a remarkable human. When a history of Alabama politics is written in coming decades, Giles Perkins will be credited for initiating overdue change.

Special recognition also goes to my law partner, Greg Hawley. We were young turks when we first met in the '78 Heflin campaign. We finally established a practice together in 2013. Along with partner Chris Nicholson, longtime friend Cissy Jackson, and Tyler, the law firm kept humming along while I pursued my campaign.

Finally, this story begins and should end with Denise McNair, Addie Mae Collins, Cynthia Morris Wesley, Carole Robertson, and their families. More than any other event from the civil rights era, the girls' deaths galvanized the conscience of a President, the Congress, and the American public. An important part of the history that is often overlooked is the fate of the "fifth little girl," Sarah Collins Rudolph, who has lived with her injuries and the horror of the day for most of her life. With the support of husband, George, Sarah's faith has sustained her.

The girls' families deserve a special place in history. They have made enormous personal sacrifices so we could all be enlightened and enriched. I am thankful that some of them lived long enough to see some manner of final justice for their children.

INDEX